Praise for *The IABC Handbook of Organizational Communication, Second Edition*

"Looking to expand your professional abilities? Learn new skills? Or hone your area of expertise? This book delivers an amazing and practical study of our profession—and a guidebook for strategic communication best practices. The *Handbook* explores the many aspects of our profession with expert insights of the best of the best in communication."

—John Deveney, ABC, APR, president of Deveney Communication

"It is a real pleasure to read the latest version of *The IABC Handbook of Organizational Communication*. It presents a sound, research-based foundation on communication—its importance to organizations, why the function must be strategic, and what it takes to get it right. From Paul Sanchez's detailed and insightful analysis of organizational culture and its influence on employees to Mary Ann McCauley's discussion on the significant role that CSR has come to play as organizations seek new and innovative ways to increase visibility, reputation, and brand awareness with key stakeholders, this is a valuable text that professional communicators should embrace and refer to often for guidance and planning."

—John G. Clemons, ABC, APR, corporate director of community relations, Raytheon

"All myths about organizational communicators being brainwashed, biased corporate journalists are out the window with this *Handbook*. This stellar compendium from dozens of authors, researchers, and editors of high professional stature is timely and forward-thinking. I know these people, and I am in awe of their work. Communication students particularly will benefit from understanding the complex disciplines that intertwine and drive effective organizational communication."

—Barbara W. Puffer, ABC, president, Puffer Public Relations Strategies, and associate professor, Communications Studies and Professional Writing, University of Maryland University College

"Chalk up a win for Team IABC. Editor Tamara Gillis has assembled a winning lineup of the best communicators to compile this useful, readable *Handbook*. Not another how-to-do-it tactical manual, this volume draws from theory and global best practices to explain the strategic reasons behind modern communication. A must-read for anyone interested in understanding the communication profession and a useful desktop companion to the professional communicator's dictionary and style guide."

—William Briggs, IABC fellow and director, School of Journalism and Mass Communications, San Jose State University

THE IABC HANDBOOK OF ORGANIZATIONAL COMMUNICATION

A Guide to Internal Communication, Public Relations, Marketing, and Leadership

SECOND EDITION

Tamara L. Gillis
Editor

Foreword by Natasha Nicholson

JOSSEY-BASS
A Wiley Imprint
www.josseybass.com

IABC INTERNATIONAL ASSOCIATION OF BUSINESS COMMUNICATORS

Published by Jossey-Bass

A Wiley Imprint

989 Market Street, San Francisco, CA 94103-1741—www.josseybass.com

Figures 7.1, 7.2, and Exhibit 7.1 are used courtesy of RBC.

The bulleted list on pages 308–309 is reprinted by permission of Waveland Press, Inc. All rights reserved.

Jossey-Bass books and products are available through most bookstores. To contact Jossey-Bass directly
call our Customer Care Department within the U.S. at 800-956-7739, outside the U.S. at 317-572-
3986, or fax 317-572-4002.

Jossey-Bass also publishes its books in a variety of electronic formats. Some content that appears in
print may not be available in electronic books.

Library of Congress Cataloging-in-Publication Data

The IABC handbook of organizational communication : a guide to internal communication, public
relations, marketing, and leadership / Tamara L. Gillis editor ; foreword by Natasha Nicholson. —2nd
ed.
     p. cm.—(A joint publication of the Jossey-Bass business & management series and the
International Association of Business Communicators)
   Includes bibliographical references and index.
   ISBN 978-0-470-89406-4 (cloth); ISBN 978-1-118-01633-6 (ebk); ISBN 978-1-118-01634-3 (ebk);
ISBN 978-1-118-01635-0 (ebk)
   1. Communication in organizations—United States.   I. Gillis, Tamara L.
   II. International Association of Business Communicators.
   HD30.36.U5I25 2011
   658.4'5—dc22

                                                                        2011002089

Printed in the United States of America

SECOND EDITION

HB Printing   10 9 8 7 6 5 4 3 2 1

A JOINT PUBLICATION OF

THE JOSSEY-BASS

BUSINESS & MANAGEMENT SERIES

AND

THE INTERNATIONAL ASSOCIATION OF BUSINESS

COMMUNICATORS

CONTENTS

FOREWORD

Organizational communication as a profession is relatively young when compared to other business disciplines, tracing it roots back less than 100 years. But as current world events such as the Toyota recalls and government buy-outs of American auto manufacturers have shown, it is a valuable, serious, and essential business component that is necessary for organizations to thrive, grow, and sustain misfortunes.

The profession's emergence and growth is closely matched to the growth and evolution of the International Association of Business Communicators (IABC). This association came together in 1970 with a band of bold visionaries at its helm—ready to serve an emerging need for a profession of the future. It sought to help its members find their way in the business world and to demonstrate the true value of communication. What started as a group of people who called themselves "industrial editors" grew into a varied assembly of "communicators" responsible for many facets of organizational communication.

As the profession has grown, so has IABC. A milestone of that growth is this *Handbook*. At this book's foundation is the definition of organizational communication as a profession and details about what that means in today's business world—adhering to a set of principles that are applied in a number of specialties that affect the successful operation on an organization. When I, or anyone who is close to IABC, describe the association, we often list specialties like media relations, marketing communication, and employee communication as a means of describing the goals and intent of organizational communication. We also acknowledge that the profession is continually growing and evolving to address the current best practices in communication strategy that affect organizational communications. We do this because it is this composition of specialties that breathes life into communication. This composition of complementary specialties shows that organizational communication is not a neat and tidy package. It is a complex array of communication disciplines that connect to shape an organization's destiny—creating the difference between an engaged workforce and one that is wrought with malaise, offering the ability to relate the vision of a brilliant company or convey a sadly backward entity.

This second edition of this *Handbook* signifies the progression of a profession—separated into specialties that are worthwhile and essential to today's business world. IABC, with outstanding guidance from Tamara Gillis, has collected the best and brightest in the communication world and included into this book their thoughts, perspectives, concerns, and analysis. It is a must-read for every communicator who wants to understand the real value of communication. And it is very much like IABC's members themselves: a collection of great communicators, sharing best practices, analyzing what works and what does not, and striving to make organizations stronger through communication.

This collection of organizational communication practices complements IABC's research agenda as well as its vast and ever-growing library of resources. I welcome you to learn more about IABC by visiting www.iabc.com.

February 2011   Natasha Nicholson
                                            Vice President, Publishing and Recognition
                                            Executive Editor, *Communication World*

PREFACE

May you live in interesting times.

Seems like we have all been cursed: we are living in interesting times. The landscape of business communication continues to evolve to meet the demands of the business world around us. The International Association of Business Communicators ([IABC], 2010) continues to meet the needs of professional communicators tasked with maneuvering that ever-changing landscape through professional development programs and groundbreaking research that shares "best global communication practices, ideas and experiences that will enable communicators to develop highly ethical and effective performance standards" and this second edition of *The IABC Handbook of Organizational Communication*.

In 2009 I conducted a series of surveys, interviews, and content analyses to create a snapshot of competencies and expectations of professional communicators today (Gillis, 2009). Not surprising, communication thought leaders and employers around the world came to similar conclusions, and members of the IABC Accreditation Council agreed that the following findings set a foundation for business communicators today—and the foundation for this book:

- Business communicators must have business acumen.
- Business communicators are expected to provide sound communication counsel.

- Business communicators are expected to think and act strategically.
- Business communicators are expected to support decision making with sound research, measurement, and evaluation.
- Business communicators are expected to make ethical decisions.
- Business communicators are expected to leverage communication technology to meet business goals.
- Business communicators are expected to cultivate organizational trust and credibility.
- Business communicators must embrace diversity.
- Business communicators are expected to be able to manage communications to support organizations in times of change.
- Business communicators must be prepared to handle crisis communication.
- Business communicators are expected to build relationships with the media.
- Business communicators are expected to keep up with current best practices in their discipline.
- Last but not least, business communicators must have excellent basic skills in writing and editing.

Regardless of the issue at hand, these basic principles continue to ring true: You need a sound plan, well-crafted messages that deliver on business strategies, delivered by appropriate media that reach the target audiences, and a means to measure your accomplishments. Our publics are demanding clear, concise, and reasoned communications from business enterprises, nonprofit organizations, and government entities alike.

We live in interesting times. A time when as communicators our strategic communications empower employees; educate analysts and investors; encourage suppliers; and comfort customers. We communicate twenty-four hours a day, seven days a week with media representatives who are often biased and jaded because of their lack of preparation and research as they meet deadlines for a voracious and frustrated public.

Robert Dilenschneider (2008) reminds us that in the end "it is the role of communicators in our society today to sustain confident communications. We need to find ways to communicate confidence and reduce panic through genuine communication so that solutions can be found and shared."

It is in these "interesting times," our finest hours as communicators, that we leave a legacy of communication strategy that defines corporate communication, organizational communication, and both public and internal communication strategies.

My sincere thanks to the chapter authors; their expertise and wisdom made this book possible. Special thanks go to the IABC Accreditation Council for their insights into the process of developing this *Handbook*. It is my hope that communication practitioners at all levels, educators, and those outside the communications field will find in this book insights and understanding that contribute to organizational success.

Who Should Read This Book?

This book is designed and organized with a number of different readers in mind. If you are new to the world of corporate communication, the chapters in this book bring to the fore issues that are critical to understand and master in any organization. If you are a professional communicator, this book provides new insights on traditional and emerging issues in organizational communication. If you are a corporate executive outside the communication discipline, this book will help you understand the importance and reach of communication within your organization and with external stakeholders.

Understanding occurs when people ask questions and share information. This book follows suit. Like any other handbook, it may be read in a number of ways. First, it may be read from cover to cover. If you are interested in all facets of organizational communication, you will enjoy starting at the beginning of this book and reading through to the end. The book's organization builds from general topics to specialty interests.

Second, readers may choose to skim the book for topics of interest or topics related to a current challenge. This book touches on issues of interest to those new to the field of organizational communications as well as seasoned professionals.

How This Book Is Organized

In developing the content for this second edition, a review of the 2006 edition was conducted in addition to the competency research referenced earlier. The Accreditation Council and other communication leaders agreed that this new edition would benefit from more case studies and examples, a greater focus on measurement, and less redundancy. In this edition readers will find more examples of principles and practices that support the foundational elements of business communication. The topics addressed in this *Handbook* represent what our experts agreed was most relevant for communicators and other organization associates to understand about the process of organizational communication.

This book is organized into five parts. Part One serves as an introduction to business communication and addresses some universal premises concerning corporate communication. The chapters in this part introduce readers to complexities and structures of corporate communication. The universal concepts of excellence, trust, culture, ethics, social responsibility, and measurement are reviewed to set the foundation for the role of corporate communicators today.

Part Two focuses on the current challenges of managing corporate communications and organizational communication. Cultivating a culture of communication is critical within any organization. The authors share insights into successful planning, implementation, and management of corporate communication. The strategies they review are fundamental to successful communication management.

Part Three contains seven chapters that explore evolving issues in the practice of employee communication and internal communication networks. At the heart of each excellent organization or corporation is a trusted internal communication program. Integral issues of relationship building, employee engagement, diversity, and internal branding are highlighted here as key to developing trusted internal programs.

Part Four apprises readers of the role of public relations in the corporate communication program. A host of external publics await business communicators. These stakeholders will have an impact on the reputation and success of our organizations in reaching their goals. The chapters demonstrate the need for a strategic approach to managing external relationships.

Part Five addresses key concepts of marketing and brand management and their place in the corporate communication program. The chapters in this part bring to life the internal impact and external challenges of marketing communications. Here, professionals share their insights and expertise for developing excellence in corporate performance through marketing communication programming.

Acknowledgments

The process of compiling a volume of knowledge like *The IABC Handbook of Organizational Communication* is an arduous one, with many twists and turns along the way. I am grateful for the assistance and friendship that I received from Amanda Aiello, Natasha Nicholson, and Heather Turbeville. I especially thank all the chapter authors who contributed their time and wisdom. Their expertise will help countless professionals make the right choices for their organizations. A special thank you to the accredited business communicators who helped in the preliminary stages. And one big thank you to Jeffrey for all his support during the process.

February 2011   Tamara L. Gillis
                                                                     Elizabethtown, Pennsylvania

References

Dilenschneider, R. (2008, October 13). Communicating during turbulent times, *Keynote address to the 2008 IABC Heritage Regional Conference*. Hartford, CT.

Gillis, T. (2009). *It's your move: Competencies and expectations*. (Proprietary research). San Francisco: International Association of Business Communicators.

International Association of Business Communicators [IABC]. (2010). *IABC's mission, vision and brand*. Retrieved July 22, 2010, from www.iabc.com/info/about/aboutiab.htm.

ABOUT THE AUTHORS

Rob Briggs is director of internal communications for the international division of RBC Wealth Management, one of the world's largest private banks and based in London, UK, and Jersey, Channel Islands. He provides strategic counsel as well as the implementation of internal communication campaigns, executive communications, and community relations programs. Briggs is a past chairman of the Europe and Middle East Region of IABC. He holds an M.Sc. with Merit in corporate communications and reputation management from Manchester Business School; a B.A. in Philosophy from the University of Reading; an advanced diploma in communication studies from the Communication, Advertising and Marketing Foundation; and the financial planning certificate from the Chartered Insurance Institute. He is accredited by the British Association of Communicators in Business and is a Fellow of the Royal Society for the Encouragement of Arts, Manufactures and Commerce.

Steve Crescenzo is a consultant, writer, and seminar leader who has helped thousands of communicators improve both their print and electronic

Editor's Note: The following designations are used to identify accredited communicators: ABC designates Accredited Business Communicator through the International Association of Business Communicators; APR designates Accreditation in Public Relations through the Public Relations Society of America.

communications efforts. Recognized as one of the nation's leading experts in corporate communications, Crescenzo is the leader of the popular Strategic Creative Communication seminar and speaks around the world on employee communication, social media, writing, integrating print and online, and creativity. He was the number one rated speaker of IABC's International Conferences in 2002, 2008, 2009, and 2010 and has been asked to speak in IABC's "All Star Track" for the past five years. He also writes a regular column on employee communications in *Communication World* magazine.

Roger D'Aprix, ABC, IABC Fellow, is an internationally known communications consultant, author, and lecturer. He has assisted scores of Fortune 500 companies in developing communication strategies, designing communication initiatives, and training for managers and supervisors. He is a vice president of ROI Consulting, a Silicon Valley–based consultancy. For fifteen years he held senior positions with two of the leading human resource consulting companies: Towers Perrin and Mercer. He is the author of seven books on employee communication. His latest book published in 2009 by Jossey-Bass is *The Credible Company: Communicating with Today's Skeptical Workforce.* His consulting career follows two decades as a corporate communication executive for Xerox Corporation and General Electric.

Melissa D. Dodd is a doctoral student focusing on communication/public relations at the University of Miami's School of Communication. Dodd is a co-organizer for the International Public Relations Research Conference and a coauthor for the instructor's manual companion to Don W. Stack's *Primer of Public Relations Research*, second edition. She received the Brigham Young University Top Ethics Paper Award in March 2010. Dodd has gained practical public relations experience through several public relations and marketing positions and internships. She earned her master of arts in public relations from Ball State University and will graduate with her doctorate in 2012.

Nick Durutta, ABC, is a senior communications manager for The Capital Group Companies, a global investment management firm based in Los Angeles. Prior to joining Capital in 1996, he was a communications consultant for many years, specializing in internal change communication. He holds a bachelor's degree in journalism from California State University at Fullerton. A member and a past director of the IABC, he has served as chair of the organization's international awards program as well as president of the Los Angeles chapter.

Jennifer Frahm, Ph.D., is the founder of Conversations of Change®, a boutique consultancy that specializes in change communication, building change capability in house, coaching change agents and leaders, and conducting off-site retreats on career and work-life change. She has change management experience in financial services, higher education, energy, innovation, human services, and manufacturing. This work has involved providing strategic advice to senior management, diagnosis of communications problems, and analysis of change interventions with an emphasis on change program effectiveness. She holds a doctorate in management, is the 2010–2011 IABC Victoria Australia chapter president, blogs on the IABC eXchange, and can be found on Twitter (@ jenfrahm).

Kellie Garrett, ABC, is senior vice president of strategy, knowledge, and reputation at Farm Credit Canada (FCC). She is responsible for FCC's business strategy, knowledge management and strategic intelligence, and reputation, including corporate communications. Her team has won dozens of awards for innovative and best practice programs in diverse areas. She is a frequent speaker in her areas of expertise and a passionate volunteer for boards in the areas of corporate social responsibility and autism. Garrett was chair of IABC's Research Foundation Board in 2006. She holds an M.A. in leadership and is a certified executive coach.

Diane M. Gayeski, Ph.D., is internationally recognized as a thought leader in organizational communication and learning. Currently she is the dean of the Roy H. Park School of Communications. For more than thirty years, she has been both an academic and a professional specializing in corporate communications strategy and management. She leads Gayeski Analytics and consults with clients worldwide such as General Electric, U.S. Navy, Abbott Nutritionals, Tompkins Financial, and Johnson Controls. The author of fourteen books, she is a frequent speaker at conferences and private executive briefings.

Tamara L. Gillis, Ed.D., ABC, is professor and chairman of the Department of Communications at Elizabethtown College, Pennsylvania. She has also served as a communications consultant with Cooper Wright LLC. In her career, she has led communication programs for higher education institutions, associations, and a health care corporation. She has served as faculty in Swaziland, Namibia, and the Semester at Sea program. The IABC Research Foundation honored her with the 2004 Foundation Lifetime Friend Award. In 2001–2002 she chaired the IABC Research Foundation. She has held leadership positions at the district and international levels of IABC, and she recently led the organization's efforts to revise the ABC accreditation program. The author of numerous articles and book chapters, she is coauthor of *Essentials of Employee Communication: Building Relationships that Create Business Success* (IABC, 2008) and *IABC Profile Study: Trends in Communication Profession Compensation* (IABC, 2008), and author of *The Human Element: Employee Communication Practices in Small Businesses* (IABC, 2008). She holds a doctorate in education from the University of Pittsburgh (Pennsylvania).

Patrick Grady is senior vice president and managing partner of CMS Communications International, an innovative communication agency based in Los Angeles. He heads up the CMS consulting business and is based in Orlando, Florida. Prior to joining CMS he held numerous positions in marketing communications, events management, and strategic and internal communications with companies including RadioShack Corporation, commercial radio stations, and an international television network. His career has included media production, executive producer, on-air talent, and presentation coach as well as strategic communicator.

Lin Grensing-Pophal, M.A., SPHR, PCM, is a communications consultant and business journalist with an extensive background in strategic marketing, corporate communications, and employee relations. She has led several strategic planning initiatives in the areas of crisis management and marketing planning. As a National Baldrige examiner, Pophal has been involved in the development of applications and the individual and consensus review and scoring of Baldrige applications for large and small organizations. She is the author of several books, including *Marketing with the End In Mind* (IABC, 2005) and *Human Resource Essentials* (SHRM, 2002). She is the coauthor of *Writing a Convincing Business Plan*, third edition (Barron's Educational Series, 2001).

James E. Grunig is professor emeritus in the Department of Communication at the University of Maryland. He has won three major awards in public relations: the Pathfinder Award for excellence in public relations research of the Institute for Public Relations Research and Education, the Outstanding Educator Award of the Public Relations Society of America (PRSA), and the Jackson, Jackson and Wagner Award for behavioral science research of the PRSA Foundation. He also won the prestigious lifetime award of the Association for Education in Journalism and Mass Communication, the Paul J. Deutschmann Award for Excellence in Research.

Larissa A. Grunig is professor emerita in the Department of Communication at the University of Maryland. She served as special assistant to the president of the university for women's issues. She has received the Pathfinder Award, sponsored by the U.S. Institute for Public Relations, for excellence in public relations research, the Outstanding Educator Award of the Public Relations Society of America (PRSA), and the Jackson, Jackson and Wagner Award for behavioral science research of the PRSA Foundation. She coauthored the first book on women in public relations.

Shel Holtz, ABC, IABC Fellow, is principal of Holtz Communication + Technology, a consultancy that helps organizations apply online technology to their organizational communications. He has spent more than thirty years in the communications field as a director of corporate communications for two Fortune 500 companies and as a senior communications consultant for two human resource consulting firms. He is the author of *Public Relations on the Net* and *Corporate Conversations.*

John Larsen, ABC, is principal of Corpen Group, Inc., an independent consultancy specializing in reputation management and government relations. He has held senior communications positions with various orders of government and in the corporate sector, including manager of executive communications for the City of Calgary and associate vice president with an international public affairs and government relations consulting agency. Larsen has lectured at four Canadian colleges and universities, is a popular industry and academic conference speaker, and has a graduate degree in communications; he is an Accredited Business Communicator, a certified member of the American Institute for Crisis Management, a member of the U.S.-based Issue Management Council, and holds formal United Nations status as an International Permanent Observatory Expert. John is also a senior reserve officer in the Canadian Forces Public Affairs Branch.

Wilma K. Mathews, ABC, IABC Fellow, has more than three decades of experience in domestic and international public relations and communication management. She is author and coauthor of numerous books and a contributor to several magazines, newsletters, and reports. Mathews is an internationally known speaker, provides counsel to organizations on strategic and media relations planning, and currently serves as chair of the IABC Ethics Committee. She previously served as chair of the IABC Research Foundation and the Accreditation Council and as a member of the IABC executive board. She is a Gold Quill winner for media relations and writing. She is a member of the Rowan University

PR Hall of Fame and has taught at the Walter Cronkite School of Journalism & Mass Communications at Arizona State University.

Mary Ann McCauley, ABC, president and principal of Catalyst Communications, provides strategic communication counsel to a broad spectrum of businesses and nonprofits. McCauley provides general communication counsel with a focus on strategic communication planning and implementation. Prior to founding Catalyst Communications in 1987, she held positions in corporations including Hallmark Cards, United Technologies Communications Company, and First Union Bancorporation. A former journalist, she was a reporter at an Iowa daily and later owned and operated a community newspaper in Kansas. She holds a bachelor of journalism degree from the University of Missouri.

Mark McElreath, ABC, APR, Ph.D., is a professor at Towson University in Maryland, and a member of IABC for more than thirty years. He can be reached at mmcelreath@towson.edu.

George McGrath is a partner and founder of McGrath Matter Associates, a public relations and public affairs consulting firm. Over the course of a twenty-five-year career in communications, McGrath has helped clients identify issues that are key to their success and develop business strategies and communications campaigns to influence the course of debates over public policy. He has worked with businesses, trade associations, and nonprofit organizations on a range of issues, including environmental protection, energy competition, health care delivery, and education. He served on the IABC international board between 1989 and 1994 and was IABC's international chairman between 1992 and 1993.

Rita Linjuan Men is a doctoral student in public relations at the University of Miami's School of Communication. She is a member of Association for Education in Journalism and Mass Communication and Public Relations Professionals Association in Hong Kong. She is a co-organizer for the International Public Relations Research Conference and a coauthor for the instructor's manual companion to Don W. Stack's *Primer of Public Relations Research*, 2nd edition. She earned her master of philosophy in communications studies from Hong Kong Baptist University and a B.A. in communication from Zhejiang University.

Sherwyn Morreale is associate professor and director of graduate studies in communication at University of Colorado at Colorado Springs. For eight years, she served as associate director of the National Communication Association. She has written or coauthored numerous journal articles, books, monographs, and book chapters. She holds communication degrees from University of Colorado at Colorado Springs and University of Colorado, Denver, and a Ph.D. in communication from University of Denver.

Alistair J. Nicholas is a frequent writer and commentator on reputation management. His career of more than twenty-five years spans journalism, politics, diplomacy, in-house communications counsel, and communications consulting across Australia, the United States, and China. He is currently the president and CEO of AC Capital Strategic Consulting, a firm he established in Beijing in 2003 to provide reputation management, public affairs, and issues and crisis management services to organizations operating in China. The firm's clients include global Fortune 500 companies, Chinese state-owned enterprises, Chinese and foreign government agencies, and nonprofit organizations.

Morgan Leu Parkhurst is owner of Blue + Linen, an organization focused on helping businesses to develop their marketing communications strategies. She has been a subject matter expert on integrated marketing communications for SCORE and Small Business Development Center seminars, has taught marketing communications courses to business owners and managers, and has been a featured speaker at business conferences. She has written for nationally and internationally distributed publications on the topics of entrepreneurship, marketing, media relations, networking, and consumer behavior. She has an MBA in marketing from Iowa State University. She is the past president of IABC/Iowa.

Lester R. Potter, ABC, MBA, IABC Fellow, is a senior lecturer in the Department of Mass Communication and Communication Studies at Towson University in Maryland. He is also a doctoral candidate in instructional technology at Towson. He serves as faculty advisor to Towson's Student PR Group, which includes PRSA and IABC student chapters. Potter blogs about strategic communication and public relations and integrated marketing communication in *More with Les*, at http://lespotter001.wordpress.com. Prior to joining Towson's faculty, Potter was president of Les Potter Incorporated, an international consultancy that he founded. Potter was chairman of IABC from 1991 to 1992. He had previously served on IABC's executive board, accreditation board, and as a trustee of the IABC Research Foundation. He is the author of *The Communication Plan: the Heart of Strategic Communication* (IABC, 2008) and *Business Management for Communicators: Beyond Strategic Communication* (IABC).

Paul M. Sanchez, ABC, APR, is founder of CSF Consulting, a research and communications firm. Prior to his current position, he worked for Mercer, Stoorza Communications, and Watson Wyatt Worldwide. His past IABC activities include executive board member, executive committee finance director, ethics committee chair, board member of IABC's U.K. chapter, and chairman of the IABC Research Foundation (2005–2006). He has a B.Sc. in psychology and a M.Sc. in organizational communications. He also attended the Executive Leadership Development at the Harvard Business School. While in the United Kingdom he was elected to the Royal Society of Arts and Mechanics. He has contributed to professional journals and wrote *Transformation Communications*, published by IABC.

Caroline Sapriel is the founder and managing director of CS&A, a global risk and crisis management consulting firm with offices in Hong Kong, the United Kingdom, Belgium, France, the Netherlands, the United States, the United Arab Emirates, and Singapore. She regularly speaks at international conferences and seminars on risk and crisis management, has written numerous journal articles, and has been a guest lecturer at the graduate school of public administration of Leiden University. She has been a member of the IABC since 1987 and serves on the board of its Belgian Chapter. She holds a B.A. in Chinese studies and a B.Sc. degree in international relations from the Hebrew University of Jerusalem.

D. Mark Schumann, ABC, is passionate about all things brand and communication related. As a consultant, he has created employer brands for more than a hundred companies around the world; as an author, he has coauthored two books on employer brands, *Brand from the Inside* and *Brand for Talent*, and, as a volunteer, he is a past chair of IABC and an active participant in the development of the association's brand. He is the winner of seventeen IABC Gold Quill Awards and a frequent IABC speaker and author. Today, he maintains a daily blog, www.acommunicatorsview.com, and leads a consultancy, How Brands Engage, based in Ridgefield, Connecticut.

Pamela Shockley-Zalabak is chancellor and professor of communication at the University of Colorado at Colorado Springs. She also is president of CommuniCon, a consulting group that specializes in leadership development, conflict resolution, and development of team-based organizations. The author of six books and numerous articles, Shockley-Zalabak focuses on large-scale organizational assessment and planning. She received her B.A. and M.A. from

Oklahoma State University and her Ph.D. in communication from the University of Colorado at Boulder.

Lorenzo Sierra is a marketing communication and public affairs consultant based in Arizona and the marketing and public relations manager for LVM Systems, a software company for health care call centers. Before joining LVM, Sierra was the regional marketing director for a Fortune 100 health insurance company and a communication consultant at a Fortune 500 human resources consulting firm. He sits on the boards of BMA Phoenix, the Arizona Hispanic Chamber of Commerce, and Parenting Arizona. He is also an appointed commissioner on the Arizona Governor's Commission on Service and Volunteerism. Lorenzo holds a B.A. in journalism from Arizona State University.

Don W. Stacks is professor and associate dean for Faculty Research and Creative Activity at the University of Miami's School of Communication. Stacks is the author of numerous articles, chapters, books, and professional papers dealing with public relations. He is a member of the Arthur W. Page Society and Commission on Public Relations Measurement and sits on the board of trustees for the Institute for Public Relations. He earned his doctorate from the University of Florida.

Karen Vahouny, ABC, is a founding partner of Qorvis Communications. Earlier, she was vice president of corporate communications at PRC, an information technology company. She was elected to the board of trustees for the National Endowment for Financial Education in 2010. Twice named Business Communicator of the Year for IABC/Washington, Vahouny has served on the IABC executive board, the IABC Research Foundation board, presented at several international conferences, wrote articles for *Communication World*, and chaired the IABC Think Tank and the IABC investment committee. She serves on the board of directors for the Capital Area Chapter of the National Investor Relations Institute. She holds a B.S. in marketing from the University of Virginia and an M.B.A. in finance and management from George Mason University.

Mark Weiner is the chief executive officer of PRIME Research North America, one of the world's largest public relations and corporate communications research and consulting providers. He is the author of *Unleashing the Power of PR: A Contrarian's Guide to Marketing and Communication* (Wiley) and has contributed chapters to three other texts. He is a frequent speaker and a visiting professor for The Executive Education Programs, S.I. Newhouse School of Public Communications at Syracuse University, and has guest-lectured at many of the nation's leading public relations programs. He is a regular contributor to leading communication and public relations professional media and sits on the editorial advisory boards of the *Strategist* and *PR News*. Weiner is a member of The Institute for Public Relations, PRSA, IABC. He is a graduate of the University of Maryland.

Patricia T. Whalen is an educator and consultant with more than twenty years of professional work experience. She has served as the head of corporate communications for a Fortune 300 company and as marketing director for an international telecommunications firm. Since 2006 she has served as the graduate director for DePaul University's master's program in public relations and advertising. Prior to that, she spent eight years as a full-time faculty member in the Medill Integrated Marketing Communications graduate program at Northwestern University. She wrote *How Communication Drives Merger Success* (IABC, 2002). She has also written books on corporate communications and marketing public relations. She holds a doctorate in mass media from Michigan State University, a master's of science degree in business administration from Indiana University at South Bend, and a bachelor's degree in English from the Ohio State University.

Brad Whitworth, ABC, IABC Fellow, is senior communication manager at Cisco, based in San Jose, California. His work has earned him recognition as a thought leader in the field of internal communications. A former broadcaster, Whitworth speaks regularly to business executives, communication groups, and university classes around the world. Before joining Cisco in 2007, he led communication programs at HP, PeopleSoft, and AAA. While at HP he developed the merger communications for the $20 billion HP-Compaq PC business and managed the company's Y2K communications program. He holds bachelor's degrees in both journalism and speech from the University of Missouri and an MBA from Santa Clara University. He served as IABC chairman in 1989–1990 and has won six IABC Gold Quills.

Anna Marie Willey, ABC, is president of Total Communications Services Ltd., a communication consulting corporation based in Saskatchewan, Canada, with interest in local, national, and international projects. She has more than thirty years experience specializing in strategic communications management and planning and organizational development and implementation. Her prior roles have included overall responsibility for government communications while chief of communications for the Government of Saskatchewan, vice president of communications with SaskPower, and other executive-level strategic positions within government and major institutions. Throughout her career, she has received a number of honors and awards and has enjoyed many roles as an active volunteer with IABC serving at the local level as well as the international level as chair of the IABC Accreditation Council.

John Williams is president of Joe Williams Communications, Inc., a twenty-five-year-old communications research, training, and consulting firm. John has conducted communications measurement, including surveys, focus groups, and audits, for organizations of all sizes and industries. He developed his firm's Performance Impact Analysis program, which identifies the key communications drivers of organizational performance. Joe Williams Communications has conducted communications surveys for more than a hundred companies and has a database that represents more than 500,000 global employees. You may reach John at john.williams@JWCom.com, or visit www.jwcom.com.

THE IABC HANDBOOK
OF ORGANIZATIONAL
COMMUNICATION

PART ONE

FOUNDATIONS OF BUSINESS COMMUNICATION

CHAPTER ONE

CHARACTERISTICS OF EXCELLENT COMMUNICATION

James E. Grunig, Larissa A. Grunig

When the International Association of Business Communicators (IABC) Research Foundation issued a request for proposals in 1984 for research on "How, Why, and to What Extent Communication Contributes to the Achievement of Organizational Objectives," we first thought of the opportunity to move beyond evaluating individual communication programs such as media, community, or employee relations, where we had previously conducted research, to construct a theory of the overall value of the public relations function to the organization. Thus, the Excellence study offered the possibility of constructing a theory of how public relations contributes to organizational effectiveness.

At the same time, our collaborators on the project (David Dozier, William Ehling, Fred Repper, and Jon White) noted that the project would make it possible to integrate a number of middle-range concepts that explained how the communication function should be organized to increase its value to the organization. James Grunig brought his concepts of publics, organizational theory and decision making, models of public relations, evaluation of public relations, and research on employee communication to the project. David Dozier contributed his and Glen Broom's roles theory. William Ehling contributed his knowledge of operations research and his views on the controversy over public relations and integrated marketing communication. Larissa Grunig brought her knowledge of gender, diversity, power, activism, and organizational structure and culture. Jon White contributed his ideas about public relations and strategic management. To this mix, Fred Repper, our practitioner member of the team, added his understanding of how theories worked in practice. The package became what we now know as the Excellence theory.

Based on our research, we developed a *generic benchmark* (Fleisher, 1995) of critical success factors and best practices in communication management. In most public relations benchmarking studies, a researcher compares a communication unit with other units in its own industry that are generally recognized as the best. The Excellence study, by contrast, identified best practices across different types of organizations—corporations, government agencies, nonprofit organizations, and associations. Generic benchmarking is more valuable than benchmarking a single case because it is unlikely that one organization will be "a world-class performer across the board" (Fleisher, 1995, p. 29). In the Excellence study, we found that a few organizations exemplified most of the best practices, many exemplified some, and others had few of these characteristics. A generic benchmark does not provide an exact formula or detailed description of practices that a communication unit can copy to be excellent. Rather, it provides a set of principles that professionals can use to generate ideas for specific practices in their own organizations.

We tested the Excellence theory through survey research of heads of public relations, chief executive officers (CEOs), and employees in 327 organizations (corporations, nonprofit organizations, government agencies, and associations) in the United States, Canada, and the United Kingdom. The survey research was followed by qualitative interviews with heads of public relations, other public relations practitioners, and CEOs in twenty-five organizations with the highest and lowest scores on a scale of Excellence produced by statistical analysis of the survey data. Three books were published from the research (Grunig, 1992; Dozier, Grunig & Grunig, 1995; & Grunig, Grunig, & Dozier, 2002).

In our first book, *Excellence in Public Relations and Communication Management*, Repper (1992) explained how the theory of Excellence can be used to audit communication programs: "One thing communicators never have been able to do is to compare our communication programs with a program that is considered the best and most effective. However, the normative theory provided in the book gives us an opportunity to measure the effectiveness of our communication programs against that of an ideal program" (Grunig, 1992, p. 112). Any professional communicator or executive to whom the communication function reports could conduct a formal or informal audit to compare that function with the generic benchmark we have developed. Professional communicators asked to serve as peer reviewers for other organizations could use the characteristics as a qualitative benchmark to frame their evaluation.

The Value of Communication to an Organization

IABC's emphasis on explaining the value of public relations stimulated us to put measurement and evaluation into a broader perspective than the program level. Although program evaluation remained an important component of our theory, we realized that it could not show the overall value of the public relations function to the organization. Our review of the literature on organizational effectiveness first showed that public relations has value when it helps the organization achieve its goals. However, the literature also showed that it has to develop those goals through interaction with strategic constituencies (stakeholders and publics). We theorized that communication adds value when it helps the organization identify stakeholders and segment different kinds of publics from stakeholder categories. CEOs in the qualitative portion of the study, for example, emphasized that the communication function has value because it provides a broad, diverse perspective both inside and outside the organization. Second, we showed that public relations increases its value when it uses symmetrical communication to develop and cultivate relationships with strategic publics. If it develops good relationships with strategic publics, an organization is likely to develop goals desired by both the organization and its publics and to achieve those goals because it shares the goals and collaborates with publics. Similarly, CEOs emphasized the value of public relations in helping the organization deal with crises and conflicts with activist groups.

Although we concluded that it is difficult to place a monetary value on relationships with publics and the outside perspective of public relations, our interviews with CEOs and senior public relations officers revealed numerous examples of how public relations had reduced the *costs* of litigation, regulation, legislation, and negative publicity caused by poor relationships, issues, and crises; reduced the *risk* of making decisions that affect different stakeholders; or increased *revenue* by providing products and services needed by stakeholders. Those examples provided powerful qualitative evidence of the value of good relationships with strategic publics.

In addition to explaining the value of communication, the Excellence study provided solid theory and empirical evidence of how the function should be organized to maximize this value. The characteristics of an excellent public relations function can be placed into four categories, each containing several characteristics that can be audited.

For public relations to contribute to organizational effectiveness, the organization must empower public relations as a critical management function. Empowerment of the public relations function includes four characteristics:

1. *The senior communication executive is involved with the strategic management processes of the organization, and communication programs are developed for strategic publics identified through this process.* Public relations contributes to strategic management by scanning the environment to identify the publics affected by the consequences of decisions or that might affect the outcome of decisions. An excellent public relations department communicates with these publics to bring their voices into strategic management, thus making it possible for publics to participate in organizational decisions that affect them.

2. *Communication programs organized by excellent departments to communicate with strategic publics also are managed strategically.* To be managed strategically means that these programs are based on formative research, that they have concrete and measurable objectives, and that they are evaluated either formally or informally. In addition, the communication staff can provide evidence to show that these programs achieved their short-term objectives and improved long-term relationships between the organization and its publics.

3. *The senior public relations executive is a member of the dominant coalition of the organization or has a direct reporting relationship to senior managers who are part of the dominant coalition.* The communication function seldom will have the power to affect key organizational decisions unless the chief communication officer is part of or has access to the group of senior managers with the greatest power in the organization.

4. *Diversity is embodied in all public relations roles.* The principle of requisite variety suggests that organizations need as much diversity inside as in their environment if they are to interact successfully with all strategic elements of their environment. Excellent public relations departments empower both men and women in all roles as well as practitioners of diverse racial, ethnic, and cultural backgrounds.

Communicator Roles

Public relations researchers have identified two major roles that communicators play in organizations: the manager and technician roles. Communication technicians are essential to carry out most of the day-to-day communication activities of public relations departments, and many practitioners play both roles. In less excellent departments, however, all of the communication practitioners—including the senior practitioner—are technicians. If the senior communicator is not a manager, it is not possible for public relations to be empowered as a management function. Three characteristics of excellence in public relations are related to the managerial role:

1. *The communication unit is headed by a strategic manager rather than a technician or an administrative manager.* Excellent public relations units must have at least one senior communication manager who conceptualizes and directs communication programs. Otherwise, members of the dominant coalition who have little knowledge of communication management will supply this direction. In addition, the Excellence study distinguished between a strategic manager and an administrative manager. Administrative managers typically manage day-to-day operations of the communication function, personnel, and the budget; they generally are supervisors of technicians. Strategic managers provide communication strategies that support the business goals. If the senior public relations officer is an administrative manager, the department usually will not be excellent.

2. *The senior communication executive or others in the public relations unit must have the knowledge needed for a strategic role.* Excellent public relations programs are staffed by practitioners who have gained the knowledge needed to carry out the strategic manager role through university education, continuing education, or self-study.

3. *Both men and women must have equal opportunity to occupy the managerial role.* The majority of public relations professionals are women. If women are not considered for managerial roles, the communication function is diminished because many of the most knowledgeable practitioners are excluded from that role. When that is the case, the senior position in the communication department often is filled by someone from another managerial function who has little knowledge of public relations.

Organization of the Communication Function and Its Relationship to Other Management Functions

Many organizations have a single department devoted to all communication functions. Others have separate departments for programs aimed at different publics such as journalists, employees, the local community, or the financial community. Still others place communication under another managerial function such as marketing, human resources, legal, or finance. Many organizations also contract with or consult with outside firms for all or some of their communication programs or for such communication techniques as annual reports or newsletters. Two characteristics are related to the organization of the function:

1. *Public relations should be an integrated communication function.* An excellent public relations function integrates communication programs into a single

department or provides a mechanism for coordinating programs managed by different departments. Only in an integrated system is it possible for public relations to develop new communication programs for changing strategic publics and to move resources from programs designed for formerly strategic publics to the new programs.

2. *Communication should be a management function separate from other functions.* Even though the communication function is integrated, it should not be placed under a management function such as marketing or human resources. When the public relations function is sublimated to other functions, it cannot be managed strategically because it cannot move resources from one strategic public to another—as an integrated public relations function can.

Models of Public Relations

Public relations scholars have conducted extensive research on the extent to which organizations practice four models of public relations—four typical ways of conceptualizing and conducting the communication function—and to identify which of these models provides a normative framework for effective and ethical public relations. These models are the (1) two-way symmetrical model of dialogue, collaboration, and public participation; (2) press agentry (emphasizing favorable publicity); (3) public information (disclosing accurate, but mostly favorable, information and conducting no research or other form of two-way communication); or (4) two-way asymmetrical (emphasizing the interests of the organization and excluding the interests of publics). The two-way symmetrical model produces better long-term relationships with publics than do the other models. Symmetrical programs balance the interests of organizations and publics in society.

The research for the Excellence study refined our understanding of these models by identifying four dimensions that underlie them: (1) symmetrical or asymmetrical, (2) two-way or one-way, (3) mediated or interpersonal, and (4) ethical or unethical. The two-way symmetrical model embodies the most desirable of these characteristics: symmetrical, two-way, both mediated and interpersonal, and ethical. The other models possess some but not all of these characteristics.

Four characteristics of Excellence, therefore, are related to models of public relations:

1. The public relations department and the dominant coalition share the worldview that the communication department should base its goals and its com-

munication activities on the two-way symmetrical model of public relations.
2. Communication programs developed for specific publics are based on two-way symmetrical strategies for building and maintaining relationships.
3. The senior public relations executive or others in the public relations unit must have the professional knowledge needed to practice the two-way symmetrical model.
4. The organization should have a symmetrical system of internal communication.

A symmetrical system of internal communication is based on the principles of employee empowerment and participation in decision making. Managers and other employees engage in dialogue and listen to each other. Internal media disclose relevant information needed by employees to understand their roles in the organization. Symmetrical communication fosters a participative rather than an authoritarian culture as well as good relationships with employees.

Extending the Excellence Theory to a Global Theory

Through several studies conducted around the world, the Excellence theory has been expanded into a global theory that includes *generic principles* and *specific applications*. This theory falls between a theory that suggests an organization should practice public relations in exactly the same way in every country—usually the way it is practiced in the country where the headquarters of the multinational organization is located—and a theory suggesting that public relations must be practiced differently in every country because of cultural and other contextual conditions. *Generic principles* means that in an abstract sense, the principles of public relations are the same worldwide. *Specific applications* means that these principles must be applied differently in different settings.

As a starting point for research, we proposed that the characteristics identified in the Excellence study are generic principles. We also proposed that public relations professionals must take six contextual conditions into account when they apply these principles: culture, including language; the political system; the economic system; the media system; the level of economic development; and the extent and nature of activism.

Our research and that of others has provided evidence supporting this theory. The most extensive research was in Slovenia. We replicated the quantitative portion of the Excellence study in thirty Slovenian firms and found the same cluster of characteristics as we did in the United States, Canada, and the United

Kingdom in spite of a different cultural, political, and economic context (Grunig, Grunig, & Verčič, 1998). To deal with such differences, communicators in Slovenia had to apply the generic principles differently than in the Anglo countries. For example, we learned that communicators needed to counsel CEOs to empower public relations managers. They also developed continuing education for communicators to deal with their lack of public relations knowledge, and they had to emphasize employee relations because of the negative context inside Slovenian organizations.

The Strategic Management Role of Public Relations

Although the Excellence theory incorporates a number of middle-range theories, its most important component is the strategic role of public relations. Since the completion of the Excellence study, scholars have continued to do research to help professionals understand and fulfill this role.

To contribute to strategic management, public relations should be an integral part of the management of every organization. The public relations function helps the organization interact with its stakeholders both to accomplish the organization's mission and to behave in a socially responsible manner. In a strategic role, communicators manage communication with *top managers* and with *publics*. They manage communication between management and publics to build *relationships* with the publics that are most likely to affect the organization or that are most affected by the organization. Communication processes that facilitate dialogue among managers and publics influence *organizational behaviors*. Dialogue among managers and publics, in turn, can produce long-term relationships described by characteristics researchers (Grunig & Huang, 2000; Grunig & Hung, 2002) have identified and defined: trust, mutuality of control, commitment, and satisfaction. Relationships can be measured and evaluated to determine the long-term effectiveness and value of public relations (Hon & Grunig, 1999; Grunig, 2002).

An excellent public relations staff cannot serve this role, however, unless research and measurement are an integral part of the function. Formative research is necessary to identify strategic publics with which an organization needs relationships and to determine how to cultivate relationships with them. Communicators can use Grunig's (1997) situational theory of publics—especially as it has been updated (Kim, Grunig, & Ni, 2010)—to segment stakeholders into publics. The Excellence study showed that the most common categories of stakeholders are employees, customers, investors, the community, government, members of associations and nonprofit organizations, the media, and donors to nonprofit organizations. The situational theory segments these categories of stakeholders into publics with different levels of activity, including activist (belonging to activist groups), active, passive, or nonpublic. The more active the public, the more likely it is that communication programs will have an effect. Evaluative research then is necessary to determine the effectiveness of communication programs. Evaluative research can determine the short-term effects of communication programs on the cognitions, attitudes, and behaviors of both publics and management and the long-term effects of communication on organization–public relationships (Grunig, 2008).

New Research to Enhance the Strategic Role of the Communication Function

Although research-based knowledge of publics and the evaluation of public relations has been available for years, other concepts and tools related to the strategic management role of public relations have been developed within the last twenty years. Some examples of research to develop these new concepts and tools include:

- *Environmental scanning:* Research to identify problems, publics, and issues and to evaluate information sources to bring information into the organization (Chang, 2000).
- *Publics:* Research to develop the situational theory and to explain the social nature of publics (Aldoory, 2001; Kim, 2006; Kim, Grunig, & Ni, 2010; Sha, 1995).
- *Scenario building:* Research to develop this technique for explaining the behavior of publics to management and potential issues created by publics (Sung, 2004).
- *Relationship cultivation strategies:* Research to expand the concepts of symmetrical and asymmetrical communication to identify strategies for cultivating relationships that produce high-quality relationships with stakeholder publics (Hung, 2002, 2004; Rhee, 2004).
- *Interactions of relationships and reputation:* Public relations practitioners and management scholars have paid a great deal of attention to an organization's reputation in recent years, in the belief that reputation is an intangible asset that adds both monetary and nonmonetary value to an organization. Our research (Grunig & Hung, 2002; Yang, 2005; Yang & Grunig, 2005) has shown, however, that reputations are largely a byproduct of management behavior

and the quality of organization–public relationships. Thus, attending to relationships will ultimately improve an organization's reputation. Reputation, however, cannot be managed directly; it is managed by influencing the behavior of management and through the cultivation of relationships.

- *Development of an ethical framework* for public relations practitioners to use as they participate in strategic management (Bowen, 2000, 2004).
- *Empowerment of the public relations function.* Research to clarify the nature of the dominant coalition in an organization and how public relations practitioners become part of or gain access to empowered coalitions (Berger, 2005).
- *Specialized areas of public relations.* Research to extend the generic principles of excellence to specialized areas of public relations, such as fund raising (Kelly, 1991), investor relations (Schickinger, 1998), employee relations (Kim, 2005), community relations (Rhee, 2004), and government relations (Chen, 2005).
- *Public relations and global strategy.* Research to develop the global theory of generic principles that can be applied in many cultures and political-economic settings and specific applications to adapt them to different contexts (Grunig, Grunig, & Verčič, 1998; Verčič, Grunig, & Grunig, 1996; Wakefield, 1997, 2000). Researchers also have applied this theory to a multinational military organization (NATO) (Van Dyke, 2005), public diplomacy programs of governments for publics in other countries (Yun, 2005), and globalized and localized relationship strategies of multinational organizations (Ni, 2006).

References

Aldoory, L. (2001). Making health communications meaningful for women: Factors that influence involvement. *Journal of Public Relations Research, 13,* 163–185.

Berger, B. K. (2005). Power over, power with, and power to public relations: Critical reflections on public relations, the dominant coalition, and activism. *Journal of Public Relations Research, 17,* 5–28.

Bowen, S. A. (2000). *A theory of ethical issues management: Contributions of Kantian deontology to public relations' ethics and decision making.* Unpublished doctoral dissertation, University of Maryland, College Park.

Bowen, S. A. (2004). Expansion of ethics as the tenth generic principle of public relations excellence: A Kantian theory and model for managing ethical issues. *Journal of Public Relations Research, 16,* 65–92.

Chang, Y.-C. (2000). *A normative exploration into environmental scanning in public relations.* Unpublished master's thesis, University of Maryland, College Park.

Chen, Y. R. (2005). *Effective government affairs in an era of marketization: Strategic issues management, business lobbying, and relationship management by multinational corporations in China.* Unpublished doctoral dissertation, University of Maryland, College Park.

Dozier, D. M., with Grunig, L. A., & Grunig, J. E. (1995). *Manager's guide to excellence in public relations and communication management.* Mahwah, NJ: Lawrence Erlbaum.

Fleisher, C. S. (1995). *Public affairs benchmarking*. Washington, DC: Public Affairs Council.

Grunig, J. E. (1992). (Ed.). *Excellence in public relations and communication management*. Hillsdale, NJ: Lawrence Erlbaum.

Grunig, J. E. (1997). A situational theory of publics: Conceptual history, recent challenges and new research. In D. Moss, T. MacManus, & D. Verčič (Eds.), *Public relations research: An international perspective* (pp. 3–46). London: International Thomson Business Press.

Grunig, J. E. (2002). *Qualitative methods for assessing relationships between organizations and publics*. Gainesville, FL: Institute for Public Relations, Commission on PR Measurement and Evaluation.

Grunig, J. E. (2008). Conceptualizing quantitative research in public relations. In B. Van Ruler, A. Tkalac Verčič, & D. Verčič (Eds.), *Public relations metrics* (pp. 88–119). New York: Routledge.

Grunig, J. E., & Huang, Y. H. (2000). From organizational effectiveness to relationship indicators: Antecedents of relationships, public relations strategies, and relationship outcomes. In J. A. Ledingham & S. D. Bruning (Eds.), *Public relations as relationship management: A relational approach to the study and practice of public relations* (pp. 23–53). Mahwah, NJ: Lawrence Erlbaum.

Grunig, J. E., & Hung, C. J. (2002, March). *The effect of relationships on reputation and reputation on relationships: A cognitive, behavioral study*. Paper presented to the International, Interdisciplinary Public Relations Research Conference, Miami, FL.

Grunig, L. A., Grunig, J. E., & Dozier, D. M. (2002). *Excellent public relations and effective organizations: A study of communication management in three countries*. Mahwah, NJ: Lawrence Erlbaum.

Grunig, L. A., Grunig, J. E., & Verčič, D. (1998). Are the IABC's excellence principles generic? Comparing Slovenia and the United States, the United Kingdom and Canada. *Journal of Communication Management, 2*, 335–356.

Hon, L. C., & Grunig, J. E. (1999). *Guidelines for measuring relationships in public relations*. Gainesville, FL: Institute for Public Relations, Commission on PR Measurement and Evaluation.

Hung, C. J. (2002). *The interplays of relationship types, relationship cultivation, and relationship outcomes: How multinational and Taiwanese companies practice public relations and organization-public relationship management in China*. Unpublished doctoral dissertation, University of Maryland, College Park.

Hung, C. J. (2004). Cultural influence on relationship cultivation strategies: Multinational companies in China. *Journal of Communication Management, 8*, 264–281.

Kelly, K. S. (1991). *Fund raising and public relations*. Hillsdale, NJ: Lawrence Erlbaum.

Kim, H. S. (2005). *Organizational structure and internal communication as antecedents of employee-organization relationships in the context of organizational justice: A multilevel analysis*. Unpublished doctoral dissertation, University of Maryland, College Park.

Kim, J.-N. (2006). *Communicant activeness, cognitive entrepreneurship, and a situational theory of problem solving*. Unpublished doctoral dissertation, University of Maryland, College Park.

Kim, J-N., Grunig, J. E., & Ni, L. (2010). Reconceptualizing the communicative action of publics: Acquisition, selection, and transmission of information in problematic situations. *International Journal of Strategic Communication, 4*, 126–154.

Ni, L. (2006). *Exploring the value of public relations in strategy implementation: Employee relations in the globalization process*. Unpublished doctoral dissertation, University of Maryland, College Park.

Repper, F. C. (1992). How communication managers can apply the theories of excellence and effectiveness. In J. E. Grunig (Ed.), *Excellence in public relations and communication management* (pp. 109–114). Hillsdale, NJ: Lawrence Erlbaum.

Rhee, Y. (2004). *The employee-public-organization chain in relationship management: A case study of a government organization.* Unpublished doctoral dissertation, University of Maryland, College Park.

Sha, B. L. (1995). *Intercultural public relations: Exploring cultural identity as a means of segmenting publics.* Unpublished master's thesis, University of Maryland, College Park.

Schickinger, P. (1998). *Electronic investor relations: Can new media close the symmetry gap?* Unpublished master's thesis, University of Maryland, College Park.

Sung, M. J. (2004). *Toward a model of strategic management of public relations: Scenario building from a public relations perspective.* Unpublished doctoral dissertation, University of Maryland, College Park.

Van Dyke, M. A. (2005). *Toward a theory of just communication: A case study of NATO, multinational public relations, ethical management of international conflict.* Unpublished doctoral dissertation, University of Maryland, College Park.

Verčič, D., Grunig, L. A., & Grunig, J. E. (1996). Global and specific principles of public relations: Evidence from Slovenia. In H. M. Culbertson & N. Chen (Eds.), *International public relations: A comparative analysis* (pp. 31–65). Mahwah NJ: Lawrence Erlbaum.

Wakefield, R. I. (1997). *International public relations: A theoretical approach to excellence based on a worldwide Delphi study.* Unpublished doctoral dissertation, University of Maryland, College Park.

Wakefield, R. I. (2000). World-class public relations: A model for effective public relations in the multinational. *Journal of Communication Management, 5*(1), 59–71.

Yang, S. U. (2005). *The effect of organization-public relationships on reputation from the perspective of publics.* Unpublished doctoral dissertation, University of Maryland, College Park.

Yang, S. U., & Grunig, J. E. (2005). Decomposing organizational reputation: The effects of organization-public relationship outcomes on cognitive representations of organizations and evaluations of organizational performance. *Journal of Communication Management, 9,* 296–304.

Yun, S. H. (2005). *Theory building for comparative public diplomacy from the perspectives of public relations and international relations: A macro-comparative study of embassies in Washington, DC.* Unpublished doctoral dissertation, University of Maryland, College Park.

CHAPTER TWO

THE CORPORATE COMMUNICATOR

A Senior-Level Strategist

Nick Durutta

Corporations are subject to the same communication dynamics as any other human interaction. Whenever people get together—in a personal relationship, a social group, or a business venture—communication inevitably happens. The larger and more structured the group is, however (such as a corporation or nonprofit organization), the greater the need for communication to be managed for it to be effective.

Most corporations or large organizations acknowledge, sometimes grudgingly, that communication is important, yet the concept is often misunderstood. "We need more communication!" is often heard in corporate boardrooms when things are going wrong. In fact, too much of the wrong kind of communication might be the problem.

Executives who demand "more communication" usually want a more effective flow of information in their organization. This means seeing that the right information gets to the right people in the right way. But each of these elements can be challenging and complex. What is the "right" information? Who are the "right" people? What is the "right way" to communicate with them?

The corporate communicator is the individual who provides comprehensive answers to these questions. To do this, he or she must be thoroughly integrated into the organization, working closely with senior and middle management, rank-and-file employees, and other key publics in the media, the community, and industry. The communicator needs to know and understand the information requirements, concerns, and goals of these audiences to devise a communication solution that meets the organization's greatest needs.

In this chapter, we examine the role of the corporate communicator as a strategist and senior-level adviser to the organization.

A Strategic Role

To be most effective, corporate communicators must play a strategic role, regardless of the type of organization or corporation in which they work. This means that they must take a broad and in-depth look at the organization, truly understand its needs, assess where communication would be most effective, and develop a plan to make it happen.

It is the responsibility of the corporate communicator to manage communication that:

- Supports organizational goals and objectives
- Ensures a healthy flow of information in and among all levels of employees and management (*healthy* means that the most useful information is flowing to the people who need it, when they need it)
- Is consistent throughout all the organization's activities
- Keeps the organization honest (ethical behavior is most effectively supported by open and honest communication)
- Avoids or mitigates potential crises

To carry out these responsibilities most effectively, the communicator must be proactive—that is, he or she must anticipate needs rather than react when needs arise. This requires that corporate communicators be senior-level managers, working alongside the chief executive officer (CEO) or president and other senior corporate officers when issues are discussed and key business decisions are made. Communicators at this level are strategists rather than tacticians; they often manage others who perform specific tasks and execute tactics (Dozier, 1992).

Too often, however, communicators assume a tactical role, responding to dictated requests: to create a website, for example, or send out a news release. In this mode, communicators are frequently more reactive than proactive. This prevents them from taking the broader view necessary to assess the communication approaches that are truly needed.

When they are positioned at a senior strategist level, communicators are more likely to understand the organization's true communication needs. They know the organization's goals and objectives, even if these are not explicitly stated in a strategic planning document. They know the human and interpersonal dynamics of the organization, which usually are not explicitly stated anywhere. They are aware of issues and concerns among the organization's employees, and within the organization's community, to which other senior managers may not have access and are able to identify potential opportunities to address these issues as well as other obstacles that may stand in the way. They are able to identify and head off looming crises before they hit the front pages of a newspaper. They are able to address potential ethical breaches or conflicts.

A Senior-Level Adviser

In a corporation, the president or chief executive officer oversees a dizzying array of factors that contribute to the well-being of the organization: research and production; customer and client service; marketing; employee relations; human resources; legal, safety, and security; facilities and asset planning; and many more. Directors responsible for each of these areas usually report directly to the CEO. Communication is one of the primary needs a CEO must address, and the corporate communicator should be prominent among the senior adviser staff.

Particularly in the current media-saturated environment, when even the slightest perceived organizational misstep can trigger a storm of public interest (whether in the mainstream media or the blogosphere), a senior communicator can be a CEO's most valuable adviser. The senior communicator should work closely to carefully consider (and foresee, when possible) the implications of any actions, planned or unplanned, on target publics.

Accordingly, the corporate communicator should be one of the least isolated members of the senior management team. While some roles, such as sales and marketing, might exist largely in their own silos, it is essential that communicators be in continual contact with all parts of the organization. That is the only way they can gain the knowledge necessary to make strategic decisions.

A Communicator's Portfolio of Skills

Which skills should a corporate communicator bring to her or his role? We are aware of the need for the critical ability to strategically analyze an organization and recognize areas in which more effective communication is needed. But the communicator's tool kit must contain many other skills.

A corporate communicator must have basic communication skills—that is, be able to write and speak well. Yet too many senior-level communicators may be effective on a strategic level yet freeze when making a speech or attempting to write a well-crafted sentence. Because communicators never know which aspect of communication they may need to address, a repertoire of basic skills is essential:

- *Writing and editing.* The ability to write well is the most critical and basic communication skill. Writing well means understanding the basics of grammar, spelling, and punctuation and having the ability to present an issue or topic in a way that is understandable to the target audience—whether it be a broad group of people with varying levels of education and background or a narrower group with specific communication needs. It also means being able to capture an audience's attention, persuade and convince them, and trigger their emotions. Good editing requires much of the same knowledge as good writing, but is a distinct skill. (There are great editors who are not great writers, and vice versa.)

- *Design sense.* The wide range of communication tools that a communicator uses—from websites to press materials to PowerPoint decks—often involves making graphic design decisions. Although a communicator does not need to be a designer, a basic understanding of design principles can be invaluable to planning and managing this function.

- *Speaking.* Sometimes the focus on written communication overshadows the importance of good oral communication. A good communicator knows how to put words together for maximum understanding and effect, in speech as well as in text. He or she must be able to speak effectively, whether in a private conversation, addressing a roomful of people, or in an interview on national television.

- *Listening.* The ability to actively listen—to absorb not only the surface facts of a situation but the many more subtle factors communicated by an individual or group—is an essential skill for communicators. Communication is often viewed as a one-way process: delivering information to a particular audience. But an equal part of the process is receiving feedback from the audience, both before the information or message is delivered and after. In this regard, research and measurement become important tasks for a communicator.

Research involves collecting relevant information before crafting and delivering a message. The more effectively communicators can understand factors influencing an issue—particularly those pertaining to the target audiences—the more effectively they can craft and deliver a message. If an issue is particularly complex or sensitive, research can become quite extensive and may involve professional research firms or specialists. Sometimes the necessary research has already been gathered and might be available from a private firm or a public database; at other times, the communicator may need to conduct independent research.

Measurement is the process of determining whether communication is meeting its goal or objective. Alarmingly, this is a step that is often overlooked; yet, conducting communication without measurement is like buying a lottery ticket and never checking the winning numbers. Unlike other activities such as sales or production, the results of communication can be challenging to measure, because they involve gauging softer, more subjective outcomes: the perceptions, opinions, and actions of groups of people. Yet such measurement is possible. There are many effective measurement tools and resources available to communicators today.

• *Strategic thinking.* The ability to put everything together—to assess a business or organizational situation (within the context of many influencing factors) and develop a plan to implement the right combination of communication skills and tools at their disposal for maximum effectiveness—is possibly a communicator's most valuable skill. Some practitioners call this "seeing the big picture"—moving beyond day-to-day activities to view a long-term solution. Strategic planning follows a prescribed process of assessing organizational needs, identifying goals, setting objectives, developing a solution, carrying it out, and measuring the results. It is through the strategic planning process that communicators can truly demonstrate their value as strategists rather than just tacticians who perform isolated tasks.

Beyond this kit of essential skills, there are certain qualities that are found in good communicators, some of which cannot be learned. It is important, for example, that a communicator be curious. The environment in which a communicator works, both internally and externally, is always changing, and staying one step ahead of changes is critical to ensuring success. A curious communicator is always researching new business and industry trends, technologies, and best practices.

The most successful communicators understand that communication is an ongoing process, similar to a continuing conversation. It involves continually checking with key audiences and stakeholders to make sure the message is being properly received and being open to changing strategies and tactics.

What Corporate Communicators Need to Know about Their Organizations

An effective corporate communicator must have thorough knowledge of the organization, with a good understanding of its industry, mission and strategic focus, management structure, products or services, customers and clients, community, history, employees (their demographics and issues), and culture.

There is typically a ramp-up period when a new communicator comes into an organization, during which he or she absorbs as many of the details of the environment as possible before initiating communication. It helps, of course, if the communicator has previous experience in the organization's industry or in a related field, but this may not always be the case, particularly in today's increasingly global and mobile job market. It is not unusual for communicators to move from one industry, or even country and culture, to another many times within their careers.

Communicators should realize that none of the key organizational elements listed previously (with the possible exception of history) remain static. Most successful organizations reinvent themselves to some degree on a regular basis, shifting their business focus in response to competitive and environmental factors. Even something as seemingly constant as a corporation's industry may shift significantly over time (think of large corporations such as General Electric or Philip Morris). The communicator must be able to develop communication strategies to adapt to these changes.

Understanding an Organization's Culture

Of the key aspects of an organization or corporation, possibly the most challenging to understand is its culture, since culture is often undefined. Even corporations that print their cultural values on wallet cards or lunchroom banners might not be fully communicating the nuances of their cultures.

Understanding the underlying aspects of an organization's culture might be a communicator's most important challenge, since these can hold the key to effectively overcoming communication obstacles and identifying opportunities. An organization that proudly and publicly proclaims integrity and ethics as cornerstones of its culture, yet makes business decisions that appear to benefit only a select few (rather than the organization overall) is not walking its talk.

Similarly, a corporation that publicly applauds employee loyalty, yet discards long-term employees in favor of bringing in younger employees (at lower pay grades), will quickly lose the trust of its workforce. One of a communicator's most important functions is to identify for management any disconnect between stated cultural values and the way the organization actually works, particularly when those practices might have legal and ethical ramifications.

An organization's culture also can have a profound influence on how it communicates. The style and tone used in communication is often an important, and typically unstated, indication of a company's culture. This can translate to using or not using certain words or terms, or even certain media.

Corporate cultures come in all styles, colors, and flavors. They often manifest in subtle ways and can be very fluid. Some are formed and cultivated by design and intention; other cultures simply happen. Accordingly, not all cultures are effective; some can serve as impediments to organizational effectiveness and success, while others can act as catalysts. Different cultures may frequently exist in different parts of the same organization.

Most often, organizational cultures are cultivated by behaviors that are modeled and rewarded rather than through words and slogans. Employees will exhibit preferred behaviors only if there is a perceived benefit or reward attached, such as a bonus, chances for promotion, or even a kind word from the boss. Communicators can reinforce and promote cultural values by showing them in action and making the benefits clear to managers and employees alike.

Types of Organizations

Another key factor in determining how a corporate, senior-level communicator performs is the nature or structure of the corporation or organization itself. Some primary distinguishing identifiers include:

- *Privately owned versus publicly traded.* Public companies have mandated communication responsibilities to their shareholders and the investment community, and the public perception of a company and its products and services can have a direct impact on the value of its stock. The communicator must be aware of any issues that could change this perception (such as unwanted media attention) and develop plans for addressing these issues, preferably before they surface on the front page of a newspaper or on a nightly news broadcast.
- *Small versus large.* The larger the organization is, the greater the number of audiences that may be affected by its fortunes and activities. A small organization might be concerned primarily with its immediate customers, investors, and employees. Larger organizations might be more concerned about publics within a larger sphere of influence: the community, government entities (at the local, state, federal, or international level), and other diverse external audiences.
- *Service provider versus manufacturer.* Organizations that provide services, such as consulting firms, financial services companies, and governmental agencies, can have different communication issues than companies that manufacture or distribute goods, such as automakers or computer firms. For example, service providers are more dependent on the actions of their employees to embody the firm's quality; the reputations of manufacturers can be damaged by flaws in their products.

• *For-profit versus nonprofit.* The communicator in a profit-making organization is largely focused on ensuring that the organization remains profitable and meets its revenue goals. This involves ensuring that customers and clients are aware of the organization's products and services and appreciate their quality, integrity, and value. For-profit organizations are often assisted in this effort by a marketing and advertising staff. In a nonprofit organization such as a charity or foundation, the communicator is often focused on fundraising, relying primarily on media exposure to convey the value of the organization's mission and activities to potential donors and volunteers. The two roles have similarities, but the tone and content of their communication may vary.

• *Union versus nonunion.* If a communicator's organization includes employees represented by a bargaining unit or employees who are considering organizing in this way, another level of complexity is added to the audience mix. Communication to employee groups must have the right tone and content.

• *Local versus multinational.* More and more corporate communicators are finding that their organizations are developing a global reach. This introduces new parameters that can influence communication: multiple cultures, multiple regulatory environments, and multiple languages.

Many corporate communicators specialize in working with specific types of organizations. There are corporate communicators, for example, who may work only with nonprofit health care groups or multinational pharmaceutical companies. Through this focus, a corporate communicator can build a specialized knowledge base that can certainly be valuable, but not all communicators have the opportunity to be so specialized.

It is essential, therefore, that a communicator be a generalist—that is, fully familiar with the basic principles of effective communication—to be of value within nearly any type of organization, regardless of industry, location, or size. (Moreover, in a quickly shifting job market, a generalist communicator, with experience in many types of organizational environments, will be much more marketable.)

Corporate Communicator Roles

A corporate communicator may apply these basic skills to several roles. During their careers, communicators may find themselves in multiple roles. The nature of their organizations, to a large extent, helps determine the roles for which they are responsible.

Public Relations

An organization's public profile—how it is perceived, regarded, and valued by the outside world—is often one of the most critical factors in its success. Regardless of the actual quality and integrity of its products or service, an unfavorable public image can destroy (and has destroyed) an organization. Similarly, a favorable public image can boost, even if only temporarily, an organization whose products and services may be of lesser quality.

Gone are the days when public relations practitioners were fast-talking "flaks" who would do anything to get their organization's or client's name in print or on the air. In today's world, the communicator's responsibility is to represent the client or organization fairly and honestly, with the goal of cultivating a positive image or countering any unwarranted negative publicity as quickly as possible.

In this role, a communicator works closely with the entities that most influence the perception of the organization (and its products and services) among potential clients or customers. These can include the media, community groups, and other key audiences (publics). The communicator must build a relationship of responsiveness and trust with these publics, so that the information received is considered accurate and honest.

Because of the importance of print, Web, and broadcast media to the public image of an organization, media relations is often a primary aspect of the public relations role and is frequently considered a discipline unto itself.

Investor Relations

Publicly traded companies must pay particular attention to opinions of their organization held by the investment community, which includes financial analysts, brokers, and traders. It is to the organization's advantage that these audiences develop trust in the company's management and its ability to meet the organization's business goals. That trust may lead to recommendations to purchase or retain the company's stock. The communicator is the investors' conduit to the organization, from whom they learn of developments, positive or negative, that could influence the company's stock price. This role has become particularly critical in this age of greater transparency and mandated disclosure of financial information.

Community and Government Relations

Most organizations are not immune to oversight and regulation from a government entity, regardless of the scope or nature of their business. The company may work with local city planners when opening a new office or facility, a state review board when revising an employee pay policy, or a federal agency when introducing a new product. Cultivating a relationship of full and open communication with these entities is as important as doing so with any other key public. The more highly regulated the organization's industry (such as energy, financial services, or transportation), the more critical the communicator's role becomes. It must involve effective relationships with key government agencies but also close ties to the organization's lobbyists who work to influence legislation.

Internal Communications

An organization's employees constitute one of the most significant and challenging groups for whom communication must be managed. An informed workforce that feels acknowledged and listened to is an invaluable asset. Building trust, dedication, and loyalty among employees should be a primary goal of all managers. But the communicator occupies a special position in this effort. Quite often, communicators become the catalysts, and the conduits, for communication between and among management and employees.

In this respect, the internal communications role resembles working with any other audience or public. It is important that it be a two-way effort that encourages employee engagement. Perhaps more than other roles, this one requires a great degree of listening.

Marketing Communications

How an organization's products or services are marketed—through advertising, promotions, branding and imagery, or sales campaigns—should be directly linked to its communications to other audiences. If a computer company's ads portray a hip, youth-oriented, and innovative image, yet it cultivates a stodgy, sluggish image when communicating to and interacting with key publics such as investors, employees, or community leaders, it can be a damaging misalignment. The consistency of a company's brand and its competitive values throughout all its communications (and actions) is essential.

The way in which a corporation markets itself can also have an effect on other business facets, including, significantly, its efforts to recruit new employees. Many potential job candidates know an employer from its public image, generally fostered through advertising and public relations. An organization needs to ask if this is the image of the company they want employees, both current and future, to hold.

Corporate communicators may not be directly responsible for marketing communication activities, but because of the importance of this linkage, they should have a relationship with the responsible company officer. The marketing communications manager should have at least a dotted-line relationship with the senior corporate communicator.

Executive Adviser

Quite often the most effective communicator in an organization—whether with employees or outside audiences—is the president or chief executive officer. This person is often consulted first when a situation arises that requires a corporate voice. Corporate communicators can help the CEO and other key executives become effective spokespersons when required, coaching them on working with the media to deliver key messages. Management itself is an important audience, often requiring specialized communication to help executives better understand their role in shaping the organization's culture and success.

Additional Roles

There may be other roles that a corporate communicator may be called upon to perform (benefits communications, event planning, or technical communications, for example). In many cases, the nature and size of the organization will dictate the corporate communicator's key responsibilities. It is not unusual for the communicator to be responsible for any or all roles, in varying degrees and emphasis. But no one role should be considered or performed in isolation. Consistent organizational messages and cultural values should be clearly understood in all communications to all audiences.

Managing Communication During Change

The true test of a corporate communicator's skills comes during periods of significant change. Major changes, whether perceived as beneficial (profound growth, new business, expansion) or negative (downsizing, takeovers, mergers, bankruptcies) can be disruptive and can challenge an organization's culture, values, and business focus. Change produces stress, fear, and disorientation.

Corporate communicators prove their value at such times by helping the organization stay focused, understanding the needs of all stakeholders, and ensuring a continued flow of well-targeted and timely information. When situations or conditions are changing rapidly, the danger of miscommunication and rumors is at its greatest. The surest way to rein in escalating chaos is through responsive, thoughtful, and targeted communication.

It is common for companies undergoing drastic change—particularly unwelcome change—to cut back on communication. This may occur because the situation has not been anticipated and no response plan exists, or because the severity of the situation is underestimated and companies prefer to remain silent, hoping that the situation will blow over.

But it is precisely during those times that well-coordinated communication is most needed. Corporate communicators who are part of the senior management team become key advisers in periods of major change. They need to develop the best communication strategies to help stabilize the situation.

Often periods of change may take a long time; indeed, some organizations are always experiencing some degree of change. During such times, communicators should seek to reinforce what is remaining constant and articulate the ultimate goal beyond the change.

Communication itself cannot correct a serious misstep, such as the chief financial officer who has embezzled the funds in a company's pension plan. But it is an essential first step in turning around the situation. Without effective communication, chances are much greater that the situation will cause lasting, and perhaps irreparable, damage to the organization.

A Corporate Communicator's Ultimate Responsibility

This chapter explained the significance and breadth of the corporate communicator role and its importance within organizations. Clearly, it is a role that requires broad-based strategic thinking and the ability to respond quickly to rapidly changing environments.

But how objective should corporate communicators be? To whom are they responsible? Are they advocates for senior management, employees, or the public at large? Is their role similar to that of an investigative reporter: telling the whole truth, no matter how raw or ugly?

The answer may seem obvious: the communicator's responsibility is to ensure the continued business health and integrity of the organization. But what if the communicator notes unethical or illegal behavior or, worse yet, is asked by management to be party to this behavior?

It is in such circumstances that the most important responsibility of the communicator takes precedence: to uphold the principles of ethical and honest communication and ensure the integrity of the profession. Here communicators can take guidance from the IABC Code of Ethics (2005) and work to ensure that they communicate legally, ethically, and in good taste.

Today's communicators work in an exciting and opportunity-filled time. Increasingly, their role is perceived as an essential, value added, senior-level one, as opposed to a necessary evil that exists mostly to help the organization react to problems.

The burden of ensuring that this trend continues lies with communicators. They must challenge management and work to enact communication that is honest, strategically focused, and proactive. It is a responsibility that takes a certain degree of daring and risk taking. It is one that will not only result in greater respect for organizational communication as a profession, but also in more effective organizations.

References

Dozier, D. M. (1992). The organizational roles of communication and public relations practitioners. In J. E. Grunig (Ed.), *Excellence in public relations and communication management* (pp. 327–356). Mahwah, NJ: Lawrence Erlbaum.

International Association of Business Communicators [IABC]. (2005). *International Association of Business Communicators code of ethics for professional communicators.* Available at www.iabc.com/about/code.htm.

CHAPTER THREE

ORGANIZATIONAL CULTURE

Paul M. Sanchez

Organizations continue to struggle with the realities of globalization, incorporating wave after wave of technological developments and complex, subtle demographic shifts. Current operating environments are also fraught with the challenges from the overhang of the global recession, where economic and political forces exert even more pressures on organizations of every type of enterprise. In guiding and managing organizations, in all sectors of human activity, leaders must deal with this landscape of economic, social, demographic, technological, and regulatory issues. To not only meet these challenges but to maximize the opportunities inherent in these times, leaders must attempt to understand the beliefs and values of their workforces around the world to enable managers and supervisors to set norms for workforce behaviors.

It is the people at all levels in organizations who must be aware and motivated to accept and support change when necessary. Attitudes and industry of the workforce ultimately determine how the missions of their organizations are accomplished, how products and services are made and delivered. To accomplish this daunting task of leading organizations in these perilous times, leaders must not only know their organizations' current culture, but they must also know what must be done to preserve beneficial elements of existing cultures and how to approach the building of new culture.

Most approaches to organization and management theory are in agreement: culture is one of the key factors used in explaining organization performance and results. The question is how to change and redirect an existing culture to ensure organization success. Is culture tangible? Is it a construct that translates into a reality amenable to practical actions to shape it? Is culture manageable? Can culture be the object of change management? Can leaders, managers, and supervisors play a role in helping change an organization's culture? These are questions that weigh on the corporate mind and occupy those who study organization dynamics.

When Louis V. Gerstner Jr. (2002) took over a failing IBM in 1993, he described his data gathering and analysis of the IBM situation. He was convinced that above all the factors he identified as contributing to IBM's plight, the deeply rooted culture of IBM had to change if this iconic company was going to survive. "I came to see, in my time at IBM, that culture isn't just one aspect of the game—it is the game" (p. 182).

The concept of organizational culture, including practical applications for strategy and tactics, is explored in this chapter. Culture must be assessed and the learnings of change management applied to develop architecture for addressing culture change.

Defining Culture

In its basic definition, culture is *how* an organization accomplishes all that it has to do to fulfill its mission or purpose. Culture can be observed in the ways that things get done—in the processes that everyone in the organization knows must be followed for work to be successfully accomplished. This meaning of culture is embodied in the statement "This is the way we do things around here."

A pragmatic approach was framed by Fons Trompenaars, who defined *culture* as "the way in which a group of people solves problems and resolves dilemmas" (Trompenaars & Hampden-Turner, 1997, p. 6). Geert Hofstede (1994) described culture in a more philosophical way: "Culture is a deeply rooted value or shared norm, moral or aesthetic principles that guides action and serves as standards to evaluate one's own and others' behaviors" (p. 68).

These definitions demonstrate that culture is indeed a first principle of organizational functioning—that although culture is not concrete, it is absolutely a potent force that can either foster and support or impede and frustrate operational change.

If these widely held definitions are accepted, then it can be seen that all the overt and subtle patterns of behavior in organizations do indeed weave themselves together to create an unmistakable personality or character of the organization—its culture. This personality endures over time and can be both a blessing and a curse as an attribute of organizational functioning. If the organization demonstrates long-term success, its abiding culture is identified as the cause of its capacity not only to cope in challenging times but to thrive and prosper, to maintain its focus, and develop an aligned workforce. If the organization is unable to resist forces that sap its energy, distract from its mission, or weaken its brand delivery, then these failures are identified as problems due to its culture.

Further, when an organization fails, its culture can be blamed for being change resistant: closed to new ideas, lacking an innovative spirit, and too slow to respond to fast-changing customer needs. The history and plight of the U.S. auto industry is replete with case studies. Culture in this view is seen as closing the corporate mind on life-saving information, internal or external, that would allow the organization to recognize and deal with the forces that have a material impact on its fate. Culture can be both barrier and constraining force that keeps an organization from freely developing responses to changing external forces.

The Impact of Culture on Organizations and People

Culture is the pervasive driver of how an organization functions over time, unless there is a threat that commands change. It determines how an organization responds to its business environment, organizes its work, structures its day-to-day activities, and deploys the skills and talents of its managers and employees. Culture also determines the patterns of social interaction used to accomplish work and shape relationships inside the organization. Culture dramatically shapes the contract between the organization and its employees, where the expressed values of the organization are made manifest in the transactions between management and the workforce. Equally important, people interacting with the organization exert their collective influence on the culture. They also reflect their national cultures in the symbiotic relation between the organization and its workforce components.

Equally important is the cultural orientation to customer or client service. Because of this impact on an organization's practical behaviors, culture has enormous strategic significance. To be successful, an organization must endeavor to shape its culture to support its mission and implement its strategy. Work processes must be aligned with the types of products or services offered, and human capital practices should be developed and with the same care. Thus there is no one right or wrong culture. In fact, different organizations within the same industry can have very different cultures. In large multinationals, there are microcultures that reflect operating differences within the umbrella of the corporate identity.

The issue for leaders is whether the current culture is keeping pace with the demands of its operating environments and challenges. Does the culture support the business strategy and the component operations and functions? The benefits of this sort of inquiry can be significant; risks of ignoring the state of the culture are enormous—as seen in the IBM example and the case of the U.S. auto industry. Alignment between culture and operating strategy enables effective processes and helps the organization deliver positive results to all stakeholders and, in particular, customers and employees. When there is misalignment, dysfunctions and suboptimal performance result. The organization may be profitable and successful in the short term, but over time, it will fail to achieve its potential. Where the culture and the strategies are not aligned, organizations may lose valuable employees who have the critical skills and experience to move easily to another organization.

Organization Building Blocks and Culture

Every organization—large or small, public or private, for profit or nonprofit—has only four basic components with which to create an organization for its enterprise: strategy, structure, people, and processes. These four elements flow from a clear statement of the organization's mission or purpose. These building blocks are used to formulate, shape, integrate, and manage the assets of the organization. Thus, the organization's culture is formed, shaped, and reinforced through the interplay of these elements. For example:

1. *Strategy* articulates how resources will be focused and applied to accomplish the organization's mission.
2. *Structure* determines positioning and arrangement of resources the organization will need to carry out this strategy to ensure the mission is achieved.
3. *People* are deployed within the structure to carry out the required work.
4. *Processes* are the implementation of work and the ways the organization functions.

The interplay of these four components enables mission accomplishment and forging of culture. When they are in balance, there is harmonious operation and functioning; the culture is positive and supports mission accomplishment. When there is an imbalance among these four elements, the organization's performance will inevitably be suboptimal. Poorly defined strategy; outdated structures; dysfunctional, inefficient processes; and a lack of the right people at critical levels will cause disappointment and bring the organization to an untimely end if left unaddressed. Culture is formed by the continual interaction of these four building blocks.

Assessing an Organization's Culture

There are many approaches to understanding and working with concepts surrounding organizational culture. Adopting and working from a model provides a foundation and frame of reference. Organizational culture models and assessment tools have been developed by leading organizations such as Gallup, Human Synergistics, Denison, BlessingWhite, and many others to help leaders not only understand the organization's current culture but also in formulating response initiatives and change management programs.

Leaders can use any one of the models as the basis for diagnostic instruments, such as employee and management audits, and as part of workforce engagement studies. Such research can reveal the nature of an organization's current culture and help leaders determine which aspects of the culture may be preventing it from achieving peak performance.

Most tools are built to assess aspects of organization processes or functioning, such as openness of communication, empowerment, decision making, uses of power, risk taking, and achievement orientation; others look to the ethos of the organization as experienced in espoused and practiced values, importance of rituals, nature of workforce interactions and relationships, pace of change, and how symbols and stories are used.

Measuring Culture at the Source

Culture measurement can only take place at its source: those who work within the culture, its members at all levels of the organization. No single group of employees is likely to provide a complete picture of the culture. This applies across operational and functional areas, where differing groups within an organization may share common values but have different practices and procedures. People at various organizational levels, from senior executives and middle management to assembly line workers, will experience the organization's culture through the lens of their own experiences.

With this in mind, it can be helpful to conduct a survey for either all employees or a representative sample of the workforce. This approach offers numerous benefits when developing a comprehensive view of organizational culture; for instance:

• A survey is one of the best ways to involve employees in the process of developing and enabling a new business strategy, such as part of merger integration. The survey communicates to employees the issues that management feels are important for the future of the company. It also serves as a tool to manage employee expectations about coming changes. Particularly powerful in this regard is how the research findings are communicated back to the workforce.

• Employees can provide perceptual information in a quantifiable way so that the company policies and practices can be evaluated for efficacy. Surveying may probe beyond the examination of formal structures and processes to provide insights into the drivers that have an impact on motivation for work and organizational challenges. An employee survey also provides quantified information on employees' views of their relationships within the company. Research limited to cataloging formal policies and procedures alone cannot reveal whether employees believe they are being treated equitably, whether they trust management, or whether they feel pride in the company.

• Employees provide valuable perceptions of how things really work throughout the organization. More than expressions of employee morale, when analyzed professionally such results become essential information about the current culture to be used by management in planning for both the company's future and addressing near-term issues. Although a comprehensive culture survey can be a complex project, it is an important and necessary first step in undertaking a culture shift.

Current Culture Versus Ideal Culture

Once an organization has a clear picture of its current culture, leaders may find that the culture is not aligned with the future vision and business strategy in ways that facilitate mission achievement and maximum performance. When this occurs, the process of change begins by defining the organization's ideal culture— the culture that enables and facilitates fulfilling the vision and business strategy. A clear picture of the ideal culture will be used as a guide by leaders as they assess the differences between where their organization is versus where it needs to be. It is an aspirational view that often finds its way into vision statements.

Ideal culture research and formulation should be informed by the organization's business strategy and by those employees who are closest to the business strategy and its customers or clients. These individuals are truly in positions to help define the ideal culture. By asking leaders *and* rank-and-file employees about their perceptions of the current and ideal cultures, an organization can develop a panoramic view that informs and guides efforts to confront the challenges of a change management program. This gap analysis can pinpoint areas so that leaders can direct the process of moving the current culture toward its ideal culture.

Collecting Leaders' Views of the Culture

A cultural audit of an organization's senior leaders can complement the insights gathered in the employee culture survey and provide a framework for discussion among decision makers about the impact of culture on an organization. In particular, it also offers a picture of the different views of culture that exist within the leadership team. Executives are able to see agreement within their own ranks on the ideal culture, how it is shaped through the various change levers, and their perceptions of the current culture.

For many leadership teams, this usually leads to discussions about the implications of these gaps, what could change by closing the gaps, which culture building blocks should have priority, and which will have the biggest impact on the organization.

A cultural audit with senior leaders could be offered as part of an executive workshop or retreat. Coupled with employee survey results, the information gathered through the audit tells the story of the culture within the organization. Taken together, these results highlight the organizational culture and show how culture manifests itself in the behaviors that people expect from each other in the organization. These results may also provide a high-level view of how differences in certain individual characteristics (such as tenure in the organization, level in the organization, or other demographics) affect people's perceptions about expected behaviors.

Analyzing Results and Evaluating Gaps

The results of the employee survey and the executive audit can be analyzed in a number of ways:

• Comparing the current culture as described by the employee survey with the current culture described by the executives in the executive audit. This enables organization leaders to determine the extent to which their perceptions match overall employee perceptions of the current culture.

• Evaluating employee survey results across different functional groups within the organization or even across such variables as organizational level.

This helps to identify subcultures within an organization, which can be particularly valuable in revealing areas or groups that can be either change champions or barriers to change. To the extent that such subgroups can be identified early in a change process, attention and resources can be applied that will facilitate a smoother change process.

• Comparing culture assessment results in depth helps business leaders understand the culture gaps that exist across the organization. By probing the gaps, business leaders can make the strategic decisions that map ways to change or shape the culture.

Of course, not all gaps need immediate attention. For instance, in an organization where attention to detail is particularly important (such as an accounting firm or a precision tool-and-die maker), gaps between the current and desired cultures around reward and recognition may be ignored in order to concentrate on more significant gaps—for example, in perceptions about work processes aimed at accuracy and reliability. Selecting which gaps to close can be as important as the methods employed to close them.

In addition, the gap analysis and selection process should lead to a discussion about change implementation and the practical issues surrounding it. Leaders may need to initiate further discussions to determine whether proposed changes have management buy-in, assess whether the organization is ready and prepared to embrace change, identify potential roadblocks to broad change, and decide which resources and tools will be required to achieve and sustain change that move the culture.

Communications and Culture

One of the clearest manifestations of culture is communication. Communication as a process, a function, and a result is both a reflection and cause of the organization's culture. How an organization conceives and manages communication tells more about its culture than any other single process element.

The manner in which an organization approaches communication policy, staffing, planning, and budgeting paints a clear picture of how it thinks of itself and how it wishes to relate to employees and its external constituencies: shareholders, customers, and the public at large. One of the most important aspects in this regard is whether the values of the organization's external brand are communicated to, and reflected by, the internal behavior of its employees. Whether brand values are reflected in how employees are treated, how human resource programs are fashioned, and how they are communicated become a potent force for shaping the desired culture.

Openness, a willingness to actively gather perception and opinion, information sharing, communication planning, the integration and application of technology, and preparation and development of supervisors to communicate effectively with their people all paint a clear picture of the organization's culture. These very tools can help guide and shape a new culture.

Communications Is a Critical Process for Cultural Change

Although organizational culture is persistent and tenacious, it is not immutable. With a clear strategy based on a valid rationale, detailed implementation plans and concerted effort sustained over time, an organization's culture can be changed.

Many process elements must be integrated to shape and develop a sustainable culture. These elements include basic steps in change management: presentation of the rationale for change and development of support processes, such as the design of reward systems (including pay, benefits, performance management, and training and development) to the more strategic framing of vision and defining values. But all of these are ultimately dependent on the act of communicating them: of conveying their purpose and implementation of each program for management and employees throughout the enterprise. Thus, communication moves to center stage in the matter of bringing about cultural change.

The true power of communication as a force to help implement and sustain a culture change is its ability to win the hearts and minds of employees—to establish trust in a climate of transparency. Such communication creates a value chain that can result in improved customer service, productivity, and ultimately mission accomplishment. To win hearts and minds of employees at all levels, however, requires comprehensive communication planning, from strategic to the tactical program execution. It requires sustained activity across a spectrum of communication channels and stakeholders, from face-to-face to mass communication activity. It also demands leadership interactivity and participation throughout the organization, from the boardroom to the mailroom. Only when communication becomes two-way, open and trust building, rather than the downward dissemination of information, can culture change initiatives be undertaken with a realistic hope of success.

The Relationship between Organizational Culture and National Culture

One important aspect of organizational culture is the interrelationship between organizational culture and national culture. Globalization is a fact of life, connecting businesses and markets across distances wider and more complex than ever before. Sales offices, manufacturing operations, staff and line functions now span the globe far from an organization's traditional headquarters. Leadership and control functions, aided by technology, impose the corporate brand of the corporate culture through the filter of the local national culture. Global organizations are learning more about how to conduct business simultaneously in many different economic, social, and political environments through standardized procedures and continual communication, but the role of national cultures may not be fully appreciated nor understood.

When considering the fit between business strategy and culture, a multinational organization must consider differing national values and customs that may place constraints on corporate practices in its various branch and plant locations. Too often managers find that an accepted home office procedure does not translate easily into operations halfway around the world, and it is more than just a language issue.

Multinational organizations are affected in two ways. First, organizations often reflect the national culture of their country of origin. A commonly cited example is Japanese businesses in comparison to U.S. businesses; in Japan, group behavior and performance are emphasized over individual performance. Thus, business strategies that require a high degree of teamwork will benefit from the Japanese model rather than the U.S. model, which often encourages individual innovation and achievement.

Second, organizations doing business outside their home country that have succeeded have learned to adapt their usual approaches and permit differences in areas deemed nonessential; they require compliance only in those areas that are business essential, mindful that *business essential* determinations require analysis and careful implementation. For example, organization A from the United States believes in taking a fair amount of risk in expanding its lines of business. But its operation abroad does business in an environment that does not value risk in financial dealings. To expand its lines of business in that country with money borrowed locally may have been thought advisable. Local banks, however, may not consider this organization a good candidate for a loan because they perceive its behavior as too risky. Successful multinational organizations consciously decide to modify their business practices to harmonize with local organizational practices, particularly those likely to touch national cultural values. This is particularly true when dealing with workforce issues—from hiring to setting wage and benefit levels to dealing with local labor laws and employee communication practices.

Modern trends in global communication coupled with the globalization of trade may ultimately lead to a more accepting global business culture that will soften or blur national differences relative to business operating cultures. But currently it is critical to recognize and understand the potential incompatibilities between national and organizational cultures, while not overlooking the points of common interest and common practice.

Case in Point: America Online and Time Warner

On January 10, 2000, Stephen Case, cofounder of America Online, and Gerald Levin, CEO of Time Warner, announced the merger transaction between AOL and Time Warner—a deal that had been valued at $350 billion. It would become the largest merger in American history and a groundbreaking combination of size and scale in the media industry. But as many now recall, it is also believed to be one of the most unsuccessful transactions in history (Arango, 2010).

In 1999, when the two organizations began talks of a merger, the vision was to "create unprecedented and instantaneous access to every form of media and to unleash immense possibilities for economic growth, human understanding and creative expression" (Arango, 2010, p. 1). AOL and Time Warner would combine a leading content provider with the world's leading Internet provider to create countless synergies and deliver enhanced services, economies of scale, promote media convergence, and ultimately increase revenues. As the two primary leaders in their distinct media markets, the companies believed that the combination was designed to be both profitable and groundbreaking (Albarran & Gormly, 2004).

The Impact of People and Culture

But only two years after the merger received regulatory approval (in January 2001), the transaction had already been labeled as a failure due to one colossal blunder: the mismanagement of people and organizational cultures. One key reason that mergers do not achieve intended business results is that many companies do not spend enough time evaluating the impact that the merger will have on employees (Gale, 2003). Also, the chance of success is increasingly hindered if the corporate cultures of the organizations are vastly different. "When a company is acquired, the decision is typically based on product or market synergies, but cultural differences are rarely examined or even acknowledged" (Gale, 2003, p. 60).

In the case of AOL/Time Warner, both sides were aware of cultural differences prior to the final transaction. AOL's fast-paced, youthful culture represented a significantly different approach to day-to-day operations than Time Warner's long service, to which the veteran employees were accustomed. Time Warner employees had their longtime benefits and profit-sharing program taken away; the replacement did not yield the same returns. AOL's top-down management style clashed with Time Warner's self-governed business units. Some employees claimed that key positions formerly held by Time Warner veterans were quickly reassigned to AOL staff—rapidly degrading employee trust and engagement during the time of change and increasing attitudes of oppression and rebellion among legacy Time Warner employees (Albarran & Gormly, 2004). Strategy and structure were different, as were key processes from planning, budgeting, and human resource management. The magnitude of these differences and how to proceed in the face of the challenges of culture integration and change management was underestimated.

"To be successful in a merger, you have to show respect for the acquired company's culture and ways," said Bill Belgard, president of the Belgard Group. "Your goal should be to achieve something together that neither company could do alone" (Gale, 2003, p. 60). But as Richard Parsons, former co-chief operating officer and later CEO, recalls, "I remember saying at a board meeting where we approved this, that life was going to be different going forward because they're very different cultures, but I have to tell you, I underestimated how different" (Arango, 2010, p. 1).

Ten Years Later

Experts and executives alike recall the impact of the merger on the companies in subsequent years with countless job losses, devastated employee retirement accounts, and even investigations by the Securities and Exchange Commission and the Justice Department. In present-day calculations, the combined values of the companies, which have since been split, dropped to nearly one-seventh of their worth as of one day before the merger (Arango, 2010). In a final thought, Parsons stated, "The business model sort of collapsed under us, and then finally this cultural matter. As I said, it was beyond certainly my abilities to figure out how to blend the old media and the new media cultures. They were like different species, and in fact, they were species that were inherently at war" (Arango, 2010, p. 1).

References

Albarran, A. B. & Gormly, R. K. (2004). Strategic response or strategic blunder? An examination of AOL Time Warner and Vivendi Universal. In Robert G. Picard (Ed.), *Strategic responses to media market changes* (pp. 35–46). Jönköping, Sweden: Jönköping International Business School.

Arango, T. (2010, January 11). In retrospect: How it went so wrong. *New York Times*, B1.

Gale, S. F. (2003, February). Memo to AOL Time Warner: Why mergers fail. *Workforce Management, 82*(2), 60–63.

Gerstner, L. V., Jr. (2002). *Who says elephants can't dance?* New York: HarperCollins.

Hofstede, G. (1994). *Uncommon sense about organizations: Case studies and field observations.* Thousand Oaks, CA: Sage.

Trompenaars, F., & Hampden-Turner, C. (1997). *Riding the waves of culture: Understanding diversity in global business.* New York: McGraw-Hill.

CHAPTER FOUR

COMMUNICATION AND THE HIGH-TRUST ORGANIZATION

Pamela Shockley-Zalabak, Sherwyn Morreale

The global financial crisis, which began in 2008, generated fear that circled the globe and resulted in what many have called an unprecedented trust crash. While it is impossible to understand all aspects of the financial crisis, most agree that trust and distrust are affecting actions of diverse stakeholders: corporations, governments, customers, the public, individual investors, regulators, and global alliances, to name only a few. In an age of globalization, scandals in all types of organizations, fast-paced change, and new pressures for innovation in processes, forms, and relationships place increasing importance on the somewhat elusive notion of organizational trust. Trust is considered pivotal for networks, alliances, uses of information technologies, workplace diversity, customer loyalty, decentralized decision making, and the list goes on. Yet, few people fully understand what it takes for an organization to be considered trustworthy. Trust influences a wide range of employee and stakeholder behaviors and is directly linked to overall organizational performance. However, the evidence is clear: few leaders and communication professionals regularly focus directly on trust.

This chapter argues that organizational trust is a fundamental leadership responsibility and a growing area of responsibility for communication professionals. We go so far as to claim that trust is the *main thing* for organizational excellence. We outline our work from 2000 to the present with regard to building the high-trust organization. We describe organizational trust, identify its impact on excellence, present our five-driver model for trust, and apply the model to diverse organizational roles and functions. We conclude that building trust is an increasingly important responsibility for all communication professionals.

Understanding and Valuing Organizational Trust

Numerous definitions of trust concern trust that results from positive expectations about another's conduct, and distrust reflecting negative expectations of another's behavior. The key is behavior. While everyone has individual intentions, and even entire organizations have intentions, the trust-distrust evaluation is determined not by what we intend but by our behavior. There are numerous examples of individuals and organizations intending to deceive or at the very least mask the full reality of a situation. Often these deceptions have been successful with behaviors and, at least initially, judged to be trustworthy. We also can remember entering a group and distrusting what might happen. When we contrast that experience with entering a group where trust levels were high, we quickly realize past behaviors and experiences influence our expectations of future behaviors and experiences. Based on our research, we describe and utilize the following definition of organizational trust:

> The organization's willingness, based upon its culture and communication behaviors in relationships and transactions, to be appropriately vulnerable based on the belief that another individual, group, or organization is competent, open and honest, concerned, reliable, and identified with common goals, norms, and values. (Shockley-Zalabak, Ellis, & Cesaria, 2000, p. 4)

Organizational trust has many faces. Our experience helps us understand that *trust is multileveled*. This means trust interactions include leader, coworker, team, organization, multi-organization, and stakeholder relationships. *Trust is culturally rooted*. It is closely tied to the norms, values, and beliefs of the organization. It also relates to broader national and regional cultures. Trust building cannot ignore existing cultures of trust or distrust. *Trust is communication based*. It influences and is the outcome of communication behaviors such as providing accurate information, giving explanations for decisions, and demonstrating sincere and appropriate openness. Trust is directly linked to strategic organizational communication. *Trust is multidimensional*. It is cognitive, based on facts and analysis. It is emotional, based on reactions to people and events. It is behavioral, based on what organizations collectively and individually do as a result of cognitive and emotional reactions to people, events, challenges, and opportunities. Finally, *trust is dynamic*. Trust is continually changing and can cycle through phases of building, stabilizing, and dissolving. Just as trust can range in degree from distrust to optimal trust, it also can vary from fragile to resilient. Fragile trust develops out of perceptions of short-term outcomes, while resilient trust usually is based on a long-term history of integrity.

The organization structures relationships and environments for individuals and groups, subject to trust evaluations. It is hard enough to trust family and friends, let alone individuals we barely know or with whom we have little or no face-to-face contact. We usually do not get to choose our bosses, team members, customers, or other stakeholders. In fact, the hierarchy and relationships defined by the organization chart can be described as a trust blueprint. By describing who has the right to decide and where the linkages are supposed to take place, the organization chart is a complicated way of describing how organizational trust should work. While at some level the organizational chart describes how trust flows, few individuals with organizational experience will say that adhering to the chain of the chart is what generates a high-trust organization. As networks, alliances, virtual groups, and other organizational forms replace older and more bureaucratic models, fewer and fewer organizations are operating as hierarchies. Thus, trust through control is replaced by trust through relationships.

It is fair to conclude that organizational trust encompasses a wide variety of organizational relationships. However, organizational trust is a more inclusive concept than simply integrating complex relationships. It encompasses relationships, but it also includes a variety of environmental influences and basic organizational competencies. These aspects of trust are more fully described later in this chapter when the trust model is discussed for both leaders and communication professionals.

Our Research Work on Building High-Trust Organizations

We began our efforts to understand trust in 2000 with a grant from the International Association of Business Communicators (IABC) (Shockley-Zalabak et al., 2000). We wanted to understand what many today find critical to success: in the face of the changing organizational landscape, with its reduced interpersonal familiarity among employees scattered around the globe, how can trust contribute to an organization's ability to work effectively? We reviewed more than 3,500 articles in the research literature on trust and worked with hundreds of organizations on issues related to improving communication and leadership effectiveness. We interviewed and talked with leaders in organizations in more than twenty-five countries, including the United States, Asia, Africa, Europe, Australia, and the Middle East. We collected data worldwide, in multiple languages, to determine whether we could identify critical drivers of organizational trust that would be stable across cultures and types of organizations. The answer was solidly in the affirmative. We conclude from our research and our practical experiences that trust has both human and financial costs (Shockley-Zalabak, Morreale, & Hackman, 2010). It is a myth that we cannot do anything about trust—everything we do is about trust. Trust is directly linked to organizational excellence and measurable organizational outcomes. Our conclusion is clear: trust is the main thing in any organization.

Trust and Organizational Excellence

High-trust organizations have increased value, accelerated growth, enhanced innovation, improved collaboration, stronger partnering, better execution, and heightened loyalty. A 2002 study showed that high-trust organizations outperformed low-trust organizations by 286 percent in total return to shareholders (stock price plus dividends) (Kramer & Cook, 2004). A 2005 study supported these findings suggesting high-trust organizations earned more than four times the returns of the broader market over the prior seven years (Covey & Merrill, 2008; Covey, 2008). By contrast, low-trust organizations appear to face a bleak future. Recent examples, ranging from Enron to Bear Stearns, Lehman Brothers, AIG, and Toyota, support the notion that without trust organizations cannot thrive and achieve excellence. It is near-impossible to pick up a newspaper or tune in to the nightly news without hearing of yet another example of fraudulent or dishonest conduct by local, national, or international organizations and their leaders. C-SPAN regularly broadcasts congressional investigations of chief executive officers (CEOs) whose integrity had once been unblemished by scandal. For example, after two years of international crises in financial markets, a degree of stability had returned to the economic sector. Then in April 2010, markets were stunned by news that U.S. securities regulators had charged Goldman Sachs, the world's top commodities broker, with fraud in connection with mortgage derivatives (Story & Morgenson, 2010). Asian stock markets tumbled following Wall Street's slide, after this major investment bank was charged with fraud. Such news of untrustworthy behavior in the financial sector fought for headlines with Toyota and consumers' claims regarding the safety of that company's vehicles in the United States. Distrust, or the lack of trustworthiness, appears omnipresent in some if not many of today's top companies and organizations.

Summarizing the research we reviewed, it is possible to conclude that trust is the basis for stability in both markets and in organizations. Trust is related to diverse customer and stockholder behaviors. Specifically, high levels of organizational trust have been associated with (1) more adaptive organizational forms and structures, (2) the ability to form strategic alliances, (3) effective crisis management, (4) reduced litigation costs, (5) reduced transaction costs, (6) product innovation, and (7) economic performance. Trust consistently has been linked to employee perceptions of overall job and communication satisfaction. High trust levels in both face-to-face and virtual teams predict a higher level of performance than moderate and low trust levels. High trust levels contribute to more open communication, high-quality decision making, improved risk taking, low employee turnover, and more overall organizational commitment. Trust in top management often is based on organizational policies, processes, programs, and perceptions of justice in dealing with employees and other stakeholders. In fact, our research (Ellis & Shockley-Zalabak, 2001) strongly suggests that trust in top management is more important than trust in immediate supervisors in overall employee perceptions of satisfaction and effectiveness. In addition, perceptions of trust in leadership as well as trust in peer groups are linked to perceptions of organizational competence. The intriguing reality is that employees may trust that management is honest with them, but if they do not trust that organizational members (including themselves) are competent to meet organizational challenges, they will have low trust levels (Story & Morgenson, 2010).

The Organizational Trust Model

We hope the argument for doing something about organizational trust has been convincing. Yet the obvious questions remain: What can be done? How can trust building become more intentional and less elusive or accidental? There is no final answer, but we think identifying five critical drivers of trust provides a framework for both leaders and communication professionals to begin to consciously and intentionally build trust.

Earlier we referenced the research we conducted that was sponsored by the International Association of Business Communicators Research Foundation. We described our review of more than 3,500 research studies describing organizational trust. The specific research that forms the basis of the five drivers we are proposing began in fifty-three organizations in which we translated our survey work into multiple languages. We compiled a large database to develop normative comparisons. The comparison data were gathered in the United States (twenty-five states), Italy (eleven cities), Sydney, Singapore, Hong Kong, Tokyo, Bombay, and Taiwan. The industries represented in the database include banking, telecommunications, manufacturing, computer software and hardware,

FIGURE 4.1 PATH MODEL OF THE FIVE DIMENSIONS OF ORGANIZATIONAL TRUST

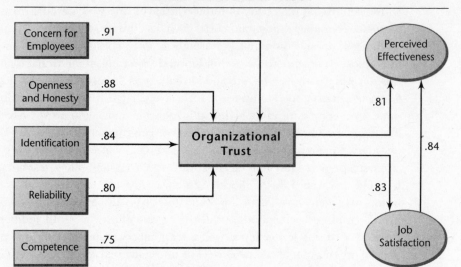

education, and sales and customer service. Company sizes ranged from approximately 100 to 146,000 employees. The work resulted in an expansion of Aneil K. Mishra's (1996) four-dimensional model of trust to the five-dimensional model presented in Figure 4.1.

In Figure 4.1, 1.00 represents a perfect relationship between a dimension of trust and organizational trust, and between organizational trust and perceived effectiveness and job satisfaction. The higher the number in the figure, the stronger the relationship of the driver to trust and perceived effectiveness and satisfaction.

The definitions of the five dimensions or drivers of organizational trust are as follows.

1. *Concern for employees.* Concern for employees includes the feelings of caring, empathy, tolerance, and safety that are exhibited when we are vulnerable in organizational activities. Sincere efforts to understand feelings contribute to high trust levels in relationships.
2. *Openness and honesty.* *Openness* and *honesty* are the words people use most often when they are asked what contributes to organizational trust. This driver involves not only the amount and accuracy of information that is shared but also how sincerely and appropriately it is communicated.

3. *Identification.* Identification reflects the extent to which we hold common goals, norms, values, and beliefs associated with our organization's culture. This dimension indicates how connected we feel to leaders and coworkers, products or services, and overall mission of the organization.

4. *Reliability.* Reliability is determined by whether leaders, coworkers, teams, suppliers, and organizations act consistently and dependably. In other words, can we count on them to do what they say they will do? Does congruency exist between words and actions?

5. *Competence.* As it relates to organizational trust, competence involves the extent to which we see not only our coworkers and leaders as effective, but also our organization as a whole. Competence reflects how strongly we believe our organization will compete and survive in the environment.

Application of the Trust Model for Organizational Leaders and Business Communicators

We now apply the five dimensions or drivers of trust from our model to diverse and critical organizational roles and functions.

Top Leaders

Organizational leaders at all levels have responsibility for trust. While most leaders would agree with this statement, few focus directly on their trust responsibilities. Leaders need to develop a more comprehensive understanding of what constitutes trust behaviors, with specific emphasis on the distinction between interpersonal and organizational trust. Many leaders rely on their personal integrity without understanding that the positions they occupy provide few within the organization the opportunity to interact with them on an interpersonal basis. Although integrity and intentions are critical, the impact of leadership is interpreted through multiple networks of relationships, behaviors, and events, making communication behaviors and decisions the currency of trust.

The use of the trust model can facilitate leaders' understanding and development. Increased understanding is important but insufficient to build the high-trust organization. The question is, What else needs to be done?

Monitor Trust Levels. First, leaders need to develop an ongoing process for monitoring the trust levels within their organizations. Leaders regularly collect performance data for their organizations, yet few collect data that directly assess trust levels. Even organizations that conduct regular employee and customer satisfaction surveys usually do not include reliable and valid trust measures. Earlier in this chapter we described links between trust and organizational performance. A clear understanding of an organization's trust level can provide leaders with important data that may precede or forecast changes in performance outcomes.

Develop an Understanding of Trust in Particular Contexts. Second, leaders need professional development in (1) distinguishing between interpersonal and organizational trust, (2) understanding trust within particular organizational contexts, and (3) examining leadership activities within the organization for their contributions to the trust environment. This usually can be accomplished through training and the development of a leadership communication plan.

Examine Organizational Decisions and Practices Using the Trust Model. Third, leaders should be challenged to examine their strategic directions, decisions, and communication plans within the framework of the trust model. How does the organization understand competence from the direction and decisions articulated by leadership? Does the organization believe leaders are open and honest? If full disclosure of information cannot be made for a variety of strategic reasons, how can leaders communicate directly what can and cannot be made known? How can leaders directly address the inevitable seeming contradictions brought about by changing circumstances? What can leaders do to remain open and honest when uncertainty is high and important decisions remain in a pending state? These are complex questions, yet research supports the perspective that leaders are more trusted when they increase communication messages during times of uncertainty and express the "I do not know" perspective with directness and a commitment to bring information forward when possible.

Leaders are responsible for the policies and processes that are interpreted as concern for employees. Organizational policies and practices should be regularly examined for expressions of concern and for implicit and explicit messages about trust. Performance evaluation systems, accounting and reporting practices, monitoring of employee behaviors (for example, use of time, telephone and computer use), access to information, involvement in decision making, reward programs, and a host of other practices and processes all are subject to trust evaluations.

Closely related to the assessment of concern for employees is the trust dimension of reliability. Are processes and practices consistent across employees and key stakeholders? Do leaders do what they say they are going to do? Does the organization regularly bring important information to those affected? Reliability should not be confused with sameness. Reliability as a trust dimension refers to consistent behaviors that exhibit competence, honesty, and concern, not necessarily unwavering support for past decisions.

Clearly, leaders need to develop and articulate organizational goals, norms, values, and beliefs. This development and articulation is critical to the identification dimension of trust. Do goals, norms, and values include employees and key stakeholders? Can employees relate their own futures to the direction of the organization? Can vendors and customers see in these strategic directions their own desired connectedness to the organization? How does leadership know whether identification is present or absent?

Structure the Organization for Trust Building. Fourth, leaders are responsible for the professional communication functions within the organization. Human relations, corporate communications, advertising, marketing, public relations, and other information functions are designed and staffed as a result of how top management views the importance of these operations. The leaders of communication functions shape trust levels by their own understandings of how the functions contribute to important organizational outcomes. The very design of the organization reflects assumptions about trust and who has responsibility for trust building.

Communication Professionals

Communication professionals are organizational leaders in both job function and specific job knowledge provided for other leaders. Nonetheless, until recently, the role of the communication professional has focused mostly indirectly on trust building. Increasingly, communication professionals are challenged to explicitly develop programs and processes for building organizational trust. The following discussion describes important professional areas linked to trust building. The list is not meant to be exhaustive but points to key responsibility areas.

Monitor Trust. For organizations to effectively develop high-trust environments, regular understanding of levels of organizational trust must be developed and interpreted for a host of planning decisions. This monitoring responsibility usually resides in human resources, internal communication, or corporate communications functions. Trends in trust levels, when related to trends in performance data, provide powerful information important to the evaluation of communication planning, training and development, appraisal systems, and other strategic initiatives. The communication professional becomes responsible for guiding top management in determining the type of data to be collected, who should collect the data, the assessment of the reliability and validity of the data,

data interpretation, and the dissemination of the data to be included in the planning processes of the organization. Instruments published by IABC (Shockley-Zalabak et al., 2000) and Jossey-Bass (Shockley-Zalabak et al., 2010) provide psychometrically sound ways to begin measurement. *Building the High-Trust Organization* (Shockley-Zalabak et al., 2010) provides extensive guidance for data collection.

Review Policies and Practices. Policies, processes, and a host of organizational practices carry implicit and explicit messages about trust. Human resource and internal communication professionals increasingly are tasked with reviewing policies and processes regularly used by the organization with employees, vendors, and stakeholders for their impact on trust. Marketing and sales professionals often provide this same review with regard to customers and competitors. Policy and procedure manuals, employee benefits, disciplinary processes, supervision responsibilities, performance appraisals, hiring and promotional practices, and other processes can be evaluated in each of the dimensions of the trust mode. For example, an employee orientation manual may effectively describe how employee contributions will be evaluated (competence), how communication exchanges among supervisors and work groups are to take place (openness and honesty), how equitable salary and benefits programs are to be administered (reliability), and what the core goals, values and beliefs of the organization are (identification). A review of the orientation manual may reveal that, while four of the five dimensions of the trust model can be identified in the manual, no messages that communicate real concern for employees are present. It is not that the organization does not want to express concern, but the preparation of an important document simply is not comprehensive in its expression of trust messages. Of course, at times it will be more than the messaging that needs to change. These comprehensive reviews may reveal policies and procedures that need improvement to build trust. Additionally, legal and compliance policies and practices have significant consequences for trust. The use and monitoring of technology is subject to trust evaluations. All policies and practices across all organizational functions have the potential to contribute to the trust profile of the organization.

Develop Training and Awareness. Training is an important component of most effective trust-building efforts. Leaders usually do not understand the comprehensive nature of organizational trust. Leader, manager, and supervisor training should include development of an understanding of organizational trust and its importance to organizational performance. Next, training should address how individuals contribute to organizational trust with both their individual behaviors and their more strategic communication activities. Employees also can benefit from an awareness of the importance of organizational trust. Increased job satisfaction, the ability to innovate, and the ability to identify with a successful organization all are related to perceptions of trust. Both individual and team training can focus on how employees contribute to trust networks. Mandatory training is of particular importance. Management development, employee orientation job training, compliance training, team training, and process training (for example, performance appraisals, disciplinary reviews, legal responsibilities) all should incorporate comprehensive messages utilizing the basic dimensions of trust. Concern for employees should be visible in new employee orientation as well as in introductions to the performance appraisal processes. Openness and honesty is fostered when any type of training supports an atmosphere in which questions can be raised about inconsistencies or seeming inconsistencies. Several organizations have successfully utilized visible mission statements and core values statements along with strategy and goal maps to foster identification. Training as a function is charged with building the competency and reliability of the organization.

Engage in Strategic Organizational Communication. Internal communications, corporate communications, public relations, advertising, marketing functions, and others (whether in one combined or separate departments) literally plan and develop strategy for how the organization describes itself to its various publics. Planned organizational communication reflects strategic direction, change initiatives, new products or services, competitive positioning, and responses to crises. Planned communication becomes the reality of how diverse stakeholders experience the organization. Message crafting and delivery are critical responsibilities in the trust-building process. Organizational responsiveness and listening are gaining in importance. Social media and the Internet provide complex opportunities for professionals to create interactive strategies for trust building. Of course, strategic direction must have integrity in order to build high trust with stakeholders. Nonetheless, integrity without communication that is trusted will not build a high-trust environment in and of itself. Employees identify with organizations in which communication goals include putting messages into contexts that employees understand, not just what leaders understand. Concern for employees is exhibited when employees learn of important news prior to more public stakeholders. Consistency of corporate messages fosters reliability. Communication professionals know this. However, more professionals have been trained to develop accurate and attractive messages with less awareness of what these messages communicate about trust.

One Fortune 500 employee relations and communication department provides an interesting example of how trust building has become an intentional department strategy. The vice president for employee relations and communication adopted the five-dimensional trust model described in this chapter as a framework for his department. He and his staff, with the assistance of an outside consulting firm, reviewed the mission and values of the organization, a year's worth of internal communications, and the annual responses to the employee satisfaction survey to determine which dimensions of the trust model were regularly present and where opportunities existed for improvement. They discovered competence and identification were the least represented of the dimensions. They developed a strategy to incorporate stories in their monthly newsletter focusing on employee achievements and advancement opportunities. They asked for and received commitment from the entire leadership team to review all speeches for elements of the trust model. They added trust development to their supervisory training programs. Finally, to measure trust, they incorporated new scales into their employee satisfaction survey. Within two years, the department was able to present to top management employee satisfaction survey improvements and reduced turnover rate data for several divisions of the company. We do not claim their experience was directly related to their new emphasis on trust, but they believe, as do we, that trust played an important part in their improved performance.

Conclusion

We conclude by emphasizing what we know is true: trust matters and, in fact, trust is the main thing!

Organizations with high trust levels have better results than do those with low trust levels. Although this makes sense, not enough effort has been expended in intentionally trying to build trust. In the past, we as leaders have treated trust as too subjective to strategically direct our focus. That is a mistake. Trust influences communication and results from communication. We can build trust with competent people who have integrity and know the importance of strategically using a variety of effective communication processes. We can build trust by focusing on competency, openness and honesty, concern for employees, reliability, and identification. In sum, it is fair to say the communication professional has a core responsibility for trust building. That responsibility, however, cannot be executed without close collaboration with top leaders. With this collaboration, the communication of trust can be far more intentional than it has been in most organizations. The communication of trust is both a primary leadership responsibility and a core competency for communication professionals. The challenges are real, but the benefits are enormous.

References

Covey, M. (2008). Trust is a competency. *Chief Learning Officer, 7,* 54–56.

Covey, S.M.R., & Merrill, R. R. (2008). *The speed of trust: The one thing that changes everything.* New York: Free Press.

Ellis, K., & Shockley-Zalabak, P. (2001). Trust in top management and immediate supervisor: The relationship to satisfaction, organizational effectiveness, and information receiving. *Communication Quarterly, 49,* 382–398.

Kramer, R., & Cook, K. (Eds.). (2004). *Trust and distrust in organizations: Dilemmas and approaches.* New York: Russell Sage Foundation.

Mishra, A. K. (1996). Organizational responses to crisis: The centrality of trust. In R. M. Kramer & T. R. Tyler (Eds.), *Trust in organizations: Frontiers of theory and research* (pp. 261–287). Thousand Oaks, CA: Sage.

Shockley-Zalabak, P., Ellis, K., & Cesaria, R. (2000). *Measuring organizational trust: A diagnostic survey and international indicator.* San Francisco: International Association of Business Communicators.

Shockley-Zalabak, P., Morreale, S., & Hackman, M. (2010). *Building the high-trust organization.* San Francisco: Jossey-Bass.

Story, L., & Morgenson, G. (2010, April 17). For Goldman, a bet's stakes keep growing. *New York Times.* Retrieved from www.nytimes.com/2010/04/18/business/18goldman.html.

CHAPTER FIVE

COMMUNICATION ETHICS

Think Like a Professional: Don't Be Idealistic When Sorting Out Right from Wrong

Mark McElreath

The ideal virtuous professional communicator is not a naïve, idealistic fool. Streetwise and savvy about the ways of the world, she or he knows how to make ethical decisions and how to help others make ethical decisions anywhere in the world—even in the most corrupt societies.

Transparency International (2010) has classified the countries of the world into four quadrants, from the most corrupt to the least corrupt, using what the nonprofit agency calls the "Bribe Payers Index." The index is based on annual interviews with 11,000 business executives from around the world who are asked the likelihood of a corporation operating in a specific country being asked to engage in "extra payments or bribery" in order to do business. The researchers then classify countries into four clusters; for example:

1. *Least-likely-to-bribe cluster:* Switzerland, Sweden, Australia, Austria, Canada, United Kingdom, Germany, Netherlands, Belgium, United States, Japan
2. *Next-to-least-likely-to-bribe cluster:* Singapore, Spain, United Arab Emirates, France, Portugal, Mexico
3. *Next-to-most-likely-to-bribe cluster:* Hong Kong, Israel, Italy, South Korea, Saudi Arabia, Brazil, South Africa, Malaysia
4. *Most-likely-to-bribe cluster:* Taiwan, Turkey, Russia, China, India

Imagine a professional communicator—you—working for an international firm with operations in each of these quadrants. Imagine your firm is engaged in a coordinated global communications campaign focused on the roll-out of a new product. Now imagine that journalists in each of the countries tells the local public relations manager practically the same thing: that the journalist will not publicize the new product as requested without something extra. In other words, the journalist would like a payment of some kind—a bribe.

In this hypothetical case, how would you answer these questions:

- Would you expect the professional communicator in each country to respond to the bribery suggestion in exactly the same way—or would cultural values and local economic conditions affect how a professional would deal with the attempted bribery?
- What would the ideal virtuous professional communicator do in each country?
- Would the professional communicator involve others in determining what to do—or act alone, deciding for herself or himself the best action to take?
- What factors should the professional communicator take into consideration before making a final decision?

These questions are analyzed in this chapter from a number of points of view. First, the strengths and weaknesses of cultural relativism are examined. Then the advantages of ethical pluralism are highlighted for professional communicators, especially those working in a global environment. A triage approach to ethical decision making is presented, and factors that affect ethical decision making at seven levels of analysis are explained.

The key points in this chapter:

- Professional communicators should not spend the same amount of time and energy on each ethical choice that confronts them. Rather, professional communicators should do as medical doctors and nurses do: perform triage. They should learn to sort through and classify their choices involving ethical situations, problems, or dilemmas.
- It is the people in an organization who make the ethical—and unethical—decisions. Consequently, ethical dilemmas need to be analyzed at the small group, interpersonal, and intrapersonal (within the person) levels.
- Ethical decisions are affected by organizational factors; by competitors and other organizations, including professional associations, outside a particular organization; by laws and public policies; and by cultural values and beliefs.

By definition, ethical decisions are not easy because they involve questions about what is right and wrong and what constitutes a good life—challenging questions throughout history. In the twenty-first century, *applied ethics* can be defined as the criteria people use to decide what is right, what is wrong, and what constitutes a flourishing, robust life.

Ethical choices for professional communicators are not easy to make because these decisions often involve other individuals, many of whom are powerful and have different worldviews, cultural values, and beliefs.

Cultural Relativism

Cultural relativism is a weak concept because some of its assumptions are weak, if not false, especially in today's global economy. Cultural relativism claims that what is good or bad and/or what constitutes a good life are culturally relative. These are the key assumptions of cultural relativism:

- Morality is culturally specific; ethical guidelines come from society; ethical judgments are relative to the culture in which they are made.
- Unless you are part of a culture, you cannot understand all the reasons for why something is considered right or wrong in that society; therefore, you should not judge that society's morality.
- Just as you should not judge another culture's morality, people from other cultures should not judge your morality.
- Everyone should be tolerant of those living in other cultures, as they should be tolerant of you.

A major fallacy in the logic of cultural relativism is to jump to the conclusion that because there are different sets of cultural values, there is no objective truth in ethics—that right and wrong are only matters of opinion, and opinions vary from culture to culture.

Another fallacy of cultural relativism is that it implies that we should decide what is right and wrong by looking at the society within which we are operating. From this point of view, if a corporate policy conforms to a particular society's set of ethical standards, then it is ethical. This is a false assumption because few people within any society think their society could not be improved; most think all societies can be improved.

The strength of cultural relativism is that it stresses tolerance and encourages people to learn more about a culture before passing judgment. The weaknesses of cultural relativism are that it assumes you cannot make judgments about another culture, even if horrendous acts are committed there, and that no culture can be improved.

Most professionals today work for organizations significantly affected by the global economy and are very aware of not only the importance of tolerance and learning about other cultures but also the importance of establishing corporate communication policies that are global—that cut across and operate effectively in all cultures.

Ethical Pluralism

Ethical pluralism is a strong concept because it claims there is no supreme cultural value, and its assumptions are plausible. Ethical pluralism is not the same as ethical relativism. Ethical relativism is similar to cultural relativism: it claims that what is right or wrong is relative to the circumstances.

Ethical pluralism is not the same as multiculturalism. Multiculturalism emphasizes tolerance of others without necessarily celebrating the possibilities generated by diversity. Ethical pluralism is more than tolerating the cultural values and beliefs of others; it is expecting the interaction of multiple cultures to generate greater understandings between and among societies and a better world.

The main argument of ethical pluralism is that we have many incompatible and irreducible moral values, and that these values are not derived from a single supreme value or hyper-norm. Ethical pluralism makes the case that conflicting, irreducible values are what people experience in their lives; it is realistic. Ethical pluralism acknowledges that paradoxes and ethical dilemmas in our lives cannot be avoided; therefore, we should seek common ground among conflicting values—not with an expectation to find a supreme value but with the expectation that the search will generate new and better ethical insights.

These are the assumptions of ethical pluralism:

- There is no single truth; but seeking the truth, especially for professional communicators, is important.
- It is best to avoid the extremes of absolutism (that there is only one truth and one right set of answers) and relativism (that there is no truth and that what passes for truth is based on power and perceptions of reality).
- Seeking the middle ground between absolutism and relativism means accepting a certain amount of uncertainty and acknowledging and appreciating the wisdom within all cultures and belief systems.

A better understanding of the world—and, therefore, a better world—is possible from the interaction of multiple approaches to the truth, ethics, and morality.

The weakness of ethical pluralism is that it does not satisfy extremists—neither absolutists nor relativists. The strength of pluralism is that it is a global version of Aristotle's Golden Mean ("Aristotle's Ethics," 2010). It recommends avoiding extremes and doing what is right based not on a compromise but on the best ideas from the wisest men and women in the world.

Who Is an Ideal Virtuous Person?

The ideal virtuous person is not an unrealistic fool, someone with unreasonable idealism. The ideal virtuous person is an individual who, as Aristotle would say, has "practical wisdom." The ideal virtuous person is streetwise and savvy.

The ideal virtuous person is not dogmatic or driven by ideology but knows how to integrate the best ideas of the best thinkers and to act accordingly, leading by example and not by edict. The ideal virtuous person demonstrates authenticity and moral authority. Aristotle would add that the ideal virtuous person has the right motives, traits, and commitments.

Almost everyone knows someone in his or her life who is an ideal virtuous person ... some of the time. Rarely is anyone an ideal virtuous person all the time. Different individuals at different times in their lives and in different circumstances will serve for others as examples of the ideal virtuous person.

According to Aristotle, the hallmark of the ideal virtuous person is that he or she knows the right thing to do at the right time ... and, if asked, is able to explain his or her actions to others.

Ethical Triage

Professional communicators should learn to perform triage when confronted with ethical choices. All ethical choices are not the same. It is a waste of time to treat them all alike. It pays off to know how to distinguish among ethical situations, problems, and dilemmas.

Ethical situations are fairly simple and straightforward; and to solve them, all a professional needs to do is to act professionally—to do what is right. There is really not too much to be debated—although you may need to spend some time educating the misinformed or misguided. For example, someone asks a communicator to omit legally required information from a press release or to put an unsubstantiated statement in an advertisement. The professional knows what to do, because that is what a professional is expected to do. It may require educating and explaining to others what is required and why; but for the professional, it is a relatively simple matter of just doing it right the first time.

Ethical problems have a number of possible ethical solutions—and there can be a genuine debate among equally sincere, good people about what should be done. For example, an editor under deadline pressure wants to use a photograph taken in public of a public figure but it shows the person in a bad light and might hold that person up for ridicule or embarrassment. It would be legal to publish the photograph; but would it be ethical? There are a number of creative, ethical solutions to the problem. The professional should take the time to engage in that discussion. The difficulty is learning how to frame the issue so that a genuine dialogue can occur without stirring up emotions and defensive reactions. The key to solving an ethical problem is seeking a "win-win" solution—and giving you and your colleagues enough time to come up with a creative, ethical solution.

Ethical dilemmas create a damned-if-you-do, damned-if-you-don't situation for the decision maker who must choose the lesser of two evils. Regardless of what is done, someone will be hurt. For example, a senior executive is involved in a sex scandal that violates corporate policies and has the media calling for an official statement. No matter what the professional communicator does, the executive, the company, and others also may be hurt. But the facts are facts and need to be disclosed. The key is to limit the amount of harm to innocent individuals and to lessen the negative impact on the corporation. Ethical dilemmas require crisis communications management.

Factors that Affect Ethical Decision Making

A number of characteristics affect how each individual communicator makes decisions about what is right and what is wrong:

- *Maturity.* Some people, even as children or teenagers, have more ethical maturity than others. Maturity is not necessarily related to chronological age.
- *Professional experience.* The less experience a person has with making ethical decisions, the more difficult those decisions are—and the more likely some of those decisions will be wrong.
- *The ability to deal with uncertainty.* Some people become rattled and cannot think clearly when the pressure is on; others become very focused, rise to the occasion, and make good decisions under difficult circumstances.
- *Formal education in ethics,* whether from hearing sermons, attending lectures, reading, or other venues. The more knowledge a person brings to bear

and the more factors a person considers in making an ethical decision, the better.

Interpersonal Factors Affect Ethical Decision Making

The relationship between two individuals also affects ethical decision making. For example, superior–subordinate relationships in the workplace powerfully influence who says what to whom with what effect. Regardless of status differences, the level of trust between two individuals affects communication. With greater trust, colleagues are more likely to make ethical decisions. Without trust, it is more difficult to make innovative, ethical decisions.

The natural tension between a public relations professional and individual reporters and editors in the media—each depending upon and needing the other, each working under different pressures and deadlines—can affect how ethical issues involving the media are resolved. The best media relations are built on mutual respect and trust between the communicator and media representative. That trust can only be established and maintained if accurate information is the currency of the relationship.

Small-Group Factors Affect Ethical Decision Making

Peer pressure is very apparent in small-group meetings. Sometimes peer pressure can be positive—encouraging reason and fairness. At other times, especially when a group is tired and running out of time, peer pressure operates against creative, ethical considerations. Effective group leaders learn to be alert to these tendencies and avoid "groupthink." Unethical leaders know how to manipulate groupthink to their advantage.

"Not enough information and not enough time" is one of the biggest excuses that individuals and small groups give for making decisions that, later, are judged to be unethical. Time pressures affect individuals, but it especially affects small-group decision making. Too many deadlines are artificially imposed for ulterior purposes. While "drop dead" deadlines and a genuine lack of information may be unavoidable, in many situations it is the perception of a lack of time that adversely affects decision making. Ethical leaders know when to stress absolute deadlines and when to search for, and find, more time and information to make the best decision possible.

As one corporate code suggests, "When in doubt, don't." If you sense you are about to make an unethical decision, then stop the decision-making process. Give yourself and your colleagues more time to think through the issues. Ethical leaders know when and how to stop a rush to judgment.

Organizational Factors Affect Ethical Decision Making

Organizational factors affect the quantity and quality of ethical decisions. The size of an organization makes a difference in a number of ways. Ethical issues in a firm with three employees are not the same as they would be if those same three individuals were part of an organization with 30,000 employees. Not only would the ethical problems be different, solutions to these problems would be different. Large size requires a different set of management skills.

Certain types of technologies breed their own set of ethical situations, problems, and dilemmas. Consider, for example, nuclear power industries, hospitals, universities and school systems, grocery stores, and food-processing firms. Professional communicators learn, too often the hard way, that the basic work of the organization carries with it certain ethical dilemmas.

The mindset of senior management may be one of the biggest predictors of success or failure in dealing with ethical issues. If candor and honesty are the hallmarks of senior management, this set of attitudes and behaviors will spread throughout the organization. If the actions of senior management generate distrust, these negative attitudes will affect a wide range of decisions, especially those that require a judgment about what is right and what is wrong.

Many organizations have developed processes for dealing with ethical issues. Some—especially organizations anxious to be in compliance with governmental regulations—have established training programs and departments dealing with ethics. Most mature organizations develop their own code of ethics—and recognize that the process of developing and revising the code may be as important as the code itself.

Factors Outside an Organization's Immediate Control Affect Ethical Decision Making

Competitors help keep you honest. Misstate a fact about a competitor's product or service and you will find out how closely your corporate statements are watched. The activist public scrutinizes a corporation's words and actions, as do regulators. Lots of people outside the control of an organization help keep it honest.

Professional associations such as the International Association of Business Communicators (IABC) and the Public Relations Society of America, to name two of the largest in this field, are significant sources of pressure. There is a Global Alliance of professional communication associations; its website has information and resources that communicators can use to identify and resolve ethical issues.

There is a predictable amount of redundancy among the various professional codes in this field. They offer guidelines that essentially encourage telling the truth and not engaging in harmful business practices. The IABC code clearly addresses the relatively universal nature of ethical corporate communication. The IABC code states it is "based on three different yet interrelated principles of professional communication that apply throughout the world" (IABC, 2005, para. 2).

These principles assume that just societies are governed by a profound respect for human rights and the rule of law; that ethics, the criteria for determining what is right and wrong, can be agreed upon by members of an organization; and, that understanding matters of taste requires sensitivity to cultural norms (IABC, 2005, para. 3).

According to the IABC code, "these principles are essential: Professional communication is legal. Professional communication is ethical. Professional communication is in good taste" (para. 4).

It is beyond the scope of this chapter to discuss legal issues affecting communicators. Most professional communicators are expected to be both legal and ethical. But, it is possible for a professional communicator to be ethical yet not legal. Consider, for example, civil disobedience involving public communication, such as an animal rights campaign that deliberately violates the law in order to gain media attention, with members of the organization willing to pay the consequence of breaking the law.

Cultural values and beliefs strongly influence ethical decision making. Profound differences in cultures can be seen at the international level. But they also occur among small communities. Ethical communicators take cultural values and beliefs of key stakeholders into consideration when developing campaigns. While these cultural differences are important, practically all cultures around the world agree to three basic concepts: seeking and telling the truth; treating others as you wish to be treated; and doing no harm to the innocent. Scholars, religious leaders, and ethicists have acknowledged that these ethical concepts are important in most cultures in the world, especially those where professional communicators are employed. For professional communicators, there are more similarities than differences among cultures in what is the right way to communicate.

Case in Point: Media Bribery

In this analysis, assume that the media bribery case took place in Canada (Cluster 1), France (Cluster 2), South Korea (Cluster 3), and China (Cluster 4). Each country is from a different quadrant used by Transparency International (2010) to classify countries according to degrees of corruption.

Question: Who are the moral actors? Are they the same in each country?

  Answer: The principal moral actors (the local public relations manager and the local journalist, among others) are the same, but the web of contacts and significant others who may become involved in the bribery scheme may expand in the more corrupt countries. For example, the concept of *Guanxi* in China emphasizes the importance of mutually beneficial relationships when conducting business: it supports the notion of an expanded network of relationships both for legitimate business dealings and illegal arrangements such as bribery schemes. The emphasis on individualism in Canada and France would suggest fewer and smaller networks of relationships for both legitimate and or illegal activities than might be expected in South Korea or China where collectivism is a longstanding cultural value.

Question: Is it an ethical situation, problem, or dilemma? Is it the same in each country?

  Answer: If the bribery situation is not discussed (for example, it is assumed to be a regular part of business), it does not become a problem—it is considered "business as usual." If the situation is discussed, then it becomes an ethical problem with a possible win-win solution (for example, among co-conspirators new arrangements might be made including one in which the undercover bribery decreases and payments become more open, transparent, and eventually legitimate). For example, we would expect a reporter's attempt at bribery in Canada (where the rule of law is strong) to be treated as an ethical situation: the public relations manager would reject participation out of hand and report the actions of the journalist not only to the reporter's bosses but also to professional associations and, possibly, to law enforcement agencies.

Question: What is morally permitted? What is morally prohibited? Is it the same in each country?

  Answer: Bribery, by definition, is illegal. But not everything that is illegal is necessarily unethical. If bribery causes harm to the innocent, then the act is unethical. Even if there is little or no harm, bribery is unethical because it does not promote a greater good. Bribery might create short-term gains for a limited number of people; but it does not elicit the best from others, nor create a greater good for society. For example, in China media bribery may be more common than in South Korea or France; and not participating in a bribery scheme in China may have more harmful consequences than in France or South Korea. From a utilitarian point of view, engaging in bribery in France or South Korea may not be morally permitted because there are legal and ethical options for voiding it. But in China, in extreme circumstances (for example, when there is the threat of violence if someone does not participate), it may be morally permitted to participate in a bribery scheme if not participating would create more harm. Highly corrupt economies can make conditions "on the ground" such that participating in bribery may be the lesser of two evils and, therefore, morally permitted, if other actions are taken to reduce bribery and other forms of corruption.

Question: Would the ideal virtuous person act differently in each country?

Answer: Yes, the ideal virtuous person would take into consideration cultural differences; but the ideal virtuous person would also synthesize the wisdom in all cultures and act according to principles that would apply across all cultures. For example, the core values of a professional communicator traveling to and from and working in Canada, France, South Korea, and China would not change dramatically; but in each country, the professional communicator would take into consideration specific cultural values and beliefs. If confronted with a media bribery scheme, the ideal virtuous professional communicator would try, in the short term, to make the transactions as transparent as possible—if not immediately, as soon as possible. The professional communicator would work, in the long term, to reduce the root causes of the bribery in that economy and to turn the clandestine criminal activity into an openly discussed legitimate transaction.

Our analysis indicates the weakness of cultural relativism, which would argue that we cannot judge the rightness or wrongness of media bribery in other parts of the world. You can and should make judgments about media bribery: wherever it occurs, it is wrong. Even in extreme circumstances when violence is threatened and it may not be avoidable, media bribery is still wrong; it is just the lesser of evils.

Our analysis also points out the strengths of pluralism. Ethical pluralism embraces the contradictions of values that force people to make choices among the lesser of evils. Ethical pluralism does not look for a supreme value or the simple right answer but only the possibility of new ethical insights. Even in the most corrupt economy, a professional communicator using ethical pluralism as a framework for making ethical decisions will focus on long-term solutions to the root causes of corruption, will acknowledge irreducible and conflicting values in society, and search for innovative and ethical solutions to the problem of media bribery.

Ethical pluralism allows the professional communicator to avoid the extremes of righteously saying "Never, never ever" engage in media bribery; or the silly relativist's expression of "Whatever," do it if that is what everybody else is doing. Applying the framework of ethical pluralism to media bribery keeps the focus on finding common ground among conflicting values and seeking new insights into ethical decision making.

Conclusion

From a personal and a corporate point of view, it pays to think through ethical choices before they happen—to know in advance how you intend to manage communication ethically—and to recognize the many factors that influence ethical decision making.

Cultural relativism is a weak concept, useful only because it emphasizes tolerance. Pluralism is a strong concept for two reasons: (1) because it is based on Aristotle's Golden Mean: it avoids the extremes of absolutism and relativism; and (2) because it seeks the wise person's common ground where new insights can emerge from conflicting values, principles, and loyalties—if the wise person holds steady and listens hard.

Basic assumptions and principles of ethical communication apply throughout the world—for example, to seek and tell the truth; to be fair by treating others as you wish to be treated; and to do no harm to the innocent.

Here are some practical suggestions for professional communicators who want to make better ethical decisions:

- Know yourself. Write your own personal code of ethics based on one of the professional codes. It will help you think through how you would deal with ethical dilemmas before they happen.
- Learn how to recognize and deal creatively and professionally with ethical situations, problems, and dilemmas.
- Know your colleagues—especially how they act in small groups—and the internal and external characteristics of your client or employer.
- Respect the cultural values and beliefs of all your stakeholders. Recognize that they, too, if they are good people, share your values of seeking and telling the truth, being fair, and doing no harm to the innocent.

References

International Association of Business Communicators [IABC]. (2005). *International Association of Business Communicators code of ethics for professional communicators.* Available at www.iabc.com/about/code.htm.

Aristotle's Ethics. (2010, March 29). *Stanford encyclopedia of philosophy.* Available at http://plato.stanford.edu/entries/aristotle-ethics.

Transparency International. (2010). *2008 bribe payers index.* Available at www.transparency.org.

CHAPTER SIX

CORPORATE SOCIAL RESPONSIBILITY

The Communicator's Role as Leader and Advocate

Mary Ann McCauley

Corporate social responsibility (CSR) encompasses a broad range of business initiatives that have a common thread. Each aims to improve our world, whether by operating an environmentally friendly business, ensuring human rights, enabling employees to volunteer their time and talents, or providing financial support to organizations engaged in improving the quality of lives. A Google search for a definition of CSR turns up more than 26 million results and many different labels. These labels include corporate responsibility, corporate accountability, corporate ethics, corporate citizenship, sustainability, stewardship, triple bottom line, and responsible business. Most of the postings indicate there is no standard definition.

The World Bank definition appears to be among the most global: "Corporate social responsibility is the commitment of businesses to contribute to sustainable economic development by working with employees, their families, the local community and society at large to improve their lives in ways that are good for business and for development" (2010, para. 2).

Communicators have the opportunity to take a larger leadership role in CSR business strategy than ever before because of the expectations of our organizations' stakeholders. Stakeholders—from customers to investors and employees—increasingly are making decisions and developing opinions about our organizations based on how they treat the environment, their communities, and the people who live and work in them.

This chapter describes in-depth the impact of corporate social responsibility strategies on our organizations' business models and how CSR strategies are implemented.

Toward Standardization of CSR

The phrase *corporate social responsibility* was coined in 1953 when Howard Bowen wrote the book *Social Responsibilities of the Businessman*, in which he addressed the question of the business community's moral obligations to society. As CSR evolved, businesses around the world have moved from simply making contributions and providing volunteers to community causes to incorporating CSR into their primary business strategies. Today, CSR is a way of doing business for many companies worldwide. Corporate social responsibility is becoming an essential component of the business model as shareholders, business partners, customers, and vendors give voice to expectations that any organization with which they do business meet certain standards for ethical, environmental, and human rights.

According to London-based International Institute of Business Ethics (Zaki, 2010), companies demonstrating a public commitment to high standards of corporate behavior on average post 18 percent higher profits. For example, in Australia, an increasing number of institutions managing retirement investments report that they "are starting to judge companies on their environmental, social and governance issues" (Gettler, 2007, para. 7).

According to ethicist Attracta Lagan, "Business will determine the quality of the air we breathe, the fuel we burn, the food we eat and the water we drink. So too, it is business that will shape the emergence of a global society by determining who is included, who is informed, who gets what and which human rights are enshrined in the global workplace. Business now has to have the potential to enhance or destabilise social progress in equal measure" (as cited in Gettler, 2007, para. 2).

Many companies have responded to stakeholder and regulatory pressures with CSR programs that are focused on improving the global community. Communicators are poised to embrace leadership roles because the success of CSR initiatives is tightly tied to the effectiveness of the communication supporting them. In Europe some countries, including France and Denmark, have passed laws that require reporting based on the triple bottom line model, which requires business performance to be addressed based on its impact on the economy, environment, and society.

As global standards for lean, sustainable business operations have been developed and are required in some sectors in order to conduct business, guidelines have come into existence that outline the key elements of any CSR report. There are vast selections of aids accessible in creating and deploying effective communication programs. Three of the most important tools to understand are Global Reporting Initiative (GRI) Sustainability Reporting Guidelines (www. globalreporting.org); AccountAbility (AA) 1000 series (www.accountability21.net); and International Standards Organization (ISO) 26000 standard (www.iso. org/sr).

Global Reporting Initiative

CERES, an environmental organization, and the United Nations Environment Programme developed the GRI guidelines in 1997 as a collaborative effort. Updated in 2006, the guidelines are the most widely used standard for CSR reports. They identify eight key elements of creating a report:

1. Collecting, analyzing, and organizing data
2. Identifying impact
3. Engaging stakeholders
4. Determining substantive issues to include
5. Defining scope
6. Discussing management approaches
7. Communicating significant data
8. Assessing progress and priorities going forward

In summary, the report must provide context to the content and be more than just a litany of data with no assessment of lessons learned, progress, and impact.

Telefónica (2008), one of the world's largest telecommunications companies, is an example of an organization that follows the GRI guidelines. Their report includes information about initiatives in twenty countries, GRI indicators, case studies, and other information that shed light on Telefónica's achievements and future challenges in the field of CSR.

AccountAbility 1000

The AA1000 series was developed by AccountAbility, a global organization dedicated to accountability for sustainability. The series provides guidance related to sustainability practices and data through three standards:

1. The AA1000 AccountAbility Principles Standard (AA1000APS) 2008 provides a better framework for an organization to use in order to better identify, understand, prioritize, and respond to its sustainability challenges.
2. The AA1000 Assurance Standard (AA1000AS) 2008 is a leading international standard used to provide assurance on publicly available sustainability information, particularly CSR/Sustainability reports.
3. The AA1000 Stakeholder Engagement Standard (AA1000SES) 2005 provides a framework to help organizations ensure that stakeholder engagement processes are robust and deliver results.

International Standards Organization 26000

The ISO 26000 standards were launched in November 2010 and provide a practical guide for communicating sustainability. The standards encompass seven core subjects: organizational governance, fair operating practices, environment, human rights, labor practices, consumer issues, and community involvement.

While most of these subjects fall outside the control of communicators, it is essential that we fully comprehend how our organizations address and implement strategies in these areas. As stated in the codes of ethics of all professional communication associations, we have an ethical responsibility to communicate truthful information.

That puts communicators in the position of being the organization's conscience. As companies have learned the value of *being green*, some have been accused of *greenwashing*. Greenwashing is a term used to describe a product, company, or service that claims to be environmentally friendly and contribute to a more sustainable world when in fact that claim is at least questionable or even untrue. To avoid possible accusations, we need to understand the life cycles of the products our companies produce to make certain that those products and their components, even if we outsource them, are produced according to sustainable guidelines from inception to distribution to consumption and disposal.

Being responsible for communication challenges us to ask questions about the CSR goals and strategies, such as:

- What is the board policy related to sustainability?
- How is that being implemented?
- How and who is monitoring compliance?
- What are employees' roles and opportunities to contribute?

An organization committed to a corporate social responsibility agenda provides significant opportunities to build trust among all stakeholders. It means walking the talk and assuring that CSR communication is a high priority. Based on the BSR/GlobeScan State of Sustainable Business Poll (2009), 66 percent of those responding indicated they planned to increase external and internal communication about their CSR programs. In addition, 50 percent reported plans to increase chief executive officer (CEO) involvement, and 38 percent planned to increase staffing levels. It is clear there is a strong commitment to CSR communication within many companies.

Before a CSR report is produced, much work must precede it. Communicators' responsibilities should focus on strategies such as leading employee engagement, aligning brand reputation with CSR initiatives, and leveraging the CSR initiatives through public relations, traditional, and social media relations.

Integrating CSR Communications

Strategic planning is as critical to CSR as it is to any other initiative. The key is to align the CSR communication plan with business, corporate communication, and marketing plans.

CSR communication programs cannot be separated from other corporate communication initiatives. It should be considered one of the many elements used in positioning a company and its products or services. The opportunities to leverage a company's CSR initiatives are too beneficial to miss.

Depending on program size, CSR may need a dedicated person or staff to manage it. If this is the case, it is important to keep this effort integrated with other public relations, corporate communications, and marketing activities. If the public relations, marketing, or corporate communication departments are not directly responsible for CSR, it is the responsibility of their respective communication professionals to establish the links among the three initiatives.

Being integrated through a planning or structural organization will make the task of managing CSR more effective, since many of the initiatives, including contributions, have the potential for external visibility. Internally there is much to be gained by keeping employees informed.

CSR programs offer companies a wealth of opportunities to be visible. Public relations and advertising strategies should consider CSR initiatives when plans are being drawn to market the company and its products or services. One of the reasons cause-related marketing is seen as valuable is that it creates an opportunity to market in ways that speak to a common interest.

For the company that has a business-to-business product or service, gaining visibility in the community can be difficult, since the average reader of the local newspaper or viewer of local newscasts has no direct interest in what you market.

Visibility through your CSR community relations efforts can be a great asset. Enabling key audiences to see your company active in local sustainability projects, local charity events, meet employees volunteering on boards and committees, and see your company's name among contributors to nonprofits all help to create a positive image of your company.

Telefónica's (2009) program, Intégrame, teams with local governments in rural areas to reduce poverty and promote development. Through these public–private partnerships, Telefónica has installed the infrastructures needed to enable telecommunication access to thousands of people in the most isolated locations. More than 200 communities have access to fixed, mobile, and public wireless telephony and broadband, benefiting more than 58,000 people. They use YouTube to tell their stories.

Visibility can include publicity resulting from special events, announcements about board appointments, equipment, product or service donations, and sponsorships. If you are considering cause-related marketing initiatives as part of your community relations effort, there are additional criteria to consider:

- Is the opportunity aligned with CSR goals?
- Is there a logical tie between our products and services and the proposed sponsorship?
- What do we expect from this relationship: leads, selling product or services directly, higher visibility, volunteer opportunities?
- What is the probability this organization can meet our expectations?
- What does the organization expect from us: product or services, higher visibility, in-kind support, financial support, volunteers?
- What will it cost us to affiliate with this organization: time, money, inventory?

Impact of CSR on Brand Reputation

Corporate and product brands are especially vulnerable to public opinions based on individuals' perception of our organizations' impacts on the environment and our communities. A poll commissioned by the U.S.-based Better Business Bureau (2008) revealed that during a six-month period from September 2007 to April 2008 U.S. businesses averaged a 14 percent drop in trust across 13 of the 15 industries polled. These included businesses that provide basic products and services, such as pharmacies and drug stores, banks, grocery stores, department stores, and home improvement centers.

Communicators have the opportunity to see that CSR initiatives are aligned with brands whether we are on the brand management side or the CSR side of the equation. For example, The Body Shop (2010) was one of the early adopters of aligning business goals and values with sustainability. Their marketing has focused on their socially responsible approach to their products, from sourcing through economic development of small businesses for women in underdeveloped companies to manufacturing products that do not harm the environment.

Body Shop founder Anita Roddick is a role model for business leaders who are committed to a set of values that enable communicators to align values with brand. On the company's website she concisely articulated those values: "We believe there is only one way to be beautiful, nature's way. We've believed this for years and still do. We constantly seek out wonderful natural ingredients from all four corners of the globe, and we bring you products bursting with effectiveness to enhance your natural beauty and express your unique personality. And whilst we're doing this, we always strive to protect this beautiful planet and the people who depend on it. We don't do it this way because it's fashionable. We do it because, to us, it's the only way" (Body Shop, 2010, para. 1).

More recently, in 2008 Timberland announced a long-term CSR program based on four strategic goals, or pillars. Each pillar is supported by several key initiatives with near- and long-term quantitative targets and was vetted through a rigorous stakeholder engagement process:

1. *Energy:* Become carbon neutral by 2010
2. *Products:* Design recyclable product
3. *Workplaces:* Fair, safe, and nondiscriminatory
4. *Service:* Community greening

One of the unique qualities of Timberland's program is an invitation for consumers to actively participate in the company's quarterly CSR progress reports by providing feedback.

Communicators need to understand how the life cycle of a product from component or ingredient supplier to production to packaging and finally consumption and disposal meets our organizations' stated values about sustainability. If all elements align, we have a great opportunity to enhance brand reputation. If they do not, we risk damaging brand reputation through greenwashing while violating our professional code of ethics.

Engaging Employees in the Community

Businesses have a great deal to gain by creating strong employee volunteer programs. These programs can range from providing time off to participating in corporate-endorsed community activities to providing matching financial gifts for specific amounts of time volunteered by the employee.

The benefits to the employer and employee are many. U.S.-based Walker Information cites a study (Drizin, 2007) that indicates 7 of 10 employees who favorably view their employers' community support state they will remain with that employer two years longer than those who do not have favorable views of their employer's community programs.

Many volunteer opportunities give employees a forum in which to strengthen existing skills or hone little-used skills. Such activities also benefit nonprofits since they get assistance at all levels, from entry level to senior management, that they could not otherwise afford. Some initiatives that have global applications for companies doing business internationally include:

- Literacy programs
- Tutoring students at all levels of education
- Mentoring programs for youths
- Hunger-fighting programs
- Health care projects for the poor
- Housing programs for the poor or disaster victims
- Small business development in impoverished or distressed communities

Opportunities such as these frequently align well with the corporate CSR goals.

Inviting employees from a variety of business units and skill levels to sit on the contributions committee allows an organization to align its contributions goals with the interests of its employees and needs of the community while gaining internal buy-in for the CSR programs. It is a morale builder to ask a representative group of employees to participate in this important decision-making process. It also is an opportunity for an employee to develop leadership skills, learn more about community's needs, and get a firsthand look at what a socially responsible company means to the company and to the community.

For example, in Hong Kong the nonprofit organization, Business in the Community (2009), and its ENGAGE network of businesses organize the annual Journey of Opportunity, through which volunteers from many businesses engage with disadvantaged youth. In 2009, they paired 52 employees as mentors from 18 leading Hong Kong companies with 65 young people from schools in Tin Shui Wai—one of the poorest districts in Hong Kong. The 2009 program represented a 44 percent increase in young people participating and an 18 percent increase in volunteers from 2008. This program gave young people a chance to learn that there are opportunities to rise out of the poverty in which they live. For the volunteers, it was one way in which they could share their work experiences and provide some inspiration for disadvantaged youth.

Regular surveys of community involvement by employees will provide a sense of the issues that are important to employees and allow communicators to see trends and identify commonalities. This is important information as you plan community relations programs, especially if one goal is to gain employee support for your initiatives. You also may find an existing connection through an employee's involvement in an organization, which gives your firm the opportunity for a special initiative that will benefit both the community and your company. In establishing criteria, consider these questions:

- Where are the greatest unmet needs in our community?
- How do these align with our CSR goals and strategies?
- In what ways do those needs match our strategic business goals?
- What values do these organizations have in common with us?
- What are some benefits to the company and our employees if we support an organization?
- In what ways are we able and willing to contribute?

Another way in which employees can become more engaged is to serve on the company's contributions committee. Many organizations take their contributions programs to more grassroots levels with guidelines that enable branch offices and remote locations to make grants without first coming to the corporate committee. Retailing giant Walmart (2010) has a community grant program that enables store managers and regional vice presidents to award local grants based on corporate guidelines without further corporate approval.

The Green Mountain Coffee Roasters, Inc., Community Action for Employees (2010) program gives employees the ability to volunteer 52 hours annually during regular work hours. Their website states, "We believe volunteering is a great way for employees to develop leadership skills, connect to their communities, and feel better about themselves and their work. Since 1993, we have provided paid time off for employees who want to volunteer for nonprofits in their communities" (para. 1). For fiscal 2008, 42 percent of Green Mountain employees donated more than 5,700 hours of volunteer time in their local communities.

The business case for such volunteer programs is validated in a study conducted by Corporate Citizenship of London (2010). The study analyzed 16 London businesses whose 546 employees were engaged in an education-based volunteer activity. They found that the average cost for the skill development through volunteer activity was £381 compared to £400 annually per employee for relevant training costs.

Finally, the overall community relations program needs to be evaluated regularly against its goals and desired outcomes. This often includes quarterly as well as annual evaluations of individual initiatives, usually involving site visits, interviews with employee volunteers, and a review of the agency's balance sheet. That an agency will be held accountable is increasingly an expectation of most funders.

Using CSR as a Public Relations Tool

Companies committed to CSR have the challenge of enhancing their corporate reputations using public relations, traditional media relations, and social media channels while achieving the delicate balance between promoting the CSR initiatives to keep key stakeholders informed and being seen as using CSR as a gimmick. This presents an opportunity for communicators to provide strategic counsel that achieves the appropriate tone, timing, and tools.

Just as with any communication strategy, we have to begin by becoming knowledgeable about the realities of any CSR initiative we chose to promote. Once we are assured that we have all the needed data and have validated them, we can develop public relations goals and strategies that will leverage the CSR program. The channels selected depend upon the stakeholders to be reached. Again, balance is essential when choosing traditional and social media channels. Management team members should be able to rely on communicators' experiences to select those channels.

Media relations presents a conduit to those we want to educate or influence about specific areas of a corporate CSR program. For example, Macy's ("Reading Is Fundamental," 2010), a U.S.-based retailer, uses media relations tools to announce a literacy program; their *Reading Is Fundamental* multi-year campaign partners with consumers to raise funds to support children's literacy programs. The editorial coverage:

- Raises awareness about the importance of enabling children to read
- Provides a means by which consumers can contribute to an important program in easy ways
- Positions Macy's cause-related marketing program in a positive light

Nonprofit organizations also use public relations effectively in their advocacy programs for CSR. In Australia, the Australian Centre for Corporate Social Responsibility (2009) advocates for the integration of CSR into the corporate environment. One of their key tools is to publish opinion pieces in leading national business publications. The centre also has garnered coverage on national television and radio programs. Their public relations program is rounded out with numerous speaking engagements at national and international conferences.

All these outlets serve to keep CSR top of mind and to educate business leaders about the benefits and obligations of an effective CSR program.

Social media tools should be evaluated as communicators develop plans for CSR in the same way they would evaluate using all other tools to determine when and how the communication channel aligns with the appropriate stakeholders. For example, consumer businesses have become adroit at using Facebook to communicate aspects of their CSR programs to customers. U.S.-based Target Corporation (2010) uses Facebook for its "Turn Summer Play into Summer Learning" program developed in conjunction with the Search Institute.

Twitter accounts for global organizations including CERES (@ceresnews) and the GRI (@GRI_Secretariat) encourage ongoing conversations about CSR.

Bringing It All Together—Why CSR Matters

The Reputation Institute's (2010) research in 2008 and 2009 shows that CSR's impact on corporate reputation accounts for 40 percent of an organization's overall reputation. The institute also reports that for the most part consumers develop their opinions from corporate communications, media coverage, and word of mouth.

The GlobeScan Corporate Social Responsibility Monitor (2010) survey reports that 84 percent of executives in 116 countries agreed with the statement that business should "generate high returns to investors but balance that with contributing to the broader public good." In addition, the editors of the *Economist* ("Just Good Business," 2008) reversed their long-standing position of companies engaged in CSR as "do gooders" to state that CSR now is mainstream in businesses worldwide.

The communicator's role is to guide the communication surrounding CSR and to ensure that corporate and brand reputation is aligned with reality. This requires transparency in how we communicate and that we be fully engaged in our organizations' strategic planning, implementation, and evaluation.

References

Australian Centre for Corporate Social Responsibility. (2009). *About us/Our sustainability report 2009.* Available at www.accsr.com.au/html/sustreport2009_impacts.html.

Better Business Bureau. (2008). *BBB/Gallop trust in business index.* Available at www.bbb.org/us/storage/0/Shared%20Documents/Survey%20II%20-%20BBB%20Gallup%20-%20Executive%20Summary%20-%2025%20Aug%2008.pdf.

The Body Shop. (2010). *Values and campaigns.* Retrieved July 25, 2010, from www.thebodyshop.com/_en/_ww/values-campaigns/index.aspx.

Bowen, H. (1953). *Social responsibilities of the businessman.* New York: Harper.

Business for Social Responsibility (BSR). (2009). *Innovating for sustainability.* Available at www.bsr.org/files/bsr_report_2009.pdf.

Business in the Community. (2009). *ENGAGE in Hong Kong.* Available at www.bitc.org.uk/resources/case_studies/engage_in_hong_kong.html.

Corporate Citizenship of London. (2010, May). *Volunteering: The business case.* Available at www.corporate-citizenship.com/archive/volunteering-the-most-cost-effective-way-to-train-and-develop-your-staff.

Drizin, M. (2007, February 3). Do employees care that employers give? *Walker Information.* Available at www.walkerinfo.com/knowledge-center/walker-library/article.asp?id=180.

Gettler, L. (2007, August 14). Social responsibility. *WA Today.* Available at www.watoday.com.au/executive-style/management/social-responsibility-20090518-ba3g.html.

GlobeScan. (2010). *2010 corporate social responsibility monitor.* Available at www.globescan.com.

Green Mountain Coffee Roasters, Inc. (2010). *Employee volunteerism.* Retrieved July 25, 2010, from www.gmcr.com/en/csr/SupportingLocalCommunities/EmployeeVolunteerism.aspx.

Just good business. (2008). *The Economist, I*(8563), 3–6.

Reading Is Fundamental and Macy's launch book a brighter future. (2010, June 30). *CSRwire* Retrieved from www.csrwire.com/press_releases/29952-Reading-Is-Fundamental-and-Macy-s-Launch-Book-A-Brighter-Future.

Reputation Institute. (2010). Why CSR matters in 2010. *Reputation Intelligence, 2*(1), 4–10.

Target. (2010). *Turn summer play into summer learning.* Retrieved July 25, 2010, from www.facebook.com/target#!/target?v=app_118532098173841.

Telefónica. (2008). *The report in brief.* Retrieved July 25, 2010, from www.telefonica.com/ext/rc08/en/telefonica/INFORME_EN_BREVE/index.html

Telefónica. (2009). *Geographic divide: Intégrame.* Available at www.crandsustainability.telefonica.com/en/innovation/geographic_divide.php.

Timberland. (2008). *CSR strategy.* Retrieved July 25, 2010, from www.timberland.com/corp/index.jsp?page=csr_strategy.

Walmart. (2010). *Giving programs: We work hard to give back to our communities.* Retrieved July 25, 2010, from http://walmartstores.com/CommunityGiving/8979.aspx.

World Bank. (2010). *Corporate social responsibility.* Retrieved July 25, 2010, from www.fias.net/ifcext/economics.nsf/Content/CSR-IntroPage

Zaki, N. A. (2010). Do Middle Eastern businesses really need corporate social responsibility? *Orient Planet.* Retrieved July 27, 2010, from www.orientplanet.com/Viewpoint_CSR.htm.

CHAPTER SEVEN

CORPORATE SOCIAL RESPONSIBILITY AND SUSTAINABILITY

Rob Briggs

There are many definitions of corporate social responsibility (CSR). For the business communicator, CSR covers a broad spectrum of issues: managing reputation, dealing with stakeholder activism, and sharing values-based messages with both employees and publics. The ways in which corporations behave, the ways in which they are expected to behave, and the ways they are perceived to behave are all areas in which business communicators can and do have a significant impact.

If we assume that society is a corporate constituency and that the rules, ethics, norms, and values expressed by society form part of the right of contract between that constituency and the corporation, in effect, this contract provides the firm's legitimacy, its licences to operate. One of the core tenets of CSR is the scope it gives organizations to manage this key intangible aspect of reputation.

While the author was delighted to compile this chapter, full credit for RBC's Corporate Responsibility initiatives is due to the hard work and dedication of a number of key employees: Shari Austin, vice president and head of Corporate Citizenship, RBC; Francis Binney, environment officer, RBC Wealth Management, British Isles; Nicola Carroll, community relations manager, RBC Wealth Management, British Isles; Sandra Odendahl, director, Corporate Environmental Affairs, RBC; and Lynn Patterson, director, Corporate Responsibility, RBC.

One only has to look at the website or annual report for almost any major public company to find statements of corporate values such as "We approach all aspects of our business with honesty and integrity" (McDonalds Canada) and "protecting and advancing ... freedom of expression" (Microsoft). Mallen Baker, of the United Kingdom's Ethical Corporation Advisory Board, defines CSR as being "about how companies manage the business processes to produce an overall positive impact on society" (2010, para. 2). A further common definition states, "CSR is about how businesses align their values and behavior with the expectations and needs of stakeholders—not just customers and investors, but also employees, suppliers, communities, regulators, special interest groups and society as a whole. CSR describes a company's commitment to be accountable to its stakeholders" (CSR Award, 2010, para. 2). CSR demands that businesses manage the economic, social, and environmental impacts of their operations to maximize the benefits and minimize the downsides.

Key CSR issues include governance, environmental management, stakeholder engagement, labor standards, employee and community relations, social equity, responsible sourcing, and human rights. CSR is not only about fulfilling a duty to society; it can also bring competitive advantage. Through an effective CSR program, companies can improve access to capital; sharpen decision making and reduce risk; enhance brand image; uncover previously hidden commercial opportunities, including new markets; reduce costs; attract, retain, and motivate employees.

Alternative views of CSR position social responsibility as *greenwash*—as philanthropic giving by the organization in the hope of managing its image rather than affecting real change to their operating practices. However, organizational reputation is far more than a public relations exercise. Look to companies such as Coca-Cola, where the market capitaliszation far exceeds the tangible assets. Here, goodwill and reputation have a value far greater than the tangible value of the company's physical assets. Coca-Cola's brand value in 2010 was US$68 billion.

Sustainability was defined by the World Commission on Environment and Development in 1987 as the successful meeting of present social, economic, and environmental needs without compromising the ability of future generations to meet their own needs. Corporate sustainability focuses on long-term economic and social stakeholder expectations both by optimizing their sustainability performance and by participating in networks with governments, nongovernmental organizations (NGOs), and other stakeholders that can provide the capacity for the world's sustainable development.

This chapter describes best practices of Royal Bank of Canada (RBC) in four key areas of interest to business communicators:

1. Structuring CSR in large organizations
2. Communicating corporate responsibility
3. Building community relations on a local level
4. Sustainability and reputation

RBC is recognized among the world's financial, social, and environmental leaders and is listed on the 2009–2010 Dow Jones Sustainability World Index and the DJSI North American Index. It is recognized as one of Canada's Greenest Employers, one of Canada's Best Diversity Employers, one of Canada's 50 Most Socially Responsible Corporations and one of the Best Workplaces in Canada.

RBC is also listed on the Jantzi Social Index, the FTSE4Good Index, and the Canadian Carbon Disclosure Project Leadership Index. As one of Canada's largest corporate donors, RBC supports a broad range of community initiatives, through donations, sponsorships, and employee volunteer activities. In 2009, the group contributed more than C$105 million to community causes worldwide, through donations of more than C$52.6 million and an additional C$52.5 million in sponsorship of community events and national organizations.

Structuring CSR in Large Organizations

Today, corporate social responsibility is high in the headlines—from BP's environmental disaster in the Gulf of Mexico to public and governmental distrust of financial institutions following the near collapse of the world's financial system in 2008–2009. The actions and performance of major organizations have a significant impact on people, communities, and countries. Managing that performance and meeting the expectations of both stakeholders and shareholders is essential for companies to operate. This section of the chapter presents an overview of how CSR is structured at Royal Bank of Canada.

The vision, values, and strategy of the bank set the context for RBC's CSR framework. It is overseen by various board committees, including the Corporate Governance and Public Policy Committee, the Conduct Review and Risk Policy Committee, and the Human Resources Committee.

Shareholder resolutions were made to Canadian banks in every year from 2005 to 2008 on climate change, biodiversity, and sustainability performance. Pension funds and other prospective RBC clients regularly request CSR information. The business has a dedicated Corporate Citizenship department that encompasses corporate responsibility, corporate environmental affairs, and donations. Key staff in other departments are responsible for programs and performance in issue-specific areas, including finance, investor relations, group risk management, procurement, corporate real estate, human resources, community sponsorships, and government relations. As well as a centralized communications function at global headquarters (responsible for strategy), RBC at global, national, and regional levels employs professional business communicators who are responsible for CSR communications at the local level. Each of its business units has its own framework for customer service, quality management, and government relations.

With one of its stated core values listed as "trust through integrity in everything we do," RBC considers corporate responsibility to include ethical business practices, having a positive economic impact, operating with integrity in the marketplace, providing a supportive workplace, being environmentally sustainable, and contributing to communities. These priorities are illustrated in Figure 7.1.

Companies both large and small contribute to the economies of the communities and countries in which they do business through taxes, philanthropy, and day-to-day business decisions and actions. RBC aims to have a positive economic impact by providing attractive returns to shareholders, creating employment, supporting small business and economic development, fostering innovation and entrepreneurship, and purchasing responsibly.

RBC has a formal policy that evaluates products for a range of risks and ensures they align with client needs, laws and regulations, and the voluntary consumer protection codes the bank has signed. It provides credit and banking services to companies in many industries, adhering to specific environmental responsibility and anticorruption policies. The bank is a signatory to the Equator Principles, a set of voluntary guidelines addressing environmental and social risks associated with project finance.

Protecting an organization's reputation and keeping key stakeholders informed is critical. If it does not actively engage key stakeholders, the organization surrenders influence over the CSR information agenda. Large organizations can manage their reputations through regularly providing information to the socially responsible investment community and engaging with stakeholder groups to discuss environmental issues related to policy development, operational impacts, and business development opportunities. For RBC, these groups include the Canadian Boreal Initiative, Durrell Wildlife Preservation Trust, ForestEthics, World Wildlife Fund, and Nature Conservancy of Canada.

Sustainability reporting provides information for stakeholders in a variety of formats. While there is a proliferation of interested parties, large organizations

FIGURE 7.1 RBC BLUEPRINT FOR DOING BETTER

RBC
Blueprint
for Doing Better™

Priorities

Economic impact
- Provide strong returns to shareholders
- Pay fair share of taxes
- Create employment
- Support small business and community economic development
- Foster innovation and entrepreneurship
- Purchase goods and services responsibly

Workplace
- Maintain progressive workplace programs and practices
- Respect diversity and promote inclusion
- Provide competitive compensation and total rewards, and enable growth through training and development opportunities
- Foster a culture of employee engagement

Operate our business with integrity

Marketplace
- Provide access to basic banking services
- Develop and provide products responsibly
- Protect, educate and listen to consumers

Environment
- Reduce the intensity of our environmental footprint
- Promote environmentally responsible business activities
- Offer environmental products and services

Community
- Provide donations with a lasting social impact
- Sponsor key community initiatives
- Enable employees to contribute

should devote sufficient communications resource to supply the widest range of stakeholders. The cornerstone of RBC's sustainability reporting can be found at www.rbc.com/responsibility.

Other CSR-related publications include the *RBC Blueprint for Doing Better*, an annual Corporate Responsibility Report and Public Accountability Statement (Patterson, 2009b), which features a year-end snapshot of RBC's economic, social, and environmental impact in the workplace, marketplace, and communities.

The business observes reporting guidelines suggested by the Global Reporting Initiative and regularly and proactively provides information to a number of key socially responsible research companies for the creation of indices, ratings, and rankings they provide or sell to analysts and investors. It also produces issue-specific reports, including an annual Diversity Progress Report and a submission to the Carbon Disclosure Project.

RBC has been examining topics related to natural resources and the environment since as early as the 1940s. Over the years, the *RBC Letter*, an essay series that tries to help people understand the world around them, has covered such topics as soil, forests, and water:

> There is not a business of the human race, not an art, science, comfort
> or beauty, which does not issue from a tree, and without trees the whole
> earth would be a hideous Sahara. Canada's forests are the country's water
> tap, regulating the storage and flow of water; they prevent soil waste,
> provide cover for wild life, screen the soil from the heat of the sun's rays,
> open an immense surface to the cooling processes of radiation, and give
> off an incalculable evaporation of moisture. Now the forests are calling
> upon man to repay some of that debt in care and preservation. (*RBC Letter*,
> 1944, p. 1)

Given the plethora of CSR, sustainability, and environmental issues currently extant, setting direction, strategy, goals, and focus is essential for any organization. RBC publishes three main CSR-related blueprints that form the heart of its approach. The first of these is the *RBC Blueprint for Doing Better* (Patterson, 2009b). The second is the *RBC Community Blueprint* (Patterson, 2009a), a document that lays out the bank's vision for helping create stronger communities (see Figure 7.2).

The third is the *RBC Environmental Blueprint* (Patterson, 2009c), a vision of how the bank addresses issues like climate change, biodiversity, forests, and water. Its objectives are to manage risks, drive returns, and protect and enhance reputation. The *RBC Environmental Blueprint* describes work plans for reducing the intensity of

FIGURE 7.2 RBC COMMUNITY BLUEPRINT

RBC Community Blueprint™

2009 Highlights

As a large, global financial institution, RBC is expected to support a wide range of causes. RBC has chosen to focus a portion of our community investments in the priority areas shown here, while continuing a broad base of support across all sectors.

We refer to this approach as the RBC Community Blueprint, which lays out our vision for helping create stronger communities.

Environment
Priority Area: RBC Blue Water Project™
- Committed over $4.6 million to fresh water initiatives in 2009;
- Announced significant grants to three universities for water research and programs;
- Pledged more then $21 million in total support since 2007, to 223 organizations worldwide working in the areas of watershed protection and access to clean drinking water.

Education
Priority Area: RBC After School Grants Project
- Invested almost $2.4 million with 90 of Canada's top community-based after-school programs in 2009;
- Over the last 10 years, provided more than $19 million in grants to 198 community-based after-school programs that offer learning and skill development opportunities to youth in the hours after classes end for the day.

Amateur Sport
Priority Areas: Olympic initiatives, Hockey
- Sponsored the Vancouver 2010 Olympic and Paralympic Winter Games, as well as the Vancouver 2010 Olympic Torch Relay, the Vancouver 2010 Paralympic Torch Relay and the RBC Olympians Program;
- Premier Sponsor of Hockey Canada since 1995. In addition to supporting Canada's men's and women's national and Olympic hockey teams, RBC is title sponsor of the National Junior A Championship and RBC Cup.

Employee Contributions
- Provided 2,443 grants of $500 each totalling $1.2 million to organizations in recognition of the volunteer work of our employees and pensioners;
- Since 1999, we have made over 17,000 grants and donated over $8.5 million to celebrate our employees' volunteer efforts;
- RBC employees in Canada volunteered the equivalent of almost $600,000* during working hours for United Way, Junior Achievement and Habitat for Humanity.

*Based on an estimate of 22,404 hours at an average of $25/hr.

Health and Wellness
Priority Area: RBC Children's Mental Health Project
- Donated over $2.3 million to 55 organizations across Canada dedicated to children's mental health with a focus on early intervention and public education;
- Donated over $5 million to community and children's hospitals across Canada and supported health-related initiatives around the world.

Arts and Culture
Priority Area: RBC Emerging Artist Project
- Supported the arts through the RBC Emerging Artists Project—long-term partnerships with organizations or programs that bridge the gap from academic excellence to professional careers;
- Invested over $900,000 in apprenticeship, internship and artist recognition programs at 43 agencies in 20 cities across Canada;
- Sponsored the RBC Painting Competition for the 11th year, providing funding and recognition for budding artists;
- Launched the RBC Emerging Filmmakers Competition in partnership with the Toronto International Film Festival Talent Lab.

Social Services
Priority Area: United Way, Food Banks
- RBC and our employees contributed $16.1 million to the United Way in Canada and the U.S.;
- We are the largest private sector contributor to the United Way in Canada, and one of only 77 organizations that contribute over $1 million annually;
- RBC and our employees gave over $600,000 to help replenish food banks and soup kitchens across Canada and in the southeastern United States.

Diversity
Respect for diversity is one of our key values, and the theme of diversity underscores all the programs within the RBC Community Blueprint.

the bank's environmental footprint, promoting environmentally responsible business activities, and offering environmental products and services.

Through setting its CSR framework in context and providing a full suite of blueprints, reports, and work plans, RBC can comprehensively cover most, if not all, aspects of CSR that are expected of a large organization. The rest of this chapter focuses on how RBC communicates CSR through specific programs at the global and local levels and examines how companies and their communicators can engage with environmental activists on controversial issues.

Communicating CSR and Sustainability

With a plethora of stakeholders to please, communicating CSR can be a daunting proposition. As well as regulatory requirements, organizations need to engage interested audiences such as employees, NGOs, media, and local communities.

Effective and transparent communication is vital to engaging and informing opinion leaders in each audience. Such communication aims to legitimize the organization's actions and behavior. The three key channels to focus on are the organization's social responsibility report, internal communications, and public relations.

CSR communication with employees can help create publicity and a good reputation through word of mouth. Employees' satisfaction levels and commitment are linked (Bevan & Wilmott, 2002). At the top of the house, RBC's Corporate Citizenship department actively promotes employee engagement in environmental programs such as the RBC Blue Water Project—a wide-ranging, multi-year program designed to help foster a culture of water stewardship so that people have clean fresh water today and tomorrow.

RBC first started talking about the importance of water in an open letter from 1950: "Water is benevolent, when properly managed. It can be productive and will support prosperous communities if its flow is wisely used. Our water problems are the outcome of our efforts to adapt our physical environment to our economic and social needs, without reckoning sufficiently on nature's unchanging ways. So, in spite of the fact that Canada is richly endowed with water resources, we have no room for complacency" (*RBC Letter*, 1950, p. 1).

Part of the RBC Blue Water Project is a grant program of C$50 million over ten years. Through the RBC Blue Water Project, the company aims to reduce the intensity of RBC's own water footprint, run education and awareness programs for employees and clients to promote sustainable water use, and create an understanding of the value and vulnerability of our water resources.

Today, RBC utilizes a dedicated website, a Facebook page, and public relations (PR) agencies both globally and locally to spread the word on water. Free the Children, a Canadian not-for-profit, used its RBC Blue Water Project grant of C$300,000 to launch an "H2O 4U Speaking Tour," which visited 100 schools across Canada to educate youth about global water issues and inspire them to take action in their daily lives to conserve and protect water. The students will be encouraged to fundraise to provide clean water and education programs for rural communities in China and India. Free the Children will help provide these communities with localized clean water sources and sanitation facilities.

The RBC Blue Water Project also aims to increase RBC's ability to provide financial services to innovative water technology companies and water-related services and encourage other organizations to get involved. At the local level, RBC Wealth Management in the British Isles (United Kingdom and Channel Islands) employs an environmental officer and a community relations manager to organize and raise awareness of environmental activities such as beach cleaning and helping to build a sustainable garden at the Wildfowl and Wetlands Trust's London Centre. This garden opened on September 15, 2010, demonstrates practical low-water gardening ideas, and encourages visitors to reduce their own environmental footprints.

Building Community Relations on a Local Level

Building links with the community on a local level binds employees together and illustrates firsthand how an organization lives the values it proscribes. One of RBC's main business divisions, RBC Wealth Management, employs more than 1,200 staff in the Channel Islands alone. As one of the largest local employers in a small community, RBC's CSR and sustainability programs have a very visible public impact on its reputation.

In the Channel Islands, the company supports local charities such as the Lions Club of Jersey and the Guernsey Round Table. In Jersey, RBC sponsors the Swimarathon in aid of the Lions Club, and this annual event is the largest local fundraiser on the island. Opened and supported by the lieutenant governor of Jersey, the Swimarathon attracts more than 1,000 swimmers a year and raises more than £120,000 annually. The Guernsey Harbour Carnival raises more than £10,000 for local causes. RBC volunteers support each event through administration and publicity while entering teams to take part.

On a purely practical level, RBC is committed to introducing sustainable environmental practices in its workplaces. In the British Isles region alone, the local facilities management team has implemented sustainable practices in purchasing, waste disposal, recycling, energy efficiency, and water management.

The business has achieved the Eco-Active for Business accreditation in Jersey, the Keep Guernsey Green Award, and the London Clean City Award.

The communications plan displayed in Exhibit 7.1 sets out how RBC's Wealth Management division uses effective communications to help key stakeholders both internally and externally understand the business's commitment to the environment.

Exhibit 7.1 RBC Wealth Management, British Isles and the Environment Communications Plan 2009

Project Vision

- RBC Wealth Management, British Isles to be recognised as environmentally responsible and committed to reducing our environmental impact in the locations in which we operate.

Project Objectives

- To reduce our operational environmental footprint in the British Isles.
- To build our corporate reputation locally as a socially responsible company.
- To encourage our employees to be environmentally responsible in the workplace and in their community.

Key Drivers

- RBC declaration of our company Environmental Blueprint Policy.
- Increase in external pressure for companies to demonstrate their environmental commitments, including the launch of EcoActive Business in Jersey.
- British Isles Leadership Team's commitment to reduce our environmental impact.
- Opportunity to improve our reputation internally as part of our objective to become recognised as employer of choice.

Key Sponsor

- Ron Nutter, Chief Operating Officer, British Isles

Key Audiences

Primary

- All RBC Wealth Management employees in the British Isles
- Local residents in our British Isles locations incl. prospective employees
- Local media in our British Isles locations

Exhibit 7.1 (*Continued*)

Secondary

- Local government in our British Isles locations
- Local regulators
- RBC corporate office departments, i.e., Corporate Responsibility and Corporate Communications

Communications Vision

- Become recognised internally and externally as an environmentally responsible organisation

Communication Objectives

- Raise awareness amongst the key audiences of RBC's global and local environmental commitments and initiatives.
- Achieve a minimum of ten pieces of external press coverage across the British Isles that profile our environmental efforts.
- Engage a minimum of 10% of RBC Wealth Management British Isles employees in local environmental community projects.
- Influence employee behaviour in the workplace to help achieve our environmental management targets.

Communications Strategy

- Leverage environmental initiatives and success stories in RBC Wealth Management, British Isles to communicate our key messages internally and externally.

Key Messages

- RBC is committed to being environmentally responsible and reducing our environmental impact in the locations where we operate.
- We have a long history of global leadership in this area. Our first global environmental policy was developed in 1991.
- RBC is committed to a path of environmental sustainability. This means reducing our environmental footprint, promoting environmentally responsible business activities and offering environmentally responsible products and services.
- When it comes to reducing our operational footprint, in the British Isles we are currently focused on recycling and reducing our resource use and the amount of waste we create.

(*Continued*)

Exhibit 7.1 (*Continued*)

• We believe that the preservation of the environment is fundamental to the sustainability of our communities, our clients and our company.
• One of our key global corporate responsibility goals is to contribute to a future of sustainable water resources worldwide.

Communications Tactics

Internal

Communications Tactic	Objective	Channel	Who	Timing
Announce our receipt of the City of London Clean City Award	Celebrate success and build a sense of employee pride	1. E-mail from Head of Office to London employees 2. Staff Magazine		December December issue
Profile our key achievements	Provide proof points to demonstrate our commitment to the environment	1. Intranet Environment page 2. Quarterly Senior Management meeting 3. Staff Magazine		December May October issue
Launch and profile volunteering activities across all locations	Engage and recognise our employees to be active citizens in the local community	1. E-mail from COO or head of office location 2. Intranet Environment page 3. Staff Magazine and Quarterlies		Throughout 2009
Launch full office recycling	Raise awareness of our operational improvements and encourage employee participation	1. E-mail from head of facilities in each location 2. Staff Magazine		March 2009 March issue 2009
Inform employees of our sponsorship of the Durrell Business Breakfast	Demonstrate our commitment and build a sense of employee pride	Staff Magazine		July issue

Exhibit 7.1 (*Continued*)

Communications Tactic	Objective	Channel	Who	Timing
Employee survey	Measure employees' awareness and opinions on our environmental activities	Data Collection—online survey Reporting: 1. Staff magazine 2. Quarterly Senior Management meeting 3. Intranet Environment page 4. Quarterly all staff meetings		August 1. October issue 2. Q3 meeting 3. September 4. Q3 meting
Profile our key achievements	Provide proof points to demonstrate our commitment to the environment	4. Intranet Environment page 5. Quarterly Senior Management meeting 6. Staff Magazine		December May October issue
Launch Green Tips scheme	Engage our employees in environmental activities both at home and in the workplace	Intranet Environment page		Q3
Announce EAB Level 3 accreditation	Demonstrate our leadership and on-going commitment to improving our operations.	1. BetOur memo from RN 2. Quarterly Senior Management meeting 3. Staff Magazine 4. Intranet Environment page		Q3 Q3 October issue Q3
Profile the Blue Water Project Grant scheme	Raise awareness of this global commitment from RBC	Separate working group leading on this initiative		tbc

FUTURE PROOF POINTS TO BE COMMUNICATED ONCE CONFIRMED

N.B. All internal activities to be incorporated in the monthly Core Team Brief schedule

(Continued)

Exhibit 7.1 (*Continued*)

External

Communications Tactic	Objective	Channel	Who	Timing
Announce our receipt of the City of London Clean City Award	Demonstrate our environmental commitment	Press release		January
Enter RBC for IABC Gold Quill Award for Communication Excellence	Celebrate our 2008 achievements and raise awareness of our environmental commitments	Award entry		January
Profile employee volunteering activities across all British Isles locations	Demonstrate our environmental commitment and our efforts to encourage employees to be active in the community	Photo media story		Through-out 2009
Profile our launch of full office recycling in Jersey	Demonstrate our commitment to be environmentally responsible	Press release + photo		April
Announce launch of Jersey Business Forum	Demonstrate our leadership and stewardship in being a good corporate citizen	Joint press release (tbc)		tbc
Announce our sponsorship of the Durrell Business Breakfast TBC	Demonstrate our commitment to be environmentally responsible	Joint press release/media invite Post event press release		June

Exhibit 7.1 (*Continued*)

Communications Tactic	Objective	Channel	Who	Timing
Announce EcoActive for Business Level 3 accreditation	Demonstrate our leadership and on-going commitment to improving our operations	1. Media invite 2. EcoActive for Business website and editorial profiles		Q3 Q3
Profile the Blue Water Project Grant scheme	Raise awareness of this global commitment from RBC	Tbc Separate working group leading on this initiative		tbc

FUTURE PROOF POINTS TO BE CONSIDERED ONCE CONFIRMED

Measurement

- Anecdotal evidence from staff and management
- Unsolicited positive feedback
- Benchmarking online survey to establish core levels of staff environmental management awareness
- Positive coverage in target media
- Raised awareness of environmental management progress in the British Isles and its business benefits among senior management

The environmental communications campaign has been running for two years as of November 2010. By the end of 2009, 34 percent of employees in RBC Wealth Management's British Isles region had taken part in community or environmental initiatives. Overall employee engagement scores in this region, according to RBC's biennial employee opinion survey, had risen by more than 12 percent—the biggest rise out of any region within the entire RBC Group. More than 91 percent of all RBC employees said that it was very important to them to work for a company with a strong record of corporate social responsibility.

Sustainability and Reputation

Financial services companies must carefully balance environmental concerns and economic opportunity by providing credit responsibly to all sectors. In Canada, RBC has been targeted by the Rainforest Action Network (RAN) among others for providing financial services to companies involved in oil extraction from Alberta's oil sands. RAN is a U.S.-based NGO that uses campaigning activities—usually targeted at brand sensitive, consumer-facing organizations—to make changes to practices that indirectly affect the environment.

The bank has conducted extensive stakeholder engagement with the Alberta government, NGOs, academics, Aboriginal leaders, industry associations, and corporate clients regarding the environmental and social impacts of the oil sands (Odendahl, 2010a, 2010b). Energy is a precious and increasingly scarce resource; both shareholders and employees expect banks to behave ethically with respect to the environment. There are expectations among some stakeholders that banks should not lend to polluting industries, such as the oil sands and nuclear power, and that the banks should track the emissions of their clients.

NGOs are holding banks responsible for the impacts of their clients with the aim of making access to capital a barrier to development. Among the demands made by RAN are that RBC provide evidence of consent from First Nations people (Canadian Aboriginal peoples); that RBC phases out financing to projects that adversely impact the environment, and develop an action plan to reduce the emissions of climate change pollution related to lending activities.

RAN targeted RBC over 18 months by picketing retail branches, organizing protest demonstrations, and orchestrating a letter-writing campaign aimed at the wife of the bank's chief executive officer. In response, RBC took a four-part approach to dealing with both the NGO and the issues it raised. The approach focused on engagement, providing information, acting (where necessary), and communicating.

RBC met and communicated with RAN on a periodic basis. It also engaged other key stakeholders, such as oil sector clients, governments, employees, moderate NGOs, Aboriginal groups, and other targeted banks, in oil sands discussions. The bank hosted an Oil Sands Learning Day for other banks and stakeholders and followed regulatory developments, consulted on, and researched the issues highlighted by RAN and other groups.

As a result of these investigations, RBC updated its corporate lending environmental risk management guidelines and researched the impact of oil sands extraction on First Nation groups. From a communication perspective, the bank has developed key messages for the media, kept employees and executives informed, and engaged with government on public policy around climate change, water, and energy. By confronting the issues raised head-on and engaging with multiple stakeholders, including activist NGOs, the bank has not only succeeded in managing its own reputation; it has also learned where it could feasibly do more on a controversial topic and where it could or should not.

Conclusion

For communication on CSR and sustainability issues to be effective, communication needs to be derived from corporate strategy and values. While overall policy and direction need to be set from the top, local implementation is essential in managing both employee engagement and stakeholder expectations.

Any organization looking to implement a full CSR and sustainability policy should take on a principle of operating with integrity, identifying its priorities, and actively engaging with both employees and stakeholders. Communicating CSR—both globally and locally—will require planning and patience.

References

Baker, M. (2010). *Definitions of CSR*. Retrieved August 9, 2010, from www.mallenbaker.net/csr/definition.php.

Bevan, S., & Wilmott, M. (2002). *The ethical employee*. London: Work Future Foundation/Future Foundation.

CSR Award. (2010). *Definition of CSR*. Retrieved August 9, 2010, from www.csraward.com.

Odendahl, S. (2010a). *RBC and the environment: Priorities and programs*. Presentation to RBC Wealth Management Business Communicators, Toronto.

Odendahl, S. (2010b). *RBC and the oil sands*, Presentation to RBC Wealth Management Business Communicators, Toronto.

Patterson, L. (2009a). *RBC community blueprint*. Toronto: Royal Canadian Bank.

Patterson, L. (2009b). *RBC corporate responsibility report and public accountability statement*. Toronto: Royal Canadian Bank.

Patterson, L. (2009c). *RBC environmental blueprint*. Toronto: Royal Canadian Bank.

Royal Bank of Canada. (1944). The importance of forests. *RBC Letter*, *25*(3). www.rbc.com/responsibility/letter/pdf/march1944.pdf.

Royal Bank of Canada. (1950). Life depends on water. *RBC Letter*, *31*(3). www.rbc.com/responsibility/letter/pdf/march1944.pdf.

World Commission on Environment and Development. (1987). *From one earth to one world: An overview*. Oxford, UK: Oxford University Press.

PART TWO

MANAGING
COMMUNICATION

CHAPTER EIGHT

STRATEGIC APPROACHES TO MANAGING THE COMMUNICATIONS FUNCTION

Diane M. Gayeski

Communication activity in organizations happens all the time—it is a natural and necessary means through which individuals accomplish tasks, coordinate activities with others, and forge relationships. For the most part, people as individuals speak for themselves. But who speaks for the company, both to internal and external audiences? The formal aspects of communication—establishing and managing the voice of the company—are the responsibility of professional communicators. These functions include:

- External communication, such as investor relations, media relations, public relations (PR), government and community affairs, philanthropy, corporate websites and blogs, and managing the corporate reputation
- Internal communication, such as employee newsletters, business update meetings, employee benefits and policy materials, Intranets, collaboration systems, and electronic news displays
- Marketing communications, such as advertising and sales materials, trade shows, customer help and feedback functions, mobile promotional apps, and e-commerce tools

Each of these is a complex specialty, and their issues and activities are covered in detail in subsequent chapters. The purpose of this chapter is to explore some strategic decisions that affect how and where this work gets done:

- Where do professional communications functions reside organizationally?
- How do communicators align their messages with the organization's strategy and with each other?
- Do employees or external contractors perform the work?
- How do projects and staff get funded?
- How do communications managers demonstrate value?

Where Does Communications Reside on the Organizational Chart?

Communications professionals can fill many different roles in organizations, and those jobs can reside in a variety of departments. Under the umbrella of business communicators, we find meeting planners, speechwriters, financial communicators, Web and graphic designers, social media strategists, advertising and PR managers, and communication analysts. There is no one best way to construct the reporting structures, but the strategic decisions about how to design jobs and where to place them certainly do affect the daily work life of the communicators in these positions. Typically, roles directed toward employee communication are placed within human resources (HR), while external communication may reside in a corporate communications or marketing department. Larger and more complex companies usually employ many communications professionals who fill fairly specialized roles, while small organizations may have just one person who is a jack of all trades.

In really small organizations, there is generally no one person whose total responsibility relates to communications. Employee communications, such as occasional recruiting, explaining company rules and benefits, and organizing some meetings probably falls to the person in charge of human resources. Promotional communications, such as maintaining the website, developing brochures, and developing proposals and presentations gets done by marketing. In organizations of fewer than twenty employees, the chief executive officer (CEO) takes charge of telling the company story to important customers, investors or donors, and employees. By the time an organization has more than fifty employees, it is twice as likely to have someone other than the CEO or owner designated as the primary communicator (Evatt, Ruiz, & Triplett, 2005).

While large organizations will have many professionals involved in communications, maintaining the active involvement and support of the CEO is still essential. For example, even though FedEx has grown to a company with more than 200,000 worldwide employees, founder Fred Smith remains actively engaged in FedEx's communications activities and reviews communications strategy for every major decision. The company has a communications platform called "One Vision, One Voice" that guides and integrates its internal and external messages and reputation (Argenti, 2006). Many studies of excellence in communications agree that alignment with, access to, and active involvement of the CEO and the leadership team is an essential factor in ensuring ongoing support and strategic results.

Once an organization gets larger, there may be one person designated to produce communications, usually having responsibility for both external and employee communication. So, to whom should this person report? Although this may seem like a small decision, it affects the way that communications projects get prioritized and measured. Typically, growing organizations feel the most pressing need is in communicating to potential customers or donors, so their first full-time communications professional typically resides within marketing or fundraising. However, in organizations in which an external advertising and PR agency does most of the promotional work, the first full-time communicator may be in charge of employee communications.

Perhaps the ideal place for the new communicator to reside is in a staff position reporting directly to the CEO. In this capacity, the communicator provides counsel to the executive team, looking at long-term company strategies and selecting communications interventions that relate to this level of objectives. But why does it matter where the position resides?

• The communicator's supervisor will bring his or her own lens into making decisions about funding and evaluating the work of the communicator. Therefore, if a communicator reporting to a vice president of marketing wants to install plasma screens to provide news updates to employees, that idea may not carry as much weight as a new opportunity to exhibit at a trade show. A vice president of human resources may not really know how to evaluate a promotional campaign.

• The career paths of communicators depend somewhat on where that function resides. If a person hired as a communications specialist within the human resources (HR) department wants to advance in the company, the logical choice would be to learn more about HR and work up the ladder within that function. If the communications function resides within marketing, a different set of skills will be needed to advance within that professional field.

• In order for the communicator to play a strategic role in improving business performance, he or she must have a seat at the table and have the inside track on organizational strategy and goals. If communicators get buried under a bureaucratic department and do not have regular contact with executives, then they become relegated to a role as order takers, simply designing publications or running meetings without really having the opportunity to analyze and select the most powerful interventions. This very much plays into the questions of whether communicators are business strategists or craftspeople and how they are viewed, valued, and supported by their executives.

In large organizations, professional communicators are likely to be placed within many different departments. For example, the company may have a chief spokesperson and speechwriter who may report directly to the CEO. Professionals in investor relations may work within the finance department. An entirely separate department of corporate communications may provide media relations, community relations, and philanthropy support. Employee communications and training for supervisory communications usually resides within human resources. Advertising and special events sponsorship typically is placed within marketing, but it is also very common for most advertising and PR work to be outsourced to an agency. Departments, divisions, or separate field offices all may have their own communications professionals. Even more complex situations occur in highly matrixed organizations in which managers may be part of several teams: geographical, product line, customer base, or functions; these managers may hire their own communicators, either as employees or as contractors (Jaccaud & Quirke, 2006).

Figure 8.1 presents a fairly typical organizational chart for a complex not-for-profit organization such as a health care system. Communicators reside in several places within the hierarchy, including both in internal positions and as external contractors and agencies.

The landscape of communications departments changes rapidly, and such change should be welcomed. An international benchmarking study found that within the United States, communications departments that have not changed have dipped in importance in their organizations. In this survey, a majority of participants (around 80 percent) said they felt that the perception of the importance of communication had increased during the past year. The only group that dropped significantly below average response was those working in departments that had not restructured in the previous twelve months (Barnfield, 2002).

For example, when Mass Mutual brought in a new CEO and leadership team, the communications department was charged with assessing the department's strengths and opportunities in order to become a strategic partner. They restructured the communications function to flatten the organization, eliminate more than US$1 million, and position themselves to be more responsive to business leaders. As a result, they quickly and dramatically improved results as measured both by client satisfaction and by reviews of external research sources in their website, their brand awareness and strength, and their positive PR coverage (Rhoades & Robinson, 2008).

FIGURE 8.1 TYPICAL PLACEMENT OF COMMUNICATIONS FUNCTIONS IN A COMPLEX, NONPROFIT ORGANIZATION

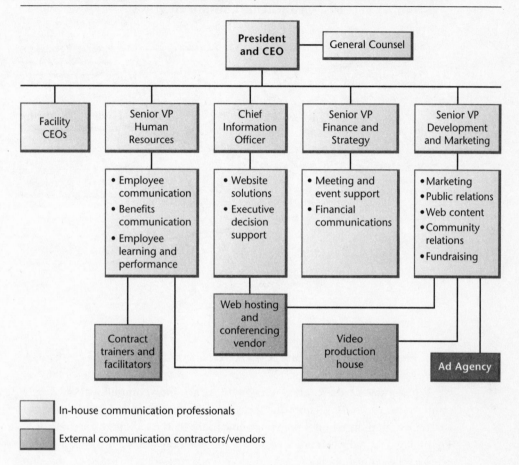

In-house communication professionals

External communication contractors/vendors

Bridging the Islands of Communication

One of the challenges facing communicators when they are dispersed across the organizational chart is coordinating the flow, load, tone, and content of messages. Employee communications, investor relations, public relations, and supervisory and executive communications are often designed and managed in separate functional silos. Professionals in these areas often have little

FIGURE 8.2 ISLANDS OF COMMUNICATION

Dis-integrated Communication

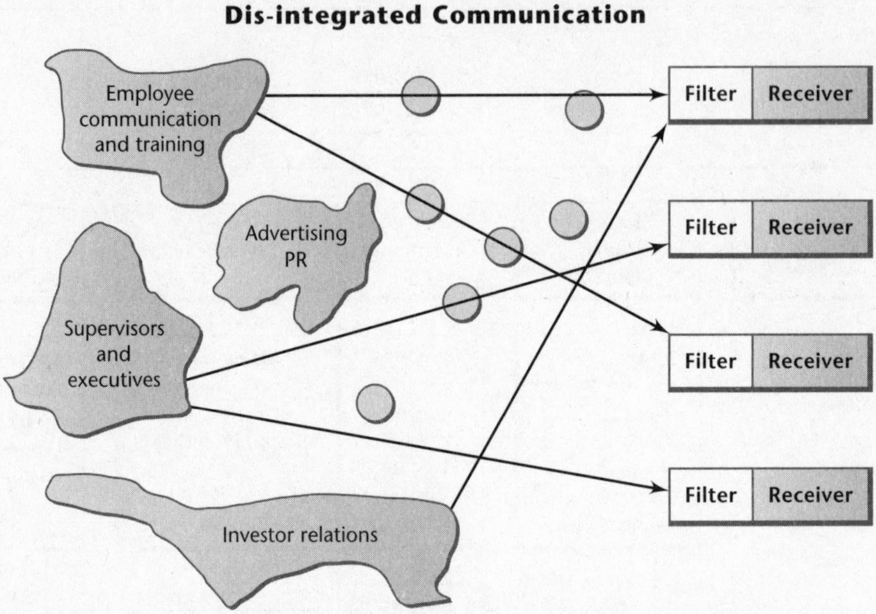

incentive—and may have many barriers to collaborating. This creates islands of communication (see Figure 8.2).

When each of these areas creates messages and communication events, communicators tend to ignore the fact that their materials and meetings represent only a small fraction of the communications load for their target audiences. They may also inadvertently contradict the content and/or the tone of other items in the communications stream. What happens then? Audiences become overloaded and form their own filters to opt out and tune out in two ways:

1. The sheer volume of information and demands on their time become overwhelming, and audiences simply opt out. They either physically delete messages or they skip meetings.
2. The inconsistency of messages and tone causes cognitive dissonance. Employees and customers do not know what to believe and just tune out. People are tired of hearing about some major initiative in the newsletter, being taught something a bit different in a required training class, and then having their supervisors tell them to ignore the whole thing because it was just a flavor of the month.

These situations cause poor performance because important messages are completely ignored—or even worse—they cause cynicism, mistrust, misdirected efforts, and inconsistent brand messages. Here are some examples of these situations. For a large Canadian bank, my consulting firm did a study to document the communications load of key roles, such as branch manager and customer service representative. We found that if they read, listened to, and attended all the materials and meetings that were expected of them, they would have no time in the week left to do their jobs! At a not-for-profit health care organization, human resources sent employees a notice that they would be receiving a less generous benefits package in the forthcoming year, and that employees would now be responsible for paying a larger percentage of their insurance premiums. In employee mailboxes that same day was a letter from the CEO asking employees to contribute to their annual fundraising effort. Not only were both the benefits and fundraising messages unsuccessful and annoying, but the CEO came across as out of touch and uncaring—a trait that branded him and cut short his tenure (Gayeski, 2007).

Studies have shown that it is essential to create an integrated approach to corporate communications. The benefits of such integration include preserving corporate brand, enhancing reputation, weathering crises, and maximizing organizational potential (Argenti, 2006). Strategies for bridging the islands of communication include:

- Creating cross-functional project teams across HR, marketing, PR, employee communications, and training for major organizational initiatives such as quality programs, the introduction of new products or services, or company reorganizations.
- Consolidating communications functions into fewer departments. In fact, in many organizations, employee communications, PR, advertising, investor relations, executive communications, and community relations are all part of one department.

For example, Hewlett-Packard (HP) centralized its global internal communications function. Internal communications reports to the company's senior vice president for corporate marketing and the executive vice president for HR. This dual reporting structure enables internal communications to help coordinate a myriad of internal messages within a framework consistent with HP's external messaging and branding. The Program Management Office (PMO) is a standing internal communications committee designed to unify messaging across regions, businesses, and functions. The PMO is a permanent version of the communications council, a central committee developing overarching guidelines around such issues as measurement and editorial message and building standard tools and templates to be used throughout internal communications worldwide (Shaw & Andrews, 2005).

Orange, a global telecommunications company that was acquired by France Telecom, has a forum of internal communicators across its various national markets. While responsibility and support for communications resides at the local level, this team has worked together to develop common standards and a "tool kit" and regularly meets to share best practices (Ridgeon, 2007).

Outsourcing

In large organizations, the complexity of communication tasks means that more communicators with increasingly specific roles and areas of expertise are hired. In these situations, a key strategic decision is whether to hire these communicators as employees or as external contractors. Over the past thirty years, the tides of outsourcing have shifted many times. In the 1980s, many organizations embraced new technologies such as videotape and videoconferencing for communicating with their employees and external audiences; in the 1990s, these technologies expanded to include desktop publishing, multimedia, and Internet/intranet sites. The first decade of the twenty-first century saw enormous growth in social and mobile media. When corporate coffers were full, staffing levels in communications grew, along with large investments in communications technologies. However, when economic times grew harder and when the new technologies were changing rapidly, the trend has been to outsource these functions.

Today, most organizations use a mix of internal and external communications professionals. Inside communicators generally handle strategy and project management; these people are close to the company, its executives, and its culture and know how to set guidelines and goals. They are easily accessible and fill key roles as spokespersons, planners, and communication coaches. Conversely, it is difficult for any one communicator to be fluent in all the skills, crafts, and technologies of communication. That is where freelancers and contract consultants and producers come in. If an organization does not need full-time help in any one aspect of communication, such as speechwriting, it is best to hire it out. Today, most video production and much Web programming is outsourced, because it is difficult for organizations to keep up with the changes in technologies and to house sophisticated studios and editing space. Likewise, most organizations use a number of hosted applications, such as blogging sites, online surveys and polling, and public sites like YouTube and Facebook.

The advantages of in-house resources are that they can be counted on to be more accessible and that they become familiar with the organization's products and politics. Therefore, they can quickly write materials and react to changing organizational needs. When dealing with sensitive material, executives are likely to prefer to work with employees rather than with outside contractors who may, in fact, also be working for the competition.

On the other hand, outsiders have the advantage of specializing in particular topics or skills such as Web programming, executive speechwriting, crisis management, photography, or evaluation methodologies. Most organizations employ one or more advertising and public relations agencies to develop and produce large-scale campaigns. External consultants as compared to employees can also provide a more unbiased assessment in some situations and are more protected from corporate politics when they need to deliver unpopular messages or recommendations. They also bring knowledge of trends and approaches from other engagements and clients. Finally, when large-scale corporate initiatives happen, such as a big change in benefits plans, a rebranding effort, or a merger, more hands are simply needed to do the work, so it is likely that major parts of those projects will be turned over to an external communications vendor. Thus, it makes sense for most organizations to employ full-time communications strategists and project managers who can then supervise and coordinate a number of ongoing contractors for ad hoc projects.

How Communications Gets Funded

Communications professionals and projects get funded in a variety of ways, and along with the organizational structure, it is one of the most significant strategies that affects the role and function of communicators. The most traditional form of funding and structure is the service center model. In this strategy, there is one central communications department that is funded by an overall tax on each corporate unit. The communications department receives an annual budget and performs projects for internal clients on a first-come, first-served basis. At the other end of the continuum of funding is the profit center model, in which the communications department charges for its projects and even takes on clients outside the organization to make a profit. A number of communications departments with unique service offerings or technologies take this route, and by bringing in a profit, they are able to protect their own jobs in times of corporate downsizing and they are able to expand their staff beyond what might be needed only for internal clients. For example, several large in-house video departments were about to be placed on the corporate chopping block when their parent companies experienced financial troubles; by turning themselves into profit centers (even separately incorporating as joint ventures between the organization and the employees of the video department), they were able to retain their jobs and facilities.

There are a number of funding and structure models that lie between the two extremes of service centers and profit centers. Many communications departments operate as cost centers whereby they charge their internal clients for services rendered. In full charge-back operations, the department charges enough to cover the cost of personnel, overhead, and out-of-pocket project expenses. For example, if the manager of quality decides to roll out a new Lean Six Sigma initiative that includes employee meetings, executive presentations, a video, and periodic newsletter articles, the employee communications department estimates what personnel (either in-house or freelance or both) will be needed and for how many hours and also comes up with a budget for actual expenses such as printing, meeting refreshments, and so on. The client is then charged either a fixed fee or is billed for actual expenses. A less aggressive approach is for communications departments to charge clients only for out-of-pocket expenses, while personnel and overhead (such as office space, equipment, and supplies) are covered in an annual budget funded by the organization.

What are the advantages and disadvantages of these approaches? In the traditional service center, clients do not have any cost barrier preventing them from working with their in-house communications professionals. The communications work emanates from a central department staffed by full-time employees. However, this ease is tempered by several problems. One is that executives often feel that communicators in such structures can become complacent because they have a captive client base. Also, it is difficult for an organization to predict how much money to budget for communications for an entire year—the budget could run out when one eager client proposes a huge project, leaving no resources for other worthy causes.

While profit centers seem like a great deal to executives, and while entrepreneurial communicators may like the prospect of selling their services to outside clients, such relationships are tricky to navigate. In-house clients may feel that they are being squeezed out by external clients, and they may dislike having to pay a market rate for communications services. In such situations, internal clients will also have the option of using external services, so a profit center may lose its best and closest customers. There are also issues of confidentiality when external customers suddenly start showing up in communications offices and media facilities.

While the previously described service, cost, and profit centers describe centralized models in which the communications department resides within the corporate headquarters, there are also variations in terms of decentralization. In organizations with multiple sites, communicators may report to a vice president or director whose office is at headquarters, but they may work at offices in other locations. For example, in a manufacturing company with several sites across the country or the globe, employee communicators will probably live and work in those locations in order to be closer to their customers. Some even have dual reporting relationships—to both employee communications at headquarters and to the local business division or plant manager.

In some organizations, individual departments or locations fund their own communications support. For example, instead of the staffing money coming from corporate headquarters to support an employee communications specialist at an individual manufacturing site, the site itself may fund and supervise that position. Shared services is a rapidly emerging model; in this approach, two or more departments or locations get together and jointly fund communications positions. For example, there are two hospitals in a national health care group that are located near each other. They may get together and fund their own media relations department to deal with the local market.

How Communications Functions Demonstrate Value

While few executives need to be convinced of the value of a company's reputation and its relationship with internal and external stakeholders, when competing for resources, the communications function often faces challenges. It is difficult to prove any direct relationship between most communications interventions and the bottom line because so many variables affect human performance and the impact of many projects takes years to show up. For example, an employee suggestion system may indeed garner some immediate ideas that reduce costs or increase profits. But beyond this, the effects of asking for employee input may raise morale and engagement, thereby making the organization a more attractive place to work. This can lower turnover and attract better candidates. However, those latter factors would be almost impossible to prove in any statistical way since so many other factors go into decisions about where to work and how much commitment to put into one's job.

Typically, communications projects are measured by either satisfaction surveys or some type of usage measure. For example, employee communication programs are usually assessed by communications audits that solicit employees' reactions to the overall climate and tools used (such as newsletters, meetings, and so on). Their opinions are gained through surveys, focus groups, and individual interviews. Usage measures include counting the number of hits to various intranet pages, gauging attendance at meetings, or counting suggestions or responses to messages. While these measures certainly do give an overall indication of opinion, they do not get to the kind of bottom line measurements that can provide a good basis for calculating return on investment.

Communications projects cannot be measured unless they start out having specific, measurable goals that influence organizational performance. For example, an intranet site that provides regulations, links to travel bargains, and paperwork for completing travel requests might reduce the costs of processing travel reimbursements by reducing staff time and gaining lower-cost travel arrangements. A communications manager could track before-and-after statistics about how much staff time is used in processing travel expenses and the average cost per trip. An employee suggestion system can track how many suggestions were implemented and how they affected costs or profits. A campaign to conserve energy can track electricity and heat costs.

But how does a communications manager measure the benefits of an electronic news system that posts the company press releases, stock price, and profiles of new employees? How does a communicator know whether the intranet helps performance or whether it is a nuisance that takes people's valuable time away from their jobs? Does the annual open house and tour of the plant positively affect the relationship to the community, and even if it does, how does that benefit the corporation? What is the impact of executives who spend their valuable time blogging?

These issues of measurement are central to the challenges and successful management of organizational communication. Thankfully, there are ways to explain the value of a good communications system in terms that executives can understand. Two powerful concepts are intangible assets and tangible assets such as human capital (Figure 8.3). *Intangible assets* are organizational factors that are not on the books as money in the bank or physical objects such as buildings and inventory. Intangible assets include the brand and reputation, good community and employee relations, loyal customers, and a smart and committed workforce. Analysts know that these factors are what drive future profitability, which directly affects stock price. *Human capital* is the workforce's collective willingness and ability to perform. This is affected by motivation, knowledge of the business strategy, and training (Gayeski, 2005).

The Communicator as Performance Consultant

To be a strategic asset, communications needs to be structured and run as a function that directly affects organizational performance. This means that, instead of taking on projects because an executive thinks it is a good idea or

FIGURE 8.3 TANGIBLE AND INTANGIBLE ASSETS

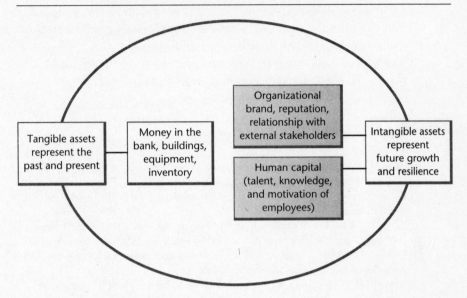

because other organizations are doing similar things, the communications manager needs to function as a performance consultant. To do this, the manager needs to:

- Maintain close relationships with management to stay on top of strategic goals and performance gaps
- Identify as precisely as possible the cost of the current performance gaps or the potential gains of successfully implementing new strategies
- Analyze the possible causes of substandard performance and the drivers of the desired goals
- Understand what motivates each audience (customers, investors, employees, regulators) and design messages tailored to the needs and styles of each
- Select communications interventions based on the probable impact on significant goals and problems
- Develop measurable and observable objectives for communications campaigns and projects
- Estimate the return on investment for each communications project
- Evaluate each project based on the stated measurable goals
- Continually benchmark best practices in organizational communication as well as major research studies that link communication to performance

The communications function, or more precisely, functions, are rapidly becoming managed as business drivers rather than as corporate frills. By carefully selecting the right organizational design, staffing roles, relationships with constituencies, funding models, and evaluation strategies, professional communicators have unprecedented opportunities to move up the ranks of their companies and become major players in organizational strategy.

References

Argenti, P. (2006). *Identity and competitiveness*. Paper presented at the Reputation Institute Tenth Conference on Reputation, Image, New York City.

Barnfield, E. (2002). *Key benchmark data for communicators—2002/3*. London: Melcrum Publishing.

Evatt, D., Ruiz, C., & Triplett, J. (2005). *Thinking big, staying small*. San Francisco: International Association of Business Communicators Research Foundation.

Gayeski, D. (2005). *Managing organizational learning and communication as business assets*. Upper Saddle River, NJ: Pearson-Prentice-Hall.

Gayeski, D. (2007). *Managing the communication function: A blueprint for organizational success*. San Francisco: International Association of Business Communicators.

Jaccaud, S., & Quirke, B. (2006, August/September). Structuring global communication to improve efficiency. *Strategic Communication Management, 10*(5), 18–21.

Rhoades, G., & Robinson, T. (2008). Creating a comms powerhouse at Mass Mutual. *Strategic Communication Management, 12*(5), 20–23.

Ridgeon, E. (2007, April/May). Creating a center of communication expertise at Orange. *Strategic Communication Management, 3*(11), 20–23.

Shaw, K., & Andrews, R. (2005). Introducing centralization in HP's global IC function. *Strategic Communication Management, 9*(1), 26–29.

CHAPTER NINE

STRATEGIC PLANNING

Timeless Wisdom Still Shapes Successful Communication Programs

Lester R. Potter

This chapter was written during a time of worldwide economic turmoil characterized by rapid change. When things are changing rapidly, can any business leader plan effectively given so much uncertainty? The answer is yes. In fact, the economic turmoil of 2008–2010 has made strategic planning more vital than ever. Strategic planning is even more important in changing times because the strategic plan provides the baseline from which to monitor and measure change (Birchfield, 2010). Strategic planning remains popular for the same reason that classical music does. Classical music conforms to certain established standards of form, complexity, and musical literacy. Strategic planning, which also conforms to certain established standards of form, content, and literacy, truly is timeless wisdom that continues to shape successful business.

This chapter reviews the concept of strategic planning as a business directive and the professional communicator's role in planning and implementing communication activities to support the mission, vision, and business objectives of an organization or business entity.

Strategic Planning

If there is any one concept that drives the planning process in today's turbulent marketplace, it is the need for *strategic agility*, the capacity to identify and capture opportunities more quickly than your rivals do (Fathi & Wilson, 2009; Sull, 2010). Writing in the *McKinsey Quarterly*, Donald Sull argues that in turbulent markets, organizational agility is invaluable. A recent McKinsey survey found that executives ranked organizational agility both as critical to business success and as growing in importance over time. The benefits of enhanced agility, the survey respondents said, include higher revenues, more satisfied customers and employees, improved operational efficiency, and faster time to market (Sull, 2010, p. 48). Along with strategic agility, a turbulent business environment calls for shorter time horizons of plans, with three to five years being the most realistic time frame (Fathi & Wilson, 2009). Highly regarded chief executive officer (CEO) Jack Welch said, "Business strategy is less a function of grandiose predictions than it is a result of being able to respond rapidly to real changes as they occur. That is why strategy has to be dynamic and anticipatory" (Welch, 2001, p. 390).

My personal journey to become a strategic planner and communicator began in the mid-1970s. One of the first strategic thinkers I studied was William E. Rothschild of General Electric and Harvard Business School. Rothschild summarized strategic planning this way: "Because of the scarcity of money and resources, most companies must become more selective and limit their investment to those companies which can provide an attractive payoff and in which they are strong. Furthermore, they must count on some business to finance the growth of others. Thus, they need a resource allocation system that will enable them to select their best prospects. This is the purpose of strategic planning" (Rothschild, 1979, p. 12). In more than thirty years of professional practice, I have facilitated strategic planning processes with for-profit organizations in many different industries, nonprofits large and small with a variety of missions, and a mix of government agencies. The common link is the value of strategic planning as a day-to-day guide on how to achieve organizational success. Business leaders, managers, or communicators who have no strategic plans as guides are at the mercy of what I call "crisis du jour."

Like many other business management practices, strategic planning has been transformed by technology. Yet like classical music, its essence remains the same. Beethoven's adagios may be even more beautiful when played using modern instruments. Strategic planning can also be enhanced by modern technology that adds tremendous speed and capability to the process. Business leaders rely on the strategic planning process to provide both the criteria for making day-to-day organizational decisions and a template against which all such decisions can be evaluated. Strategic planning answers three basic questions: First, where are we going? Second, what is the environment? And third, how do we get there? (Goodstein, Nolan, & Pfeiffer, 1993). "The strategic plan provides leadership. If done well, it gives a real vision that empowers everyone in the organization, and that is as relevant today as ever" (Birchfield, 2010, p. 56).

The Strategic Planning Process

Strategic planning usually consists of four phases: an internal review, an external review, a strategy summary, and contingency plans. The first phase begins with a systematic process to determine exactly what the organization wants to achieve. After much group facilitation, these broad descriptions are usually captured in vision or mission statements. Many organizations have both, with the vision statement at the top of the hierarchy governing the big picture of achievement. The mission is far more relevant and useful to business managers, especially communication managers. A good mission statement answers the following questions: What function does the organization perform? For whom does the organization perform this function? How does the organization go about filling this function? Why does the organization exist? (Goodstein et al., 1993). It takes a great deal of organizational analysis, often called *needs analysis* or *situational audit*, to write these short, simple statements. In strategic planning, you must analyze what businesses you are in, your customers, markets, and competition and then decide where you want to go as an organization.

The second phase consists of making assumptions about the environment through which the organization must navigate in order to achieve its mission. In this phase, an organization studies external forces, in a process often called *environmental scanning*, that it assumes will have an impact on its ability to achieve its mission over the life of the strategic plan. I usually interject self-imposed restraints into this phase of planning. These restraints relate to the organization's values and corporate culture. An organization's values come from its corporate culture, defined as "a pattern of beliefs and expectations deeply held in common by members of the organization" (Goodstein et al., 1993, p. 60). Values, in turn, give rise to situational norms ("The way we do things around here") that are manifested in observable behavior. All this is of enormous importance to the organizational communicator, especially behavior of publics.

The third phase usually consists of putting together all that the organization has learned from environmental scanning and an internal performance audit. This includes the ubiquitous SWOT (strengths, weaknesses, opportunities, and threats) analysis. SWOT analysis looks at the recent performance of an organization using some basic indexes, such as cash flow, growth, staffing, quality, technology, operations, service, profit, and return on investment, identified as critical to the strategic profile. The performance audit provides data for gap analysis, determining the degree to which the strategic business model is realistic and workable (Goodstein et al., 1993).

At this point, an organization is usually ready to formulate goals, objectives, strategies, and tactics. Goals describe future desired results toward which efforts are directed (Bedeian & Zammuto, 1991). They can be broad brush, such as "to maximize shareholder wealth." Goals should be achievable, but there have been those who urged business leaders to think big. Collins and Porras did just that in their book, *Built to Last: Successful Habits of Visionary Companies* (1995), when they urged organizations to have a long-term vision that is supposed to be so daring in its scope as to seem impossible (Reingold & Underwood, 2004). Goals that are achievable, even if considered stretch goals, work best today. For communicators, goals must be understood by members of the organization; therefore, the simpler and more achievable they are, the better. Strategic planning is not operational or annual planning because overall direction and goals do not fundamentally change in the short to medium term. A strategy that changes every year is not a strategy, but a reaction (Birchfield, 2010).

Objectives must be specifically written so that those charged with implementation can clearly see how the objective will help manifest a goal into reality. A simple acronym to remember when formulating objectives is SMART (Potter, 2008, p. 94):

S   Specific

M   Measurable

A   Attainable

R   Relevant

T   Time sensitive

Strategy is a curious little word with a big impact. Steiner (1979) observed that it originally was used by management to mean what you did to counter what a competitor did or intended to do. Sometimes the word *strategy* is used to cover every aspect of strategic planning, as with the balanced scorecard. Some speak of strategy as the answer to this question: What should the organization be doing? A strategy specifies general direction and priorities. The essence of strategy is choosing to perform activities differently from competitors so as to provide a unique value proposition (Kaplan & Norton, 2001).

Successful strategy is not a tool reserved for the for-profit sector. For-profits, nonprofits, and government agencies all have the same problem: it is not easy to determine strategy. Nonprofits and government agencies typically have considerable difficulty in clearly defining their strategies. Kaplan and Norton

(2001) have seen strategy documents extending to fifty or more pages. Most of the document, once the vision and mission are articulated, consists of lists of programs and initiatives, not the outcomes the organization is trying to achieve. These organizations must understand that, as the highly regarded Harvard Business School's Michael Porter said, strategy is not only what the organization intends to do but also what it decides not to do, a message that is particularly relevant for nonprofits and government departments (Kaplan & Norton, 2001).

Government and nonprofit organizations can be strategic and build competitive advantage in ways other than pure operational excellence. But it takes vision and leadership to move beyond improving existing processes to a strategy that highlights which processes and activities are the most important to implement (Kaplan & Norton, 2001).

However, vision cannot do it alone. The heavy lifting is done by tactics. Tactics are the step-by-step details that must happen to accomplish a strategy. Standing alone, they may be small things, but taken together, tactics have a big impact on success of the plan. I believe most strategic plans fail due to lack of effective tactical execution. Conversely, all too often, organizational communicators focus only on tactical execution of various media rather than on an overall strategic communication plan for their work. In such situations, training in strategic planning and subsequently developing a strategic approach to communication management is extraordinarily valuable.

The fourth phase of the typical strategic planning process consists of contingency planning. This phase accounts for how the organization will anticipate the unexpected and still achieve its plans. What will the organization do if things do not go as planned? Contingency planning involves the following (Goodstein et al., 1993):

- Identifying the most important internal and external threats to and opportunities for the organization, especially those involving other than the most likely scenarios
- Developing trigger points to initiate action steps for each contingency
- Agreeing on which action steps will be taken for each of these trigger points. (p. 32)

The timeless wisdom of strategic planning has helped many organizations achieve success. But each year there is some new innovation that touts itself as the newest, best way to manage. Countless new book titles about business appear every year. That is why I believe in the timeless wisdom of strategic planning, as management fads come and go. The strategic planning process makes you think and conduct research before you act, focus on the right things, and decide what you will and will not do within resource constraints. With this as a backdrop, I next discuss the communicator's role in strategic planning.

The Role of Strategic Planning in Communication Management

To survive and prosper, organizational communicators must contribute significantly and measurably to strategic management. They must think, act, and manage communication programs strategically, recording measurable results that contribute to the accomplishment of the organization's mission. This fact transcends state or province and international borders, for-profit, nonprofit, and government organization types. It is relevant to the specialist as well as the generalist practice of communication. It is true of internal and external communication. The only reason organizational communication programs exist is to build and maintain mutually beneficial relationships with key publics and to help build a positive image for the organization by recording measurable results that help the organization realize its mission. In the International Association of Business Communicators (IABC) Research Foundation's Excellence project, the research team found that excellent communication and public relations managers help to bring the values and goals of different functional managers together by working with them to build relationships with relevant publics and to bring the perspectives of those publics into strategic management (Grunig & Grunig, 2000, p. 307).

An organization's management relies on the strategic planning process to provide both the criteria for making day-to-day organizational decisions and a template against which all such decisions can be evaluated. The organization's mission, goals, objectives, strategies, and tactics are all developed in the strategic planning process. Enlightened senior leaders demand that communication programs contribute to the achievement of the organization's mission, goals, and objectives and facilitate the implementation of key strategies and tactics. That is what *managing communication strategically* means. It means that there is a causal relationship between the communication activities and the achievement of the organization's mission. It means that communication programs support successful completion of the organization's strategic activity in a measurable way. Anything less will not be tolerated. Communicators who do not practice communication strategically are often frozen out, replaced, or realigned under some other functional area that the organization values at a higher level than communications.

The Communication Plan

The heart of strategic communication management is the communication plan. It reconciles communication activity with the mission, goals, objectives, strategies, and tactics of the organization in a measurable way. For communicators, learning all they can about organizational strategic planning makes them better prepared to build and execute an effective, results-oriented communication plan, one that they can claim with all authority is strategic.

A communication plan is a written statement of what communication actions will be taken to support the accomplishment of specific organizational goals, the time frame for carrying out the plan, the budget, and the procedures for measuring the results of communication.

For decades, organizations have used strategic planning techniques to get where they want to go. Communication plans serve the same purpose: they guide the communicator to those right actions that will help the organization achieve its goals using communication as a strategic management tool. Strategic plans, marketing plans, and business plans are all similar. It follows, then, that to be considered strategic, communication plans must be structured in a similar way.

The typical strategic plan consists of four major sections, and each section may have as many as ten subsections. My model for an effective communication plan is similar, but the plan is structured somewhat differently:

1. *Title page.* This page identifies the name of the project, the contributors to the report, and the date it was submitted for implementation.

2. *Executive summary.* Write this last. It is a summary of the plan that any busy decision maker can easily and quickly read to get the main points of your plan.

3. *The communication process or background.* This is an explanation of what strategic communication is, written for decision makers who may not understand this researched-based and business-oriented way of managing communication. This section helps to educate decision makers on the function of strategic communication planning and management. It is helpful to include information on the major events that have led to the need for the plan.

4. *Situation analysis.* This is the heart of my process of strategic communication planning. This section determines the real issues that an organization must address. Formative research, consisting of primary and/or secondary research, is instrumental to this section, which seeks to separate cause from effect and disease from symptom. You can treat effects or symptoms, but until you do something about the cause, the effects will reappear. I find it helpful to list issues from research, followed by a list of the facts about each one in bullet points under

it. These facts form the basis of the actions to take to counter them or capitalize on them later. This section should treat the organization's general situation plus any organizational effectiveness issues that may help or hinder accomplishing the goals of your plan. End this section with a description of all your key strategic publics. Including a SWOT analysis is a good way to summarize the situation analysis.

5. *Strategic summary with recommendations.* This section explains what you intend to do about the problems and/or opportunities you discovered in doing research for your situation analysis. This is your overall strategy. This section should include, in this order, goals, objectives to accomplish each goal, and tactics to accomplish each objective. Bullet point format works best. Remember: Write SMART objectives as previously described.

6. *Implementation.* Now it is time to put it all together. This section should contain a timeline or schedule of your tactics. I find it best to use a Gantt chart for this purpose. To me, the plan should be an annual plan, showing the twelve months of the year and the activities plotted accordingly under each week and month of the year.

7. *Budget.* Just as in management's strategic planning, resource allocation is all-important to the communicator. Remember, strategic plans help you manage resource allocation. Budgets are always finite, and to be a successful communicator, you must accomplish your goals and objectives and stay within budget guidelines. Make sure your budget includes an accurate cost for all of your tactical items.

8. *Monitoring and evaluation.* This section explains your design for summative research. It refers to what you learned from research conducted prior to developing the plan, plus research conducted during and after the plan to evaluate the success or failure of any aspect of implementation. Monitoring and evaluation conducted during the plan allow you to make course corrections and maximize your chances for overall success. Never wait until the plan is completed to conduct measurement. If you do, then it is too late to make any necessary changes (course corrections) to accomplish the plan's goals and objectives.

The Importance of Research

Effective strategic communication planning and management begins and ends with research. Research is the communicator's firm foundation on which to build relevant, results-oriented communication plans. Practicing communication strategically, beginning with research, is relevant to the specialist as well as the generalist practice of communication. There are two types of formal research:

primary and secondary. *Primary research* is data collected for the first time, specifically for the project on which you are working. Since you do everything from scratch, primary research is generally more expensive and time-consuming than secondary research. You can hire a research firm to do it or do it all yourself. But either way, the advantage of primary research is that it is completely relevant to your current situation. The tools of primary research are interviews, surveys and questionnaires, and focus groups. *Secondary research* is data collected by others that you study and apply to your situation. It is generally less expensive and quicker to obtain, but it must be adapted to your situation. A visit to the IABC Research Foundation or the library or the Internet can yield a wealth of information for your planning purposes. Experts agree that a combination of primary and secondary research is best (Bivens, 2005).

Science provides a way of knowing through the scientific method. To the extent that communicators use the scientific method for decision making in communication and public relations management, the communicator elevates the function from the intuitive enterprise of the artist and makes it part of the organization's management system. At the core of this management system are the following aspects of research:

1. Research is conducted to define the problem (or issues) for the purpose of developing a communication or public relations program.
2. Research is done to monitor program implementation for performance accountability and for strategic adjustments.
3. Research is conducted to measure program impact or effectiveness with respect to goals and objectives (the expected outcomes) (Broom & Dozier, 1990).

Knowing how to conduct research is a fundamental strategic tool of successful communicators. With these skills, you are better able to complete a key step in the process of strategic communication planning: the situation analysis.

Strategic Planning and Strategic Management

I believe that the disciplines of strategic planning and strategic communication management can be unified. Strategic planning seeks to measure results of strategic activity. Strategic communication is built on that same premise: measuring results. However, performance measurement is a difficult task. In the early 1990s, Kaplan and Norton developed a process—the balanced scorecard—that recognizes that an organization's ability to develop, nurture, and mobilize its intangible assets is critical to success. Financial metrics alone simply cannot capture the value-creating activities from an organization's intangible assets (Kaplan & Norton, 2001):

- The skills, competencies, and motivation of its employees
- Database and information technologies
- Efficient and responsive operating processes
- Innovation in products and services
- Customer loyalty and relationships
- Political, regulatory, and societal approval (pp. 2–3).

Organizations that adopted Kaplan and Norton's balanced scorecard recognized that competitive advantage comes from the intangible assets listed. It follows that strategy implementation requires that all strategic business units, support units, and employees be aligned and linked to strategy. These organizations realized that the formulation and implementation of strategy must be a continual and participative process. Organizations need a language for communicating strategy as well as processes and systems that help them to implement strategy and gain feedback about their strategy. The adopters of the balanced scorecard realized that success comes from having strategy become everyone's everyday job.

Consider the huge implications to communicators of the balanced scorecard. As more and more companies adopt the balanced scorecard and become what Kaplan and Norton call "strategy-focused organizations," such organizations require that all employees understand the strategy and conduct their day-to-day business in a way that contributes to the success of that strategy. This is not top-down direction but top-down communication. Executives use the balanced scorecard to help communicate and educate the organization about strategic matters. When executives clearly define strategy, communicate it consistently, and link it to the drivers of change, a performance-based culture emerges that links everyone and every unit to strategy (Kaplan & Norton, 2001).

Long gone are the days of simple jobs for simple people. The challenge today as never before is to motivate the hearts and minds of employees at all levels of the organization to strive for continuous quality improvement, cost reduction, meeting customers' expectations, and countering the competition. The balanced scorecard provides organizations with a powerful tool beyond traditional strategic planning for communication and alignment. Yet Kaplan and Norton's (2001) own studies show that less than 5 percent of the typical workforce understands their organization's strategy. Therefore, organizational communicators are needed more than ever to add value to business management.

References

Bedeian, A., & Zammuto, R. (1991). *Organizations: Theory and design.* New York: Dryden Press.

Birchfield, R. (2010). The strategic plan. *New Zealand Management, 57*(3), 56–58.

Bivens, T. (2005). *Public relations writing: The essentials of style and format.* New York: McGraw-Hill.

Broom, G., & Dozier, D. (1990). *Using research in public relations: Applications to program management.* Upper Saddle River, NJ: Prentice Hall.

Collins, J., & Porras, J. (1995). *Built to last: Successful habits of visionary companies.* New York: Harper Business.

Fathi, M., & Wilson, L. (2009). Strategic planning in colleges and universities. *Business Renaissance Quarterly, 4*(1), 91–103.

Goodstein, L., Nolan, T., & Pfeiffer, J. (1993). *Applied strategic planning: How to develop a plan that really works.* New York: McGraw-Hill.

Grunig, J., & Grunig, L. (2000). Public relations in strategic management and strategic management of public relations: Theory and evidence from the IABC Excellence project. *Journalism Studies, 1*(2), 303–321.

Kaplan, R., & Norton, D. (2001). *The strategy-focused organization.* Boston: Harvard Business School Press.

Potter, L. (2008). *The communication plan: The heart of strategic communication* (3rd ed.). San Francisco: International Association of Business Communicators.

Reingold, J., & Underwood, R. (2004, November). Was built to last built to last? *Fast Company, 88*, 103–111.

Rothschild, W. (1979). *Strategic alternatives.* New York: AMACOM.

Steiner, G. (1979). *Strategic planning: What every manager must know.* New York: Free Press.

Sull, D. (2010). Are you ready to rebound? *Harvard Business Review, 88*(3), 70–74.

Welch, J. (2001). *Jack straight from the gut.* New York: Warner Business Books.

CHAPTER TEN

ISSUES MANAGEMENT

Linking Business and Communication Planning

George McGrath

Organizations today must navigate a turbulent, highly competitive and fast-changing environment in pursuit of their business goals. Like mariners on a stormy sea, an organization's leaders must continually scan the horizon for future threats and opportunities so they can avoid trouble and find the fastest, safest passage to their destinations. Such forecasting is the basis of an organization's strategic planning process. Through the issues management discipline, strategic planning also becomes a key component of communication planning.

Issues management is a process that identifies the *issues*, *trends*, and *stakeholder attitudes* that can affect the organization for better or worse and develops strategies and tactics, including communication programs, to deal with them.

The dictionary defines an *issue* as "a point, matter or question to be disputed or decided" (YourDictionary, 2010). A discussion of an issue involves a debate between different points of view, which ideally leads to agreement or resolution.

W. Howard Chase (1984), who pioneered the practice of issues management, further defined an issue as the gap between an organization's performance and the expectations of its stakeholders—such as customers, investors, employees, communities, elected officials and regulators, or interest groups.

This gap can have implications for the organization's overall business strategy as well as its communication. For example, the organization may be performing in line with shareholder expectations—or beyond expectations—but it has not told its side of the story. In this case, the issue can be resolved primarily through communication. If the organization is performing below stakeholder expectations, the issue may require an adjustment to operating strategy.

This chapter provides an overview of issues management and the critical role of communications in issues management.

How Issues Develop—and How Organizations Can Influence Them

Gaps between stakeholder expectations and an organization's or industry's performance evolve over time, driven by gains in human knowledge, demographic and social changes. Often, these gaps are crystallized by a major news-making event that puts the issue front and center with the public. For example, the development of tools for modeling data on global climate trends has raised climate change as an issue of concern to governments, the public, and business, leading to mandates for reduction of greenhouse emissions. Catastrophic hurricanes linked to global warming generate renewed calls for action to reduce emissions.

In its early stages, the problem may be recognized only by a few experts who are closely studying the area, much like the scientists in the late 1970s did with climate models. Over time, emerging issues move from the fringes to the front page, as public awareness grows and pressure increases to make changes or to legislate remedies.

By the time an issue reaches the crisis stage, an organization's response will be limited largely to damage control. When the costs and damage to the company's reputation are tallied after the crisis is over, someone will inevitably observe, "We should have seen this one coming." The earlier an organization gets involved in such an issue, the more options it has for shaping the discussion, deflecting potential threats, or adapting its business practices to meet the needs of a changing world.

The Five-Step Issues Management Process

The issues management process has five basic steps: identify potential issues; set priorities; establish a position on the issues; develop the response; and monitor the issue.

Issue Identification

Issues identification involves looking inside the organization at its business strategies, operations, and behavior—and outside, at social, economic, or political trends and developments that may affect the business in the future.

The communications manager can conduct an informal issues scan as part of the annual communication planning process. Or it can be a more comprehensive effort involving representatives of different staff and line business functions.

As a starting point, there are a few simple steps any communicator can take to identify immediate, near-term issues facing the organization—and the organization's readiness to deal with the issues.

First, review the organization's business plan and current operations. Is the organization engaged in activities or considering changes that might create controversy, debate, or dissent? Are there implications for any products or services either currently offered or under consideration? Where is the organization most vulnerable to the emergence of new competitors, changes in attitudes among customers, investors, employees, or other constituents, or new social standards that will create a gap between company practice and social norms?

Second, evaluate stakeholder attitudes and concerns. Communicators are typically on the front line dealing with employees, journalists, investors, elected leaders, communities, so this is an area in which they can provide the organization with insights and added value. What subjects are generating the greatest number of inquiries, comments, or complaints from the media or public? Where are the greatest gaps between stakeholder expectations and the organization's performance?

Third, weigh senior management's concerns. What news stories pique senior management's interest and generate requests for more information? What competitors is the organization most concerned with? What trends or events are recurring subjects in formal or informal management gatherings?

Fourth, consult with in-house experts. What does the government affairs director see as the major upcoming legislative and regulatory issues on the horizon? What technological developments is the chief information officer concerned about? What workforce trends is the human resources director following?

Fifth, scan news channels and social media for social, political, economic, technological or cultural trends and issues that have relevance and potential impact for the organization. What issues have recently made the jump from blogs to mainstream media? Where are leading commentators and pundits focusing their attention?

Finally, understand the common concerns of your industry. What key issues are being tracked by the trade or professional associations? What are the leading topics being discussed at industry conferences, meetings, and seminars? Has a competitor's negative actions affected the credibility or reputation of the industry as a whole or brought industry practices under scrutiny?

Capture Ideas and Information from the Issue Scan. Ideas, trends and information from the issue scan should be summarized, analyzed, and ultimately considered by senior management and policymakers within the organization.

The issues report can be a report or presentation to senior management that describes the trends and potential issues surfaced through the scan and their implications for the organization. The report should include a recommendation to continue to monitor the trends for further developments, conduct more in-depth research, or develop a position and response to the issue.

Issue Prioritization

Limited management time and resources as well as competing priorities will restrict the organization's ability to respond to every potential issue. The issues manager should establish priorities and create a short list of key issues.

The process for selecting key issues involves a few simple and direct questions about each potential issue surfaced in the identification phase.

- What is the issue's current or potential impact on the organization's ability to do business or its reputation: high, moderate, low?
- What is the probability that the impact will occur: high, moderate, low?
- What is the likelihood it will have an impact: now, next twelve months, next thirty-six months?

Top-priority issues are those with a major and imminent impact on the organization. They require an immediate response: the development of a statement that summarizes the organization's position on the issue, likely questions and answers, and an action plan. Medium-priority issues may require development of a position statement and supporting materials, such as responses to likely questions. Action plans can be longer term in nature. The only indicated action may be to keep monitoring the issue. Low-priority issues can be put on a list for periodic reassessment or dropped from consideration.

Develop the Organization's Position on the Issue

Before the organization takes any action, it must determine its position on the issue: how the organization views the issue and how it believes it should be handled or resolved.

The process of building an issues statement should involve all key decision makers inside the organization who are affected by the issue or will have a role in its resolution. For example, if the issue involves product safety, the sales, marketing, product quality, and customer relations groups should be actively involved in the discussion. If the issue concerns the environmental impact of a manufacturing facility, the plant manager as well as the corporate health and safety officer should be engaged in the process.

To develop a position, participants will need to reach an agreement on several areas:

- How serious an impact could the issue have on the company's reputation or ability to achieve its business objectives?
- How is the issue likely to develop over time? Absent the company's involvement, is the likely outcome favorable, unfavorable, or neutral for us?
- Which groups have a stake in this issue? What stakeholders are on our side? What groups are firmly opposed to us?
- What can we do to change the development and resolution of the issue? How should we engage in the debate with activist groups, elected officials, or the media? Should we resist changing our policies or operations, or should we take actions to adapt?
- Finally and most important, what impact can the organization have? Can we affect the resolution of the issue by taking an active role? Do we have the credibility and resources to win the argument? Do we need to work with others so we can pool resources and engage others in the debate?

Craft the Issue Statement

The end result of this process is the issue statement: a one- to two-page document that defines the issue, the organization's position on it, and the response. It includes the following components:

- *Issue summary:* A short description of background on the issue and its development, impact on the organization, current and future activity
- *Issue position:* The organization's position on the issue and actions taking place around it, including actions the organization may take on its own to deal with the matter
- *Issue owner(s):* Names and contact information for the individuals in the organization responsible for monitoring and managing the issue

The issue statement should be circulated internally to all groups that have a role in managing and resolving the issue. The organization's stated position on the issue should guide the development of talking points and external communications with stakeholders.

Assembling the Issue Team

In the process of developing the issue position, the organization should identify a senior leader as the issue owner. He or she must have the authority to recruit a cross-functional issue management team, assemble resources to support the effort, and seek changes in corporate policy or operations if required.

The issue team's size and membership depends on the scope, complexity, and impact of the issue. The team should include the stakeholders involved and participants who know the issue and who have subject matter expertise that can help develop a solution. For example, a team dealing with a potential product safety issue could include the product manager responsible for sales and marketing of the product; the quality assurance manager who deals with its manufacture; the product development or technology manager who knows how the product was developed, its components and how it works; the communication manager who knows key external stakeholders such as the news media; the customer relations manager who will have to handle inquiries or complaints from product users; the legal affairs director who may have to deal with claims arising from product problems.

Organizing the Planning Session

Once the issue team is formed, work can begin on developing the organization's action plan. An initial planning session can jump-start the effort by bringing the key players together to review the issue and brainstorm potential responses.

The agenda for the kickoff meeting could include:

- *A review of the issue, the organization's position and response.* If the description, position, and response have not yet been developed, the issue team should prepare a draft as part of its action plan.
- *Status of the issue.* What is the issue's stage of development? Are any events imminent that will galvanize stakeholders or accelerate action?
- *Identification and prioritization of stakeholders.* What groups are involved in the debate or resolution of the issue and what are their attitudes?
- *Objectives.* What should the organization seek to achieve with key stakeholders?
- *Strategies.* How should the organization marshal its resources—or align with other groups—to achieve the desired response?

- *Tactics.* What specific tools and techniques will be used to implement the strategies?
- *Measurement.* How will progress be tracked and evaluated?
- *Timing, responsibilities, budgets.* Over what time frame will the plan be implemented, by whom, at what cost?

Identification and Ranking of Stakeholders

Stakeholder analysis is a critical component of developing the action plan. Various stakeholder groups should be studied and ranked by attitudes and importance in the debate. A product quality issue, for example, has implications for many stakeholder groups.

- *Customers* will be concerned if questions arise about quality and may seek alternative products, depressing sales.
- *Employees* could see employment prospects suffer if product sales decline; morale could be affected by attacks on the company's reputation.
- *Shareholders* have a financial stake in the company; declining product sales could hurt earnings and reduce the value of their investment.
- *Interest groups* such as consumer organizations or user groups will push solutions, which could range from calls to reformulate or redesign the product to publication of consumer warnings to demands the product be withdrawn from distribution.
- *Elected officials* may become involved if the issue becomes visible in the media or constituents or advocacy groups lobby for action. They may pursue legislation to regulate the way the product is manufactured and sold or hold hearings that generate more attention for the issue.
- *Regulators* charged with consumer protection could mandate the company take action to address the issue.
- *News media* will seek to guard the public interest and educate or inform readers about the issue. They will gather positions from all parties involved in the debate and point the way toward a consensus position, if one exists. The media response will shape how stakeholders view the matter.

The issue team should rank the stakeholders to provide priorities and focus for the action steps.

Define Objectives

The organization's position and response to the issue will drive the definition of objectives for each critical stakeholder group. In the case of a product quality issue, the objectives might include:

- *Consumers:* Maintain perception that the product is effective and safe; protect the company's reputation as a manufacturer of reliable, quality products
- *Regulators:* Obtain regulatory endorsement that the product meets or exceeds all quality standards
- *Interest groups:* Avoid demands for product recalls; obtain product endorsement and support from major product user groups
- *Media:* Vigorously defend the product and ensure the company's position is included in news coverage

Objectives must be measurable and specific. This may involve baseline research, for example, opinion surveys to determine what consumers believe about product safety now, or content analysis of current media coverage to form a picture of how the issue and the company's position is currently being portrayed. The issue team can then discuss targets, for example, increasing coverage of the organization's position in major media covering the issue.

Determining the Proper Response

There are three modes of issue response: reactive, adaptive, and dynamic.

An organization in a *reactive* mode decides it is not going to change its policy, procedures, practices, or products in response to an issue and instead seeks to deflect the issue through communication or lobbying campaigns that try to slow or stop the progress of outside action by elected officials or regulators.

An organization can take an *adaptive* response to an issue and voluntarily change its policies, practices, or products *before* changes are defined by other advocates and mandated by law. The organization gets credit for exercising leadership and may be able to institute a change on a more favorable basis than if the terms had been defined by outsiders.

In the *dynamic* response, the organization models how an issue will develop: what advocates will be attracted to it, what are the likely arguments and counterarguments, and what consensus solution is likely to be acceptable to the organization and society. Then the organization can lead the way in articulating the issue and a possible solution, attract advocates, and build public support for its desired outcome.

The choice of approach depends on the timing of the issue and what is at stake for the organization. Issues that have already made the front page or legislative agenda are going to be dealt with in a reactive fashion—the best the organization may be able to do is raise enough questions to prolong the debate and postpone the outcome. It may not seem like the most enlightened approach, but when the organization is in crisis mode, with its business at stake, a defensive strategy may be the only alternative.

Strategy Selection

The selection of specific strategies will be driven by the organization's chosen response, its analysis of its strengths and vulnerabilities on the issue, and its stakeholder priorities.

Depending on the nature of the issue and the chosen response, potential strategies include:

- Conducting a communication campaign to educate stakeholders about the company's performance on the issue and close perception gaps
- Building a coalition with other organizations or stakeholders to develop a proposed solution, pool resources, coordinate activities, and communicate broad support for the position
- Communicating the organization's position directly to elected officials and their staffs to influence the content or timing of legislation or regulatory actions
- Mobilizing support for the organization's position from the grassroots—for example, by educating the organization's employees about the issues' importance to them and encouraging them to speak to friends and neighbors, write supportive letters to the editor, meet or write their elected leaders and make their views known
- Redesigning a product or developing new policies and procedures to adapt the organization to new or emerging stakeholder expectations

Issues Monitoring

Issues are not static. Once an issue is identified, it should be tracked and periodically reassessed to determine whether it remains relevant to the organization, whether the fundamentals of the debate have changed, and whether the organization's action plan needs to be modified to accommodate recent developments or new information.

Issue monitoring tools include:

- *Opinion research* such as phone polls or online surveys are used to determine attitudes of stakeholder groups on the particular issue and track changes in attitudes over time as the stakeholders receive new information about the issue.
- *Monitoring of news media coverage* on the issue helps track key developments, the level of media and public interest, the most quoted, most influential advocates, and the organization's effectiveness communicating its views through the media.

- *Monitoring websites and blogs* about the issue can help determine the views of different advocacy groups, how the topic is being debated, and what new arguments may be emerging at the frontiers of public opinion.
- *The development of legislation* can be monitored through media coverage, tracking services, postings of proposed legislation or regulatory action on government websites, and meetings with legislative staff.

Issues Management Improves Communication Effectiveness

Communicators today are being challenged to be more productive, more efficient, and more effective with fewer resources. This challenge requires targeting the areas that have the greatest impact on the health and growth of the organization.

Issues management is a tool that identifies issues that are critical to the organization's present performance and future prospects. By surfacing and prioritizing these concerns, communicators are better able to focus, coordinate, and maximize their time and resources against the greatest areas of opportunity—or points of pain—for their organizations. The communicator can also play a critical coordinating role by facilitating the flow of issues information to those who can help the organization examine the matter, respond to it, and ultimately develop a solution.

Finally, communicators have the skills essential to resolving contentious issues and bridging gaps between the organization and its stakeholders. By seeking opportunities to create a dialogue with constituents early in the development of an issue, before battle lines are drawn, we can reduce the risk to our organization's reputation and operations, and help to reach a balanced resolution that is fair to all parties.

Case in Point: Building Grassroots Support for a Development Project

National Development Corporation, a leading commercial real estate company, remediates abandoned and polluted industrial properties and redevelops the sites as shopping centers, amusement parks, and office complexes. The company typically works with local governments to obtain tax breaks or other financial support for its projects.

National Development identified a 300-acre site—a former automotive plant in the city of Zenith—that offered a promising location for a new project. The company envisioned building AquaWorld, an indoor water park, retail complex, and condominium community, at the location. The project would be an economic boon for the struggling city, which had never fully recovered from the loss of the auto plant ten years before. But National Development knew from its own experience that no development project is uncontroversial. The company needed to identify potential issues that could undermine public support for its plans and develop strategies to deal with them.

National Development formed an issues management team that included representatives from the corporate communications, government relations, legal, marketing, and real estate development departments. The team was charged with conducting an issue scan to identify local stakeholder concerns, attitudes, and issues that could affect the company's proposed project.

The issues team researched local mainstream and social media to find how similar projects had been received in Zenith. They learned that a competitor's project—an indoor ski mountain and race car track—had drawn vocal opposition three years before due to concerns about its proposed height, the impact on traffic, and the multimillion-dollar cost of the proposed tax incentives. A local environmental group had led opposition to the project and through demonstrations, petition drives, and negative news coverage eroded political support for tax incentives and forced the developer, Summit Properties, to abandon its project as uneconomic.

The National Development issues team also conducted more intensive research on attitudes of key stakeholders in Zenith. The company retained a well-connected community relations consultant—the former head of the Zenith Chamber of Commerce—to meet with local opinion leaders to investigate the likely local reaction to the AquaWorld proposal.

The research process identified some important lessons learned from the Summit Properties experience. First, Summit Properties had a mixed record as a developer and marketer of its projects, often asking to renegotiate terms of financial agreements with host communities when retail leasing did not go as well as planned. Second, Summit had taken a hard sell approach to communications with newspaper ads, charity events, and marches by local construction unions in support of the project, trying to steamroll local opponents. Third, many Zenith residents were concerned about the need to clean up environmental problems—a legacy of the city's industrial past—as well as to attract investment and jobs.

Based on these insights, the National Development issues team developed an integrated business and communications strategy to engage stakeholders, build grassroots, and secure municipal backing for tax incentives needed to make the project economically viable.

The company's issues management strategy included the following elements:

- *Project positioning statement.* The team developed an issues statement that positioned National Development's project as an economic and environmentally beneficial initiative, to be developed by a highly experienced, responsible company, in consultation with the community. This document, along with supporting key messages and proof points, was used to drive all communications.
- *Grasstops outreach.* The issues team met with influential community leaders (also known as *grasstops*), including the heads of leading businesses, economic development agencies, environmental groups, and not-for-profit organizations. The meetings included a brief overview of National Development's proposal and its projected benefits, with most of the time devoted to gaining feedback on how the project could be best advanced. The company later invited several of these influential leaders to join a project advisory panel to provide ongoing input.
- *Political strategy.* The company's government affairs staff met with Zenith municipal officials to discuss the AquaWorld project and its benefits as well as its funding needs. Based on these discussions, the issues team developed a project communications timeline that included a public announcement coordinated with the Zenith mayor's office, with subsequent hearings before the municipal zoning board, the city council, and a likely public referendum on the needed tax incentives.
- *Media relations strategy.* The issues team announced the AquaWorld project with a news conference featuring National Development executives, the mayor of Zenith, other key elected officials, and members of the recently formed project advisory panel. The event introduced National Development and its proposal to the public at large and received extensive coverage by mainstream and social media. National Development's corporate communications manager later arranged for key reporters and bloggers to visit a similar project the company had built in a neighboring state and report on its successful results.
- *Community outreach.* At the kickoff media event, National Development announced it would hold a series of community meetings at which local residents could learn about the project and provide their comments. These meetings were designed to communicate the project's benefit and identify community issues that could affect the project's chances for approval. The meetings were well attended and helped the issues team identify common concerns over traffic that would be generated by the project, the desire for more "green space" along a river that bisected the property, and whether the struggling city of Zenith could

afford to grant the developer any property tax breaks. Based on this feedback, the company repositioned the location of three parking lots to reduce potential highway backups, redrew its plans to include parkland and a restored wildlife habitat, and agreed to work with Zenith officials to approach the state for additional development funds, reducing the anticipated tax incentives required.

- *Mobilizing the grasstops and grassroots.* Through its dialogue with Zenith leaders and residents, National Development built a list of several hundred people who expressed strong support for its project. The issues team developed a series of e-mail alerts to this group to keep them posted on the project approval process and to encourage them to attend public hearings before the zoning board and city council to voice their support for the development.

- *Monitoring developments.* The issues team continued to monitor media coverage, blog posts, and public comments regarding the AquaWorld project and modified its communications strategy to address new concerns during the project approval process.

National Development listened to its stakeholders, identified key issues that could delay or damage its prospects for success, and took action to bridge gaps between the company's plans and stakeholder expectations for the project. Hundreds of supportive residents attended the zoning board and city council hearings, at which the company's plan was approved. In the subsequent public referendum, 59 percent of voters endorsed the city's plan to provide a seven-year property tax reduction for the project. With the help of the influential members of its project advisory board, National Development won additional financial support from the state's Green Projects fund, which offset the costs of developing the park and wildlife refuge. The AquaWorld project was developed with minimal delays, helping to keep construction costs within budget and generating an above-average return on investment for the company.

References

Chase, W. H. (1984). *Issue management—Origins of the future.* Stamford, CT: Issue Action Publications.

YourDictionary.com. (2010). *Issue.* Retrieved August 9, 2010, from http://www.yourdictionary.com/issue.

CHAPTER ELEVEN

COMMUNICATING CHANGE

When Change Just Doesn't Stop: Creating Really Good Change Communication

Jennifer Frahm

The ongoing and unremitting nature of new product development, shifting consumer and stakeholder priorities, and government reform creates intense pressure for the public sector to commercialize and for the private sector to be flexible. Whereas managers once could introduce a change, implement the change, and reinforce the change in a relatively simple linear process, modern business dictates a pace that prevents anything but continual change.

The optimistic view of continuously changing organizations is that they seek to be more flexible, more innovative, and more responsive to the dynamic external environment. The more cynical view is that of businesses that repeatedly fail to realize benefits from their change programs. Employees manage the discomfort of successive change programs with acquiescence and little engagement.

Arguably, many change models are founded on Lewin's (1951) three-step "unfreeze-change-refreeze" model. Regardless of the view (optimistic or cynical) of the continuously changing organization the pressure faced by organizations to change continuously renders the Lewinian three-step change models obsolete, as time to *refreeze* is rare. The difficulty for those charged with the internal communication activities associated with change is manifold.

One of the problems associated with continuous change is the resultant impact on employee receptivity to change of successive downsizings, re-engineering efforts, and multiple attempts at culture change. The change masters advocate, "Communicate, communicate, communicate." We do, and we are often faced with employees who are cynical, mistrusting, disengaged, and worn down.

Why do some organizations lament high numbers of employees who experience change fatigue and change cynicism, and others point to a highly engaged, resilient, and innovative workforce? *Really good* change communication can be the distinction.

This chapter considers the factors that make for really good change communication, including:

- A broader consideration of what change communication is
- Clarity of change communication purpose
- Alignment between change communication competence and change communication expectations, and
- Engagement with the *background talk* of change

Defining Change Communication: A Broader Consideration

For many managers, change communication means fact sheets, FAQs, road shows, and manager talking points. Good change communication means timely information that is fed to the troops and provides a consistent message and clarity in meaning. If that is the worst we get of change communication, then we are probably not doing so badly.

Others argue for a broader understanding of change communication (Frahm & Brown, 2007; Taylor & Van Every, 2000). Change communication represents a mindset that sees organizational change as the result of a series of communicative events. The communication within the organization creates the change we need to make. This perspective considers the types of conversations that occur within organizational change and how we deploy them.

Monologues and Dialogues

Organizations consist of monologues and dialogues. Monologic change communication is identified as top-down, one-way, instrumental communication. When the change communication is monologic, we speak with the same voice and shared understanding, and the power lies with those who make the decisions about the change.

Dialogic change communication is constructive. Relationships matter, different perspectives matter, and power is shared among all within the organization. The frontline employee has as much voice as the chief executive officer (CEO). The nature of dialogic communication is about creating new meaning, processes, or products out of the conversations.

Monologic and dialogic change communications suggest purposeful and deliberate uses of formal communicative action within organizational change. However, we cannot forget the informal communication of change—the conversations that go on in the background.

The Background Talk

Many conversations of change occur through the grapevine, by the water cooler, and within the corridor. The ways in which employees individually make sense of change can dominate the formal narrative of change, and this sense making produces a *background talk of change*. The background talk can serve as a barometer of how receptive employees are to changes being introduced.

In considering a broader understanding of change communication, we add complexity to the change communicator's efforts. Simplification of the complexity of change communication occurs by drilling down into what you are really trying to achieve with your change communication.

What Is the Purpose of Your Communication?

Reducing the complexity of the change communicator's considerations requires asking the questions: What is the purpose of your communication? What do you want to do? Do you want to use communication to *create some stability* within the change program? Or do you want to *create more change* with your communicative efforts?

The use of fact sheets, FAQs, road shows, and manager talking points *create stability*. In a time of uncertainty, these tools provide information that can reassure, educate, and clarify the details on those issues on which the employee is unsure.

Managers seek to stabilize the organization by communicating vision and educating employees of the benefits of the change. It is reflected in speech acts or written directives that suggest a one-way direction. This unilateral trajectory assumes a high degree of planned change and that the manager or change communicator can control the message.

To *create further change*, you need to employ dialogic communication. It is more about the relationships and less about the tools. Bokeno and Gantt (2000) suggest that dialogic communication is distinctly different than the usual patterns of management communication; it represents the ability to engage with genuine care and respect and generates reflective discussion. Authentic conversations have positive impacts on innovation and organizational change.

This dialogic approach assumes that managers and employees possess the requisite competencies to carry on dialogue. It goes beyond strong interpersonal skills; it also means high emotional intelligence and managers who are willing to suppress status and ego. Good dialogues are challenging to start and difficult to maintain. They demand higher-level skills and capabilities of the participants: you need to be able to listen, to be empathetic, and be cognizant of differences. Dialogues require managers to relinquish their power perspectives and become equal partners in the conversations.

Communicating for Stability

Some of the points that are important to consider when communicating for stability include:

- *Communicate what is staying the same.* Rather than focus on what is changing, provide employees with something reassuring.
- *Use effective media.* Many managers are overwhelmingly using e-mail as a proxy for good change management practice, and employees are already overwhelmed by overflowing inboxes. A morning 10-minute meeting can convey a lot of information and settle things down.
- *Determine the credibile source.* Who should be doing the communicating: the frontline supervisor or senior management? This has become a contentious issue with conflicting research on the answer. Some studies suggest senior management must be the ones communicating the information, others suggest that employees prefer the frontline supervisor as there is more trust in the relationship. Your answer is guided by the purpose, if you want to create stability, who will be most reassuring? That is who communicates the changes.
- *Use metaphors.* Metaphors allow us to reframe new issues in the language of the already understood. But you have to know your audience well to be able to use the correct metaphor. One CEO I worked with was fond of saying, "We are like a boat at sea on a journey to an unknown destination, and we do not have time to go into dry dock to have our paneling replaced, but we just have to do it. We know the general direction, but we do not know exactly where the winds will take us." This metaphor got turned around pretty fast by the employees: "Yes, but how will the boat get to its destination if the captain does not know where it is going?" Talk of mutiny and plank walking ensued.

Communicating for Further Change

When your purpose is to create further change, you need to think about how to enable the relational focus. This might include an emphasis on employee forums,

Web 2.0 enterprise systems, a communicative culture that values listening and eschews hierarchical structures.

- *Employee forums.* Providing forums for employees to discuss the changes required for the business is critical to creating space for dialogue. In these forums, participation is voluntary, the agenda is owned by employees, and management's role is to listen and provide authentic and candid perspectives.
- *Web 2.0 and enterprise systems.* One of the interesting things about increased adoption of Web 2.0 technology enterprise-wide is that it has introduced behaviors that enable dialogic communication, for example, collaboration, attribution, sharing, respectful commenting, and community interaction.
- *Dialogic culture.* Many communicators value control—ensuring the right message is communicated at the right time in the right way by the right person. A culture that supports dialogic communication is one that is comfortable with flexibility, experimentation, risk, and a lack of status.

Given that the norm is often quite disparate to a truly dialogic culture, bear in mind these words of caution for those pursuing organizational dialogue: Often we hear the expressions *two-way conversations*, *participative communication*, and *collaborative engagement* used to describe what are intended as dialogic initiatives. However, if these are all used as tools to achieve buy-in and successful sale of your change, then the true purpose is not to create further change but to create stability by implementing the change that those in power have determined. To use dialogic tools for the sake of appearing to be consultative is a high-risk strategy. It usually results in greater cynicism when expectations of further change are unmet.

Defining Purpose Beyond Change and Stability

The change and stability dialectic is a simple distinction, and it is not always one that captures the complexity of organizations that undergo change on a frequent and continuous basis. Cheney, Christensen, Zorn, and Ganesh (2004, p. 319) offer a more comprehensive and thoughtful model of change-related communication (see Figure 11.1).

The model presented in Figure 11.1 indicates that the question, "What is the purpose of your change communication?" can be answered by four core change-related phases:

1. *Formulation.* Sometimes known as *ideation*, this phase is the point when the organization is generating an understanding of what the change outcome might

FIGURE 11.1 A MODEL OF CHANGE-RELATED COMMUNICATION

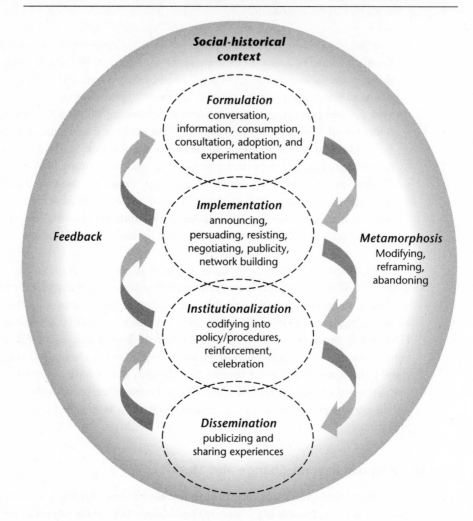

Source: Cheney, Christensen, Zorn, and Ganesh (2004), *Organizational Communication in an Age of Globalization*, p. 319. Used by permission.

be like. Note the inclusion of communicative acts such as experimentation. Rather than focus on planned change events, organizations that change continuously recognize the value of experimentation, adaptation, and flexibility.

2. *Implementation*. This maps with traditional change communication planning and implementation; it is about how the message is introduced. But it also

recognizes the importance for change communicators to build networks of influencers and that the implementation is more than a one-way process of message transfer. It is often a highly contested space of resistance and negotiation.

3. *Institutionalization.* This phase recognizes the importance of embedding the change initiatives and the communicative acts that occur to celebrate and reinforce the changes.

4. *Dissemination.* The final phase recognizes the value in publicizing the change experience, but perhaps more important sharing experiences. In an organization that changes continuously, it is important to process the lessons from the previous change experience before embarking on the next.

These four phases operate within the social historical context. What has gone on before matters. You cannot create a successful change communication experience in isolation from the history of the organization and the social makeup of the employees.

Alignment between Change Communication Competence and Change Communication Expectations

The first two phases in Figure 11.1 suggest that those charged with facilitating the change communication have control over the process. The third phase considers that default theories-in-use (best practices) are not so useful when applied to the workforce. Really good change communication ensures that there is an alignment between the communicative expectations of the employees and the competencies of those delivering the change communication.

Communication Competencies

Developing communication competencies requires a twofold approach. One aspect demands a behavioral competence within change: for instance, knowing how to deliver a clear and unambiguous message or knowing how to facilitate a dialogue. Perhaps the more critical competence is the second one: knowing when to use a monologic approach or dialogic approach.

Often change communicators have been taught that participatory communication approaches are best for organizational change. And they are, in organizations where the employees want to participate!

If the employees' communicative expectations are to be told what to do, when, and how, they will not be impressed with being invited to join a dialogue on the future of the organization. Attempts at inclusive conversations will be met with scorn and overt attempts to undermine the managers or the change communicators deploying the collaborative and dialogic communication approaches. If the employees possess monologic expectations, then they will respond with an attitude of "If you are asking me, you must not understand what you are doing, and not worthy of your title."

That is not to say that you cannot build the competencies of the employees to include the ability to have constructive conversations, but it does not happen by osmosis.

And the reverse is true. If you come into an organization that possesses strong dialogic competencies, and you take a monologic approach (top-down, information focused), you will be just as ineffective.

Ultimately the responsibility lies with the communicator. You need to understand the communicative preferences and expectations of those whom you wish to initiate change. It represents a form of primal tribalism—the need to identify whether the newcomer is one of us or a threat. If you are not communicating the way the tribe does, you are a threat and will certainly lack influence.

Identifying Expectations

When we have worked as communicators across many change programs, we often default to what we have done before. For instance, good change management means more information; good change management means involving people from the start. We can forget to pause and ask, What are our audience's communicative expectations? What do *they* consider really good communication? The types of things we should be asking about include preferred media; degree of involvement; stage of involvement; desire for detail or big picture; degree of information required; quantity of information; amount of consultation; and preferred source.

If you are in an organization that regularly conducts organizational communication audits, then you should have access to this information. Another way is to conduct some sessions unpacking the lessons learned from previous change programs. By asking the employees, "Would you tell me about the communication of change over the last twelve months?" you can expect to hear several indicators of their expectations. This can be more effective than running an organizational communication audit, as it provides the employees an opportunity for a cathartic vent, allows the organization to clear the air from previous unsatisfactory change events, and reduces some of the cynicism about future change.

In two organizations I have worked with, the employees had very different expectations of what made for good change communication. One set of employees expected that they would be provided with a step-by-step plan on how things would occur. They rejected notions of high-involvement practice to contribute their thoughts. In contrast, the employees of another company believed they should be included from the very beginning. They marveled at a new change leader because he just listened and were disappointed later in the process when their voices were not requested. The lesson was fairly simple: violate the expectation and you create mistrust and cynicism, even if you have the best of intentions.

Building Matching Change Competencies

Organizations that wish to change continuously require more dialogic approaches to communication. However, few organizations possess dialogic competencies to support change.

Building dialogic change competencies within an organization is a two-step process. In the first step, the change communicator needs to align his or her communication approach with the communication expectations of the employees. Good change communicators possess situational wisdom; they are particularly skilled at knowing what approach to use depending on the needs of the employees. They know when to employ a monologic or authoritarian information-based style that unequivocally reduces the anxiety. The highly competent change communicator can also switch to a softer style that emphasizes listening, engagement, empathy, and learning when there is a need to enter into conversations about change.

Most managers have learned the former style, set the boundaries, make it clear what is to happen, and establish themselves with formal power. It is less comfortable for managers to encourage risk taking, acknowledge what they do not know, and treat employees as equal partners in the change effort. Empathetic engagement and a genuine interest in another person's position can be a challenging task, politically unwise, and potentially career limiting.

Once trust and satisfaction with the change communication has been established by matching competencies and expectations, then management can look at introducing a program to build the change competencies across all levels of the organization.

One way is by modeling the behaviors and building rewards into the performance framework on considered risk taking and the demonstration of empathy and respect. If you are using 360-degree feedback tools, then consider measuring the communication competencies beyond information provision.

It is very difficult to engage in constructive discussions when some of the participants do not have the skills to do so. To automatically employ dialogic approaches in an organization with low dialogic competencies is to render the change communication problematic.

It will also pay to address the physical space in the organization and ensure opportunities for constructive communication. Do you have breakout rooms? Do you have open-door policies? Who is situated on what floor? Ensuring that dialogue can occur easily from a spatial sense is important to good change communication.

Engaging in the Background Talk of Change

The final element of really good change communication is the importance of engaging with the background talk of change. Those working in change programs have traditionally operated within a paradigm of problem solving where the change to be introduced represents a solution to an organizational problem. Taking the optimistic view noted at the beginning of the chapter, a shift has occurred to more positive interventions that reflect a focus on continuous changes. In essence, the business does not need to be broken to fix it! Sometimes we just want to make it better.

With the shift toward more positive interventions, there is an accompanying focus on linguistic-based interventions: interventions that are designed to focus on the language, words, and meaning that matter to employees and managers. The challenge for communicators is how to intentionally shift and shape the conversations to create new organizations, ones that are simply better. Part of the conversational shift requires a conscious and deliberate engagement with the background talk by change communicators.

Background Talk

Background talk emerged as an expression within my doctoral research on communication and organizational change, when one of the employees was explaining how the real communication of change occurs in the background of the change. He meant the ways that employees made sense of changes in light of little formal change communication or how they responded to official and formally sanctioned messages of change. This background talk revealed key narratives within the business. The informal talk occurring in the background of the change efforts was taking precedence over the formal communication. With formal communication lacking, employees relied on the background talk to make sense of what was happening.

Background talk can be a very important barometer of change when you gauge the success of change initiatives. It is a place to establish where there may be a lack of understanding that will impede your change efforts. It can also be the site of better ideas.

The benefits of engaging with background talk are numerous, so it makes it all the more surprising that managers usually do everything *but* engage with the informal conversations going on around them at an employee level. One study (Crampton, Hodge, & Mishra, 1998) found that despite a widespread perception from management that there should be some form of engagement with the grapevine (for example, monitoring, feeding information, and correcting misinformation), 92.4 percent of organizations had no policy to deal with the grapevine, and managers and organizations were usually reluctant to take an active role in managing informal communication networks. This is a surprising insight, as previous research suggested that 70 percent of all organizational communication occurs at grapevine level (De Mare, 1989). The communicator who consciously engages in the background talk of change has considerable opportunity to shape the conversations.

Case in Point: StateSmart and People Change

Meet Donella, the internal communications manager of a public sector agency, StateSmart, in Australia. StateSmart has 1,000 employees who typically work in a wide variety of roles including advisory, administration, policy development, and all associated business support functions (human resources, finance, legal, communications, and so on). The People Change initiatives include restructuring divisions, sometimes in response to external factors, and cultural change programs. Donella gives us her perspective of what makes for *really good* communication and how her staff cope with continuous change.

Question: How does StateSmart view continuous change?

Answer: The view of the senior leadership team is largely optimistic in that it needs to be considered as business as usual. Having said that, there is strong awareness that this can be tough for people, and strong communication and leadership is vital so people can understand why the change is occurring and what it means for them.

Question: When your CEO asks you to handle the change communication, what is his perspective? What is he looking for?

Answer: The CEO and the senior leadership take a monologic perspective. The CEO is looking for a robust plan detailing aspects of the change and its effect on people and advice regarding the messaging of the business rationale (case for change). He wants to know who will be accountable for what elements and that the management of the affected team(s) is prepared to lead the change through to implementation. Once he is comfortable with the plan, we are trusted to work with the business and just get on with it, providing regular updates along the way. Stability is a key motivation for the CEO.

Question: How does this perspective differ from what you deliver?

Answer: The senior leadership team may not ask for it, but they also get much unsolicited advice and coaching! A big part of the change comms team's role is a dialogic approach to continuously test assumptions and foster empathy. How would you feel if you were being told this news? How can people have their say? How can we explain this well, without using *corporate speak*? What's the context—is anything else in the pipeline that people should know about now?

Often you have to say things that management does not want to hear! However, that can be a positive turning point in a project, when people start to understand their responsibilities in the change and acknowledge that you cannot outsource leadership responsibility. In this way, we *change* the way we change. Getting in an external consultant to *do the change* may not be the best approach long term!

Question: What is the impact of background talk in StateSmart?

Answer: Any good communicator is listening to the word on the street as part of their job, so being across the background talk during change is especially important. Sometimes it is a way of letting off steam and processing the change, other times it may signal a lack of clarity or misinformation about the change, and then there are times you have vocal blockers. You do need to acknowledge this, in whatever way or style that suits the team concerned.

Question: What do you define as your change communication purpose in StateSmart?

Answer: The change communication purpose differs according to the change and different needs of different parts of the organization. We tend to focus on *implementation*—the traditional change comms' work—but there are projects that require flexibility and adaption, the "What if we do this?" approach. We have found it useful to share experiences or *disseminate* from other change programs, especially asking leaders to address others to help prepare for change and build the "guiding coalition" which Kotter (1996) refers to.

Question: How would you describe the change communication competencies within StateSmart?

Answer: Mixed. We have great teamwork between communications and HR, and skills have built up over a number of years working on significant change programs. Some leaders are great at the "big presentation" announcement change stage (for instance, monologic), but not so much the open-door, listening and showing empathy skills (dialogic). The focus can be too much on "announcement day" rather than the time and energy that's going to be required in the days and weeks and maybe months afterward.

Question: What are the change communication expectations within StateSmart?

Answer: Again, mixed. We survey employees each year, and many questions are about change communication—to capture information about whether people felt they were communicated with well, that leaders explained the change, and so on. It doesn't always mean they agreed with the change or were happy with the end impact on them. If you have built up a positive culture over time, hopefully there is goodwill among people to trust in the process and know that they will be heard—they may not get their way, but they will be heard and their opinions will be respected. Sometimes this basic human need can get lost in the "formal updates of progress" dialogue. One senior leader was great at the technical information updates, but I encouraged him to address what people are really thinking and feeling, which has nothing to do with the project update. What will it mean for me? Can I trust you that you will listen to feedback? Can I trust you when you say there will be no job cuts?

If leaders are truly able to put themselves in their team members' shoes, this empathy will shape the change process and contribute greatly to its success.

Conclusion

As professional communicators charged with supporting corporate leaders through repetitive, relentless, and often painful change, we carry a heavy burden. We are expected to be counselors, magicians, educators, creatives, disciplinarians, and innovators and put aside our own concern for what the change means for us. The four elements of really good change communication discussed in this chapter are offered as a starting point for reflection. You may find it becomes easier and you are able to move toward creating a resilient workforce that looks forward to opportunities for transformation.

References

Bokeno, R. M., & Gantt, V. W. (2000). Dialogic mentoring. *Management Communication Quarterly: MCQ, 14*(2), 237–270.

Cheney, C., Christensen, L. T., Zorn, T. E., & Ganesh, S. (2004). *Organizational communication in an age of globalization—Issues, reflections, practices.* Prospect Heights, IL: Waveland.

Crampton, S. M., Hodge, J. W., & Mishra, J. M. (1998). The informal communication network: Factors influencing grapevine activity. *Public Personnel Management, 27*(4), 569–584.

De Mare, G. (1989). Communicating: The key to establishing good working relationships. *Price Waterhouse Review, 33*, 30–37.

Frahm, J., & Brown, K. (2007). First steps: Linking change communication to change receptivity. *Journal of Organizational Change Management, 20*(3), 370–387.

Kotter, J. P. (1996). *Leading change.* Boston: Harvard Business School Press.

Lewin, K. (1951). *Field theory in social sciences.* New York: Harper & Row.

Taylor, J. R., & Van Every, E. J. (2000). *The emergent organization: Communication as its site and surface.* Mahwah, NJ: Lawrence Erlbaum.

CHAPTER TWELVE

CRISIS COMMUNICATION

Moving from Tactical Response to Proactive Crisis Preparedness

Caroline Sapriel

Globalization, the interdependencies of systems and stakeholders, the increasing politicization of events and their developments, climate change, instant media coverage, and the viral social media scene are but a few of the key factors compounding the complexities of crisis management in the early twenty-first century. There have always been crises—political, diplomatic, business, and others—but when we consider the Toyota and BP crises of 2009–2010, we cannot but reflect that today, their scope and impact have changed.

We are witnessing increasing stakeholder outrage at corporate misbehavior, and hatred and blame across all ranks in society seem to reach levels previously unattained. This finger-pointing phenomenon is slowly being exposed (Friedman, 2010; Kellaway, 2010), if not yet academically researched. Learning lessons, closing gaps, and making responsible parties accountable are all critical parts of the crisis management process; but more than ever, the ability to anticipate, prevent, and mitigate crises before they occur must be high on the agenda of corporate leaders and their communication chiefs.

Defining Crisis

Taking a step back, it is useful to set the scene by first defining what a crisis is. The International Association of Business Communicators (IABC) describes a *crisis* as an event, revelation, allegation, or set of circumstances that threatens the integrity, reputation, or survival of an individual or organization. It challenges the public's sense of safety, values, or appropriateness. The actual or potential damage to the organization is considerable and the organization cannot, on its own, put an immediate end to it.

Generally speaking, it is commonly agreed among today's crisis management academics and practitioners that there are two broad categories of crises: sudden and smouldering.

According to the Institute of Crisis Management (ICM, 2010), a *sudden crisis* is "a disruption in the company's business which occurs without warning and is likely to generate news coverage, including fires, explosions, natural disasters and workplace violence and may adversely impact: employees, investors, customers, suppliers or other publics; offices, plants, franchises or other business assets; Revenues, net income, stock price, etc.; reputation—and ultimately the good will listed as an asset on the balance sheet" (p. 1).

ICM (2010) defines a *smouldering crisis* as "any serious business problem that is not generally known within or without the company, which may generate negative news coverage if or when it goes 'public' and could result in fines, penalties, legal damage awards, unbudgeted expenses and other costs" (p. 1). Examples include:

- Sting operation by a news organization or government agency
- Customer allegations of overcharging or other improper conduct
- Investigation by a government agency
- Action by a disgruntled employee such as serious threats or whistle blowing
- Indications of significant legal/judicial/regulatory action against the business
- Discovery of serious internal problems that will have to be disclosed to employees, investors, customers, vendors and/or government officials (ICM, 2010, p. 1).

Crises are often further subdivided by types, including accidents, natural disasters (acts of God), industrial action, civil disturbances, third-party hostile action, or security-related (extortion, arson, tampering, hostage taking, terrorism, bomb attacks, and computer hacking), environmental, health- and safety-related crises, commercial and financial, and others such as rumors and white-collar crime (fraud, embezzlement, corruption).

With the increasing sophistication and interdependencies of our societal systems, more types are added to the list, and there is frequent overlap between two or more types, making the distinction and classification ever more challenging. This is not merely a puzzle for the crisis management theoretician and practitioner. More dramatically, it is evidenced in today's multiple jeopardy crises that organizations face.

Whether sudden or smouldering, and whatever type or types a crisis may fit into, it normally consists of three components: surprise, threat, and short decision-making time. The organization must react quickly and act responsibly to respond to the threat, protect lives, the environment, assets, and its reputation—whatever is at stake in the context of the situation. This response, to be effective, cannot be improvised. It takes careful planning, extensive practice, and experienced teams to steer an organization through the chaos of a crisis.

Crisis Management and Communication

Gone are the days when the corporate spokesperson could work with his journalist contacts and mop up bad news when things went wrong in his or her company.

Crisis management is no longer primarily a corporate communication function, nor is it enough for the communications department to write the crisis manual and to arrange media training for management. The fact is crisis management today is much more than crisis communication. According to Crandall, Parnell, and Spillan (2010), "Indeed, the area of crisis management originally concentrated on communication with outside stakeholders. In fact, much of the early days of crisis management were more appropriately considered 'damage control' procedures with the media" (p. 16).

Today, crisis management is a strategic function that must be embedded in the organization's corporate management systems, driven from and by the top echelon, and implemented across all levels. It is no longer merely about tactical response preparedness but about anticipation, prevention, and mitigation. It is about sound and tested processes, competencies, practice, and ongoing risk and stakeholder mapping.

In response to the threats posed by a more complex world, crisis communication since the 1990s has become more sophisticated. Companies are increasingly emphasizing proactive approaches to crisis communication. Today, proactive crisis management and mitigation includes a more deliberate process of identifying risks and issues early and managing them before they escalate to crisis levels.

From its early focus on tactical media response, crisis communication has taken on a strategic role that is integrated in the organization's crisis structure along with other critical corporate functions such as security, health, safety and environment, human resources (HR), and legal, among others.

According to Gilpin and Murphy (2008):

> Most authors trace the origin of the crisis communication field to the first Tylenol tampering case in 1982. … As the field has matured, its assumptions have become increasingly complex, and it is possible to discern phases of development in which the emphasis shifted. In the broadest sense, during the 1980s the field was concerned mainly with tactical advice that prescribed specific plans and checklists. During the 1990s, crisis specialists began to give more attention to strategic issues, noting the impacts of contingency and uncertainty along with the possibility of multiple outcomes. Most recently, those who study crisis have focused increasingly on organizational culture and transformation. Elements from each phase have carried over into the next so that it is possible to speak of a "dominant" view of crisis communication representing an accretion of 20 years of study. Overall crisis specialists have given increasing attention to the open-endedness of crisis, the role played by multiple stakeholders, and the interaction between internal and external drivers of crisis. This evolution points toward a model of crisis as a complex adaptive system. (pp. 17–18)

The role of communication in the organization has become increasingly sophisticated since the 1990s. Beyond a focus on media relations, communicators are now tasked with engaging multiple stakeholder groups; developing corporate and business plan positioning, brand and reputation strategies, internal communication plans, product messaging; and becoming social media experts. Communicators are driving a variety of critical deliverables for their organization and have to play the role of internal and external antennae. Therefore, they are uniquely positioned to integrate crisis communication into the overall business strategy and consequently help anticipate, detect, and mitigate crises.

"Professional communicators understand the environment their organization operates in, which provides them with a keen understanding of emerging discrepancies that can evolve into a crisis," says Dr. Arjen Boin, U.S. editor of *Public Administration* (Louisiana State University, Public Administration Institute; cited in Sapriel, 2007, p. 25). Because professional communicators have their fingers on the public's pulse, Boin continues, "They also have a good grasp of the credit level remaining for an organization hit by crisis. This allows for a smoother transition back to a state of normalcy."

Statistics (ICM, 2009) show that in the Western world, most business crises today are non-event-related, or so-called smouldering crises. This implies that a great majority of business crises could be prevented or mitigated. Consequently, organizations are shifting their focus to issues and risk management to monitor new and unimagined threats and, if possible, to anticipate and prevent their escalation.

Therefore, there is a growing recognition among corporations that crisis management must be institutionalized and that all key business functions must address crisis prevention and management formally as part of business planning. Organizations must take a holistic view and establish an integrated business contingency planning framework (see Figure 12.1) of which crisis management is but one element. The framework should encompass three key pillars:

• Risk and issues management as loss prevention function
• Emergency and crisis management as loss response and management function
• Disaster recovery and business continuity as loss recovery function

Crisis management involves being prepared to handle adversity and minimize impact most effectively and facilitating the management process during chaos.

FIGURE 12.1 BUSINESS CONTINGENCY PLANNING FRAMEWORK

Business Contingency Framework

Pre-Loss	Loss	Post-Loss
Risk and Issues Management	Crisis Management Emergency Response	Business Continuity/ Disaster Recovery

Strategic Planning
Stakeholder Management and Communication

Preventive	Reactive	Curative

Anticipation	Response	Resumption	Recovery	Restoration

Return to business as usual

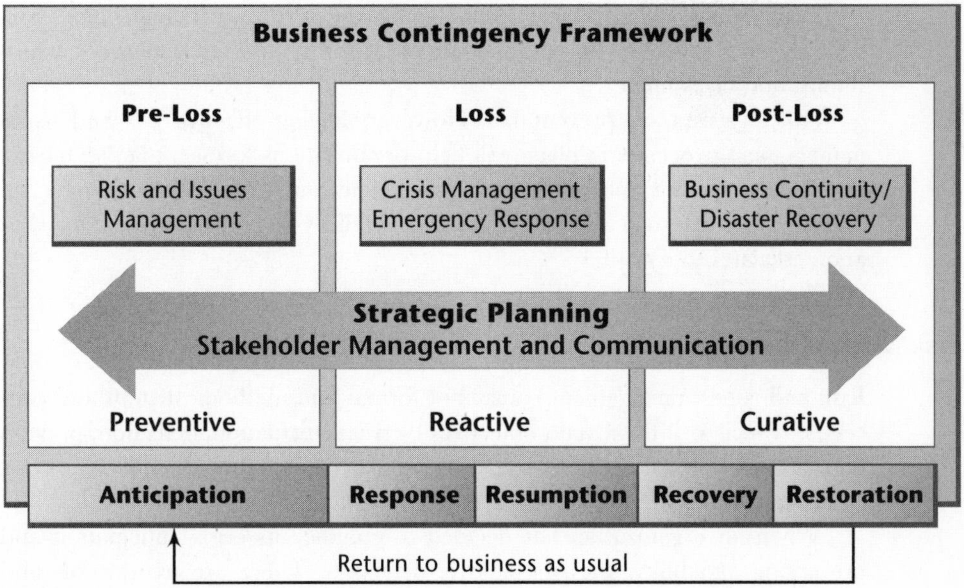

Source: Used with permission from CS&A International Risk & Crisis Management.

Best practice shows that integrating issues and risk management with crisis management enhances organizational resilience and vigilance. However, risk management, crisis management, and business continuity are often managed independently by different functions. This lack of coordination often generates gaps and/or overlaps in processes that reduce overall effectiveness. To provide an integrated approach to crisis anticipation, prevention, mitigation, and recovery, it is essential to assign ownership of the entire business contingency management process to a custodian, whether an individual senior staff member or a department, and embed it into corporate management planning.

When the business contingency management process is not assigned to a custodian in the organization, the corporate communication department is often called upon to take on its coordination role.

For the many organizations that have crisis management plans in place and have matured in their overall crisis response capabilities, the next step is to enhance their crisis anticipation, prevention, and mitigation abilities. This includes the scanning and detection of new and unimaginable threats and risks, mapping the ever-changing web of stakeholders, and developing worst-case scenarios and mitigation plans.

When the risk management process is integrated with issues management in the organization, the crisis prevention capability is noticeably strengthened. This is particularly the case for smouldering crises.

Risk management and issues management are critical yet challenging, particularly when involving the complexities of corporate structures, mergers, acquisitions, and divestments.

Not all crises are preventable. However, having effective risk and issues management processes in place will help organizations foresee, plan scenarios, and decide whether to take, treat, transfer, or terminate the risk. Moreover, an organization with such a proactive culture will likely be better prepared if a situation escalates to a crisis.

Risk Management

Risk and issues management consists of formal and methodical steps and processes. A review of their main objectives—crisis anticipation, detection, prevention, preparation, and mitigation—is useful to articulate the role of today's crisis communicator.

When an organization has decided to enhance its crisis anticipation and prevention capability, the first step is detection. There are many tools and mechanisms to detect warning signs inside and outside the organization. This includes macrodata such as intelligence reports, media monitoring, employee surveys, and so on, and other information drawn from staff reports, risk committee meetings, and the like. Whatever method is used, a framework of criteria must be drawn up as a necessary and practical starting point.

According to Fearn-Banks (2007):

> The detection phase may begin with noting warning signs, or what Barton (1993) referred to as prodromes or the prodromal stage. Some crises have no noticeable prodromes, but many do .... The Exxon Valdez oil spill was a prodrome to other companies as well as Exxon itself .... There are other less obvious prodromes. Employee discontent over any issue is a sign of a brewing crisis.... The same prodromes can be early signs of workplace violence.... To detect early signs, organizations form employee committees that function like lighthouse keepers watching for vessels at sea, watchdogs, or whistle-blowers.... Crisis detection also refers to a system within the organization in which key personnel are immediately notified of a crisis. An organization has a considerable advantage if it knows about a crisis before its publics do, especially before the news media get the tip. This gives the organization time to draft a statement, make preparations for a news conference, notify the crisis team, and call in spokespersons. (pp. 11–12)

The ultimate purpose of detection is to anticipate, if possible prevent, but at least mitigate the risk or escalation to a crisis. "Mitigation tries to eliminate or reduce the risks. Some risks can be eliminated. For instance, an organization uses a hazardous chemical in its production process. The presence of hazardous chemical presents the risks of a hazardous chemical release. The risk of hazardous chemical can be eliminated if the organization can find a nonhazardous chemical to replace the hazardous one it uses. Most risks cannot be eliminated. For instance, workers can always make mistakes or become violent. Training and monitoring can be used to reduce the risks that cannot be eliminated" (Coombs, 2005, pp. 217–218).

The risk management process consists of specific steps to be managed by the organization's risk committee and implemented through nominated risk owners. This includes adoption of a common risk matrix, population of an integrated risk register, and development of mitigating action plans for each and every risk rated as critical. Even when not appointed crisis custodian (see previous), the communicator must take an early and active part in this process and follow it through to the crisis preparation phase alongside colleagues in other key corporate functions.

According to Coombs (2007):

Prevention involves seeking to reduce known risks that could lead to a crisis. Preparation involves creating the crisis management plan, selecting and training the crisis management team, and conducting exercises to test the crisis management plan and crisis management team. Both Barton (2001) and Coombs (2006) document that organizations are better able to detect and handle crises when they (1) have a crisis management plan that is updated at least annually, (2) have a designated crisis management team, (3) conduct exercises to test the plans and teams at least annually, and (4) pre-draft some crisis messages. The planning and preparation allow crisis teams to react faster and to make more effective decisions. (para. 5)

Across industry sectors, best practice organizations are busy designing sustainable crisis anticipation, prevention, mitigation, and recovery capabilities and building proactive crisis management cultures—in which the continuous drive to detect problems and identify issues early, encourage reporting, plan for different scenarios, and mitigate effects can unveil opportunities for improvements and enhance efficiency across the business.

Moving up the crisis management culture ladder from pathological to reactive to calculative to proactive and finally generative (see Figure 12.2), organizations must examine the external context more closely and listen to their stakeholders' perceptions and needs while staying on track with business goals. In crisis mitigation, the communicator is often best placed to link these efforts.

Within the context of this macro-model, the communicator's arsenal holds two tools to help advance the organization from the crisis detection phase to prevention and mitigation: stakeholder mapping and scenario planning.

Stakeholder Mapping

When one considers the complexities of some recent crises (Toyota, BP), it becomes apparent that the multitude and diversity of intertwined stakeholder pressures compounded these crises to previously unseen dimensions. There cannot be a clearer sign that stakeholder mapping must be high on the priority list of any well-trained crisis manager today. This is not an improvised task. It requires skills and a process.

Stakeholder mapping consists of identifying all audience groups (no matter how small or remote to the crisis situation) who have a stake in the crisis, categorizing them in at least three groups: allies, neutral, and opposition. Defining what their specific issues are about the crisis situation, whether they are likely to take any action, whether the organization has any influence on this stakeholder group (and if not, instead focus on the ones where there can be influence), what would

FIGURE 12.2 THE CRISIS MANAGEMENT CULTURE LADDER

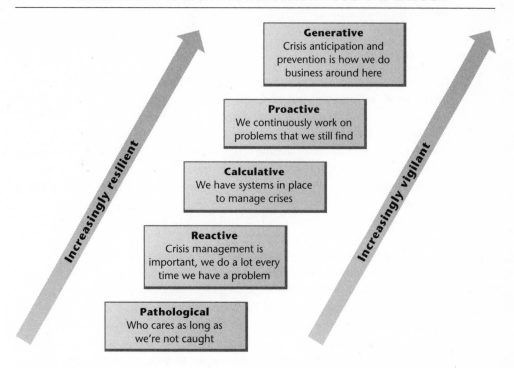

Source: Used with permission from CS&A International Risk & Crisis Management.

be the desired outcome, strategy, and key message. This process is an ongoing one during the crisis; it is not done only once and put aside. It must be reviewed, adjusted, and fine-tuned as the situation develops.

According to the research of Johnson, Scholes, and Whittington (2008): "Stakeholder mapping identifies stakeholder expectations and power and helps in understanding political priorities. There are different ways in which stakeholder mapping can be used to understanding of stakeholder influence. It underlines the importance of two issues: (1) how interested each stakeholder group is in impressing its expectations on the organisation's purposes and choice of strategies, (2) whether stakeholders have the power to do so" (p. 18).

The very nature of crises is that they are unpredictable; we do not know how long they will last, how they will twist and turn, and how they will end up. One thing is always almost for certain, though: they get worse before they get better. One of the well-known characteristics of crises is that however long they last, there are periods of intense activities with information overload within very short time spans, and other times of virtually no development and senseless waiting for endless hours.

Scenario Planning

Crisis teams can use stakeholder maps to develop scenarios, build strategies, think out of the box, and generate solution-focused approaches. Under day-to-day circumstances, scenario planning involves building at least three permutations on the current situation: worst case, status quo, and optimistic. In a crisis, considering time pressures, building different worst-case scenarios is most useful. Besides helping to develop strategies to address each scenario, scenario planning is also invaluable to keep spirits up during the crisis "downtimes" referred to previously.

According to the research of Hill and Jones (2009):

> Scenario planning involves formulating plans that are based on what-if scenarios about the future. In the typical scenario planning exercise, some scenarios are optimistic, and some are pessimistic. Teams of managers are asked to develop specific strategies to cope with each scenario. A set of indicators is chosen as signposts to track trends and identify the probability that any particular scenario is coming to pass. The idea is to get managers to understand the dynamic and complex nature of each environment, to think through problems in a strategic fashion, and to generate a range of strategic options that might be pursued under different circumstances.... The great virtue of the scenario approach to planning is that it can push managers to think outside the box, to anticipate what they might have to do in different situations, and to learn that the world is a complex and unpredictable place that places a premium on flexibility rather than on inflexible plans based on assumptions about the future that may turn out to be incorrect. As a result of scenario planning, organizations might pursue one dominant strategy related to the scenario that is judged to be most likely, but they make some investments that will pay off if other scenarios come to the fore. (pp. 26–27)

In a crisis, the problem cannot always be fixed or controlled quickly, as we have observed from the Toyota and BP cases, and crisis management efforts become more of a management of stakeholders, their conflicting agendas and perceptions. This has no right or wrong per se and is more a question of holding the fort and credibly addressing stakeholder issues. Stakeholder mapping and scenario planning are invaluable tools and skills for the prevention and mitigation of crises, mighty assets in the midst of crises.

Case in Point: Crisis Management at a Multinational Organization

Not all crises can be prevented, but many can be anticipated and mitigated.

This is the case of a multinational organization in which corporate communication, the legal and health, safety and environment departments, plant operations and senior executives and board members jointly and proactively prepared for a court hearing that, three years after the event, was to rule on the company's guilt in a plant explosion that killed several workers and injured a number of others.

The timing of this event was critical, as the organization in question was in the midst of a merger with another major multinational group. The court hearing date was set to take place two months before the company's final annual general meeting (AGM) set to vote on the merger.

While the company could in no way influence the court hearing, a strategic plan was essential to try and contain news coverage, mitigate potential escalation and its consequent negative impact on the AGM and related decision on the merger.

The team assembled early and developed a comprehensive, proactive crisis mitigation plan that consisted of the following elements:

- A detailed stakeholder map that was regularly reviewed, updated, and fine-tuned
- Detailed research of similar cases and their outcomes
- Development of several possible outcomes of the court hearing (including various permutations of a worst-case outcome)
- Articulation of strategies and action plans to cope with each scenario
- Position papers for each strategy and messages for each key stakeholder group; the organization in question was particularly careful not to lose sight of the human tragedy of the accident at the expense of commercial, legal, and business priorities
- Extensive media training and grilling for each scenario
- A contingency plan for worst-case outcome

The efforts paid off. Although the court handed down a partially guilty verdict and a considerable fine was imposed, media coverage was mostly contained to local and national news focusing primarily on the victims and their next of kin. When international news media organizations enquired, the company's response was wholesome and credible. Therefore the level and scope of inquiries did not escalate.

The spread of bad news resulting from this court hearing (whatever its outcome) could have catapulted the company into a repeated crisis, affected its share price and the vote on the merger. This case demonstrates that a deliberate and strategic approach to proactively map stakeholders, plan for worst-case scenarios, and prepare accordingly reflects the kind of crisis management culture that organizations need to be able to hold the course and ultimately do the right thing in the midst of chaos.

Conclusion

If we accept the hard reality that, despite having a proactive crisis management culture in place to anticipate, prevent, and mitigate them, crises will occur, much care must be placed on what it takes to manage them effectively.

Sound and tested processes and practiced competencies are essential, but less tangible yet equally critical are the human factors that can make or break a crisis. Research (Coombs & Holladays, 1996; Dean, 2004) shows that organizations appear to experience less reputational damage when their crisis responses include an expression of concern and/or responsibility.

The willingness and ability to own up to a problem and express concern and regret early on rests on the organization's very values and principles. Rarely are these tested more dramatically than in a crisis. They are often proudly displayed in corporate lobbies, yet in times of trouble, leaders sometimes forget their true essence and power and instead bow to legal or insurance pressures, to name a few, instead of using them as pillars to hold on to when the storm gets really rough.

Human factors, such as values and culture, in a crisis, which are less tangible, must not be underestimated but are far more difficult to harness. Quick response, ownership, and transparency are values that many organizations espouse and actively communicate. When these promises are broken, stakeholders are merciless.

Effective crisis management today is no longer just about fixing the problem, having the perfect crisis plan, the right processes, and the trained teams in the right places at the right time. It is about all those, but more than ever, it involves facing up to the complexities and threats of our globalized world. Crisis management is first and foremost about having a highly adaptive mindset and culture in place. A culture in which management and employees assess risks, monitor issues, map stakeholders, and plan scenarios to anticipate, detect smouldering problems early, and help prevent and mitigate escalation as part of day-to-day smart business conduct. The crises of 2009–2010 have shown that while traditional crisis communication principles still apply, organizations must shift their approaches to withstand the magnitude of impact they are likely to face in a crisis.

References

Barton, L. (1993). *Crisis in organizations.* Cincinnati, OH: South-Western.

Barton, L. (2001). *Crisis in organizations II* (2nd ed.). Cincinnati, OH: College Divisions South-Western.

Coombs, W. T. (2005). Crisis and crisis management. In R. L. Heath (Ed.), *Encyclopedia of public relations* (Vol. 1. pp. 217–221). Thousand Oaks, CA: Sage.

Coombs, W. T. (2006). *Code red in the boardroom: Crisis management as organizational DNA.* Westport, CN: Praeger.

Coombs, W. T. (2007). *Crisis management and communications.* Institute for Public Relations. Available at www.instituteforpr.org/essential_knowledge/searches/18ecf35d1cd01d29ea14fa659a93f13d.

Coombs, W. T., & Holladays, S. J. (1996). Communication and attributions in a crisis: An experimental study of crisis communication. *Journal of Public Relations Research, 8*(4), 279–295.

Crandall, W., Parnell, J. A., & Spillan, J. E. (2010). *Crisis management in the new strategy landscape.* Thousand Oaks, CA: Sage.

Dean, D. H. (2004). Consumer reaction to negative publicity: Effects of corporate reputation, response, and responsibility for a crisis event. *Journal of Business Communication, 41*(2), 192–211.

Fearn-Banks, K. (2007). *Crisis communication: A case approach.* Mahwah, NJ: Lawrence Erlbaum.

Friedman, T. L. (2010, June 11). This time is different. *The New York Times,* p. 10.

Gilpin, D. R., & Murphy, P. J. (2008). *Crisis management in a complex world.* New York: Oxford University Press.

Hill, C., & Jones, G. (2009). *Strategic management theory: An integrated approach.* Mason, OH: South-Western.

Institute of Crisis Management [ICM]. (2009). *2009 Annual ICM Crisis Report.* Available at www.crisisexperts.com.

Institute of Crisis Management [ICM]. (2010). *Crisis definitions.* Available at www.crisisexperts.com/crisisdef_main.htm.

Johnson, G., Scholes, K., & Whittington, R. (2008). *Exploring corporate strategy.* Harlow, UK: Financial Times Prentice Hall.

Kellaway, L. (2010, June 18). BP is the company we all love to hate. *The Financial Times.* Available at www.ft.com/cms/s/0/9c732c98-7b01-11df-8935-00144feabdc0.html?SID=google.

Sapriel, C. (2007). Taking the long view. *Communication World, 24*(5), 24–27.

CHAPTER THIRTEEN

THE ROLE OF COMMUNICATIONS IN COMPANY BUSINESS STRATEGY

Kellie Garrett

As a professional business communicator, you know how to craft communications strategy that produces measurable outcomes. You know how to shift stakeholder opinions. You incorporate internal and external audience analysis in your work and devise initiatives and tactics to realize communications strategy goals. In short, you know your craft.

So how would you rate your knowledge of your company's *business* strategy? What is the value proposition? What are the key metrics on the corporate scorecard? Does the work you are doing further the business strategy? Does it contribute to increased customer loyalty or enhance employee engagement? How will the operating environment affect your company? The communications function can and should play a critical role in the successful execution of business strategy. A few fortunate communicators can contribute to strategy formulation. Unfortunately, many communicators possess much less knowledge about what drives their companies' success than do the accountants and operations folks.

My career morphed from communications to marketing and then to business strategy. I served as an executive in all three roles. Along the way, I had three fundamental *aha*'s:

1. A communications background is an amazing strength when crafting business strategy, integrating diverse concepts, influencing change, and then communicating the strategy to internal and external audiences.

2. Communicators are usually relegated to communicating the business strategy once it is cooked. Communication tends to be an event rather than a continuous connection of everything a company does to plan and implement its business strategy.
3. Most communications professionals do not really understand what makes their companies tick.

Communicators look at the world differently than do many other business professionals. This is a strength, particularly related to strategy. However, our unusual vantage point makes us unique and at times misunderstood.

In this chapter, you will learn how you can increase your ability to add value to the strategy process as well as its communication. The chapter also presents ideas on how to enhance your knowledge of your company's business strategy, including its financial drivers.

Love (2002) says, "To add value, we need to look at how we can address business problems with communication solutions. . . . Communication is expected to get more involved in the development of business strategy, public policy and positioning" (pp. 16–27).

Communication plays an integral role in leadership, change management, employee engagement, customer loyalty, and stakeholder relations. Why? Leaders need to galvanize employee action in a way that is aligned with business strategy, and that takes frequent, consistent, and inspiring communication. A great strategy is nothing without effective execution, and it is employees who execute. Good change management hinges on dialogue and education through all stages: from awareness and acceptance of the change through to its implementation. Employees who understand what is expected of them, how they can succeed and feel that they are valued are more engaged and therefore more positive and productive. Customers need to feel that employees care about their needs, which means customers need to feel heard and see that actions occur as a result. Finally, stakeholders form opinions about companies based on communication—word of mouth, advertising, newspaper articles, the Web, interaction with a firm's employees—you get the picture.

It is impossible to effectively run a company and realize its long-term business strategy without stellar communications. A *Forbes* study of 163 chief executive officers (CEOs), senior strategists, and communications professionals revealed that "the importance of communications to the overall success of strategic initiatives was unilateral among respondents with CEOs (90 percent), strategists (86 percent) and corporate communicators (96 percent) agreeing that communications is critical, very critical or extremely critical to strategy development, execution and ultimate success." One CEO suggested, "There is no strategy without communications" (Forbes Insights, 2009).

However, without fully understanding your organization's vision, competitive advantage, value proposition, external market challenges, financial plan, measures and targets, and long- and short-term strategies, you will have limited ability to provide strategic counsel to your executives and create communications that support what your company is trying to accomplish.

How can you gain that kind of knowledge without getting an MBA? Here are some ideas for you.

Understand Business Strategy Fundamentals

There is no one definition of strategy. As Harvard Business School professor and strategy guru Gary Hamel says, the real problem with strategy is that while we can all recognize a great one when we see it, no one really knows where it comes from (Mintzberg, Ahlstrand, & Lampel, 2005).

Many companies around the world have adopted some form of Kaplan and Norton's (2001) famous "balanced scorecard," which calls for strategic objectives in four areas—customer loyalty, employee engagement, employee efficiency, and process excellence—all leading to profitability or, in a not-for-profit's case, realization of its mission. The rationale for including the four areas is that it is not enough to focus on profit or mission. You can have a great product but no customers, and fantastic employees but insufficient financial viability to sustain the organization. Norton says:

> To execute strategy is to execute change at all levels of an organization. . . . Our research into successful Balanced Scorecard organizations . . . identified five principles applied by every organization:
>
> • Mobilize Change through Executive Leadership—(executives) take the initiative for managing the change required to support the strategy.
> • Translate the Strategy to a Balanced Scorecard—create a Balanced Scorecard which translates the strategy to operational terms.
> • Align the Organization to the Strategy—use the Balanced Scorecard to link the goals of corporate, lines of business, and support units.
> • Make Strategy Everyone's Job—educate, empower, and incent those at all levels of the organization to execute the strategy.
> • Make Strategy a Continual Process—through the Balanced Scorecard, link the governance process (budgeting, reporting, planning, reviews) to the strategy. (Norton, 2002, pp. 1–2)

Private sector companies are market driven, that is, they must publicly report on their financial and business results at least quarterly. If publicly traded, stock prices are an ever-present factor in corporate decisions, not the least of which is resource allocation. Competition is a major consideration. Today's public sector organizations are much more aware of the need to produce results that are connected to constituents' needs and wants. Not-for-profit organizations need to demonstrate results in order to secure continued funding and support from government and the publics they serve.

Whether public or private, all organizations operate in an era of increasing transparency and accountability, which has major implications for communications. Is the organization proceeding toward its vision and realizing its targets? Is the business strategy clear to employees and external stakeholders? Are spending practices prudent and not wasteful? Communicators have a role in identifying and answering these questions.

Many organizations labor over creating the right business strategy. The amount of time invested in strategy execution is a different story. Ninety percent of well-formulated strategies fail due to poor execution (Kaplan & Norton, 2001). The challenge is implementation. Translating ideas into action means inspiring employees to pull in the same direction in a way that obtains results that forward the strategy.

"You're better off with a strategy that is 80% right and 100% implemented than one that is 100% right but doesn't drive consistent action throughout the company" (Gadiesh & Gilbert, 2001, p. 74). "The ability of frontline employees to execute a company's strategy without close central oversight is vital as the pace of technological change accelerates and as companies . . . become increasingly decentralized" (p. 79).

Communication is vital at every stage of strategy execution and, ideally, as strategy is being conceived.

Understand Finance Basics

If you do not have a background in finance (and most communicators do not), I urge you to take a course or read a layperson's guide to finance. Until you can read a balance sheet, you will not understand a major component of company performance. There are lots of ways to learn the basics without becoming a financial geek. If you are good at learning on your own, a book like *Finance for Dummies* is very helpful. If you prefer interactive learning, look for courses with names like "Finance for Nonfinancial Persons." Everyone in the class will be there for the same reason you are, to learn something new. Or contact a peer in finance and ask that person for advice or suggestions. Once you have read what the finance person recommends, go and ask him or her more about the concepts. You may be amazed at how he or she warms to the topic. Many people love to feel knowledgeable and share their expertise. There is nothing like a very willing and interested pupil—you!

Interview Your Strategy Office

Many communicators have written portions of the company's annual report. We get the financials from our accountant colleagues and make sure they are laid out correctly and proofed, but that is as far as most of us go. If you have taken in the previous point, you now can read the financial statements and notes and jot down questions about them. Often, we receive the balanced scorecard report from the strategy office and add it to the annual report layout. Take the time to absorb what the strategy is and the report against it, and write down any questions you have about that too.

Now that you are armed with questions about the business strategy and the financials, make an appointment with someone in the strategy office and tell that person that you are interested in learning more about the company business strategy so that you can communicate it as effectively as possible. The person on the other end of the phone may faint. Most folks do not darken the strategy office doors unless necessary. Once the shock has worn off, she will be happy to share everything she knows. Once you understand the strategy, you can start adding more value.

For example, even if you are not involved in strategy formulation, you play a key role by probing for clarity about the strategic intent of words in the business strategy. Hobbs (2008) tells a story about how "individual interpretations of 'large' varied dramatically [at a food processing company]. To some, it meant most profitable, and to others, it meant garnering the greatest revenues. Some thought it meant processing more food each year than any other firm, and others believed it meant having more physical locations than anyone else. The CEO thought it meant being the industry leader" (p. 48). Unless the communicator is certain about the interpretation, the communication will be skewed. The goal is to share the meaning of the strategy with the full workforce such that actions throughout the company are aligned.

Imagine how impossible a Hollywood Western movie's cattle drive would be if John Wayne had to personally tell each steer which way the herd was going to go. Instead, Big John makes sure the cowboys all know the plan, so they can steer the herd once they get it moving. While modern employees are considerably more intelligent that the average steer, the work force as a whole does share many herdlike traits. Therefore, all of the management "cowboys" must be aligned before getting the employees into motion. (Hobbs, 2008, p. 178)

Once you understand the full intent of the strategy, it is time to create communications that will bring it to life and incite momentum to realize the strategy. The Harvard Business School change management guru Kotter (2008) says, "Emotions influence action. . . . Martin Luther King Jr. did not reduce anger among blacks and contentment or anxiety among whites by announcing 'I have a strategic plan.' [King] pounded away at people's gut-level feelings with poetic rhetoric and passionate words about justice and morality. He hit hearts in a way that converted anger and anxiety into a commitment to move, do the right thing, and *now*" (p. 46). Kotter goes on to say that "mindless emotion is not the point. . . . The winning strategy combines analytically sound, ambitious, but logical goals with methods that help people experience new, often very ambitious goals, as exciting, meaningful and uplifting—creating a deeply felt determination to move, make it happen, and win, now" (p. 47).

If you can do anything resembling that, you have an amazing gift and you are in the right profession.

Learn About the Business

Most communicators are in the enviable position of attending a wide cross-section of meetings because we often have to write about them. Get yourself invited to even more. What is preoccupying your salespeople? What about marketing? What are the trends in customer complaints?

Take peers from other areas out for coffee and interview them. Surf the company intranet in areas you know nothing about. Go to optional webinars if they are available. Get on the list for reports about business metrics.

All of these ideas will contribute to a sound understanding of the business strategy, which will allow you to make more and more connections. This context will allow you to make better sense of how various initiatives are connected to each other, and in turn, create clarity for employees and stakeholders.

Tie Communications Work to Corporate Metrics and Business Strategies

Good communications professionals always connect the communications plan to the business strategy. But many focus on a particular aspect of that strategy rather than the big picture. We can also feel like we spend the majority of our time fighting fires or reactively working on internal and external news. So it is important to carve out time to be proactive.

As Woods (2004) says, "The first step is to identify the strategic corporate goals that can benefit from the successful planning and execution of communications initiatives. These goals may include: driving sales leads and revenue; increasing customer retention or loyalty; increasing employee satisfaction; building brand reputation" (pp. 15–16).

Once you have identified the company goals and metrics that require communications counsel and assistance, you will need to ensure that the majority of the team is focused on work that furthers the business strategy.

No matter how much you plan, you will still need to handle the work that pours in from various areas of the company. However, if you have done your homework and fully comprehend the complexities of the business strategy, you can apply that knowledge to everything you do. For example, if you are asked to write a piece about employee benefits, do you write about that or tie it to the big picture? For example, if the war for talent is a company's top enterprise risk, and there is a corporate strategy to create an effective recruitment and retention strategy, the benefits communiqué needs to be connected to the risk and the strategy. Another example: if you need to write a communiqué regarding the latest customer loyalty results, it should be connected to reputation and employee engagement.

Measure and Report on Management's Promise Record

Faith or trust in a leader's integrity influences employee engagement, customer loyalty, and ultimately, a company's profit. Watson Wyatt's *Human Capital Index* (2001) states, "Improving the trust and integrity associated with company leadership builds shareholder value by 2.3 percent" (p. 6), and, "When a company makes a significant improvement in creating a culture where employees at all levels can offer input to senior management, it is associated with a 0.7 percent increase in shareholder value" (p. 8).

Mastrangelo, Eddy, and Lorenzet (2004) echo this view: "Effective leaders engage in both professional leadership behaviors (e.g. setting a mission, creating a process for achieving goals, aligning processes and procedures) and personal leadership behaviors (e.g. building trust, caring for people, acting morally)" (p. 435). In a fast-paced corporate world, many leaders focus more on professional behaviors than personal ones. Communicators can help leaders to gain heightened trust with employees and external parties.

Before you recommend a communications strategy or write anything, find out what the executives, your annual report, and others have already said or promised—internally and externally. Companies are good at publicly reporting against the key aspects of their business strategy. However, there is generally less accountability to employees. Hundreds of promises are made to employees during the course of the year. Many are formal, such as communiqués sent to all staff or a particular division. Others are contained in e-mails or pledged in meetings: "I'll get this to you by Wednesday." Employees notice which colleagues and bosses keep their promises, as well as those who do not. Sometimes, the issue could easily be resolved by explaining the reason for not fulfilling the promise. In all cases, it is clear that not closing the loop is a source of irritation and a trust breaker.

Examine the actions taking place in your company and hold up a mirror to management. "Neither corporate leaders nor their communication advisers typically plan for nonverbal communication. That's a huge missed opportunity. . . . The impact of implicit, nonverbal communication and explicit, verbal communication (that is, the written norm) is never equal. The two are never even close to equal. One of them—the same one—will always trump the other" (Lee, 2008, p. 26). Consider tracking management's promise fulfillment record and reporting it to employees.

When I was a young person, I could be strident and judgmental, which meant that my observations often fell on deaf ears. As I matured, I learned that disconnects between actions and words (yes, even from management) were often unintentional. Eventually, I learned to present my opinions more constructively. So while you should examine any disconnects between actions and words within your organization, do not stop there. Look at your own track record. You just might find some room for improvement.

"There is an old Japanese proverb that says, 'The reputation of a thousand years may be determined by the conduct of one hour.' . . . Such is the fragile nature of integrity. We live in an uncertain world; don't let the sincerity of your word be uncertain. At the end of the day, all relationships—business or personal—are built on trust. If you make promises and don't deliver, how is that different than lying?" (Dao, 2004, p. 4).

MyComm (IABC, 2010) is a fabulous resource on www.iabc.com. There is a "say-do" matrix there that helps you measure any disconnects between messages and words.

Contribute to Business Strategy Formulation

Unfortunately, communications is a largely tactical role, primarily supporting and communicating organizational strategies (Kay, 1995). Try to get a seat at the management table when strategy is being created. If you are not in a senior role, sometimes you can get there if you ask to attend as an observer to increase your understanding so that you can better communicate the strategy.

Even if you are not part of the strategy discussion, you can "identify and interpret important communication issues at the strategy formulation stage" (Moss & Warnaby, 1998, p. 20). Find ways to ensure that communications has input whether or not you are at the table. You know the current business strategy. Put together a one-pager with ideas or questions that should be considered during the meetings. Your executive will think you are proactive and may even come back to you with some answers.

Ask Senior Executives What Bugs Them About Communicators and How You Can Better Meet Their Needs

Years ago, during a senior management retreat, each member of our senior management team shared how he or she felt our peers got in the way of high performance. Our chief financial officer (CFO) told me that he did not respect me because he felt that I did not consider return on investment and that my division was too large for its function. I silently fumed. A few weeks later, I interviewed him. He was happy to share the reasons for his comments and quite surprised that I wanted to delve into them. I then went back to my team and said that we had a major influencing campaign to conduct. We knew how to shift employee and stakeholder opinions, so we used the same principles to shift his. It took quite a while, but the CFO is now a very supportive colleague.

In most companies, we do not obtain such direct feedback. Consider proactively soliciting positive and negative feedback. What does your function do well? What is missing? You do not need to agree with the comments you receive. It is valuable feedback that you can use to shape how you interact with other areas of the company and communicate progress.

If You Must Ask for Resources (Human or Financial), Make a Business Case

Remember my story about the CFO? Although I do not believe I squandered corporate resources prior to his criticism, I certainly have been much more frugal since becoming aware of his perceptions. Every nod to a new idea consumes capacity. And how much capacity should be devoted to communications in an organization? There is no one right answer. Suffice it to say that the communications function is overhead, along with finance, human resources, information technology, and many other services. It is important to invest in communications, but not at the expense of the other services vying for resources, or the front line, which is customer facing. If you must ask for more resources, first satisfy yourself that it is truly necessary. What can you quit doing that is not adding value directly connected to the business strategy? What is a "nice to do"? If there really is not any excess capacity, put a business case together that shows the return on investment for the additional resources (monetary or additional personnel, which in essence is monetary) that is directly connected to corporate metrics. It will demonstrate to your boss and the executive that the corporate hat was squarely on your head when you made the decision to recommend additional investment in communications.

Communication guru Fraser Likely (2002) has these suggestions for thinking strategically: be attentive to signals within the organization and its external environment; look for connections among the past, present, and future of the organization as well as internal and external implications of those connections; become comfortable with cognitive dissonance; be open to multiple solutions to corporate challenges; become comfortable with the natural boundary-spanning qualities of organizational communication to connect people from numerous levels of the organizational hierarchy; counsel organizational leadership regarding potential outcomes of decisions and actions; and by all means keep the organization grounded in reality.

These are just some of the many ways you can enhance your role as a communicator in your company's strategy and performance. You need to explore what is right for you and your company. Whatever you do, believe that you can make a difference.

Communicators often complain that they are not at the executive table and that our profession is not sufficiently valued. Complaining exhibits a victim mentality. In my experience, if you have compelling ideas that are practical and will further the business strategy, you are already on the road to being valued. If you are also viewed as a team player who is trying to build upon what is already in place rather than just critiquing it, you will gain management's ear. Executives need great ideas that work. We care whether those ideas come from a credible source, that is, someone with a proven track record. Once you have a reputation for getting things done and making a difference, it does not matter whether you are a financial professional, a middle manager, or a communicator. If you are also known for focusing on implementing ideas more than just talking about them, you may even find yourself at that mahogany table.

References

Dao, F. (2004, November). Forget the free sodas—They don't motivate anyone. *Executive Action, 122,* 1–4.

Forbes Insights. (2009, June). *The powerful convergence of strategy, leadership and communications: Getting it right.* Available at www.forbes.com/forbesinsights/FDStrategy/index.html

Gadiesh, O., & Gilbert, J. L. (2001). Transforming corner-office strategy into frontline action. *Harvard Business Review, 79*(5), 72–79.

Hobbs, L. (2008). *Strategic DNA.* Chicago: B2 Books, Agate Publishing.

IABC. (2010). *MyComm.* Retrieved June 28, 2010, from www.iabc.com/mycomm1/popup/essentials.html#saydo

Kaplan, R., & Norton, D. (2001). *The strategy-focused organization.* Boston: Harvard Business School Press.

Kay, J. (1995). *The foundations of corporate success.* Oxford, UK: Oxford University Press.

Kotter, J. P. (2008). *A sense of urgency.* Boston: Harvard Business Press.

Lee, T. J. (2008). Actions speak loudly. *Communication World, 25*(4), 24–28.

Likely, F. (2002). What it takes to be a communication strategist? *Strategic Communication Management, 6*(3), 26–29.

Love, M. (2002). Communication 2002—the SCM roundtable. *Strategic Communication Management, 6*(1), 16–21.

Mastrangelo, A., Eddy, E. R., & Lorenzet, S. J. (2004). The importance of personal and professional leadership. *The Leadership & Organization Development Journal, 25*(5), 435–451.

Mintzberg, H., Ahlstrand, B., & Lampel, J. (2005). *Strategy bites back: It is far more, and less, than you ever imagined.* Upper Saddle River, NJ: Prentice Hall.

Moss, D., & Warnaby, G. (1998). Communications strategy? Strategy communication? Integrating different perspectives. *Journal of Marketing Communications, 4,* 131–140.

Norton, E. P. (2002, January-February). Managing strategy is managing change. *Balanced Scorecard Report, 4*(1), 1–5.

Watson Wyatt. (2001). *Human capital index.* Washington, DC: Watson Wyatt.

Woods, J. A. (2004). Communication ROI. *Communication World, 21*(1), 14–18.

CHAPTER FOURTEEN

THE IMPACT OF TECHNOLOGY ON CORPORATE COMMUNICATION

Shel Holtz

Since the 1960s, computer and network technology have had a great impact on organizational technology—altering everything from the skills communicators need to convey messages and engage audiences to stakeholders' ability to organize and influence company behaviors.

Since the early 1990s, we have witnessed the introduction of e-mail to the business world, followed by the World Wide Web and social media. In two decades, we have gone from a print-centric communications environment to one in which the death of print has been widely predicted. We have seen the Internet's impact on communications evolve from an afterthought to the primary channel through which people get their information. The ability to access content online has transitioned from a privilege available only to a few to ubiquity, with an increasing amount of access occurring through mobile phones.

So much change has put unprecedented pressure on communicators to adapt to a communications environment that would have looked like science fiction just a few years ago.

This chapter covers the following dimensions of technology's impact on communications:

- The conditions that led to the rise of online communication
- The key tools communicators need to know
- The shift in communication behaviors

The Perfect Storm

Technology has always driven the way organizations communicate. The introduction of the printing press introduced the notion of mass media, which forever changed communication from the face-to-face, oral tradition that had characterized it for centuries before.

The introduction of video as a technology available to communicators altered the way we communicate externally (look at video news releases) and internally (with video used to explain employee benefits, expand the audience of town hall meetings, and summarize company news). Because of computer technology, the past two decades have seen video transform from a process that involved hundreds of thousands of dollars' worth of equipment manipulated by a professional editor to something that can be shot with a mobile phone and edited on a computer by anybody using free software—or right on the mobile phone.

Desktop publishing removed the paste-up stage from the print production process. Fewer and fewer communicators today—among those working with print—recall what it was like to produce galleys of text that had to be waxed and carefully pressed onto a board that was then photographed so it could be turned into a negative that was used as the basis of a metal printing plate. Desktop publishing, introduced in the mid-1980s, opened a number of doors for communicators who could now produce content more frequently at less cost.

The Web introduced the next phase of communications technology, and again we saw the inevitable transition from content creation by specialists to something anyone could do. In each case—desktop publishing, video, and the Web—content proliferated as the people who formerly could only *consume* content became producers.

But not all consumer-generated content rose to the standards of professional communication. With desktop publishing, it was not unusual to see newsletters boasting fourteen fonts in eight columns on a single sheet of paper. The publishers of these travesties believed desktop publishing put the power to communicate in their hands, obviating the need to work with a professional communicator.

Communications challenges resulted. So many newsletters were distributed around some organizations that information overload became an issue. Several newsletters conveyed conflicting information. Many were difficult to read. Many more were poorly written. Ultimately, communications departments were tasked with getting their arms around the problem. Policies were crafted to do departmental journalism, bringing the organizational communications process back under one roof.

It was the last time organizations were able to control communication.

The Web introduced a variety of tools that enabled anyone to become a publisher. Those newsletters could now be published as websites thanks to tools like Microsoft FrontPage and Macromedia Dreamweaver that, like desktop publishing, let anybody create a website. Blogging software and sites like Blogger.com and WordPress.com made it even easier. Those videos anybody could shoot and edit could now be shared on YouTube and other video-sharing sites.

Not only could employees publish, so could customers, consumers, activists, critics, and just about anyone else who formerly fit neatly into the category of *audience*. This capability has forever altered the practice of communication as the entire dynamic between organizations and their stakeholders has undergone a fundamental shift.

A number of factors have driven this transition, reaching critical mass at the same time.

Trust

Public trust in institutions has been declining steadily, chronicled by studies such as the annual Edelman Trust Barometer. The spectacular failures of companies such as Enron, along with more general circumstances like a long-running economic recession, have taken their toll on the trust people place in traditional institutions.

Consequently, people place little credence in the pronouncements of senior executives and official corporate spokespersons, finding third-party sources and frontline employees more believable. Consumers have also lost any confidence they had in advertising, with some studies reporting that as many as 94 percent of consumers do not trust ads (Weber, 2007).

Consumer Frustration

The decline of trust in organizations has been coupled by a concurrent rise in frustration in dealing with companies. There are several catalysts for a consumer desire to redefine the relationship between organizations and their constituencies, such as the growing remoteness (or detachment) of the customer from the people in large organizations who can help solve their problems or address their issues.

The pre-social relationships among consumers and companies may seem to be the long-standing natural order, but it is actually rather new in the scope of human history. We began movement toward the current relationship with the beginning of the Industrial Revolution. Consider how people did business before the Industrial Revolution. Put yourself in the role of a consumer in, say, the 1500s who needs a pair of shoes. First, you visit the marketplace and talk to others you trust about which cobbler offers the best service, price, and quality. Once you know the cobbler you want to use, you visit his shop. He explains what kinds of shoes he makes and you respond with the features you want in your shoes. He takes measurements of your feet, then makes your shoes for you. If the sole separates from the rest of the shoe, you can return it to the cobbler who made it to have it fixed.

Now consider the shoe-buying experience today. You visit a store that most likely offers shoes from dozens of manufacturers. The styles, sizes, and colors were determined long before you entered the store. Not only do you have no direct contact with the shoemaker, it is unlikely you will ever interact with anybody at the manufacturer. Your contact is with the store salesperson. The salesperson has some knowledge of the shoes the store carries, but no power or ability to customize the shoes to meet your individual needs.

Even when customers deal directly with the company that made the product they bought, their connection is with a customer service representative, usually a call center employee who responds to queries from a database of canned answers. Technical support works the same way. Unless you have been invited to participate in a survey or focus group, you have virtually no influence. You are several steps removed from the people in the organization you really want to talk to: the people who design and make the products.

Rather than engage customers in a conversation, organizations have found newer and more intrusive ways to deliver one-way, top-down messages to their audiences. Marketing has become the pervasive communications model, even for nonconsumer audiences such as investors and employees; most communication is delivered from the organization to the audience with no feedback loop (or one that is so formal and constrained, like focus groups and town hall meetings, that it does little to satisfy the customer's desire for engagement).

As this isolation from the organization continues to grow and the ability to engage the company and its leaders diminishes, customers are becoming increasingly fed up. Any organization that can find a way to treat customers as partners and engage them in a conversation that involves as much listening as talking is likely to build the kind of loyalty that has been deteriorating over the past several decades.

The Crumbling of Barriers

The barriers that initially kept the average person from creating content on the Web have evaporated over the past ten years.

The technical requirements for content development initially included knowledge of HTML, the code used to create web content, and the ability to use FTP, the protocol that transfers content from a computer to a server. Additional technologies were added to the mix over the years, including scripting languages like PERL, tools that enabled multimedia like Java and Flash, and code that added functionality to the Web like Javascript.

In addition, there were large costs involved in publishing to the Web. If you did not know the technology, you needed to hire someone with the expertise to develop your Web presence. Then there was the cost of servers, high-speed connections to the Net, domain names were far more than $4.95 from GoDaddy, and other assorted costs made a website prohibitive for anybody but organizations with deep pockets and the most dedicated enthusiasts.

The world has changed considerably since then. Easy-to-use tools ranging from hosted blogging utilities to social networks like Facebook and file-sharing sites like Flickr and SlideShare are free (with low-cost premium services) and enable anybody to publish content to the Web.

In addition to other effects, this has led to the end of the era of the destination website. Typical organizational websites once dominated the Web. Increasingly, they represent just one category of Web content, along with content-sharing sites, collaborative sites (like wikis), social networks, blogs, status update sites (like Twitter), and others. By some estimates, by 2011 user-created content will occupy more of the Web than any other kind of content (MacManus, 2010).

Word of Mouth

Word of mouth has always been a powerful channel, but its influence has been amplified by the rise of social media. Since people trust other people more than they trust representatives of institutions, it makes sense that they would turn to one another for recommendations and information. Because it has become so much easier to find others who share common interests, word of mouth has become even more important, with marketers working to develop campaigns that drive word of mouth.

Studies conflict over whether online or offline word of mouth is more important, but even if people share their experiences and observations more offline than on, social media remains critically important because of its ability for word of mouth to jump clusters.

In the real world, word of mouth tends to remain confined within a cluster. For example, let us say a professional communicator reads a great book on a topic related to communications but also relevant in other fields, such as human resources and organizational development. At professional association meetings, the communicator tells her peers about the book, and they in turn tell *their* peers. At some point, everyone in that circle has heard about the book, and the word of mouth dies out.

Online, when the same communicator shares the information in an online communications community, it is safe to assume that some members of that community are also members of other communities. Once they have heard of the book, they are likely to share that information with their other communities, which could include human resources or readers of business books, to name just a few.

According to Emanuel Rosen (2000), it was a carefully orchestrated online campaign that generated the word of mouth that propelled the book *Cold Mountain* to the bestseller lists. The book had several strikes against it: it was a work of literature, it was about the Civil War, and it was published by a small independent publisher. By producing online buzz, word of mouth initiating in a cluster of people who like literature jumped into the cluster of Civil War buffs and fans of indie publishers, among others.

Online word of mouth can do more than help sell products. It can drive traffic to a website, raise awareness of a cause, and influence public opinion about an issue.

Access

When the Internet evolved from an academic tool to a consumer resource, the only way individuals could access the network from home was by dialing in over a telephone line. Retrieving e-mail, visiting Web pages and performing other online tasks were time-consuming activities. This low-speed connection inhibited optimal use of the resource. Even more noteworthy is the fact that users were online only when they needed to be online; when they were finished doing whatever it was they dialed in to do, they disconnected.

The introduction of broadband connectivity has altered the way people use the Internet. Initially broadband connectivity was expensive and complex, but plummeting prices and simple setups have led to rapid adoption. Wireless technology has untethered computers from cables and the development of mobile smartphones has led to increased access without computers. One study concludes that mobile access to the Internet will outpace computer access by 2014 (Meeker, cited in Ingram, 2010).

Consequences

These converging factors have resulted in a wide array of disruptive changes to work and society.

The Shift to Digital

While traditional media will continue to offer value to communicators, there is an indisputable shift away from these tools to digital resources. Newspaper and magazine subscription rates are plummeting, and publications are going out of business. For the 2009 holiday season, Amazon.com reported for the first time that the sale of digital books for its Kindle reader outsold hardcover books.

Advertising and marketing is shifting to digital as well. The Pepsi soft drink brand gained considerable attention when it announced it would not buy television advertising in the 2009 Super Bowl, opting instead to allocate those dollars to online venues. Companies are investing vast sums into online advertising, from banner ads to pay-per-click models like that offered by Google.

This transition to digital advertising, marketing, and public relations makes sense considering the number of people whose attention is being drawn by online media. Among younger demographics, it is as likely that a television show will be viewed online through a channel like Hulu.com as on cable or satellite TV. Devices like smartphones and tablets are primarily media consumption devices (unlike computers, which are also content creation tools).

Steve Rubel (2008), a senior vice president with Edelman Digital, has projected the demise of all "tangible media." "By January 2014 I will wager that in the US almost all forms of tangible media will either be in sharp decline or completely extinct. I am not just talking about print, but all *tangible forms* of media—newspapers, magazines, books, DVDs, boxed software and video games" (para. 1). Rubel's projection may be extreme, but his point is inescapable: "We're moving fast toward becoming a society that consumes media entirely in digital format" (para. 4).

The Nature of Work

These pervasive connections have significant repercussions on work and society. People can be connected twenty-four hours a day, seven days a week. They can access e-mail and other work-related resources from anywhere, on a wide range of devices from laptops to iPads, effectively ending the notion of *work-life balance*. Members of the millennial generation have grown up with such connectivity and do not see the need for such distinctions. Work, they believe, is just a part of life; they can work anywhere, any time, and do not understand why they should confine their work to a scheduled block of time in an office.

Today the workday extends beyond the traditional nine-to-five hours and the workplace extends past the traditional office walls to any location that is Internet accessible—the kitchen, the airport lounge, or the beach. Knowledge workers increasingly expect to be able to collaborate internally as well as externally. A study (Bulmer & DiMauro, 2010) conducted by SAP and the Society for New Communications Research found that decision makers with access to their social media peer groups made better and faster decisions on behalf of their organizations. Frontline workers bring value to the organization through their broader social networks as well, getting answers to questions they cannot find inside the organization.

Employees also increasingly look to their organizations to provide the means to network internally the same way they do externally, through social networks and microblogging tools.

The Ability to Organize Without Organizations

The Internet has provided individuals with the ability to organize quickly around any issue without the assistance of an organizing entity. This characteristic is one that is often overlooked by businesses, but it is one of the most powerful dimensions of the online phenomenon.

Consider activism in the pre-networked world. An organization would expend considerable resources finding and organizing like-minded people to take action on an issue. Social media has not only strengthened the ability of these organizations to mobilize supporters; people who share a common interest no longer need such organizations at all.

In 2009, an American living in the United Kingdom undertook an effort to raise money for a charitable organization that brought drinkable water into developing communities where water was scarce. She quickly created a website that explained the concept. Organizers in local communities would arrange "tweetups," in-person gatherings of people who communicate with each other on the microblogging service Twitter. The organizers would charge a small admission fee for this event, which would be held on the same day in communities around the world, and forward the funds to a central location where they would be tallied and then donated. Since the original Twestival, additional events have been held, raising more than $1.2 million within 14 months for 137 nonprofits, according to the Twestival site, which adds, "All local events are organized 100% by volunteers and 100% of all ticket sales and donations go direct to projects" (2010, para. 1).

Individuals use the same techniques for professional development. Gatherings with names like Casecamp and unconferences routinely draw hundreds of people to learn from one another, without the need for a professional association or academic institution to provide a location or identify speakers.

These are hardly the only examples of organizing without organizations. Activists have used social channels to drive change, as in the case of Nestlé. YouTube's removal of a Greenpeace video at Nestlé's request sparked the action. The video pointed to Nestlé's use of rainforest-sourced palm oil in its KitKat product as a contributing factor in the eradication of the orangutan's habitat. As word spread (by word of mouth), individuals of their own volition posted outraged comments to Nestlé's Facebook page. The volume of commentary on the Facebook page attracted mainstream media attention, which led to even more commentary posted to the Nestlé Facebook wall. Ultimately, the actions of individuals who shared the same environmental sensibilities led Nestlé to announce it was changing its policy and would obtain palm oil elsewhere—at higher costs to the organization.

The speed with which word of mouth can spread online enables individuals to take action in ad hoc groups, both in support of organizational actions as well as in opposition. Organizations can take advantage of this organizing ability; they also need to recognize its power and be ready to address it. Nonprofits whose primary mission is raising money need to recognize that individuals may opt to make their contributions through social channels like Twestival rather than through organizations that contribute only a portion of the funds they raise because they keep some of it to cover the costs of traditional organizing.

Access to Information

Organizations are routinely surprised by the volume of information available online to those who are willing to spend the time looking for it. Asked once about the availability of material that could be sensitive, confidential, or damaging, Google CEO Eric Schmidt replied that everything indexed by the Google search engine was publicly available. To test his assertion, a News.com reporter used Google to assemble a dossier on Schmidt and write a story that included his net worth, political contributions, and home town. (Schmidt was so incensed that he ordered a year-long boycott of access by C|Net, which owns News.com.)

Computer equipment manufacturer Belkin is another company that was surprised by the availability of information online. A graduate student discovered simply by using available online information that the company was offering to pay people to write positive reviews of its products and to dispute negative reviews. When the story blew up, Belkin insisted it was the action of a single individual and was not reflective of the company's culture. In online communities, several former Belkin employees rejected the assertion, claiming that in their experience, the behavior was typical of the company.

The easy access to information that was easily kept hidden in the pre-Internet world is another compelling reason for organizations to adopt a culture of transparency in which communicators will play an active role.

Information in Real Time

Communicators once scheduled their efforts around news cycles. These cycles were based on the routine distribution of news and information by mainstream media: the morning and evening editions of newspapers, the 6 and 11 p.m. local newscasts, the 7 p.m. network newscasts.

Today, there are no news cycles. News now spreads via real-time Web services like Twitter's and Facebook's status update features.

The impact of the real-time nature of news is no better exemplified than by the remarkable landing of US Airways flight 1549 in New York's Hudson River on January 15, 2009. Janis Krum, a passenger on a commuter ferry that joined in the rescue effort, took a picture with his smartphone of the crew and passengers standing on the plane's wing and life rafts, then uploaded the photo to Twitter, where his followers immediately retweeted it (that is, they forwarded it to *their* Twitter followers). The photo was accompanied by Krum's brief tweet: "There's a plane in the Hudson. I'm on the ferry going to pick up the people. Crazy."

As a result, the world knew of the incident before the mainstream media did, and before US Airways officials could begin the process of managing communications around the event.

The growing importance of real-time content on the Web has resulted in the launch of several search engines dedicated to real-time content. Unlike Google, which can take weeks to index the content on static Web pages, services like Collecta can provide links to content as recent as a few seconds ago from sources ranging from Twitter and blogs to mainstream news organizations like Associated Press.

Google, recognizing its importance and unwilling to cede the business to newcomers like Collecta, has begun adding real-time content to its search engine results pages (SERPs).

For communicators, this means there is less time to react. The communicator in the digital era will be prepared to respond quickly without waiting for reviews and approvals; these should be obtained proactively rather than reactively, with legal and other departments who traditionally review content before it is released working with the communications team to ensure they are prepared to communicate in a heartbeat without putting the organization at any risk.

The Return to the Marketplace

All of the consequences of the encroachment of digital technology on business means that organizations are returning to the pre–Industrial Revolution marketplace, where customers have direct access to the organization and to one another. As a result, communicators need to incorporate a new set of skills.

New Skills for Communicators

The communicator in the digital era needs to be conversant in a number of skills, including the following:

RSS. When most people talk about RSS (really simple syndication) today, they suggest that the notion of a news reader, an aggregator that collects news and updates from news sources, never really gained widespread adoption and is now a fading technology. They fail to understand that news readers or aggregators represented only one way to consume RSS feeds. In fact, RSS is the infrastructure for the delivery of news and information throughout the Web. As a result, while the average consumer can ignore it, communicators must be familiar with RSS and how it works.

At its core, really simple syndication allows publishers to make their content subscribable. RSS is built into many content management systems that automatically produce and publish the feeds, but that does guarantee that organizational content is always made available by RSS, which ensures that it can be incorporated into a variety of external news sources and websites that rely on RSS to publish current information.

RSS is based on the XML scripting language. Communicators are not obligated to learn how to code RSS, but they must be as conversant in it as they traditionally have been in the technical aspects of printing.

Search Engine Optimization. Good content is meaningless if audiences cannot find it.

Communication processes of the past involved the push of content through a limited number of channels. As one advertising executive noted, a 30-second spot on the nightly newscasts of the three major television networks guaranteed that 80 percent of the target audience would see it. Today, much of the content people see is uncovered during online searches. It is therefore a requirement that communicators know how to optimize their content to be more likely to appear high in SERPs.

Search engine optimization (SEO) has been a skill practiced only by specialists, but increasingly writers of Web content are learning the basics, if not the intricacies, of SEO in order to produce content that is both compelling and discoverable.

Content Curation. Traditional communications was contained in packages such as newspapers, magazines, and newscasts. The publication or news show staff produced the content. With the introduction of hyperlinks, communicators are becoming more than producers of content. They are also curators of content produced by others.

At its core, *curation* means that communicators identify credible, relevant, and useful content elsewhere on the Web and link to it and use it to enhance their communications efforts. Curation is already gaining traction in the journalism world, with publications ranging from the *Washington Post* to the *Huffington Post* providing links to outside content related to their own coverage and sometimes incorporating those links into reporting resources like maps and timelines.

For communicators, it will become a routine practice to vet and link to content produced by others, both internal and external.

Monitoring

All communicators will need to be skilled at monitoring what stakeholders are saying about the company, brands, and issues and analyzing those conversations in order to determine how (or whether) to respond to them.

PepsiCo brand Gatorade recently established a social media mission control operation, a glass booth in the middle of its marketing operation in which a five-member team monitors multiple screens that display in real time various social conversations and metrics related to the brand. By maintaining so close a watch on the conversation, they can respond quickly to what people are saying. For example, when buzz emerged around a song played in the background of a video, the team was able to post a YouTube video of the song, which generated additional word of mouth and further spread the Gatorade brand through the social media space.

Video

Video, once an expensive proposition used only under specific circumstances, has become an "essential, competitive differentiator that drives SEO and

TABLE 14.1 A COMPARISON OF COMMUNICATION STYLES

Traditional	Early Twenty-First Century
• Transmit a message one-way, top down	• Engage and participate in conversations
• Preach the company's message	• Advocate for the company's point of view
• Exercise command and control	• Influence and persuade stakeholders
• Use formal and instructive text	• Use informal and conversational material
• Tell your audience	• Build community
• Focus on institutions, such as the press	• Focus on people and relationships
• Manage deadlines	• Function in real time
• Honor the power of the media	• Recognize the power of networks
• Focus on target audiences	• Focus on communities

increases brand identification," according to the blog SearchEngineLand (2010, para. 1).

Thanks largely to YouTube, anyone can produce videos with devices ranging from inexpensive cameras that connect via USB directly to a computer to a smartphone that allows the uploading of video directly from the device.

Communicators will need to be as comfortable shooting and editing video as they are at producing text.

Communication Styles

In the highly socialized world of modern communications, traditional communication styles must give way to styles that are more effective. These styles are contrasted in Table 14.1.

Integration

Listening to many of those writing and speaking about the new communication landscape, one might conclude that all communication is social and older methods of communication are relics of a bygone era.

Nothing could be further from the truth. Throughout history, new media has never completely killed old media. Rather, old media adapts to the realities of the new landscape, often (but not always) shrinking as they continue to exist based on their strengths. For example, radio did not die when television became popular. However, much of the programming that filled the radio airwaves was abdicated to television: soap operas, variety shows, dramas, and comedies. Radio thrived, though, by presenting content best suited to audio: music and talk.

Smart communicators will seek to integrate new and old media. The best recent example comes from a traditional advertiser: Old Spice. The men's grooming product advertising was awarded to innovative agency Weiden & Kennedy, which introduced the Old Spice man, portrayed by actor and former football player Isaiah Mustafa. The popular television commercial—a medium many have written off—led to an innovative social campaign in which people tweeted questions to the Old Spice man, who replied to many of them with short YouTube videos.

Ultimately, communicators will succeed if they approach the online space as strategically as they have treated traditional communication, focusing first on goals and last on tactics. (See Chapter Nine for details, and apply those principles to your use of digital and social technologies.)

The Speed of Change

Nobody saw Twitter coming. Introduced only in 2007, it is now one of the most influential channels for communication.

The lesson is clear: Do not get hung up on tools or the latest shiny new object. You have no way of knowing what somebody is cooking up in a startup or garage that will become the next highly influential communication channel.

Still, it would be foolish to ignore important trends or remain ignorant of what may well become vitally important communication tools. It is incumbent upon communicators to stay as current as possible on the emerging technologies that will shape their efforts in the future.

References

Bulmer, D., & DiMauro, V. (2010). *The new symbiosis of professional networks: Social media's impact on business and decision-making.* Available at http://sncr.org/wp-content/uploads/2010/02/NewSymbiosisReportExecSumm.pdf

Ingram, M. (2010, April 12). *Mary Meeker: Mobile Internet will soon overtake fixed Internet.* Retrieved August 17, 2010, from http://gigaom.com/2010/04/12/mary-meeker-mobile-internet-will-soon-overtake-fixed-internet/

MacManus, R. (2010, May 31). *The coming data explosion.* Retrieved August 16, 2010, from www.readwriteweb.com/archives/the_coming_data_explosion.php

Rosen, E. (2000). *The anatomy of buzz*. New York: Doubleday.

Rubel, S. (2008, November 14). *The end of tangible media is clearly in sight*. Available at www.micropersuasion.com/2008/11/the-coming-end.html

Searchengineland.com. (2010, August 3). *Video is now a must-have feature for competitive SEO*. Available at http://searchengineland.com/ video-is-now-a-must-have-feature-for-competitive-seo-4768

Twestival.com. (2010). *What is Twestival?* Retrieved August 16, 2010, from http:// twestival.com/about-twestival-global-2010/

Weber, L. (2007). *Marketing to the social web: How digital customer communities build your business*. Hoboken, NJ: Wiley.

PART THREE

INTERNAL COMMUNICATION

CHAPTER FIFTEEN

INTERNAL COMMUNICATION

Brad Whitworth

Organizations—whether they are community hospitals, nonprofit associations, or multinational oil companies—exist for one reason: people can accomplish more when we work together as teams than we can as individuals. To create a truly effective team, each member of that team must understand the organization's vision, goals, and objectives and then move in that direction. That is relatively easy for small organizations to accomplish.

When an organization grows in size or complexity or spreads across international borders and time zones, it needs a formal internal communications program to help keep its team in sync. Think of it this way: with a little practice, a pianist and a violinist can create magic as a two-person team. But a 107-person symphony orchestra needs a director to be able to reach its musical goals.

This chapter provides an overview of internal communications as an essential element of successful organizations.

Building Blocks of Internal Communication

There are three fundamental building blocks to any internal communications program: *hierarchical communication*, in which chief executive officers (CEOs), vice presidents, directors, managers, and frontline supervisors play key roles in the communications process; *mass media communication*, in which newsletters, e-mail,

FIGURE 15.1 BUILDING BLOCKS OF AN INTERNAL COMMUNICATIONS PROGRAM

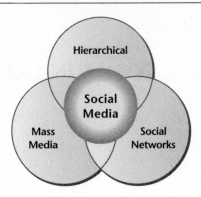

videos, blogs, and other vehicles reach broad employee audiences; and, often overlooked, the *social networks* of invisible communicators who organically spread the word.

Layered on top of these three elements are the comparatively new *social media* tools—such as LinkedIn, Facebook, Twitter, Delicious, YouTube, Plaxo— that are migrating from the real world into the corporate environment (see Figure 15.1).

Hierarchical: Starting at the Top

The simplest internal communications programs historically relied on an organization's existing hierarchical structure to move information to employees. Patterned after military command-and-control structures, such programs started with top-down messages driven from the highest levels of the firm, typically the chairman, president, or CEO. Successive layers of executives, managers, and supervisors were expected to push or cascade the messages down until they reached every employee. The more levels of management and geographical sites there were, the more difficult it was to ensure timely and consistent delivery of information. This cascading practice still exists and can work effectively for some organizations, particularly smaller and simpler ones. However, far too many companies rely on managers as their only means of communicating with their workforces. A big drawback to this cascading form of internal communications is that some managers do a far better job of communicating with their teams than do others.

Over the years, many organizations have been removing extra management layers and flattening their hierarchical structures, largely as cost-cutting moves so as to be more competitive. An unintended benefit has been improved internal communication. However, instant messaging, e-mails, texting, and *word of mouse* routinely move messages faster than any hierarchy can.

The Manager's Communication Role. Studies have consistently shown that most employees expect their immediate managers to share important company information and put it in context. Larkin and Larkin (1994) describe five decades of research that proves the importance of communicating change through frontline supervisors. The research shows that immediate supervisors are employees' preferred source of information and have more credibility with employees than do senior executives.

Yet organizations generally have done a poor job of telling supervisors about their communications responsibilities, training them to communicate effectively, measuring how well they communicate, and rewarding the ones who do it well. Some managers are natural communicators; others require more coaching and training. It is not an easy thing for many managers to do, particularly those who have been promoted for their technical expertise rather than their interpersonal and leadership skills. Communication professionals can help by providing messages, structure, training, and coaching for supervisors and managers to help build their communications prowess and effectiveness.

Supervisors must make sure that information moves smoothly and quickly to their direct reports and ultimately to every frontline employee. But managers must do far more than *tell* today. They also own the responsibility of putting information into context for their employees. They need to help interpret top-down messages and engage employees in dialogue about the relevance of the information. They need to ask all members of their teams the right questions to make sure they know what is happening.

It does not stop there. Supervisors are responsible for moving the information that they glean—good and bad—from the front line back up to top executives. An organization's seniormost managers must know what is happening throughout the organization, particularly in areas where frontline people work with customers.

The real goal of creating this two-way exchange is not merely to tell employees what their executives want them to do or inform executives what customers are saying. The ultimate prize is to engage all employees, improve their abilities to make informed decisions, and turn them into active advocates for the organization.

Managers and supervisors should continually engage in a two-way dialogue that moves the organization closer to fulfilling its goals. It is just as important for managers and supervisors to know how to listen as it is to talk.

Managers must be skilled in all forms of interpersonal communications, starting with one-on-one conversations. The immediate supervisor is the only one who can explain changes in job assignments, set individual goals, recognize on-the-job performance, and deliver appropriate individual rewards. The immediate manager is also in the best position to hold one-to-many discussions with her team about the group's role, create aspirational goals, highlight performance, and reward the team's accomplishments.

A supervisor's one-to-one and one-to-many conversations are best done face to face. But as organizations grow and spread, employees often find themselves reporting to remote managers. That means that managers must be comfortable with electronic substitutes for face-to-face communications, whether conference phone calls, web conferences, or telepresence sessions.

There is abundant research to show that there are times when the immediate supervisor is *not* the best person to lead the communications effort. Measurement guru Angela Sinickas (2005) has two decades of data proving that supervisors are not an employees' preferred information source on most company subjects. She suggests that informal focus groups or a custom-tailored survey can uncover which subjects workforce and management believe deserve the most communication content. The next step is to identify the preferred sources of information for each subject.

For example, the chief financial officer—and not the immediate supervisor—may be seen as the most credible person to describe corporate financial results, and a human resource manager would likely be the preferred source for information about a complex benefits change.

The Third Dimension. Diverse organizations must also find effective ways to move information across their business units, breaking down the structural silos that they unknowingly build around departments. For example, a nurse in a hospital's neonatal unit needs to know a lot about his own department's goals and processes. He may not need to know equivalent details about the hospital's intensive care unit, but he should know *something* about what is going on there.

It is a natural desire of executives and communicators to have every employee know everything that is going on everywhere within an organization. Although this is certainly an admirable goal, it is also an unrealistic one in a large or complex organization. We cannot expect every employee either to know everything that is taking place or, more important, to *want* to know everything. Everybody needs to know something, but nobody needs to know everything.

Senior Leaders as Communicators. It takes more than middle managers and frontline supervisors to create an effective communications environment for an organization. It also requires senior leaders who take communications seriously and are model communicators themselves. Employees expect senior executives to share their vision for the organization and their ideas and perspectives with the entire team. Employees deserve to know that their contributions are valued by senior leaders. They expect open, honest, credible communication. They expect leaders who are visible, approachable, and conversational. They want leaders who can tell compelling stories.

Effective executive communication is not merely a CEO's monthly column or an occasional e-mail message to all staff. It also includes a mix of regular staff meetings, video blogs, all-employee gatherings, instant messaging, informal meetings, brown bag lunches, and many other communication opportunities. It means that the top executives practice MBWA (management by wandering around) to engage employees firsthand in two-way discussions. It is listening to employees' concerns and sharing observations. It is talking about work-related topics and getting to know employees as individuals. It is asking about an employee's sick child as well as discussing a competitor's latest product innovation.

MBWA should not be limited to the organization's chairman or CEO, though it needs to start at the top. All members of the senior leadership team must be active participants in creating an effective communications environment. Senior leaders cannot afford to hide in meetings or wait in their offices for issues to show up on their doorsteps. They must be out and about—in sales offices and break rooms and on the factory floor—actively asking questions of employees and providing answers when asked. And they should demand the same behavior from their direct reports.

A critical component of effective senior management communications is credibility. When a senior leader tells a story, it has to be believable. When a leader sets a direction, it has to be clear. And when a leader makes a decision, it must be in alignment with the words he or she has been saying. The old adage, "Actions speak louder than words," is certainly true in the corporate world. Communicators, who often help craft leaders' messages, must continually check to make sure that their leaders' actions and words are in sync. If the messages delivered by top leaders are not matched by their actions, employees have little choice but to believe the actions. Credibility suffers as a result.

Mass Media: Filling the Gap

Organizations cannot rely solely on managers and senior leaders to communicate with the workforce. While many managers take to communications naturally and embrace their communications roles; others never share information with their employees. Still others leave out key information or add unwanted detail. Many never receive needed skills training in communications.

As a result of this managerial inconsistency, communicators began bolstering their companies' internal communications programs with newsletters, magazines, bulletin boards, and other mass media solutions aimed at employee audiences. They started simply, with modest publications that were often called house organs. Organizations turned to communications professionals with journalism and mass communications experience to produce these publications. The introduction of mass media channels provided a tremendous amount of control over the timing of the message and the consistency of the wording. Over the years, these mass media channels have expanded from their humble beginnings of mimeographed news sheets and bulletin board programs to include the latest electronic delivery mechanisms: videos, satellite TV networks, e-mails, intranet sites, webcasts. Internal communications programs have evolved over time, too. Many early employee newsletters focused on company picnics, bowling leagues, employees' service anniversaries, and the births of employees' children. Photos were often staged grip-and-grin poses with a senior company official handing a trophy to a proud employee while shaking hands and mugging at the camera. You would be hard-pressed from the earliest employee publications to determine anything about a company's products, services, strategic business direction, competitors, or industry news.

That has changed over the years. Today, the best company communications deal honestly with an organization's strengths and weaknesses, its market successes and failures. The best internal magazines and newsletters deliver good news and bad news. The reporting and writing are powerful. The stories are about employees and their accomplishments. The publications invite customers to freely discuss what is going on in the organization and suggest ways to make things better. Photojournalists provide strong images that make the stories compelling and effective.

The best internal communications programs go far beyond publications. They mirror the broad range of mass media available in the world outside work and reflect the way technology has shaped our communication habits.

At first, technology's impact was limited to making the communicator's job easier. Technology was still relatively expensive in the 1960s and 1970s; its applications started with number-crunching back office functions that cried for automation. Gradually electric typewriters replaced clunky manual models. Linotype machines disappeared when computer-set type arrived. In the 1980s and 1990s, industrial video shoved 16mm film aside. Fax machines moved documents around the world in minutes instead of days. Word processing, publishing software, and personal computers simplified and sped up the writing, design, and production processes for newsletters and magazines.

As the price of information technology continued to drop and the size of computing devices continued to shrink, employee publications began to disappear in favor of e-mail and then online newsletters. As companies put personal computers into employees' hands for e-mail and Internet access, the formula changed forever. Passive recipients could become participants in the communications process. The one-way push of information from management to employees was now technologically enabled to become a two-way dialogue. Producing a sophisticated employee newsletter became less important than providing the appropriate electronic forum for two-way interaction between employees and the organization's leadership.

Employees' expectations were changing at the same time. As people bought personal computers, printers, digital cameras, and smartphones for their personal use at home, they began to demand more at work. Why can't I access my benefits information online the way I can conduct online banking? If I can post a video clip of my kids' soccer match on YouTube, shouldn't it be just as easy to post a sales training video on the company's intranet?

While evolving mass media channels have overcome many of the shortcomings of top-down managerial communications, they are not perfect either. Readership studies show that not all employees read publications, e-mail, or intranet content. Video programs face distribution challenges that limit employee viewership. The personal computer has given huge numbers of employees access to vast amounts of information via e-mail and intranet sites. Many employees suffer from information overload, and important messages can be lost in the daily barrage of e-mail. However, certain groups of employees still do not have easy access to personal computers because of the nature of their jobs. They do not sit at a desk eight hours each day. They are driving forklifts, teaching classes, or assembling automobiles. Even if they do have access to information with a personal computer or smartphone, they may not have time or interest to do so.

Social Networks: Communicating Naturally

A lot of company news has never moved through mass media channels or the company's hierarchy. Instead, it has always flowed naturally through an invisible network of employees who give, take, shape, and accumulate information: the coworkers who eat lunch together every day in the company cafeteria, the group of smokers from several departments who gather around the communal outdoor ashtray and compare notes about the latest executive promotion, and the company's softball team that chats about a new product over a couple of beers after the game. All of these groups share information that they have heard from their managers, read in a company newsletter, or saw on the local TV station. They discuss the messages and always uncover the inconsistencies.

These informal networks are often dismissed by company executives and slapped with negative labels like the "rumor mill" or the "grapevine." They are seen as maverick communication factories that produce inaccurate information. However, smart communicators are tapping the power of these hidden communications links and making them a key component of their internal communications programs. Because it does not cost anything to build these networks—they occur naturally in all organizations—the return on investment for using these networks is extraordinarily high. These social networks are efficient, quick, and highly credible.

The study of these invisible networks is an emerging practice that draws on anthropology, mathematics, chemistry, and subatomic physics. One of the leaders in the field, Karen Stephenson, who teaches at Harvard and the University of London, developed and now markets software that builds a visual map of an organization's social networks. The software uses algorithms to analyze data from employee surveys that ask people whom they communicate with the most. The graphic representation looks like a giant spider web of multicolored lines interconnecting all individuals in an organization. Some people are extraordinarily well connected; others have only a few links outside their immediate work group. The network map spotlights the invisible influencers in an organization: people who carry quiet corporate clout but may not have important job titles.

Stephenson (2005) has dubbed people in those roles the *hubs* of the network, the best connectors among people and information. She labels other key roles as *gatekeepers* (the information bottlenecks who make themselves indispensable by controlling contact with the rest of the network), and *pulsetakers* (who carefully cultivate relationships to monitor the ongoing health of the organization).

Malcolm Gladwell (2000) similarly describes three roles individuals play in social networks. *Connectors* are sociable people who bring people together. *Mavens* like to pass along knowledge. *Salesmen* are skilled at persuading the unenlightened. Although Gladwell uses different terms to define slightly different roles, his point is the same as Stephenson's: messages and behaviors spread like viruses through these social networks by word-of-mouth epidemics triggered with the help of those role players.

There are ways for communicators to tap the power of these social networks. For example, suppose you stage a monthly breakfast meeting for the CEO and a randomly selected group of employees from across that organization. If you sprinkle a few *mavens* and *hubs* into the mix, you are almost guaranteed that messages from the CEO will spread quickly and effectively through the network as soon as the breakfast is over. Or instead of designing and printing posters to invite employees to a town hall event, let the *salesmen* work their network magic using *word of mouse* to distribute a personal invitation by e-mail.

Used effectively, social networks are an excellent way for internal communicators to connect effectively and inexpensively with their employees.

Social Media: Bringing the Pieces Together

Most employees entering the workforce today have grown up in a digital world surrounded by consumer electronics: personal computers, CDs, DVDs, cellular phones, and video games. They are comfortable sharing information with friends on Facebook, posting pictures on Flickr, installing apps on their iPhones, and staying connected in real time with texts and instant messaging. They expect their corporate IT infrastructure to be as progressive as those they can access outside of work. Sometimes they expect more.

Those expectations have fundamentally changed the organization's communications formula. Today's employee expects to have access to the company and industry information she needs to do her job and to be able to easily connect with her coworkers and leaders, the same way she does at home. If she does not know the answer to a problem, she asks for a little help from her friends. Participation, albeit electronic, in the communications process is a given for workers today and an important objective for any communications organization.

The authors of *The Cluetrain Manifesto* (Levine, Locke, Searls, Weinberger, & McKee, 2009) nailed it: Forget one-way, hierarchical communication. Today, it is all about the conversation. The authors explain that the Internet has enabled people to invent new ways of sharing relevant knowledge at blazing speed. They explain how conversations taking place on websites and message boards, in e-mail, text messages, and chatrooms, give employees a voice that can radically alter traditional businesses by challenging a slow and cumbersome top-down communications hierarchy.

Progressive communications teams are fulfilling their employees' expectations with solutions that blend mass media coverage, social networking pragmatism, and executive leader content.

Social Networking at Work: Turning Play into Profit

Some companies have blocked employee access to social media sites such as Facebook, Twitter, Delicious, YouTube, and MySpace to keep workers from *wasting* their work time online. Yet other companies have not only embraced social networking tools, they have imported them or developed their own to improve employee productivity.

One of the first to see the business benefits of social networking was IBM. The conservative computing giant has built a suite of tools that foster teamwork among its 400,000 full- and part-time employees who work in IBM offices, at client sites, and, increasingly, from their homes.

IBM's internal phone directory, the Blue Pages, lays the foundation for internal networking. Employees control most of their own content beyond the basic information (name, title, location, phone, e-mail) pulled from IBM's human resources (HR) database. For example, employees can replace their company-issued ID card photo with pictures with their kids or from a ski vacation. They can tag themselves to highlight skills or professional experiences. They form communities around common interests and can search for coworkers who have certain skill sets. Need to find a software developer who speaks French and has experience selling to financial services companies? An online search of the Blue Pages will connect you with that select subset of coworkers the same way Facebook can match you with people with whom you share hobbies or interests.

Over time IBM added other tools to the mix. There are wiki sites on which any employee can add, edit, or delete documents, often around a collaborative project. There is an application called Dogear that lets employees tag, organize, and share their bookmarks to websites (think Delicious). An IBMer can start a blog at any time. To create the company guidelines for blogging, employees started a wiki to post helpful how-to advice.

Other companies have put social networking tools to work inside the firewall, too. Networking giant Cisco deployed across the company its own version of YouTube called Show and Share. Employees can post everything from short training videos for salespeople to recordings of speakers at all-hands meetings. The intranet application has also accelerated the use of video capture devices, including the company's own inexpensive Flip digital camcorder.

The internal successes at IBM and Cisco convinced both companies to market their social networking tools as commercial products. IBM brought Lotus Connections to market in 2007, and Cisco started selling Show and Share to customers in 2010.

Exactly Who Is an Employee?

It used to be fairly simple to answer that question: someone was either an employee or was not. The person received a paycheck from the company or did not. He or she was invited to staff meetings, went to the company holiday party, received the company newsletter, and bowled in the company's bowling league—or did not.

Today it is harder to define the boundaries of an internal audience. Organizations have full-time employees, part-time employees, contractors, consultants, temporary employees, and just about every other kind of worker. Add to that mix all the workers in franchises, strategic partnerships, independent distributors, and other allied organizations that are not officially part of the corporate structure. All of these people have information needs, but their needs are as varied as their jobs. To do their jobs effectively, some people who are near the fringe of the organization may need more information than regular, full-time employees.

Communications professionals must take these audience demographics into account as they develop internal communication plans. Employee communications are like bathing suits: one size does not fit all.

The line between internal and external communications is increasingly blurry. Consider a Microsoft engineer living in Redmond, Washington. Chances are very good that she uses Microsoft products (and receives Microsoft's customer communication), owns Microsoft stock (and receives shareholder communication), and watches Seattle television (where she sees her company's media communications efforts played out). It is critical that internal communications programs work in concert with media relations, investor and customer communication, striving for consistency in messages and timing.

In addition, communicators recognize that information can easily ooze across these fuzzy boundaries. An e-mail intended for an employee-only audience can (and usually does) find its way beyond an organization's borders. While it has always been possible for a paper copy of an internal company document to be shared with outsiders, it is much simpler for digital information to move anywhere at the speed of light. Communicators must assume that any information they produce that is targeted at an employee audience is likely to be seen by competitors, regulators, retirees, and journalists.

Recognizing Limitations

When we start an internal communications function in an organization, we discover that there are a few people and departments who completely ignore us.

They do not seek our help to develop plans, they send out important messages without our input, and they stage employee events without letting us know what they are doing. In an organization with unlimited resources, we could be involved in all of those activities, in addition to managing employee portals, producing newsletters, writing executive announcements, and doing the thousands of other things on our never-ending to-do lists.

Communicators will recognize that there are finite limits to their capacity for involvement. Most of the communications that take place inside their organizations will not, and probably should not, pass through internal communications programs. We cannot stage every staff meeting, script every telephone call, or review every employee's tweet. We cannot edit every e-mail message. But we can prepare strategic meetings about impending changes and craft key messages for an all-employee voicemail. We can develop guidelines for proper use of social media and share them across the organization.

The key role any internal communicator can play is to create the environment in which employees at all levels of the organization can easily exchange the information they need to do their jobs. We can set the stage and provide critical information for the formal and informal communication that takes place among employees, supervisors, managers, senior leaders, customers, and stakeholders.

References

Gladwell, M. (2000). *The tipping point: How little things can make a big difference.* New York: Little, Brown.

Larkin, T. J., & Larkin, S. (1994). *Communicating change: Winning employee support for new business goals.* New York: McGraw-Hill.

Levine, R., Locke, C., Searls, D., Weinberger, D., & McKee, J. (2009). *The cluetrain manifesto* (10th anniv. ed.) New York: Basic Books.

Sinickas, A. (2005). *How to measure your communication programs* (3rd ed.). Irvine, CA: SCI Publishing.

Stephenson, K. (2005). *Network management.* Retrieved July 28, 2010, from http://netform.com/html/knowledge_management.html

CHAPTER SIXTEEN

COMMUNICATING WITH A DIVERSE WORKFORCE

Tamara L. Gillis

In today's organizations, diversity initiatives are "business as usual" and include commentary on demographic differences as well as on differences in perspectives among cultural groups. Often challenges regarding diversity are categorized broadly into tangible and intangible categories (Milliken & Martins, 1996). Characteristics such as race, ethnicity, disability, gender, and age are often tangible and observable, while culture and religion are examples of intangible characteristics of diversity.

Beyond fair treatment issues, at the heart of the discussion of diversity in organizations today is representation of diverse groups among internal and external stakeholders, top management's active support for diversity, and employee participation in organizational outcomes. To help readers better understand this issue, this chapter explores diversity and inclusion as well as the benefits and challenges of communicating diversity initiatives.

Diversity and Inclusion

Diversity and *inclusion* represent two related organizational approaches to diversity in the workplace. According to Roberson (2006), "Diversity focuses on organizational demography, whereas inclusion focuses on the removal of obstacles to the full participation and contribution of employees in organizations" (p. 217).

Woods (2002) provides a similar dichotomy: "Diversity is about people. Inclusion, on the other hand, is about organization" (p. 38). Often used interchangeably, these initiatives challenge communicators to respect diverse populations by managing multiple organizational strategies that employ multilingual approaches and multiple media. These two initiatives may result in different approaches to diversity in organizations (Roberson, 2006).

Common strategies used to increase employee involvement in work systems leverage learning and growth outcomes from diversity initiatives in organizations. These outcomes include the integration of diversity into work processes, greater innovation and creativity, organizational flexibility, and traditional fairness issues. Organizations recognized as leaders in diversity initiatives integrate diversity management as an organizational strategy, engage different demographic groups within and outside their organizations, and have top management's support for diversity (Douglas, 2008; Frankel, 2010; Profiles in Diversity Journal, 2010). These organizations additionally develop inclusion initiatives to facilitate employee participation and engagement in organizational decision making.

Today's holistic concept of communicating with a diverse workforce is the result of Thomas and Ely's (1996) learning-and-effectiveness paradigm and Senge's (1990) learning organization. These approaches to organizational management foster the linkage between organizational learning and diversity to organizational strategy, markets, processes, and culture. More specifically, diverse employee perspectives and approaches are incorporated into business processes to leverage the benefits that enhance organizational learning and growth (Douglas, 2008; Roberson, 2006). These organizations enjoy access to greater pools of talent, a diverse customer base, and success in the marketplace.

Many organizations describe themselves as "inclusive organizations." "Inclusive organizations not only have a diverse composition, but are also learning-centered organizations that value the perspectives and contributions of all people, and strive to incorporate the needs and viewpoints of diverse communities into all aspects of the organization. Inclusive organizations are, by definition, diverse at all levels" (Reeves & Nalty, 2010, para. 3). This concept of an inclusive organization or inclusive culture embraces the idea of engaging all members of a diverse workforce in exceeding organizational goals.

Benefits and Challenges

Valued by companies and countries in the global marketplace, diversity is a business imperative (Ahonen & Tienari, 2009).

Additionally, corporations and scholars correlate diversity in the workplace to increased innovation and creativity; improved and increased relationships with customers, suppliers, and community partners; improved conflict resolution and problem solving across the organization (Abbott, 2010; Baxter Worldwide, 2010; Cisco, 2010; Gibbons, 2010; Great Place to Work Institute, 2007; Roberson, 2006).

Many organizations strategically position themselves in the domestic and global marketplace by having diversity strategies, and they are open about their initiatives to leverage diversity as a business strategy. Organizations that identify diversity and inclusion among their business objectives are more likely to measure the results of their communications efforts with their workforces and about their diversity programs with their organizational stakeholders (Weiner, 2008). "You can look at every part of your organization and ask if diversity is showing up. A lot of the measurement with diversity comes from looking at your whole company. How is the corporate climate? Are employees satisfied? . . . Look at every part from recruitment to external vendors" (Johnson, as cited by Weiner, 2008, p. 16). For example, companies with dedicated diversity recruitment programs report corresponding increases in promotions to higher positions among employees from traditionally underrepresented groups, according to the 2010 DiversityInc. Top 50 (Frankel, 2010).

Marquez (2008) and Goetz (2008) confirm that diversity as a business concern is shared across cultures. Marquez reports that diversity initiatives are a business imperative for Japanese companies: "the main challenges [Japanese] firms face is changing the culture of their organizations" (para. 6). For many companies, diversity initiatives represent major change communication programs. In the business environment of mergers and acquisitions, Goetz reports that companies are juggling both corporate cultures and diverse national cultures, resulting in challenges of both synergy and inclusion.

Hansen (2010) notes that the current trends in diversity programming include shifting these initiatives from human resources to corporate social responsibility and the appointment of chief diversity officers as part of the C-suite to improve accountability of these efforts. Hansen warns that the majority of corporations participating in a 2009 Institute for Corporate Productivity study were lax on developing metrics regarding diversity and its impact on the bottom line. Measurement practices to consider include impact on employee retention and engagement, representation with the community and the market, a dashboard of key diversity indicators, and return on investment metrics.

Two challenges that have received much attention from management and communication scholars and practitioners are generational cohorts in the workforce and religion or spirituality in the workplace. Some researchers suggest that organizations should focus on cultural characteristics of generational demo-graphic groups, largely modeled after American classifications: traditionals, baby boomers, generations X and Y, nexters and millennials, to name a few. Other scholars warn against these dichotomies as artificial since members in the same age cohort from different cultures outside of the United States are characterized by different behavioral and motivational indicators (D'Aprix, 2010; Sullivan, 2008). "Other regions of the world don't share the same timeline in population booms, and there clearly are cultural differences that affect the expectations and wants of global employees" (Sullivan, 2008, p. 50). These same scholars and practitioners agree that employing a mix of communication strategies to reach a diverse population of employees coupled with consideration for employee motivators and life factors, is the best strategy.

According to Sue Weston, writing for *New Zealand Management* (2002), religion or spirituality in the workplace inevitably sparks a spectrum of responses from employees and management, ranging from those who feel it is appropriate to those who oppose it on the grounds that religion has no place in the workplace. "Somewhere in the middle of the spectrum reside attitudes which see spirituality as akin to values and ethics, and thus an important component of organizational success" (p. 29).

Due to this range of attitudes, employers must decide how to respectfully manage spirituality at work. Companies that claim to embrace diversity and an inclusive culture are finding ways to balance faith and the workplace. Grossman (2008) reports that faith-friendly companies value inclusion and promote diver-sity and religious self-expression; they invite employees to bring spiritual expres-sion to the workplace. Ford Motor's Ford Interfaith Network is one example. Its mission is to promote religious tolerance, corporate identity, and human dignity while promoting understanding and respect for all members of the organization. Grossman (2008) writes that faith-friendly companies report increased levels of employee commitment and engagement, according to SHRM's Religion and Corporate Culture survey.

Diversity and Communication

"There is a critical difference between merely having diversity in an organiza-tion's workforce and developing the organizational capacity to leverage diversity as a resource," wrote Roberson (2006, p. 234). And that difference comes down to communicating diversity and inclusion in the organization.

Diversity programming and communications starts with recruitment prac-tices and extends through the tenure of employees in the organization by promoting awareness and education. Collaborative work arrangements and conflict resolution processes represent means to involve employees in organizational decision-making processes. The following list includes common organizational strategies and tactics for communicating about diversity and with diverse stakeholders:

- *Diversity training.* The focus of diversity training is helping people understand and manage their biases. "Diversity training programs may have common objectives, such as developing awareness of individual feelings about diversity, disseminating information about diversity-related legal issues and policies, developing skills for a diverse work environment, and applying those skills to improve or change the organizational culture . . . . Diversity training has the added complexity of addressing not only the roots of organizational culture (inclusiveness of policies and practices), but also the values and attitudes of individual participants (their biases and fears)" (Hite & McDonald, 2006, pp. 366–367).
- *Mentoring programs.* Some organizations assign official mentors within the company to new employees to help them adjust and navigate the company environment. In some organizations this process is not formalized; employees find their own mentors or role models. In another model of mentoring, organizations partner with local diversity-based groups to pair employees with mentors and leaders in the community and conduct community outreach programs.
- *Employee resource groups.* "Employee resource groups (ERGs) are a valuable tool for both increasing employee engagement and demonstrating the value of diversity and inclusion to growth and revenue. Companies that have made ERG members a prominent part of their organizations are able to offer employees the opportunity to be heard and make tangible contributions to the revenue line. ERGs should be leveraged as inputs into the marketing and design functions, and their contribution must be communicated across the organization. ERGs themselves should concentrate on adding value to the business and aligning their activities with business objectives" (Conference Board, 2009, p. 13).
- *Diversity task forces, committees, and advisory boards.* These three terms are used to describe groups tasked with monitoring diversity and inclusion activities within organizations. Typically these groups are composed of employees and leadership from across the organization. In some organizations, these groups partner with community diversity organizations. The role of these groups is one of advising leadership on progress toward diversity and inclusion goals.

- *Diversity annual reports.* Companies are sharing their diversity and inclusion initiatives through separate diversity annual reports and dedicated sections in regular annual reports, which additionally are published on the corporate website. These reports highlight progress toward workforce diversity and inclusion programs, especially for companies that have identified diversity as a business objective.
- *Employee network support groups.* These employee groups provide professional development, support, and guidance based on shared experiences. These groups are commonly organized around dimensions of diversity. Douglas (2008) defines these affinity groups within the company as "communities within a corporation that are organized around the employees' similar circumstances and common goals" (p. 12).

Case in Point: Lockheed Martin MS2

In 2007, Lockheed Martin was facing a mammoth demographic problem: many of the company's 70,000 engineers were expected to retire within the next fifteen years. To keep its edge, the company needed to replenish a workforce that was traditionally heavily recruited from the military with young engineers, scientists, and managers drawn from all backgrounds who were able to think across traditional borders. At that time, Lockheed Martin president and chief executive officer (CEO) Bob Stevens emphasized that the solution to this workforce transition would require breaking away from the traditional engineering workforce—one that is heavily Caucasian and mostly male. Instead, he emphasized that Lockheed Martin must deliberately create a more diverse and inclusive workforce, not only of racial differences but also of differences in beliefs, backgrounds, and experiences.

In 2007, the Lockheed Martin MS2 employee communications and design team felt they needed to move beyond standard communication and messages and instead find a way to help employees understand the nuances of beliefs and backgrounds that contribute to an inclusive work environment. They wanted to explore the thoughts and beliefs around individual differences. The team discussed several options, including traditional newsletter articles, intranet postings, and the like. The final solution centered on an innovative "Embrace Diversity"

This Gold Quill award-winning case study is shared with the permission of its creators, Kathy Baier, Doug Clement, and Sue Kraus of Lockheed Martin MS2, Moorestown, New Jersey.

print postcard campaign. MS2 employees would receive a series of three post-cards over four months, with specific, thought-provoking discussion of various issues.

The intended audience for the campaign included 13,000 Lockheed Martin MS2 employees; while the majority of employees are engineers and researchers, there are a large number of employees who do not have technical backgrounds. Employees are located at seventy-six sites worldwide, ranging from groups of one to two employees who work on-site at customer locations to large complexes housing more than 5,000 employees. MS2's employee base tends to skew older, given the legacy of industry growth that occurred in the 1960s and 1970s. Overall, approximately 20 percent of employees are 55 or older, 35 percent are ages 45 to 54, 20 percent are ages 35 to 44, and 25 percent are ages 25 to 34. However, Lockheed Martin was hiring 500 to 750 new employees a year, and the percentage of employees ages 25 to 45 would continue to grow in the next several years. With this diverse audience base lay a wealth of different beliefs, backgrounds, and perspectives that could be explored through the postcard series.

The overall communications objective for the campaign was to create a thought-provoking communication tool not only to capture the attention of the employee audience but also encourage them to think about their own reactions and beliefs. Doing so would require an eye-catching design paired with bold, edgy language. With this understanding, the team established the following goals for their work:

- Engage employees by providing vibrant, consistent, and relevant diversity information to increase employee understanding and acceptance of inclusive behavior.
- Set the stage for greater employee involvement and engagement in both diversity communications and the company's efforts to create a diverse, inclusive work environment. (This acknowledges that changing a culture takes time and continuous effort. It is not a "one year and be done" program.)

Two key objectives were established:

1. Reach at least 75 percent of employees with a targeted diversity postcard series
2. Establish a solid baseline of employee understanding about what constitutes a diverse environment

The team had not measured this understanding previously, so their current work would serve as a baseline for future efforts.

The "Embrace Diversity" print postcard campaign consisted of twelve different postcards that explored themes such as generational differences, cultural and religious traditions, teamwork, military experience, sports colloquialisms, and company loyalty. During the campaign, every MS2 employee received a series of three postcards over four months, each card containing specific, thought-provoking discussion of various issues. The team decided on this approach for several reasons:

- Because of the heavy use of e-mail and other electronic communication, employees receive very little print material from MS2. The team believed a print piece would stand out from the electronic overload many employees experience.
- Multiple postcards could be created, with a selection of postcards distributed each month. This allowed the team to explore more than just a handful of issues yet remain within the project budget.
- The postcards could be strategically sorted so that each employee would receive a different postcard from a peer seated in an office or cubicle next to them. This was designed to encourage conversation among employees about the topics.

The intent was to explore the beliefs and backgrounds that contribute to an inclusive work environment by presenting realistic scenarios—issues that can arise every day in the MS2 work environment. The design focused on "conversation bubbles"—similar to those that appear in comic strips—as a way to present thoughts and reactions in a neutral way. The team wanted to avoid using stock photography or illustrations that included people, because they wanted employees to focus on the issues and language, not whether the postcard presented a gender or race issue.

The dialogue on the front of the postcards was written to be edgier than traditional company communications about diversity in order to attract employees' attention in a more thought-provoking way. The team used conversational language to present the beliefs, reactions, comments, and generational nuances that matched each of the issues explored. The back of the postcards contained a call to action—reinforcing that diversity is a business imperative for Lockheed Martin MS2. Each card contained three to four bullet points of actions employees could take to create an inclusive work environment, from specific behaviors to more subtle challenges to their beliefs and behaviors.

Given the positive reaction to the first set of postcards, the team quickly created an employee contest to generate future postcard ideas. More than fifty different ideas were submitted, and ten of them were developed into electronic diversity postcards for use as e-cards and on the website during the corporation's

Diversity Awareness Week in September 2007. The communications team took the ideas submitted and developed the creative content and language to mirror the original campaign.

The key messages and themes for the campaign included the following:

- As a corporation, Lockheed Martin's goal is to create an inclusive work environment in which all people are valued and their ideas encouraged and respected.
- A diverse and inclusive work environment is about more than accepting attributes such as race, sex, and religious beliefs. It's about accepting the variety of backgrounds, experiences, and perspectives that make each individual unique.
- The diversity of Lockheed Martin's workforce provides the competitive edge needed for MS2 to succeed in the global marketplace. A diverse and inclusive workforce allows the company to benefit from the different backgrounds and perspectives of colleagues and fosters more creative and innovative thinking throughout the organization.
- Respecting others' perspectives and backgrounds is more than a business imperative—it is also the right thing to do.

By using existing communications, design, and Web staff from across the organization, much of the campaign costs were absorbed by department payroll. The cost for the printing and shipping of the "Embrace Diversity" postcards was approximately US$6,800, or US$0.12 per employee. The campaign was developed in April and May, and distribution began in June 2007 as scheduled.

Ironically, the one challenge the team expected—getting senior executive buy-in on the postcard topics and language—did not occur. Rather, senior leadership felt the postcards were well thought-out, provocative, and dealt with pertinent issues.

The most difficult challenge was developing an accurate distribution list for employees. With the wide use of electronic communications, keeping an up-to-date list of employee office locations within each facility has not been a business priority. The team addressed this with a secondary campaign encouraging employees to update their office locations and personal information in the company database and by working closely with mailroom staff at each location. While the team did not achieve 100 percent distribution, each series of postcards achieved a higher distribution rate than the previous one.

Key to the success of the campaign was measurement of the campaign objectives.

Objective 1: Reach at least 75 percent of employees with a targeted diversity communication. Based on returned cards, a nonscientific poll of employees conducted via the intranet, as well as discussions with communication leaders and mailroom staff across locations, the team estimates that 70 percent of employees received the first batch of postcards; that number reached up to 90 percent of employees for the final set of postcards.

Objective 2: Establish a solid baseline of employee understanding about what constitutes a diverse environment. Following each of the postcard distributions, the team conducted an online survey and received nearly 1,000 responses (just under 10 percent of the workforce and thus considered statistically valid). With each of the postcard distributions, 62 percent to 65.5 percent of employees recalled receiving the postcard; 43 percent felt the diversity message was new, different, and made them think; and up to 50 percent believed the message was effective. Again, because the team had not measured the effectiveness of diversity messaging in the past, these results give them a solid baseline to work against in future years.

In late September 2007 (at which point the "Embrace Diversity" postcard campaign had been completed), the HR organization surveyed employees on their perspectives on diversity and Lockheed Martin's communication of diversity as a business imperative. It revealed the following strong metrics:

- The percentage of employees who indicated that they strongly agree or agree that MS2 is serious about its commitment to have a diverse, inclusive work environment was 85.2 percent.
- The percentage of employees who indicated that the benefits of a diverse, inclusive work environment have been clearly communicated to them was 84.5 percent.
- In addition to the quantitative feedback, the team received a number of notable e-mails from employees:

    "I like them! I thought the concept was a little 'hokey' until I actually read them. But they are very well presented and made me stop and think about my own actions and reactions."

    "You managed to touch on one of my pet peeves. I'm ex-Navy with no traditional degree and the last postcard addressed the concern I have that some folks think one has to have a sheepskin on the office wall to be effective. That's not true. Thanks for sharing that message!"

    "May I say I am not a fan of what I consider corporate group-hug efforts—strange for an old guy who would benefit from diversity-think—

but I must compliment you on your campaign . . . especially the bubble-conversation post cards I have seen. Brilliant marketing."

Conclusion

In today's business environment, large and small companies pursuing domestic and international industry are embracing diversity as a business imperative and reaping the benefits of an inclusive environment. Key to success in leveraging diversity and inclusion in the workplace is engaging employees and reaching out to all employees. Using a mix of communications strategies benefits employees as well as external stakeholders. Understanding what motivates all employees and providing them with means to positively affect their work environment and the bottom line of the organization drive the engagement of a diverse workforce in an inclusive organization.

References

Abbott. (2010). *Global citizenship our people.* Retrieved August 18, 2010, from www.abbott.com/global/url/content/en_US/40.50:50/general_content/General_Content_00280.htm

Ahonen, P., & Tienari, J. (2009). United in diversity? Disciplinary normalization in an EU Project. *Organization, 16*(5), 655–679.

Baxter Worldwide. (2010). Global inclusion and diversity. *2009 Sustainability Report.* Retrieved August 18, 2010, from http://sustainability.baxter.com/employees/inclusion.html

Cisco. (2010). *Inclusion and diversity.* Retrieved August 24, 2010, from www.cisco.com/web/about/ac49/ac55/index.html

Conference Board. (2009). Diversity and inclusion: Global challenges and opportunities. *Council Perspectives.* New York: Conference Board.

D'Aprix, R. (2010). Leadership in a multi-generational workplace. *Strategic Communication Management, 14*(2), 13.

Douglas, P. H. (2008). Affinity groups: Catalyst for inclusive organizations. *Employment Relations Today, 34*(4), 11–18.

Frankel, B. (2010). *The DiversityInc. top 10 companies for global diversity.* Retrieved August 18, 2010, from www.diversityinc.com

Gibbons, P. C. (2010). *Diversity initiative.* Retrieved August 18, 2010, from www.gibbonslaw.com/about/index.php?view_page=4

Goetz, J. (2008). Two become one: Communicating a merger at Nycomed. *Strategic Communication Management, 12*(2), 28–31.

Great Place to Work Institute. (2007). *Why is Google so great?* White paper available at www.greatplacetowork.com

Grossman, R. J. (2008). Religion at work. *HR, 53*(12), 26–33.

Hansen, F. (2010). Diversity of a different color. *Workforce Management, 89*(6) 22–26.

Hite, L. M., & McDonald, K. S. (2006). Diversity training pitfalls and possibilities: An exploration of small and mid-size US organizations. *Human Resource Development International, 9*(3), 365–377.

Marquez, J. (2008, September). Diversity challenges in Japan. *Workforce Management Online.* Retrieved August 18, 2010, from www.workforce.com/archive/feature/25/73/39/257342.php?ht=

Milliken, F. J., & Martins, L. L. (1996). Searching for common threads: Understanding the multiple effects of diversity in organizational groups. *Academy of Management Review, 21*(2), 402–433.

Profiles in Diversity Journal. (2010, July/August). 2010 International Innovation in Diversity Awards. *Profiles in Diversity Journal,* 28–37.

Reeves, A., & Nalty, K. (2010). Inclusiveness 101. *Beyond diversity: Inclusiveness in the legal workplace.* Available at www.legalinclusiveness.org/clientuploads/pdf/Inclusiveness_101.pdf

Roberson, Q. M. (2006). Disentangling the meanings of diversity and inclusion in organizations. *Group & Organization Management, 31*(2), 212–236.

Senge, P. M. (1990). *The fifth discipline: The art and practice of the learning organization.* New York: Doubleday.

Sullivan, J. (2008). A new breed of ageism. *Workforce Management, 87*(16), 50.

Thomas, D. A., & Ely, R. J. (1996). Making differences matter: A new paradigm for managing diversity. *Harvard Business Review, 74,* 79–90.

Weiner, L. (2008). Companies must set goals for diversity. *Crain's Detroit Business, 24*(15), 16.

Weston, S. (2002). Faith at work. *New Zealand Management, 49*(3), 28–30.

Woods, S. (2002, January/February). Creating inclusive organizations: Aligning systems with diversity. *Diversity Journal,* 38–39.

CHAPTER SEVENTEEN

INTEGRATING EMPLOYEE COMMUNICATIONS MEDIA

Steve Crescenzo

When I broke into the employee communications business in 1992, the internal communicator's choice of vehicles was limited, to say the least.

You had print, of course, and face to face. Most companies had some version of a town hall meeting that was really just executives giving speeches, with very little interaction with the audience.

If you had a ton of money, then you might have had a video department; but those were pretty rare and limited to really big companies.

There was voicemail and posters. And that was about it.

But very quickly, the vehicle choices began to increase. First, e-mail and intranets changed the very nature of how we communicate, allowing us to be more timely and, on the downside, to push out more *stuff*.

Then, Web 2.0 hit and social media arrived on the scene, which again changed how we communicate, allowing us to be more interactive and conversational if we took proper advantage of the tools.

Finally, the last addition came along a couple of years ago: multimedia. Today, anyone with a Flip camera can post video on their intranet; and anyone who wants to invest in an $80 digital voice recorder can add podcasts and other audio to their list of channels.

Savvy communicators now have so many more options to choose from to deliver messages to employees.

But these tools have also created a problem: information overload. Employees are buried with information these days, and some communicators are not helping the situation, by bombarding employees with the same messages in twelve different channels.

Information overload is always going to be an issue, but if used properly these new communications tools can work *together* instead of in *competition* and can help minimize the overload.

The trick, of course, is to *not* put the same messages on your intranet, in an e-mail, in a blog, on a video, in a podcast, and in your print publication. Each of those communication channels is really good at some things, and really bad at others. We need to take advantage of each vehicle's strengths and minimize its weaknesses and *then* integrate them so that each vehicle is carrying one part of the communications load.

For example, print vehicles can no longer be timely news vehicles, so trying to make them timely is a waste of time and energy. But print is great for coming in after the fact and doing what journalists call "The Day Two Story," when the news is already out there and the print publication delves deeper into that news, providing context, analysis, and background.

So you should never write a headline for a print publication that reads, "Fourth Quarter Earnings Announced." Even if you do a monthly print publication, that headline is going to be stale by the time it gets to employees.

Instead, that announcement headline belongs online, where it will be timely, and the print headline should read, "Behind the Numbers: What the Fourth Quarter Earnings Mean to XYZ Corporation."

In order to help readers better understand the strengths and weaknesses of each of our primary communication vehicles, in this chapter we look at the two big categories: print and online. Additionally, we explore a number of online tools, including audio, video, blogs, message boards attached to articles, and other social media.

The New Role of Print

The role of print has changed from that of a timely news vehicle to a more educational vehicle. It also has a crucial secondary role: to steer people to online content.

Communicators everywhere are catching on to this fact, using print less frequently but using it a lot better. More and more print publications have gone from monthly to quarterly, or even to only twice a year.

I know some companies that do just *one* print publication a year; it is beautifully done, explains the bigger picture to employees, features terrific photography and graphics, tells great stories that feature employees, and serves as a reference tool for employees throughout the year.

One communicator who grasps the new role of print is Kevin Heinrichs, a communicator at Suncor, in Vancouver, Canada. I first met Heinrichs when he was working for Petro Canada and churning out a twice-monthly publication, *In Brief*. It was a mediocre publication. With a twice-monthly deadline, Heinrichs did not have any time to do any real reporting or writing. To his credit, Heinrichs, a brilliant editor, knew the publication needed work.

After we talked through it, the solution was fairly simple: he needed to reduce the frequency and give himself time to do a better publication. In other words, communicate less, but communicate better.

Heinrichs did just that. He had the courage to start over. He changed the title from *In Brief* to *In Depth*, and he created a glorious new four-color, quarterly magazine that gave him the time, and the space, to flex his substantial creative muscles.

In Depth features stunning photos (my favorite is of a ship moving an iceberg away from an offshore drilling facility, with this caption: "How to wrestle icebergs in the North Atlantic"); feature stories loaded with personality and *voice*; and stories about Petro Canada people that make even the most boring business topics interesting. In short, the new magazine looks, feels, and reads like a consumer magazine dedicated to the company, which is the highest praise an internal editor can get.

The lesson we can take from this example is, When it comes to print frequency, less is more.

Print's secondary objective is to steer people to your great content online. The intranet is a crowded place, and it is easy for your content to get lost in the sea of electronic noise. But if you have a print publication, you can use it to push people directly to your online content. Your print publication becomes a marketing tool for your online materials.

To learn how to do it, just look to the consumer magazines, like *Newsweek* or *Time*. They use print to steer people online in two ways:

1. They dedicate an entire page of print to highlight all the great stuff that is happening on their websites. Exclusive interviews, multimedia content, discussions with authors—all of these things get advertised on the page, and readers who care about that content go online to check it out.
2. At the end of many articles, they *jump* people online for more content. For example, if they did an article on the fishing industry in Wisconsin, they may

have a tagline at the end of the article that says, "For an audio interview with Tom Jones, who has been fishing Wisconsin waters for 75 years, visit www.oursite.com."

Internal communicators can use the same technique. If you are putting print content online, do not just shovel it on there and be done with it. Web it up! While the space you have in print is finite, there are no such limitations online.

When the *New York Times* first started publishing news on its website, the editors just put the print story on the Web. But go look at www.newyorktimes.com now, and most of the stories now have additional content, multimedia sidebars (audio or video that adds to the story), and links to more information.

So when writing for print, think of the online version of the story. When you do interviews for a print story, bring a digital voice recorder and a Flip video camera. Look for the content that would lend itself to audio or video. If you sense the interview subject is really passionate about a topic, capture that passion on audio or video. That way, when it is time to put that print content online, you will already have a multimedia sidebar to go along with it.

When you are writing that print piece, and you have to start cutting it for space, save those clippings. They can all be added in to the online story when you post it.

Once you use print to steer people online, that is when the real fun starts.

Online Communication in a 2.0 World

For the longest time, most corporate intranets were stuck in the Web 1.0 era. While the external Internet morphed into a social place, and a place to watch video and listen to audio, intranets were still, for the most part, one-way publishing tools.

They were like print publications, only they happened to be electronic instead of paper. They were glorified filing cabinets—a place to dump all the forms and other paperwork that companies create by the ton. There was no interactivity, no multimedia, no social media, no sense of community.

That, thank goodness, is changing. Companies small and large are starting to take advantage of their intranets to do more two-way communication, build community, and allow employees to communicate with each other and with leadership. They are also taking advantage of multimedia channels to inform, educate, and entertain their internal audiences.

Great intranets have three components:

1. Information and work tools
2. Opportunities for employees to voice opinions, take part in work-related discussions, collaborate with colleagues, and interact with leadership
3. Multimedia components, such as video and podcasts

There is not a lot of mystery surrounding that first component: information.

Our job is to write good articles and put them where employees can easily find them and read them.

It is the second two components that cause the problems. All the stuff in the second two groups has been lumped under the term *social media*, and many organizations are scared to death of it.

They fear losing control. They fear a loss of productivity. They fear legal problems if employees are allowed to share information. And they let that fear dictate what they will and will not allow in the intranet.

But without social media, the intranet will never come close to realizing its full potential. The simple fact is, no matter what organization you work for, you *can* use the social media tools. You can use blogs. You can use podcasts. You can do interactive video. You can and should open up articles for comments. And you can do it for not a lot of money, which makes it very attractive.

Just because you can *use* the tools, that does not mean they are going to work. Like any other communication vehicles, you have to use them the right way. If you want to use social media tools successfully at your company, you need to do the following five things.

1. *Make sure they serve a business purpose.*
Doing a podcast to fulfill whatever creative urges you have been sitting on for the past fifteen years is not a good enough reason. You have to ask yourself two important questions:

   a. How will using social media help this organization?
   b. What can social media do that more traditional media cannot do?

If you can answer those questions successfully, then you can build a business case for using the new tools.

One great example of how this can work is Walmart's internal social media site, MyWalmart. I had the pleasure of seeing this intranet and learning the rationale behind it when I served as a judge in a communication awards program. MyWalmart was one of the winners of best intranet.

MyWalmart is a true community. Employees can blog, post videos, join discussions in forums. It even has a Facebook-like application that allows employees to assemble a list of friends (coworkers) just like you do on Facebook.

According to the award entry, the site was originally developed to engage associates, but it quickly took on a life of its own. It became a grassroots community that allowed employees to network with their peers *while* learning about new company initiatives, celebrating company culture, and telling the communicators (and leaders) their thoughts on everything from operations and marketing to advocacy and change management.

And here is what makes the case study truly amazing: employees are required to access it from home! Not *allowed* to access it from home; *required* to access it from home.

That seems like a recipe for disaster. What sane employee is going to finish an eight-hour shift at Walmart and then head home to surf the company intranet?

The answer is, a lot of employees. In fact, out of Walmart's 1.4 million employees worldwide, just about half, or 650,000, have registered for the site as of this writing. And another 120,284 have created public profiles in the "Facebook" section of the site.

As of this writing, 844 different topics were being discussed in the online forums, with comments from more than 30,000 different employees and hundreds of thousands of views.

But the key to MyWalmart's success is that it was done with a business purpose in mind. The company had the research to back it up. When the communications team polled the employees, they found that most people wanted to join the conversation on matters that affect them and the company. Some other numbers:

- 81 percent wanted information about Walmart when they were not at work.
- 83 percent expected Walmart to have a functioning social network.
- 78 percent were interested in connecting with other employees around the world.

Thus, MyWalmart is fulfilling a business need: engaging employees, allowing them to collaborate and voice their opinions. And the communicators use those discussions and comments to fuel their own communication efforts.

2. *Make sure you fulfill the entertainment expectation.*
This is especially true with blogs, podcasts, and interactive video. Do not let your chief financial officer (CFO) read the quarterly numbers on the intranet, and call it a podcast. Do not dump that awful chief executive officer (CEO) column

from page 2 of the print publication onto the intranet, add a comments feature, and call it a blog.

If your CFO really wants to talk about the numbers, interview him, and get the story behind the story. Then add some music to the recording, and maybe some sound effects. In other words, make it sound like a radio show.

And if your CEO really wants to blog, help him write in an entertaining, informal, conversational fashion. Because that is what people expect in a blog . . . not just an online version of the CEO column, complete with a comments function that nobody will use.

People these days have a lot of choices about what they read, listen to, or watch. In order for your social media vehicles to cut through employees' choices and get noticed, they better be interesting, relevant, and *entertaining*.

Audio and video are powerful communication tools, but they can easily be neutralized by bad content. The reason that audio and video are such powerful tools is that they can capture the emotion, passion, and personality of subjects in a way that print stories, or online stories, simply cannot do.

We neutralize that power by doing talking head videos of our executives. We suck the life from our podcasts by allowing people to read scripts, or by not adding music and sound effects and other elements that turn regular audio into more of a radio show.

When you are doing multimedia—either as a stand-alone vehicle, or as multimedia sidebars to your online stories—ask yourself this question: What can audio or video do for me that the printed or electronic word cannot do? What can it *add*? What part of the story can it tell?

Here is a good example: Colleen Hawk is a communicator at APS, a large utility in Arizona. She was doing an intranet story on safety, in which she featured a man who had been in an accident and had badly hurt his arm.

Hawk, who never goes anywhere without her Flip camera, asked the worker if she could take a 15-second video clip of his mangled arm while he described what happened.

The story itself turned out great, but it was that 15-second video that really drew readers.

3. *Make sure that* you *are involved in the content.*
Social media and multimedia need *talent*. It needs writers, talk show hosts, and video anchors. Unless you are blessed with executives or managers who can and will do all those things, you need to step up and *be* the talent.

That is what Nicole Helprin, a communicator at HP, did when she decided to do a podcast with Vyomesh (VJ) Joshi, the president of her division of HP.

Her idea: Follow VJ around on various site visits, and capture him talking to employees and managers.

"I wanted to get the story behind the story," says Helprin. "I wanted to capture the most interesting stuff . . . the stuff employees don't normally get to hear."

But how best to structure the podcast? Well, Helprin is a big fan of the NPR radio show, *This American Life*. So she decided to model her podcasts after the show, only much shorter. The only problem with that, of course, is that to do that kind of show, you need a host.

So Helprin took on that role herself, despite the fact that she had no background in radio. *She* became the voice of the podcast, and the podcast became a success.

The opportunities are limitless. You can be the radio host of an internal podcast that interviews interesting people inside and outside your company. You can do an editor's blog in which you write about important company initiatives from a personal perspective. You could do a video news broadcast during which you bring employees up to speed on the latest developments at the organization.

This is a new role for communicators, who for years have toiled in relative anonymity. Some communicators may not be comfortable with it, but it is a role we need to embrace.

4. *Make sure that you serve as a coach to your executives.*
Know this: Your executives are probably not very comfortable with social media. Many of them may not even know what it is. So asking them to blog or podcast successfully is a huge risk. You could be setting them up for failure, which is never a good idea with executives.

For social media to work with executives, we need to do two things:

a. Identify the executives most likely to succeed, then push them to start using the new tools. And,
b. Help them succeed by coaching them.

Teala Kail, who used to do internal communications at PSM, a utility in New Mexico, did exactly those two things for her boss, CEO Jeff Sterba.

Sterba was going to North Korea as part of a U.S. delegation to talk about nuclear energy with the North Korean government. Kail thought it would be a great idea to test a temporary CEO blog so Sterba could file reports from overseas for employees.

The only problem was, Sterba would have no Internet access. But Kail did not let that stop her. She asked Sterba to phone in the blog items twice a week; then she transcribed them word for word and put them on the blog, where employees could read and comment on them.

But there was one more problem. A busy executive in the middle of talks with communists probably is not going to have blogging first and foremost on his mind, so Kail stepped in to help him.

She gave Sterba a list of a dozen or so questions, such as, "According to the Energy Information Administration the country often experiences blackouts. How does this affect critical operations within the country, such as manufacturing or health care?"

All Sterba had to do was call Kail's voicemail, answer a couple of the questions each day, and presto: instant blog.

But it never would have happened if Kail had not been willing to push Sterba out of his comfort zone, get him to try something new, and then help him execute it successfully.

5. *Make sure you open up the conversation.*

Social media is about conversation. It is about dialogue. It is the antithesis of one-way, top-down communication.

A problem many organizations, and many executives, face is that they are only comfortable with one-way, top-down communication. They do not *want* to open up the conversation. They are afraid of free-flowing conversation. They like to be in control.

This is a problem, since a blog without a comments section is not a blog; it is an online column. And podcast radio shows are always better when they are interactive. The same is true with video.

So what can we do? We can open up the conversation but still control it. For example, have a comments section on your blog, but have all the comments go through you, the editor. That way, you can tell your executives if there is something submitted that might get the organization in trouble; you can kill it before it goes live.

Do the same with a podcast. Set up a voicemail or e-mail box that people can call or write in with comments; then you can vet all the comments.

Or, maybe you can have an article blog, where people can comment on articles that you have posted to the intranet; again, all the comments come through you before they go live.

There are lots of ways to open up the conversation, but not open it up all the way, and keep our executives comfortable.

Now that we have explored some of the best practices surrounding individual tactics and channels, let us look at how they can work together.

Integration: Bringing It All Together

Let us say that you are really taking advantage of each of your communication vehicles. Your print publication is a non-timely educational tool that uses longer stories, photos, sidebars, and graphics to show employees the bigger picture.

Your intranet is a thriving community through which you deliver the news and people join the conversation via various social media tools. It is a great example of *three-way communication*: you to them, them to you, and them to each other. You are also using video and audio for what those channels do best: capturing the emotion and passion that people bring to their jobs.

This is a great start. But we still need to weave the tools together and ensure they are all doing their part.

Here is a hypothetical example. Let us say that your company is going through a major change, a reorganization. Each of your channels has a role to play in keeping employees informed, answering questions, and getting key messages across.

Print

Many communicators are going to skip this section, because they killed the print publications years ago. Even if you do not have a regular print publication, there is no law that says you cannot create a one-time-only special issue for a topic as big as a reorganization.

In fact, I see quite a bit of that: using print as needed instead of having a regular publication. If you use a print vehicle, make sure it does the two things every print vehicle should do:

1. *Educate employees about the bigger picture.* In this case, the reasons behind the change. Do feature stories that show how individuals can help accelerate the process; use graphics—such as a timeline—to show progress; quote people both inside and outside the company to provide perspective; and use sidebars and other tools to define terms and clarify what is happening.
2. *Push people online.* Every story, every *article*, should direct people to go online for more information. You may want to even create an icon—a computer screen, perhaps, or a mouse—that you include in all the articles in which there is more information on that topic online.

Intranet Stories

This is where you will cover timely news about the reorganization. But do not feel the need to put yourself on a set schedule. Cover news as it happens, just like the big news sites do.

By opening up the articles for comments, you should get comments and questions that will help you develop more targeted, focused stories in the future, because that content will be based on feedback from employees.

As you write these stories, keep an eye out for multimedia sidebars that can bring the content to life. If you do an interview with a company leader, for example, a 2-minute video of him talking off the cuff about the reasons for the change can boost readership. You could do this as a one-off feature, or you could brand it as a regular feature and call it "Five Questions for [insert leader name here]."

Editors and Leadership Blog

Most reorganizations are very sterile affairs. Blogs can be a great way to put a face on the information and make it more personal. We are, after all, not reorganizing desks and chairs. We are reorganizing *people*.

If you have an editor's blog, you can write about your personal experiences going through this massive change. You can let your guard down and talk about the fear you have and the uncertainty. Then ask employees to share their stories.

If you have a leadership blog, you can have a rotating series of executives cover a wide variety of topics related to the reorganization, using a conversational, human style that will go a long way toward making the executives more *real* to employees. You can use the comments section of that blog to gather questions from employees, which will fuel future posts and other content.

Done properly, a great leadership blog is like an ongoing, never-ending town hall meeting, where the original post is the executive's speech and the comments serve as the Q&A.

Video and Audio

Besides the multimedia sidebars, you can also create stand-alone multimedia channels. You could create a podcast series called "Profiles in Change" that showcases, through interviews, how employees are dealing with the change.

You could do short video interviews with leaders, in which they talk about how their roles are changing, what can be expected in the near and long-term future, and what they hope the new company will look and act like.

You could take your Flip camera out to the hallways and do roving reporter-style interviews with employees, getting their thoughts about the reorganization. You could even use the Flip camera to gather employee questions and then interview leaders answering those questions.

In the End

The point is, you are not repeating the same message in each vehicle. You are not boring people with the same content over and over again.

Each vehicle serves a distinct purpose and helps accomplish a specific organizational or communication goal. That is true integration, and that is what every communicator should strive for in employee communication.

CHAPTER EIGHTEEN

INTERNAL BRANDING, EMPLOYER BRANDING

Patrick Grady

Any savvy business leader knows that employees are their first market and are central to the success of their companies. The concept of internal branding represents a cultural shift within an organization, in which employees become more customer focused and more business focused. Internal branding contends that employees transition from being informed, to understanding the information, to becoming committed, so that they change their behavior in support of the company goals. This improves company performance overall, from customer relations to sales to shareholder value.

It starts with employee recruitment, orientation, and communications strategies throughout the tenure of the employee with the company. Employer branding is "the sum of a company's efforts to communicate to existing and prospective staff that it is a desirable place to work" (Lloyd, 2002, p. 65).

This chapter examines the challenges and benefits of internal branding, also known as *employer branding*.

What It Means

Every day, businesses must decide whether they want the end-of-year W2 statements to be mailed to employees or ambassadors. And while internal branding cannot do the job alone, it is an important part of galvanizing a team and engaging minds toward a clearly defined set of corporate objectives.

While on the job, employees are regular subscribers to Monster.com, career-builder.com, theladders.com, and other employment sites. They spend some portion of their time browsing opportunities that end up in their mailboxes (often their work e-mail boxes—your mailbox). Employees use Facebook to complain about their job and talk about how excited they are to leave work on Friday at 5 p.m. ("Work," 2007).

Ambassadors, on the other hand, are charting their career paths within your company. They see opportunity at every turn, they are engaged, and they feel a part of something bigger than themselves. You can choose to call them something other than ambassador. Some companies have *evangelists*, *brand makers*, *customer advocates*, or *team members*. Sadly, companies with monikers like these may still have employees, much to their dismay.

Ambassadors love it when people ask them about their companies. They like tackling problems and looking for solutions. They have written goals that all relate to the company name that is on their paychecks.

Ambassadors may like Facebook, too. But you will hear them talking about things at work in a positive way: talking about their successes at work, cool new things that are happening, projects they are involved in, and more. Why? They like their jobs, they feel valued, and they look forward to contributing every day. Instead of tweeting about their jerk of a boss, they are tweeting about the good work they are doing.

Internal branding plays a part, and it is a starring role in this behavior. But you can never confuse the internal *brand* with the internal *identity*.

It is not a trick question. We all want brand ambassadors or evangelists. None of us would choose to have employees, and we can all see the difference.

Here is the tricky part: the corporate entity that is charged with developing, updating, modernizing, or revamping the internal brand *must* be connected with the seniormost team that is charged with managing, delivering, executing, and living the corporate culture.

Far too often, these two responsibilities are not connected. The internal branders are given a task; they may not be connected in the right way and to the right people. That is something that needs to be corrected, and fast.

Bad Ideas Executed Badly

Here is an example. In 2009, a large company (name withheld intentionally) was preparing for an annual sales meeting. They were spending millions of dollars to bring people in from all over the world and to tell the story of One Company

Vision (no, it was not Ford Motors). It is a good story. It is an even better story when it is told with living examples that stand up at every level of the organization. Management knew how important this meeting was, but for some reason, they were not connected to the internal communications group in the way they should have been. Internal communications was seen, as it often is, as an order taker—a pizza-and-marcom delivery service.

The chief executive officer (CEO) had meetings with her people. The president had meetings with his. The vice presidents had a few of their own, and, finally, the "get-it-done-team"—the order takers—were brought on board.

Their task was to come up with a theme and a logo for this important meeting. Where would their input come from? What was their starting point? What was the history? What themes had been tossed around, and what were the reactions to these themes? They had limited exposure to strategy, no role in creating it, and no direct interface with the leadership team.

They came up with "On Our Way to Number One!" and "Becoming the Change We Want to See" and "One Company, One Team, One Goal." Plus several more.

What they came up with was not great. The group's early ideas did not match up with leadership expectations. So, the leadership team decided, once again, that they would have to take matters into their own hands and deliver a theme; the group could come up with a logo. That was the least they could do.

The theme they delivered was "It Starts with You." The order takers crossed from their list "Come up with a theme" and went to work on "Create a great logo."

The theme had potential; there may be something in there, but some flags should have gone up in the internal communications group. They should have known that there were some serious issues throughout the organization. They should have been aware of a widespread fear (and often dislike) of some of the senior team. They should have known that there were eyewitness accounts— stories of which had already spread far and wide—of public flogging of under-performing managers. They should have known that employee engagement and satisfaction were at an all-time low.

They should have known, but they did not. Had they known, and had they the interface and the ongoing dialogue and respect of the leadership team (or at least one champion on the team), they might have been able to avert what turned out to be a catastrophe. In another company, on another day, in another year, this theme would not have been a big deal.

The leaders tried to make it work; they rallied behind the theme. They sent out memos and e-mails explaining their good intentions. They told the masses things like "Turning Our Company Around—It Starts with You."

If the leaders had been branding a college, a nonprofit, a political movement, or another kind of business that might successfully appeal to the needs and desires of one's altruistic motivations, the theme might have worked.

But when you are in an organization that is in the business of making money, you have to be clear and up-front about that. As a business, you give good product and service, maybe even great products and amazing service (think Nordstrom's), in exchange for money.

Employees—or ambassadors—are not much different. There are many studies that illustrate a list of reasons why employees change companies—and money is not on the top of the list ("Retention," 2009). It is usually fourth or fifth. Employees' motivation to leave is often centered on how they felt they were treated and whether they felt they were doing important work.

Most employees go to work in order to get paid. And if the company has done a great job choosing, motivating, and engaging the employees, it will get great work in exchange. Most people are capable of doing a better job than they deliver every day; they must be motivated to outperform their previous best.

If you are curing cancer, fighting AIDS in Africa, or providing water to communities in developing countries, you might continue working at that organization (if you could) for no pay. Chances are good that you go to work each day motivated and engaged because you care deeply about what you are doing.

So back to the theme: "It Starts with You."

Some cultural challenges existed, which we have identified. And the CEO is going to get up on stage, in front of 2,400 people (and more watching a live stream). He is going to deliver an amazing speech written by an outside speechwriter. The outside speechwriter has no knowledge of the cultural challenges employees face, and the leadership team painted the "future vision" picture quite beautifully for the outside speechwriter. So he was able to craft this eloquent prose that, at another organization or in another year, might have worked. The deliverer of this world-class speech might have gotten a huge round of applause, maybe even a standing ovation, and e-mails from grateful employees saying how moved they were. And that would be good.

But that is not what happened. The speech came off as if an outsider was delivering it. There was no acknowledgment of the challenges the organization faced. There was no reckoning with the real challenges it faced. Instead, the speech came off as a flagrantly pompous attack on the little guy.

As employees sat in their chairs, already undermotivated and underengaged, the CEO went on and on telling them, "It starts with you." The success of the company, future competitiveness, increasing market and mind-share—all of that was to start with the little guys in the seats and watching via live stream. It was not going to start with any of the members of the C-suite.

It did not work, because the real world in which everyday employees lived did not match up with the tone of the challenge.

The CEO stood there, expecting a thunderous round of applause, expecting people to throw their babies in the air and sign an irrevocable blood-oath to the company. No applause came. Because when the CEO delivered the message, what employees heard was, "All the problems we have, the challenges we face, and the difficulties we are experiencing, these are your fault." And they heard it over, and over, and over in that challenging phrase. "It starts with you."

To make a long story short, the meeting ended, the company spent wheelbarrows full of money, and people left with less motivation than when they arrived. And they had the luggage tags and T-shirts emblazoned with the "winning" theme to remind them of the meeting.

Of course, there were other things at work in this meeting. A different theme would not have necessarily saved the day, but it might have lessened the bleeding.

If they had employed a simple pronoun change and gone with "It Starts with ME" and the CEO stood on stage and claimed personal responsibility, then *shared* that responsibility with everyone watching, the company might have had an incredible moment. Candor is a powerful thing, and it is probably what was needed in that moment. Instead, the audience felt blamed for the mistakes that had been made.

Of course, the company knew that mistakes were made. What did they do to address them? The marketing communications manager was fired and the group was restructured. Shame on them? Not really. The marketing communications manager did not step up to the plate, so to speak, and instead acted like an order taker. Their team did little more than the outside speechwriter did—they did exactly what they were told. It was easier to repopulate the group and start from scratch than to retrain the manager and challenge the manager to become a leader.

It is not fair, of course. There were many people at fault in this scenario. But at the end of the day, it is about value and contribution. The manager was not perceived as adding enough of either.

Case in Point: A Great Example

Once upon a time, within a Fortune 500 company not too far away, a successful president was preparing to add CEO to his title.

This company had been enjoying record stock performance. The president was credited and with good reason for breathing new life into what had been seen by many as a dying brand. He had already spent nearly seven years as president, preparing for this increase in responsibilities, in reach, and in impact.

The employees, many of whom were in fact ambassadors, were enjoying exceptional sales results, strong profits, and as bright a future as any could remember.

So how will the president-cum-CEO make the transition meaningful? How will he use it to make an impact? How will he capitalize on the successes of the past and use it to lead this larger organization into the future?

Considering the quality of personal connections this man had made in his seven years as president, you would think he would likely have some pretty good ideas about what he would like to see happen, what he would mandate going forward. After all, the troops truly loved him. They respected him. They listened to him. So what was he going to tell them about what he wanted to do?

Let us jump back in time from the new CEO start date by almost a year. He began planning for his move even before the news was announced. He gathered the key leaders from operations, communications and public relations, and human resources.

He laid out a plan to produce a program that he believed would better engage employees (soon to be known as *team members*) and encourage better results at the corporate level and in the stores. He said, "In order for our stores to be the best place to shop, then our stores and offices must be the best place to work."

He called his program "Think Best!" and he could have rolled it out on the day he would assume his new responsibilities. Along with his leadership team, he could have come up with a meaningful, powerful list of challenges, changes, and enhancements that would excite, engage, and energize the team. He could have, but he did not.

Instead, he asked the employees. He asked them in an incredible, profound, meaningful, and powerful way. The company was RadioShack, and the leader was Len Roberts.

Roberts knew that in order to engage employees' hearts and minds, he must involve them. What began as a simple idea became a significant internal rebranding effort.

The approach was simple enough. Sixty-three people were gathered together in a room and, after listening to Roberts explain the program, were asked to vote on the most important issues that faced the company. Fifty-nine of the people participating were employees, four were spouses of employees. Roberts wanted to make sure all perspectives not only were considered, they were involved. The employees came from a wide variety of people, from newly hired to nearly retired, and from administrative to executive. They represented every facet of a complex organization.

The employees then selected nine key focus areas, things like enhancing group insurance, improving vacation policies, creating a culture of positive motivation, and updating dress guidelines. As you can see, their focus was broad.

The teams were excited and ready to get to work. It is likely that they did not have a real understanding of the amount of work they were going to (gladly) invest. Each team member was given a badge branding him or her a *change agent*, and a trained facilitator took over the meeting.

The facilitator explained how things were going to work and each of the teams would focus on one of the areas identified for improvement. Each team would spend up to six months researching best practices, benchmarking competition, working with finance on feasibility and impact, getting input from a larger audience, and more. Each team had a leader, a scribe, and a vision. And before long, each team had a mission.

Instead of answering the question "How can we improve our vacation/personal days policy?" by saying "More!" they were guided through a business approach that weighed culture, cost, and competition.

Each team was given access to an executive sponsor, a corporate officer who was challenged to advise, not guide.

An entire book could be written (and probably should be) about Roberts's Think Best program.

"Think Best" became a new internal brand.

The sixty-four people each started out with their own ideas, but ended up—nearly a year later—presenting their group findings to management. These were not the half-baked ideas that often show up in suggestion boxes; these were fully baked and included cost analysis, implementation guidelines, expected impact, and more.

The team that reviewed vacation days and personal time made the case for more vacation days and flexible use for personal days. They made the case showing the real financial impact, a benchmark analysis comparing other companies' plans.

The team reviewing "Updating Our Dress Guidelines" presented a well-thought plan for implementing business casual in the home office and the field. They supported their claim with case studies, efficiency reports, and—most interesting—a solid study that showed a more open and honest dialogue in an office where dress was more casual.

And so it went, team by team, until all nine had made their presentations.

Surely to their surprise and shock, after the last presentation was made, the steering committee, led by Roberts, pronounced definitively, "Done!" They were even more shocked when for the first time in the history of the company *every* employee was invited to a meeting to hear what all the buzz was about. That was more than 2,400 people. To ensure that the phones were answered, two meetings of 1,200 people were held at the Bass Hall in downtown Fort Worth. The meeting was videotaped and shown to virtually every employee throughout the company that same week (more than 35,000 people). The entire employee audience was thrilled to hear Len Roberts pronounce "*Done!*" to enhancements in benefits, dress code, positive work environment, and more.

"DONE" became a new internal brand. It was seen on memos at every level, on e-mails between team members, and even on presentation slides during public events projected on the walls at annual managers' meetings.

The company knew that the program was a success, not only because of a measurable rise in engagement but also by requests from managers and department heads for cards, posters, signs, even note pads that encouraged them and those around them to "Think Best."

The Earth Isn't Flat (But My Budget Is)

People in nearly every department at every company everywhere have heard some version of the mantra (or demand), "Do more with less." This rings as true in internal communications, internal branding, and employee branding as it does everywhere else in the company.

It is even more true in 2011 than it has been in the past twenty-five years. Budgets are squeezed. Money is tight. Some companies are going out of business, while others thrive—and for lots of reasons.

Something that is far too often neglected or ignored altogether, other than our amazing employees, is the fact that many enjoy and employ social media (like Facebook and LinkedIn and microblogging like Twitter).

Shel Holtz, International Association of Business Communicators (IABC) Fellow and award-winning communicator (www.holtz.com), says that today, communications is more about the 140-character sound bite (the number of characters the system allows in a tweet) than about the white paper just released. More people are connected in more ways with more affinity than at any previous time in history.

What do people write about on their Facebook posts, in their Twitter tweets, and in their LinkedIn updates? They write about everything in their worlds, including their work experiences. Remember, you want *ambassadors*.

As a professional communicator today, you have a variety of media to use to communicate your company brand to audiences outside of your company.

Consider how those same media are used inside your organization to address internal branding and employee engagement.

Does your company have a policy on Facebook at the office? Some companies still have the archaic "No personal computer use" policy. No surprise, their employees are still getting online at work on their iPhones, Droids, company BlackBerries, or whatever device they love.

There are at least two sides to this discussion on social media policy. First, who (what person or group, depending on your company's size) at your company is responsible for monitoring and reporting on social media buzz about your company? If the answer is no one, and you are not with a small company, that is not the best answer.

If your company has more than seventy-five people, or is in the high-tech arena, someone needs to be responsible for monitoring current social media and reporting on what is being said about your company. The frequency and depth and detail are up for debate, but the basic need is not.

However, the internal employee branding focus is different. Your objective should be to engage your employee audience and make them *want* to talk about your company in positive ways. Make sure your policies are modern-day and realistic. It is important to realize that when many employee handbooks were written, most of us were not carrying a cell phone, much less a smartphone or iPhone. We can connect with more people during a coffee break than most people could in an entire day of working without these modern tools.

If you do not already embrace and use these new technologies, you need to. It is just that simple. The technologies will meld and change over time, but catching up will just get harder every day.

Employees have a louder, more effective mouthpiece than they have ever had in the past. In the past, the worst thing most companies had to worry about was an employee complaining to her or his spouse, family, and a neighbor or two. If they were particularly outgoing and adventurous, you might add bowling league. But today, Twitter and Facebook are 24/7/365.

Develop a policy and a plan that recognizes that employees are tweeting and Facebooking and engage these activities in a way that encourages employees to say great things about you. Take a lesson from this chapter, and engage your employees in the development of these policies and plans. At every turn, find ways to involve employees in these decisions that ultimately will make or break their satisfaction with the company, their levels of engagement, and their willingness to advocate for your business.

Today, countless people have been hired by word of mouth. People hold on to contacts for decades longer than they did in the past. And those who are lost are getting reconnected through social media.

The average person on Facebook has an average of 130 friends ("Statistics," 2010). Those people are saying something, and their friends are listening and are influenced. If your company sells a product or service that people can buy (as in RadioShack or Best Buy, as opposed to Intel or AMD), consider "friends and family" virtual coupons that can be distributed using Facebook. That is something that can build your internal brand *with* employees, while showing the rest of the world a great image.

Inside Out

Your external image begins with your internal brand. Your employees are the frontline players with your customers and other stakeholders. So it makes sense that the internal communications group has to make sure that on every intranet site, every employee memo and e-mail, every benefit communications, employee stock plan notice, open enrollment announcement, and in every training meeting, video, and webcast, the internal brand is consistent and engaging.

It is about whom employees think their company thinks they are—human capital or brand ambassadors. Employees' perception of how they are treated and how they are communicated with will directly affect their perceptions of their value and contribution to the organization.

As with all communications media, you *must* know your audience. You must write in the voice of the sender to reach the heart of the receiver and reach them with a message that resonates from the top of the organization through to every last employee.

Internal communicators must help the company's leadership see the importance of internal branding, help them prioritize *and fund* it, and help them see your ability to help the company deliver on that promise.

Your company's employees have more interested voices and a louder volume than at any previous point in history. Their friends are listening; give them something great to say.

References

Lloyd, S. (2002). Branding from the inside out. *BRW, 24*(10), 64–66.

Managing the rising use of social networks at work. (2007). *Strategic Communication Management, 1*(6), 8.

Retention: Why people leave. (2009). *HR Professional, 26*(5), 14.

Statistics. (2010). Facebook. Retrieved August 17, 2010, from www.facebook.com/press/info.php?statistics

CHAPTER NINETEEN

COMMUNICATING FOR A MERGER OR AN ACQUISITION

Patricia T. Whalen

Since the 1960s, mergers and acquisitions (M&As) have been the most common growth strategy for corporations worldwide, despite research showing that the majority of M&As do not achieve their financial goals and as many as half of them are *demerged* in full or in part within five years of the deal's completion (Whalen, 2002). The billions of dollars invested and lost by DaimlerChrysler and AOL/Time Warner, and the thousands of employees who lost their jobs in those failed deals, should provide a cautionary tale about the risks associated with a poorly conceptualized or poorly executed merger or acquisition.

A *CFO* magazine survey of Forbes 500 chief financial officers suggested that M&As fail primarily because of people-related issues such as incompatible cultures, management's lack of understanding of the acquired company, an inability to implement change, or clashing management styles and executive egos (Forbringer, 2002).

Some of the least successful M&As were short-circuited by people issues (DiMaggio, 2010). Take the 2005 $35 billion merger of Sprint and Nextel Communications. Because the firms were in the same telecommunications marketplace, many thought this was a logical and strategic M&A. However, the two firms focused on very different target segments and had different marketing philosophies, with Sprint focusing on the low-margin, high-volume consumer segment and Nextel focusing on more specialized business customers. Shortly after the deal's completion, there was a mass exodus of Nextel executives and managers who claimed that the two cultures could not get along. These issues, combined with the slowdown of the economy and increased competitive pressures, drove down sales and ultimately caused major employee layoffs and dramatic drops in stock price (DiMaggio, 2010).

Another reason an M&A may be labeled a failure is its inability to recoup its purchase price and earn a solid return on investment. This type of problem is typically due to a gross overestimation of the cost savings and revenue increases that can be achieved from the deal (Whalen, 2002). The Quaker Oats $1.7 billion acquisition of Snapple in 1994 is a classic example of this type of failed M&A. After acquiring the quirky Snapple brand for considerably more than its book value, Quaker Oats then tried to impose a more traditional mass marketing strategy similar to what it used with Gatorade, but the strategy did not work. After just twenty-seven months, Quaker sold Snapple for $300 million, a loss of $1.4 billion (DiMaggio, 2010).

While there is little that corporate communicators can do to affect the price of an M&A, there *are* ways they can influence the outcome of the deal, including proper management of the M&A strategic planning process, identifying and addressing key targets, and creating communications tools to meet the needs of the M&A. These activities are the focus of this chapter.

Understanding the Terminology

For the purposes of this chapter, the terms *merger* and *acquisition* are used as interchangeable concepts to describe a variety of combinations that, regardless of the specific method, all require some form of merging of firms' assets and personnel. There are, however, differences in the ways firms can combine (Ozanich & Wirth, 1993):

- *Acquisition* is the direct purchase of assets of another company using cash, stock, or a note providing for payment at a specified rate and time. Usually the acquired firm continues to exist, but under new ownership.
- *Merger* refers to the combination of two corporations' assets into a single existing entity, and the acquired company ceases to exist. It typically takes on the name and identity of the acquiring firm.
- *Consolidation* takes place when both firms cease to exist as they were, and a new identity is created that incorporates both firms' identities.
- *Joint ventures* involve two or more firms that invest in a new venture, but they continue to operate their parent firms as separate and independent organizations.

Merger of Equals

In addition to these legal definitions, corporations sometimes erroneously use the term a *merger of equals* when one firm is clearly dominant. It sounds like a friendlier transaction, and executives hope that this designation will help smooth the integration process (Whalen, 2002). While a true merger of equals is possible when both firms play an equal role in deciding how the newly merged firm will be organized, it is a rare occurrence.

More commonly, a lead firm (usually the acquirer) makes most of the decisions regarding the deal, and this firm usually intends to install its own processes and managers at the acquired firm. This was clearly the case when Jurgen Schrempp, then chairman of Daimler-Benz, planned the 1998 merger with Chrysler Corporation to form the $40 billion DaimlerChrysler Corporation. Despite the German automaker's clear dominance in the decision making, Schrempp repeatedly used the term *merger of equals* when discussing the deal with Chrysler employees, shareholders, and the media. He set up expectations that never materialized. Shortly after the deal's completion, Schrempp publicly admitted that he intentionally mischaracterized the equality of the two firms to help the deal go through. This revelation caused a class action lawsuit on behalf of Chrysler's shareholders and resulted in dozens of negative news stories. DaimlerChrysler's stock took an immediate nosedive and never fully recovered. That, plus a deepening recession, caused the 2007 divorce between the two firms, with Chrysler being sold for a mere $7 billion (DiMaggio, 2010).

The lesson here is that while a merger of equals can be a sound approach to an M&A, if one firm is clearly the acquirer, it should be up-front about its role in managing the deal. Nevertheless, smart acquirers acknowledge the unique qualities of the acquired firm and show respect to its management team and workforce. After all, one assumes that the acquired firm has something to offer or the deal would not have been made in the first place.

Synergy

Another often misused and overused term is *synergy*. When an M&A announcement is made, investors, customers, employees, and the public are typically told that the combined firm will achieve great synergy, meaning that the two firms will achieve more as a combined operation than what they could achieve separately. This is the argument for paying more for a company than its book value.

The media today treats this term with a fair amount of skepticism, and the public now recognizes that there are many less than synergistic reasons that firms are acquired or merged, such as eliminating the competition, fulfilling ego needs of a CEO, or just plain greed. When real synergies exist, they tend to be in terms of increased revenues or reduced costs.

Revenue synergies come from market growth, cross-selling opportunities, and an improved competitive position, but they are particularly hard to predict. A McKinsey study found that 70 percent of mergers do not achieve their revenue synergy targets. *CFO* magazine suggests that some acquirers, such as Eaton Corporation, avoided the problem by forecasting only cost synergies and refusing "to be drawn into a game of guesswork" about revenue synergies (Frieswick, 2005, p. 27).

Cost synergies, or savings that occur due to consolidation within two firms, are slightly more predictable and more likely to be reported than revenue synergies, although the McKinsey study found that 40 percent of those M&A targets are also missed. Most cost synergies fall into one of two categories: financial synergy and operating synergy.

Financial synergy is often sought when the focus of the deal is diversification and to merge the two firms' financial assets. All M&As look for some type of financial synergy, but it is often the sole motive for conglomerates that acquire firms in unrelated fields and plan to operate them as independent businesses. Some key cost savings through financial synergies include an improved tax situation; eliminating duplicate central accounting, legal, and computer systems; a lower cost of money from lenders; and combining the merging organizations' insurance plans, employee benefits, and pension funds.

Operating synergy is often sought when two firms are in a related field and there is perceived similarities in markets and operations. Typically called *strategic mergers*, these almost always result in layoffs and consolidation of facilities. The most common operating synergies sought are integration or reduction of production facilities; achieving economies of scale in purchasing and manufacturing; and reductions in selling, administrative, and overhead expenses.

These types of synergies can be stressful for an organization and can result in employees becoming angry, defensive, secretive, and resistant to the deal. Some employees go into a siege mentality as soon as the deal is announced. Marks and Mirvis (1997) call this reaction the *merger syndrome* and suggest that the best employees will begin to leave, while those who remain will experience physical and emotional stress that lowers their performance and organizational commitment. Arbuckle (2003) found that when the firms announced that synergies would be achieved through consolidation of facilities and integration of people, the degree of conflict and culture shock that employees experienced rose significantly. Therefore, planning well in advance of the deal and knowing what to expect go a long way toward reducing employee anxiety.

Preparing for the M&A

Every corporate communicator faces the possibility of being called into the CEO's office and asked to have a news release and communications plan ready to go by the next day to announce a major merger or acquisition. In this situation, there are three things for the communicator to do:

1. Ask why the M&A is being undertaken and what synergies it is trying to achieve so this information can be incorporated into the communications strategy.
2. List all of the firm's constituencies who will be affected by this M&A and ask about each of them: Who will likely benefit and who might be hurt by this deal? Who will be most resistant and what must we do to overcome that resistance?
3. Develop a plan to address all key targets, recognizing that there are several stages to the M&A process, and different targets will take precedence in different stages (see Figure 19.1). The three broad stages are
   a. The confidential preannouncement planning stage that culminates in the public announcement
   b. The premerger planning stage that focuses on obtaining regulatory approvals and creating internal and external excitement for Day One, the official first day of the newly merged entity
   c. The postmerger integration stage, when all of the functional plans need to be put into place to integrate the businesses and achieve the promised synergies

Preannouncement Planning

At the outset of the deal, the planning team will be small because confidentiality is critical. The two main activities in this stage are to help identify any financial and cultural barriers to moving forward and to coordinate with the other firm on the wording and process for publicly announcing the deal.

Cultural Due Diligence

Due diligence refers to the homework that needs to be done up-front, before the deal is finalized. Financial due diligence is a given when an M&A deal is being considered. The accountants and lawyers look very closely at the financial

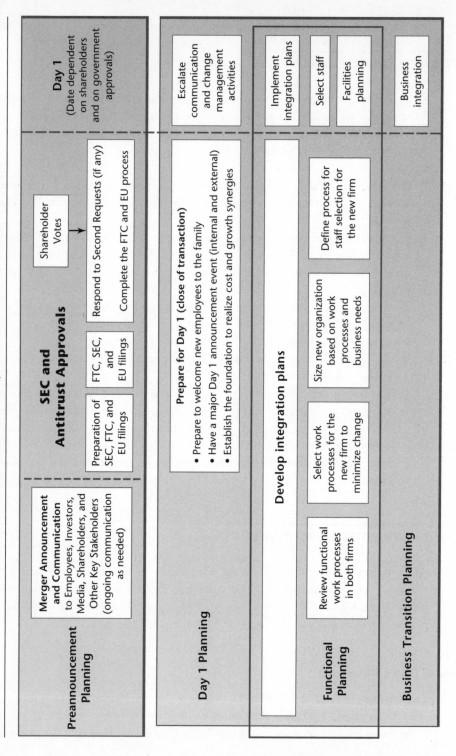

FIGURE 19.1 MERGER AND ACQUISITION PLANNING OVERVIEW

Note: SEC = Securities and Exchange Commission; FTC = Federal Trade Commission; EU = European Union.
Source: Adapted from a slide by Catherine Maxey, Dow Chemical Company, April 10, 2001.

soundness of the deal before proceeding to final negotiations. Unfortunately, internal communications experts are rarely brought in at this stage, and therefore there is little opportunity to explore the cultural compatibility of the two firms. Those companies that do undertake cultural due diligence can identify potential pitfalls for the deal in organizational culture, management styles, employee reward systems, and work ethic.

Planning for the Announcement Day

The most important activity in the preannouncement stage is creating a compelling explanation of the M&A and translating this explanation into the appropriate communications vehicles for specific audiences. These typically include a news release for the investment community, letters and intranet articles for employees, a brochure for customers, and frequently asked questions for managers.

One of the biggest challenges in the preannouncement stage is to work on the communications materials while keeping the information secret until it is ready to go public. While most firms take a position never to comment on rumors, if a rumor about the deal becomes widespread and people begin to trade on the stock based on that rumor, it could become necessary to move up the announcement date. Corporate communicators must be ready to make the announcement at a moment's notice.

Announcement Day

On the announcement day, it is useful to have one team focus on internal audiences while another focuses on the news media and investors. Other external audiences, such as customers and suppliers, will also require specialized communications, but these are typically handled by the marketing and purchasing departments, who should be brought in to the planning prior to the announcement if possible, and if not, then immediately upon announcement.

Media Interest. The corporate communicator should be prepared for the greatest amount of media interest in the deal at the initial announcement, which could make front page news or be the lead story on national news broadcasts. Accordingly, any key messages that the two firms want to convey must be incorporated into the early announcement. After that, follow-up reports about the deal tend to slow down or are buried behind more recent news. The image management firm Lippimott & Margulies found that firms that planned a name change for the merged entity should provide it during the initial announcement or risk that it will be lost in obscurity if announced later ("Name it now," 2000).

Employee Interest. It is critical on announcement day that whatever is said to the news media and other external audiences be reflected in what is communicated to internal audiences. Because of selective disclosure laws, publicly traded firms cannot favor employees by providing information about the deal in advance of the public notice, but they can ensure that the information is distributed simultaneously. The fastest way to do this is to provide a copy of the news release to employees (with some personalized message) at the same time that it goes to news media. When possible, this is done in person in large group meetings; but in global firms, e-mail may be the only way to distribute the message quickly.

At this early stage, management rarely knows exactly what the impact of the deal will be on jobs, plant consolidations, and so on, but this is exactly what employees want to know. The best approach is to be honest about the motive for the deal and to provide a timeline for when these decisions are most likely to be made and how employees will be informed about them. Newsletters, intranet articles, and other communications can follow to provide updates and clarification. Figures 19.2 and 19.3 provide a list of the most common formal and informal communication tools used in M&As and when they are most often used.

Premerger Planning

Once the announcement has been made and the initial media frenzy has dissipated, the corporate communicator moves into the premerger planning mode. During this stage, three key activities must be done simultaneously:

1. Obtaining approvals from shareholders and all of the government oversight groups, including any specific regulators in the firms' industries
2. Keeping employees in the loop while planning for the official merger kickoff on Day One of the combined firm
3. Developing the ongoing integration plans to help the two organizations work as one

Obtaining Regulatory Approvals

Before the deal can go through, the merging firms must obtain approvals from government regulators: the Securities and Exchange Commission, the antitrust division of the U.S. Justice Department, the European Commission (if appropriate), and other regulatory bodies that may have a voice in the deal. In addition, shareholders of both firms (if publicly traded) must approve the deal. Primary

FIGURE 19.2 FORMAL EMPLOYEE COMMUNICATIONS TACTICS USED DURING MERGERS AND ACQUISITIONS

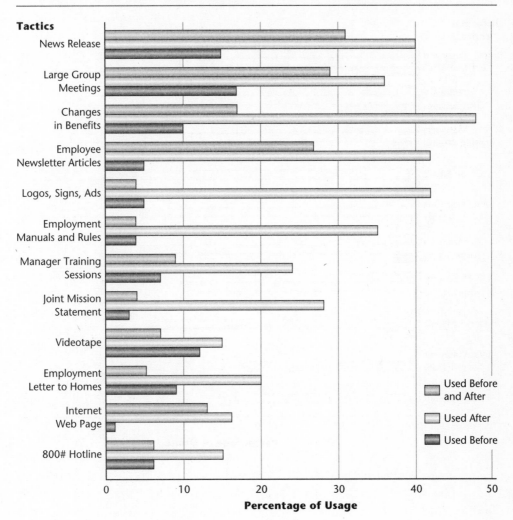

Source: Whalen (2001).

communications activities for this are typically handled by the legal, government affairs, and finance departments; a coordinated effort is critical, since all public communications will likely enter into the review proceedings. Any negative media headlines or skeptical comments from board members, investors, employees, or customers will likely hinder the approval process.

FIGURE 19.3 INFORMAL EMPLOYEE COMMUNICATIONS TACTICS USED DURING MERGERS AND ACQUISITIONS

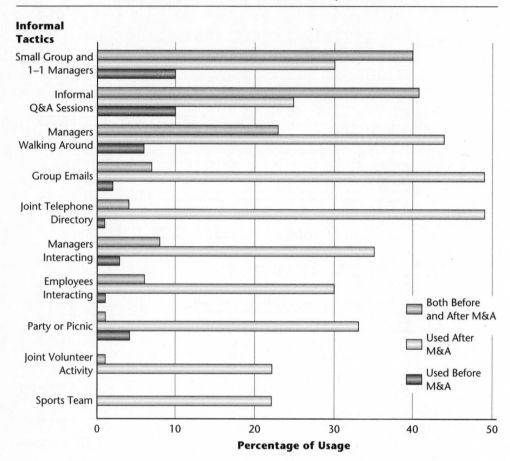

Source: Whalen (2001).

Keeping Employees in the Loop

In this premerger stage, management is often so focused on investors and regulators that they ignore employees. Their logic is that there will be no employee impact if the deal does not go through. But in the absence of direct information from the company, employees will scan every media story and blog posting to try to determine the real story about the deal. To keep anxieties as low as possible, Sally Benjamin Young (2009), vice president of communications for

Lundbeck, Inc., suggests that it is critical to create and maintain a vested interest in the deal among employees and make management accessible to them as much as possible. She cautions that productivity loss is a major issue once an M&A is announced and notes that a well-orchestrated communication effort is essential to keeping employees focused and contributing. "Creating two-way personal dialogue and demonstrating leadership's commitment to its people helps avoid the failure all too common to M&As: employees quitting without actually leaving because they have no connection to the organization's ongoing success" (Young, 2009, p. 28).

This is great advice, but establishing two-way personal dialogue is not always feasible, especially in large, widely dispersed organizations in which executives cannot have face-to-face meetings with every employee. There are three tools, however, that have the ability to personalize communication across large groups of employees: business television, town hall meetings, and CEO blogs.

Business Television. With digital technologies, the ability to stream video to employees anywhere around the world has become fairly easy, and this tool is often widely used on the day of the announcement to personalize the message for a wide array of audiences. For these one-time events, most firms hire a professional video production firm to shoot it and upload it to the Internet or for a live satellite feed. However, a growing number of firms are using business TV as an ongoing tool to keep employees up to date on the deal's status; these usually require a dedicated staff and studio to create daily broadcasts.

This tool was used in 2001, during Dow Chemical Company's $12 billion acquisition of Union Carbide and Mead Corporation, in its 2002 merger with giant Westvaco, and in 2005 when MeadWestvaco sold off its paper manufacturing operations to a holding company, forming NewPage Corporation. Both firms had utilized the technology for daily broadcasts long before their M&As, and during the M&A process management could break in to their regular content with news about the status of approvals, organizational changes, and action items that management needed employees to accomplish.

Town Hall Meetings. Town hall meetings have become common during the M&A process. These allow for more face-to-face interaction, materials tailored for a local context, and auditing to ensure that programs are successfully executed (Alexander, Lindsay-Smith, & Joerin, 2009).

But there are some risks to town hall meetings: employee cynicism, distrust, and concerns that their questions or comments may be scrutinized and that they may be punished for contrarian views (Guiniven, as cited in Woodward, 2006). To tap into employees' natural desire for connectedness, management should be there before employees arrive and should mingle, turning this formal tool into a more informal tool. Another approach has been to have executives ask questions of employees. Guiniven suggests that some sort of written follow-up to a town hall meeting should occur so that key message points can be formalized and employees feel that their concerns were noted.

CEO Blogs. A more recent tool that has been used to keep employees, as well as other stakeholders, informed about organizational activities is a CEO blog. This tool can fill in the missing gaps when face-to-face meetings are not feasible and can lend an authentic and personal quality to the communications about the deal. Demopoulous (2009) suggests that a CEO blog can put a face to top management and associate a personality with an organization. When this occurs, the CEO builds trust and likeability, essential elements in good employee relations, since people tend to trust people they know (p. 1).

But blogs, especially those with the authority of the CEO, have many potential pitfalls, including Securities and Exchange Commission restrictions on what can be communicated about a deal still in progress. Jonathan Schwartz, former CEO of Sun Microsystems, although a strong advocate for executive blogging under normal circumstances, resisted the urge to fire up his own blog for nearly nine months in 2009 during Sun's acquisition by Oracle. When he returned to the blogosphere after the deal's completion, which left him no longer CEO, he aptly titled his new blog *What I Couldn't Say* (Demopoulous, 2009). He wished the newly merged organization success but also alluded to communications constraints placed by the SEC and his sense of personal restraint under the circumstances.

In contrast, John Mackey (2010), CEO of Whole Foods Market, made extensive use of a CEO blog during his firm's acquisition of competitor Wild Oats Market. However, this blog had a professional feel that suggests that it was written and managed not by the CEO but by professional staff to describe the company's new executive team, its organizational structure, and to provide charts of the organization's financial performance. Mackey's conservative approach may have been the result of his past troubles with the SEC related to his negative blog posts about Wild Oats for which he used a pseudonym; he was investigated for trying to drive down that firm's stock price in preparation for the acquisition (Paumgarten, 2010).

Planning for Day One

Day One is the term used to describe the very first day that the newly merged entity becomes a legal entity. Often, this is the first day that the stock of the new firm is traded. Unfortunately, this can be an anticlimactic event, and many Day Ones come and go with little or no public acknowledgment because the media have lost interest in it. Therefore, a key activity for corporate communicators during the premerger planning stage is to develop materials and strategies to create interest and enthusiasm for the new entity on its first day of operation, especially with employees, investors, and customers.

This was certainly true for the Dow/Union Carbide deal in 2001 after languishing in the European Union regulatory system for nearly eighteen months. The media had lost interest, and it was difficult to maintain employee enthusiasm. To generate interest for Day One, the company held a Dow Day on Wall Street with banners streaming from the New York Stock Exchange building and greeters distributing Dow pens to traders as they entered the building. Dow's CEO rang the opening and closing bell for the first day of trading of the new Dow stock, held a news conference in New York, and granted dozens of print and electronic media interviews. Hundreds of news stories were generated about the event.

All of this was covered by a TV crew from Dow's in-house news department, which ran the story live at all Dow and Union Carbide facilities worldwide. At company headquarters in Midland, Michigan, employees watched the proceedings from an auditorium and then sat in on a live discussion with company executives about what the deal would mean for the two firms. Magazines were distributed to all employees around the world in a variety of languages detailing the history of the two firms along with a package of materials that provided answers to many questions about benefits, timetables for integration, safety rules, and other matters. In addition, an elaborate package of materials for customers of both firms was distributed to the sales force and mailed to key customers.

Postmerger Cultural Integration

In the last stage of the M&A process, the corporate communicator is focused on ensuring a successful integration of all newly merged employees and keeping the outside world informed about how it is going. This, of course, assumes a strategic merger in which cultural integration is critical for success. If the M&A is one of the few that seek only financial synergy and employees are promised a hands-off arrangement, then the M&A process is complete, and operations go back to normal with only minimal communication and interference from the new corporate parent.

However, if cultural integration is the goal, then integration teams will continue to operate well after the deal is official for as long as deemed necessary by management.

Best Integration Practices

Many factors will influence the best integration tools to use in an M&A, including the motive for the deal, how much rivalry existed between the two firms prior to the deal, size differences, geographical separation, and how much interaction will be necessary among the employees of the two firms.

For those pursuing a strategic M&A in which cultural integration is critical, successful deals use both traditional, formal communication tools such as newsletters, intranets, hot line numbers, and videotaped messages from the CEO and more informal tools to help create opportunities for members of the merging firms to interact with each other. These tools include training opportunities that mix people from both firms, managers walking around the acquired firm's facilities and meeting people, combined sports or volunteer activities, joint parties or other social occasions, as well as joint e-mail and telephone directories that help employees find their counterparts in the sister firm (Whalen, 2001).

Formal and informal communications are necessary during a strategic M&A. Information will be trusted and relied on more if the merging firms take the time to create informal interactions with members of their key constituencies to explain the strategy behind the M&A and answer questions in person (Whalen, 2001). The informal interactions are much more time consuming, and the information is harder to control for corporate communicators, but the most successful firms put strong emphasis on management training and encourage face-to-face communications about their M&As. They also anticipate most of the questions that will be asked and have FAQs for managers and the sales force well in advance of the deal's completion, so that informal interactions are as useful as possible.

Conclusion

M&A communication cannot be reduced to a single formula. Just as the types of deals and their motives vary, so should the approach to communicating about these deals. For some M&As, honest and open communication at the outset will be all that is necessary for a successful transaction. But for the majority of M&As, a great deal of planning and implementation will be necessary from the moment the deal is conceived and will continue to be necessary throughout the life of the merged organization. This will help a sound M&A reach its full potential by reducing the amount of nonproductive time spent in dealing with personality clashes and employee misunderstandings.

One of the biggest factors that separates successful from less than successful deals is the use of experienced communicators who are involved in the planning early and have created an M&A action plan that allows them to learn from their own and others' past mistakes (Whalen, 2001). Communications, no matter how well done, will not eliminate the conflict that will naturally arise when painful workforce reductions and closing or consolidation of facilities are necessary. Communications will not make up for a gross miscalculation of the synergies that can be achieved or the overpayment for those synergies. Today M&As face some of the toughest scrutiny in history. The media no longer give them a free pass. Customers have become suspicious of the motives behind them. And the investment community is no longer willing to carry the entire burden of the deals through stock-only transactions. Corporate communicators need to be part of the M&A planning process early on and need to ask the right questions and ring the alarm bell when the answers do not make sense.

References

Alexander, J., Lindsay-Smith, S., & Joerin, C. (2009). On the quest for world-class internal communication. *Strategic Communication Management, 13*(4), 32–35.

Arbuckle, G. A. (2003). Nine axioms for success in mergers. *Health Progress, 84*(1), 38–42.

Demopoulous, T. (2009, February 26). *CEO blogs: 3 reasons CEOs should blog.* Message posted to http://bloggingforbusinessbook.com/blogging_for_business/ceo_blogs/

DiMaggio, M. (2010). *Best (and worst) mergers of all time.* Rasmussen College School of Business/Rasmussen College Online, accessed from CNBC.com, Retrieved June 30, 2010, from www.cnbc.com/id/34467713/?slide=1

Frieswick, K. (2005, February 1). Fool's gold. *CFO,* 27.

Forbringer, L. R. (2002). *Making mergers work.* Olin School of Business. Available at www.olin.wustl.edu/discovery/

Mackey, J. (2010, May 12). *Keeping our executive team together for 10 more years.* Message posted to www2.wholefoodsmarket.com/blogs/jmackey/

Marks, M., & Mirvis, P. (1997, May–June). Revisiting the merger syndrome: Dealing with stress. *Mergers and Acquisitions,* 21–27.

Maxey, C. (2001, April 10). *Dow and Union Carbide—Communications and change management in mergers and acquisitions: A case study.* Presented at Northwestern University, Evanston, IL.

Name it now. (2000, July 2). *PR News.* Retrieved from www.prenewsonline.com/news.4027.html

Ozanich, G., & Wirth, M. (1993). Media mergers and acquisitions: An overview. In A. Alexander, J. Owers, & R. Carveth (Eds.), *Media economics: Theory and practice* (pp. 115–133). Mahwah, NJ: Erlbaum.

Paumgarten, N. (2010, January 4). Food fighter. *The New Yorker.* from www.newyorker.com/reporting/2010/01/04/100104fa_fact_paumgarten

Whalen, P. T. (2001). Well said: The role of communications in mergers and acquisitions. *Investor Relations Quarterly, 4*(2), 26–28.

Whalen, P. T. (2002). *How communication drives merger success.* San Francisco: IABC Research Foundation.

Woodward, N. H. (2006). Doing town hall meetings better. *HR, 51*(12), 68–72.

Young, S. (2009). Communicating through a successful merger at Lundbeck Inc. *Strategic Communication Management, 13*(6), 28–32.

CHAPTER TWENTY

THE CHALLENGES OF EMPLOYEE ENGAGEMENT

Throwing Rocks at the Corporate Rhinoceros

Roger D'Aprix

The task of engagement—that is, unleashing the energy and talent of people in the workplace—is one of today's most critical leadership challenges. It is also formidable. And, surprisingly, in some quarters it is even controversial.

For some the controversy is whether engagement is real or possible in a hierarchical organization in which command-and-control leadership dominates. For others it is the belief that engagement is a manipulative leadership technique to squeeze more out of an already overworked and understaffed workforce. These dissenters argue that unless, or until, today's democratization of information overcomes corporate autocracy, there is little hope for wholesale, voluntary engagement of a workforce.

Their conservative opposites continue to wonder whether it is even wise to engage and empower the workforce, as though sharing power is a dangerous idea. Suffice it to say that for their own reasons, not everyone is enamored with the idea of employee engagement.

At the same time the business case for engagement is so powerful it cannot be ignored. Various studies show that companies with high levels of employee engagement clearly outperform their competitors. For example, high-engagement companies are reputed to have a return on assets six times higher than those with low engagement. High-engagement companies also show on average a 19 percent increase in operating income and 28 percent growth in earnings per share year over year. Conversely, companies with low engagement numbers show a 32 percent drop in operating income and an 11 percent drop in earnings per share (Towers Perrin, 2008). These claims are difficult to dismiss.

The essential engagement vision is the creation of a work environment that inspires every employee to give his or her best effort. Despite all the talk to the contrary, we are still a society that struggles with the question of how to lead people effectively in institutional settings—in effect, to create that inspirational work environment. But change is in the air as more and more institutional leaders recognize that they are living through a revolution in which the sterile phrase *human capital* really translates to *people* as *the* vital resource that makes or breaks the organization's vision and mission. The pace of this change can only be described as remarkable. It is also very uneven from organization to organization.

Workers as Mere Units of Cost

For the most part, the history of human capital leadership both before and during the Industrial Revolution was a sad affair. It was largely characterized by a fondness for authoritarian leadership that was aided and abetted by bureaucratic management structures. The underlying, but unspoken, premise was that workers were untrustworthy, childlike creatures who needed more than anything to be parented—rewarded when they conformed to the rules and punished when they did not.

Psychologist and business critic Harry Levinson (1973) characterized this timeworn arrangement as "The Great Jackass Fallacy." His simple observation: if we are so enamored with carrot-and-stick reward systems, we need to reflect on what we typically put between those two objects—namely, a jackass.

For most managements, practices that grew up over the long history of the Industrial Revolution stemmed from the belief that the workforce was nothing more than another cost of doing business. Global competition, the emergence over time of a large body of educated workers, and the massive application of technology that could be manipulated only by talented knowledge workers, together with unprecedented access to information, have together introduced a new set of realities.

Nonetheless, too many organizational leaders have clung to the old views despite all the evidence to the contrary and have continued to indiscriminately treat the members of their workforce as interchangeable units of cost. For example, in the financial crisis of 2008–2010, 72 percent of U.S. companies chose to reduce their workforces to save money and improve their bottom lines (Towers Watson, 2010). Not surprisingly, 70 percent of employees say those actions have negatively affected how they feel about their work and their employers. Tally up the engagement costs of not appreciating and recognizing the contribution of key performers who quit in disgust. Consider also the numbers of talented people who leave organizations because they can no longer tolerate a martinet of a boss. The waste in talent and dollars is appalling.

In this chapter we examine the organizational factors that encourage or discourage engagement. A simple process to begin to address employee engagement organization-wide is also proposed.

Engagement as a Soft Issue

Those of us who think seriously about issues like engagement are often frustrated by the tendency to label them as soft, as though they were not worth discussing or so squishy that they are impossible to define or manage.

The word *soft* in the corporate lexicon is usually a derogatory term. We tend to think of soft people as weaklings. We speak of the soft-hearted, for example, as opposed to the hard-nosed or the tough-minded among us. Or we talk of soft numbers when we really mean numbers that are hard to come by or difficult to manage. Or we talk of someone who speaks softly. It is usually not a compliment. The connotation is timidity or uncertainty—qualities that in corporate life are generally not admired.

Author Umberto Eco (2005) uses a wonderfully vivid phrase to describe one of his characters in a short story titled "The Gorge." The character is a kind man who blames God for the evil around him. Eco writes, "He had it in only for God, and that must have been a real chore, because it was like throwing rocks at a rhinoceros—the rhinoceros never notices a thing and continues going about its rhino business, and meanwhile you are red with rage and ripe for a heart attack" (p. 66).

Communications professionals face a rhinoceros of their own. Metaphorically, it is that self-satisfied body of business leaders who, in their heart of hearts, long for the days of command and control and dismiss any initiative or process designed to improve human leadership as unnecessary and frivolous. In truth, the autocratic leader is a threatened species. The hard realities of global competition that demand innovation, the introduction of technological tools that give unprecedented creative power to their users, the exploding availability of information, and the increasing openness of contemporary society all make the autocratic style less suitable than at any time in modern history. Like it or not, institutional leaders must now share power and win followers who are inclined by virtue of that sharing to give their best efforts in support of the organization's goals and mission.

In reality, it is all a matter of balanced leadership. Former General Electric chief executive officer Jack Welch differentiates among four types of manager/ leaders:

1. The ruthless, who focused on the numbers regardless of the people costs
2. The people managers, who thought people and their needs were infinitely more important than any numbers
3. The incompetent, who achieved neither the financial nor the people goals
4. And then the only managers he wanted to keep: the ones who met the numbers through excellent people leadership

By and large the generation of progressive leaders who have succeeded Welch and his contemporaries are more likely to be receptive to the power sharing implicit in the notion of employee engagement—and more willing to give up command-and-control leadership in favor of consultation and collaboration. Their goal is improved performance and innovation. Engagement offers a strategy to achieve that goal if leaders can create the required inspirational environment to make it happen.

The Rock Throwers

Tolerance of autocratic management behavior, the tendency to layer organizations with unnecessary levels of approvals, and the inclination not to trust or value human assets have all given birth to this virtual rhinoceros that charges ahead, often oblivious to the rocks that are hurled at it by a multitude of persistent researchers, enlightened management thinkers, human resource professionals, and countless consultants. The rhino has managed for years to go about its nasty and costly business while the rest of us marvel at its capacity to ignore the forces aiming to tame it or end its mindless run.

Today, there is great hope. Current pressures and realities suggest that the days of the dominance of the corporate rhino are numbered. Various rock throwers are having an impact on those who believe that the soft management issues were not worth the effort to address them.

Persistent rock throwers have included the Gallup Organization, David Sirota, Frederick Reichheld, and Towers Watson (Towers Perrin before the 2009 merger with Watson Wyatt).

Gallup has been a leading advocate and popularizer of the notion of engagement. In fact, Gallup may well be the first organization to use the term. Buckingham and Coffman (1999) note the difficulty of guessing how well one company or one manager is doing in eliciting employee engagement. They emphasize that the real pressure for increased engagement is coming from institutional investors who command billions of dollars in company stock. Describing this group as "the ultimate numbers guys," Buckingham and Coffman assert that in years past, institutional investors did not concern themselves with issues like culture and employee satisfaction or engagement, seeing them as fundamentally irrelevant. Today they take a keen interest in such things as drivers of business success.

The Gallup Organization has spent the past thirty-plus years gathering engagement data from millions of people in hundreds of companies. Buckingham and Coffman note that searching for the drivers of engagement in this stack of data was like looking for the proverbial needle in the haystack. The search was to identify the core elements that help attract, focus, and keep the most talented employees. The end result of this huge research effort was what Gallup finally termed the "Q12" survey items—the twelve questions that identify which organizations had the greatest percentages of engaged people.

The twelve questions, not surprisingly, are heavily slanted toward an individual's personal relationship with the organization. Equipped with that understanding, Gallup has been able to determine the degree of engagement in any particular work organization. The items in question link to such critical issues as productivity, profitability, retention, and customer satisfaction.

Ten of the twelve questions in the research linked consistently with the organization's level of productivity. Eight are linked to profitability. Five are linked to employee retention. Of the twelve questions, Buckingham says that six were the most powerful predictors of an engaged workforce: an understanding of job expectations, the availability of the materials and equipment to do the job, the opportunity to contribute one's best at work, recognition or praise for a job well done, whether one's supervisor cared about him or her as a person, and whether there was someone at work encouraging his or her development.

It was clear in all the data that supervisors, team leaders, and managers were powerful influencers of whether people were or were not engaged. All of that is consistent with the research findings through the years that people quit bad bosses rather than bad companies. The data also emphasize the conclusion that the most powerful communication experience of any employee is the day-to-day interchange with authority figures—particularly with his or her immediate supervisor.

FIGURE 20.1 GALLUP DATA ON THE DEGREE OF ENGAGEMENT IN TYPICAL COMPANIES

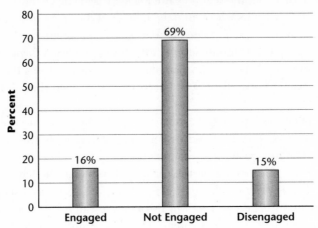

Source: The Gallup Organization.

The remaining Q12 questions deal with whether employees perceive that their opinions are listened to, whether the company mission creates individual pride, whether coworkers are perceived as committed to quality work, and whether people had a best friend at work. As Figure 20.1 shows, the degrees of engagement and of disengagement in the companies in the database were roughly equal. The group that was neither engaged nor disengaged was by far the largest at 69 percent, so the opportunity to do better is huge. The implication for communication professionals is clear: to have an impact on engagement, concentrate a significant part of your strategy on improving the typical line manager's efforts.

Researcher David Sirota comes to a remarkably similar set of conclusions after reviewing the employee data he gathered over a ten-year period. His database includes 2.5 million employees in 237 diverse public and private organizations in eighty-nine countries.

Here is what Sirota, Mischkind, and Metzler (2005) claim are the key drivers of engagement: achievement, equity, and camaraderie. By *achievement*, they mean the pride one takes in doing things that matter well and receiving the recognition that creates pride in the organization's accomplishments. The components of achievement sound very much like some of the elements of the Q12: the challenge of the work itself, the ability to acquire new skills, the training and the resources needed to do the job, the perceived importance of the job, recognition for performance, and working for a company in which one can feel pride.

The second element of the three primary goals of people at work is *equity*, the need to be treated justly in relation to the conditions of employment. The basic conditions Sirota et al. (2005) describe as physiological (a safe working environment, an equitable workload, and comfortable physical working conditions), economic (a reasonable degree of job security with satisfactory pay and benefits), and psychological (being treated respectfully with credible and consistent leadership). Again the echoes of the Q12 can be clearly heard.

The third element is *camaraderie*, "having warm, interesting and cooperative relations with others in the workplace." The closest of the Gallup Q12 questions to this element is, "I have a best friend at work." In both cases, the researchers (Sirota et al., 2005; Gallup research) are pointing out the importance of the workplace as a social community in which people can derive satisfaction from the day-to-day interchanges with coworkers. It is not surprising that the stimulation that comes from working with like-minded and compatible people is an important element in determining engagement.

Both Frederick Reichheld and Towers Watson approach the subject of engagement in similar fashion by showing its impact on performance. Reichheld (1996) reports studies showing that customer loyalty is often dependent on employee loyalty (that is, commitment). In other words, committed employees are much more likely to create loyal customers who provide the repeat business that every organization depends on. The power of this relationship lies in Reichheld's finding that a 5 percent improvement in customer retention yields a 25 to 95 percent increase in profits, depending on the industry. The performance link is both clear and powerful.

Towers Perrin (2008), in its employee engagement report, presents the results of a survey of 90,000 employees in eighteen countries. One of the primary interests of the study was to determine what common factors most influence employee engagement globally. Senior management's ability to demonstrate genuine interest in employees is the top engagement driver. The report notes, "This finding speaks to the enormous influence that a company's top leaders have on their extended global teams, even among people they have never met and may never meet" (p. 10). In rank order, the study determined these ten as the primary drivers of employee engagement globally:

1. Senior management interest in employees' well-being
2. Improved my skills and capabilities over the last year
3. Organization's reputation for social responsibility

4. Input into decision making in my department
5. Organization quickly resolves customer concerns
6. Set high personal standards
7. Have excellent career advancement opportunities
8. Enjoy challenging work assignments that broaden skills
9. Good relationship with supervisor
10. Organization encourages innovative thinking

Once again you can hear the echoes of both Gallup's and Sirota's research in these findings. Achievement, equity, autonomy, pride, resources, camaraderie, caring leadership—all of these qualities resound through their collective findings, as does the assertion that attention to these matters profoundly affects the performance of the individual and therefore the organization.

The Engagement Power of the Boss

Increasingly the rhinoceros and its handlers are an anachronism. But the important question remains: How do you create that overall work experience that supports high levels of engagement? The answer lies in aligning a number of key influencers from management behavior to what gets inspected and rewarded in an organization.

The one word that sums up the need most directly is *leadership*—not just leadership from the top but leadership at all levels of the organization, and particularly leadership at the level closest to the employee. Undeniably one of the most critical influencers of employee behavior is the behavior of the boss. *Boss* is an unfortunate word because it conjures up all of those negative images of arbitrary behavior, unmerited privilege, checking up, and "Because I said so." A more accurate term is *line manager leadership*.

What does that role entail? The model that I have found to be the most descriptive (Figure 20.2) is based on addressing an employee's engagement needs from the most basic question—What is my job?—to the clearest engagement question—How can I help? It assumes that people's engagement needs begin with a focus on the performance issues closest to them and then progress to the larger issues of how they fit into a team and then into the larger organization before they can determine how much discretionary effort and loyalty they are willing to give that organization. It is a dynamic, almost day-to-day, minute-by-minute decision-making process having much to do with how employees are treated over time. And it is profoundly affected by the nature of the work they are doing.

FIGURE 20.2 A MODEL OF THE EMPLOYEE QUESTIONS LINE MANAGERS MUST ANSWER

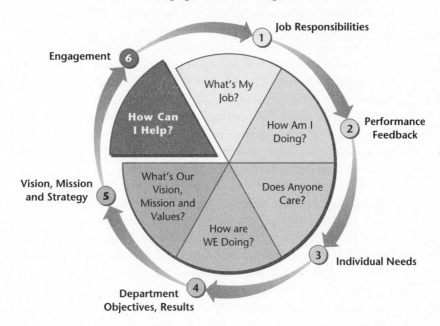

The How-to of Engagement: Moving From "I" to "We"

In all of this, the immediate manager or supervisor plays a critical role by answering the six questions of the model through his or her words and actions. Coaching, listening, providing performance feedback, recognizing accomplishments—all of these are the basics of eliciting lasting levels of engagement. This is the role of the contemporary manager in today's competitive work organizations, but it will not happen if managers are not accountable for their behavior.

In addition to training managers and holding them accountable, any line manager initiative must take into account the need for senior managers to provide the proper role modeling and prodding that is essential to sustained performance. That means consistent leadership behavior to reinforce the kind of engagement culture the organization has deemed critical to performance and business results.

That same initiative requires a selection process that accurately identifies leadership talent and puts only those in leadership positions who have the innate instincts and people skills to lead. An executive of Inter-Continental Hotels once put this selection issue in crystal-clear terms for me: "If you want people in my business who smile and welcome guests enthusiastically, hire people who are friendly and smile . . . and then teach them the hotel business." Similarly, if you want real leaders in an organization, select people with people skills, and then teach them the other things they need to know.

Finally, line managers cannot make engagement work without support and without information. There is a need to ensure that they are fully educated in the marketplace issues of the business and are provided the information and tools necessary for effective communication and leadership.

In specific terms for communications professionals, there is no doubt that improving employee engagement will also require attention to the communications role that has been most ignored in the past: the task of supporting the line manager's communications and leadership roles.

But there is an important caveat. And it may help explain the doubts that are expressed by those who are agnostics about the practical realities of engagement. Engagement is ultimately an *individual* response to an inspirational environment. The impact of such an environment on institutional success is an accumulated effect. In other words, it is the *aggregated* result of individual efforts. Any individual's engagement on any one day or even hour may be wildly erratic. Humans are not machines, so to expect them to remain highly engaged on a continuous basis is unrealistic. What we can hope for is that most of the time and in most cases where that inspirational environment exists, the environment will carry the day and keep most people at high levels of performance even when there are peaks and valleys in their commitment and energy. Engagement is like any other human relationship.

Translating It All Into Practical Actions

In the past, the communications professional has been mainly a tactician charged with delivering organizational messages as efficiently as possible. That meant essentially the task of sending out stuff. The new competitive environment calls for much more than journalistic or electronic skills geared to the efficient dissemination of information. What is now required is the ability to size up employee communication needs, collect relevant data, and use this information as the basis for strategy. It also means strong collaborative and relationship-building skills with peers in other functions. In turn, that requires analytical skills, deep knowledge of the organization's business and marketplace, the ability to synthesize information and turn it into suitable communication strategies, and the skills to counsel a preoccupied and pressured leadership. It is not a role for the faint-hearted.

Working with the senior leadership also requires the communications professional to acquire strong consulting skills. That means being comfortable in the role of influencer rather than simply program designer and implementer. In fact, one recent university study in the United Kingdom found that simply being proficient in communications craft skills was an impediment to one's success in today's environment (Watson & Sreedharan, 2010). This task of engagement is so broad and diverse that no one skill set is adequate. Also no organizational specialty can own it. It has to be a highly collaborative effort of everyone who has a stake in the game.

An illustrative example of what I mean comes from a joint effort by communications, branding, and human resource professionals at Symantec Corporation partnering with consultants at ROI Communication. Both Symantec and ROI are Silicon Valley–based organizations in the heart of the U.S. high-tech universe. When Symantec executives learned from a series of surveys and focus groups that employees had little understanding of company strategy and corporate business objectives, they were concerned that this lack of understanding could be hurting company performance.

The two top drivers of engagement are senior management's genuine interest in employees and the opportunity for employee improvement in knowledge and skills. Based on this understanding, the company leadership launched an annually recurring initiative that focuses on Symantec's vision, mission, values, business strategy, and brand promise. The goal was to use company vision and strategy to enhance employee engagement and emphasize that "Symantec Is You." The logic was that the leadership's intent to create a more informed and collaborative workforce, and greater alignment with company strategy, would be the levers to creating higher levels of employee engagement.

The initiative leverages Symantec leaders and managers as *the* primary communication channels to reach all 17,700 employees across all business units and geographies. To support managers in this effort, multimedia channels, online tools, and other electronic communications were developed. Among the specific goals of the initiative were improving employee collaboration and reducing the impact of silos as well as helping Symantec people better understand the market views of customers, business partners, and the financial community.

Manager-led, all-employee meetings were held over a six-month period across the global organization. In addition a President's Forum, a full-day, in-person meeting of the company's top 150 senior leaders was the means of launching "Symantec Is You" for the leadership team and ensuring understanding and commitment. A social network was created for Symantec managers to share messages and follow-up questions in a restricted-access online network.

The results of the effort were impressive. For example, 82 percent of employees reported having a higher awareness of how they can make a difference at Symantec. More than 80 percent of the workforce reported having a high understanding of Symantec's future vision, customer experience, and cultural aspirations. More than three-quarters of the workforce claimed a high understanding of Symantec business priorities, corporate strategy, and partner experience. The result was demonstrable proof that the leadership cared enough to invest heavily in the kind of employee understanding that is the knowledge base for greater employee engagement and improved performance.

Driving the Rhinoceros Away

Clearly engagement is not a simple matter. It is a complex human process that is vital to an organization's competitiveness and business success. The so-called Great Recession that began in 2008 with the collapse of the financial sector shows how fragile the process of engagement really is. A recent report from Towers Watson claims that in the aftermath of devastating layoffs and high unemployment, employee engagement had declined by 9 percentage points overall and an alarming 23 percentage points for top-performing employees (Finney, 2010).

That means that engagement requires a sustained and unrelenting effort by all concerned parties to attack the fundamental causes of disengagement—causes that are deeply rooted in the psyches and dysfunctional behavior of many institutional organizations, from corporations to governmental and nonprofit agencies. Like the charging rhinoceros, the perpetrators as well as the causes do not go quietly into the night. Those causes must be carefully identified through a deliberate data-gathering effort to demonstrate the harm they cause. And then they must be addressed with a carefully integrated strategy.

Communications professionals by virtue of their interests and backgrounds need to be a vital part of that collaborative effort of helping to make the business case, collecting the data that show the root causes of disengagement, lobbying for the necessary training and development, and consulting with senior leaders and their staff peers on corrective action.

The task is formidable. It is also essential.

References

Buckingham, M., & Coffman, C. (1999). *First, break all the rules*. New York: Simon & Schuster.

Eco, U. (2005, March 7). The gorge (G. Brock, Trans.). *The New Yorker*, 62–73.

Finney, J. (2010). The new, new deal. *Communication World, 27*(2), 27–30.

Levinson, H. (1973). *The great jackass fallacy*. Boston: Harvard Business School Publications.

Reichheld, F. (1996). *The loyalty effect*. Boston: Harvard Business School Press.

Sirota, D., Mischkind, L., & Metzler, I. (2005). *The enthusiastic employee: How companies profit by giving workers what they want*. Indianapolis: Wharton School Publishing.

Towers Perrin. (2008). *Closing the engagement gap: A road map for driving superior business performance*. Towers Perrin Global Workforce Study 2007–2008. Available at www.towersperrin.com

Towers Watson. (2010). *Global workforce study*. Available at www.towerswatson.com/global-workforce-study

Watson, T., & Sreedharan, C. (2010). *The senior communicator of the future—Competencies and training needs*. Institute for Public Relations. Available at www.instituteforpr.org/files/uploads/Senior_Comm_Future-Watson.pdf

CHAPTER TWENTY-ONE

MEASURING THE EFFECTIVENESS OF INTERNAL COMMUNICATION

John Williams

You have a chest pain and rush to your doctor. "Doc, I need a heart transplant right away!" The doctor says, "What? How do you know? Let me examine you." "No!" you insist, "just schedule the surgery!" Makes no sense, but many people in the communications business make important decisions and take action without any examination (research) first.

Research is nothing more than a systematic process for getting sound answers to questions you need answered before you make decisions, solve problems, and take action. If you have questions to answer before you make decisions or solve problems, research can help show you the way. Get a physical before you order a heart transplant.

Whether you do your own research or rely on an outside consultant for part or all of it, an understanding of the research process is important. This chapter outlines the five key steps for developing and implementing a measurement plan, including both quantitative and qualitative research for internal communication programs:

1. Identify the problem and assess needs
2. Develop a research methodology
3. Conduct the research
4. Analyze the data
5. Communicate the results, take action, and commit to follow-up measurement

Step 1: Identify the Problem and Assess Needs

Make sure you know what the problem is and what questions need answers. Research begins with a problem that needs to be solved, and it answers important questions so the problem can be solved and intelligent decisions made.

Before you begin any research project, you must have a clear understanding of what you want to achieve. If you do not know what the target is, you will not hit it.

Ask yourself questions like:

- What needs to be determined to solve our problem?
- What will we do with the information when we get it?
- What important questions need answers?
- What information will answer those questions?
- How and where will we get this information?

Write down your research purpose (Why am I doing this research?) as well as your research objectives (What do I hope to end up with?).

As part of Step 1 in the measurement plan, it is important to understand some key guidelines for effective measurement:

- *Determine your purpose.* What do you want your research to uncover? Do you want to know what employees think about a given issue? Do you want to assess the overall effectiveness of your communications? Having a clear objective of your purpose will help you stay focused throughout the project.
- *Involve others* in the planning process, including senior management.
- *Commit to feedback afterward.* Tell people at the outset that you will communicate your findings by an announced date in an announced vehicle (a newsletter, a bulletin, e-mail, a video, face to face, and so on).
- *Commit to using the information to make changes.* Employees become very cynical toward surveys if their input is not going to change anything. You have to act on the information you gather.

Step 2: Develop a Research Methodology

Develop a detailed "map" of how you will achieve the research objectives outlined in Step 1. Here you plan the details of your research effort; consider different options; select research methods; and develop schedules, budgets, and research instruments.

Type of Research to Conduct

In order to meet your objectives, identify what kind of research you need to conduct, such as:

- Initial research that establishes benchmarks for future efforts
- Monitoring research that looks at programs in progress
- Evaluation research that looks at the effectiveness of programs after they are completed
- Exploratory research that tells you whether there are problems within your organization
- Descriptive research that tells you about employees' perceptions, concerns, and attitudes
- Explanatory research that looks for the reasons behind things
- Causal research that examines changes and effects

Methods of Measurement

Next, you need to determine which method of measurement to use to gather the information you need. Should you do a survey, or focus groups, or both? Perhaps include management interviews? Possibly observation of workplace communication?

There are two basic methods of measurement: quantitative and qualitative. Quantitative measurement involves numbers—quantifiable data that allow for a precise measurement that can be compared against other data in a statistically valid manner. The most common form of quantitative measurement is a survey.

Qualitative data is non-numeric, typically representing descriptions of how or why people think or act the way they do. For employee communications measurement, the most common forms of qualitative research are focus groups and management interviews.

Conduct a survey when:

- You need to know *what* people think.
- You need to know *how many* people think a certain way.
- You need to compare data for various demographic groups, such as business units, departments, job levels, work locations.
- You need data that are statistically representative of the entire audience.
- You want to give people throughout the company an opportunity to provide input.

Conduct focus groups when:

- You need to know *why* people think the way they do.
- You need examples and stories about what is working and what is not working.
- You do not need results that are statistically representative of a population.
- You have a specific set of questions to ask, but you would like to ask probing questions based on the participants' responses to your first set of questions.
- You want to solicit ideas for improvement.

Oftentimes, a research methodology calls for conducting a survey first, to obtain quantitative data, then following up with focus groups to better understand the issues raised in a survey. One good way to think about it is, Surveys tell us *what* people think, and focus groups tell us *why* people think the way they do.

Administration, Logistics, and Scheduling

How long will this research take? What about budget? What resources (staff support, management support, promotional material) are available? Will you need help with questionnaire design, tabulation of data, analysis, and reporting?

Budget. Setting a budget for measurement can be a complicated task, as it involves many variables. If you are using a research firm, ideally the firm can give you a good idea of the project cost before starting the research. If your budget is limited, you can conduct a survey yourself using various online survey tools that are available. You can also conduct focus groups yourself, keeping in mind that employees may not be as open with you as they might with an external facilitator.

In-House or Consultant? The measurement plan needs to include a consideration of whether to conduct the research in-house or hire a research firm. Conducting a simple research project with in-house resources can save money, but for large-scale projects, an in-house effort can require a significant amount of staff time—time that could be dedicated to completing other essential internal projects. When you factor in the expense of staff time, a cost-benefit analysis may show that hiring a research firm is more cost-effective.

Step 3: Conduct the Research

The third step is to conduct the research, which includes preparing the survey or focus group questions, selecting employees to participate in the research, and then collecting the data. The actions you take in this step will vary depending on whether you are conducting quantitative or qualitative research, so we address each methodology separately.

Quantitative Research: The Employee Survey

Quantitative research projects like surveys require a few stages of development.

Writing the Survey Questions. A vital step in conducting a survey is drafting the questions. Poorly written questions, or questions that do not focus on the objectives of the research, can result in useless data, wasting everyone's time, energy, and resources. To ensure your survey questions are accurate and scientifically valid, follow these guidelines:

- *Focus.* Each survey question should focus on a single, specific issue or topic. Make sure that the questions are addressing the information needs identified in the research plan. One good rule of thumb is that if you have the word *and* in a question, then it is not focused. For example, the survey question, "Senior management listens and responds to employee input," really asks about two things: whether management listens and whether they respond. How do respondents answer this question?
- *Be clear and logical.* The questions should be clear and makes sense to the respondent. The majority of people reading the question should have the same interpretations of what the question is asking.
- *Be concise:* Avoid long, wordy questions.
- *Avoid jargon.* Every corporation has its own jargon, and as communicators we think everyone knows what it means. It is important to spell out acronyms and explain what different terms mean.
- *Avoid bias.* There are various techniques in writing survey questions to ensure that they do not create a bias in the responses, such as avoiding leading questions, loaded questions, and ambiguous wording; being too specific, and more.

There are many types of questions that can be included on a survey, such as multiple choice, categorical (to which respondents can only select one response option), scaled, ranking, open-ended, and more. Oftentimes surveys use what is called a Likert Scale, which requires a respondent to state his or her level of agreement in response to a statement on the survey. For example, the survey may ask respondents the extent to which they agree with the following statement: "My supervisor keeps me informed of upcoming changes." The response options might be on a scale of Strongly Agree to Strongly Disagree.

In addition to writing the questions, you also have to come up with accurate and reliable response options. All possible responses must be accounted for and listed for each survey question. You may need to provide an option for "Other" on some questions in the event that you cannot cover all possible response options.

When drafting survey questions, the assistance of a professional survey researcher can go a long way in ensuring that your survey is valid and will result in useful data being collected for analysis and action planning.

Survey Audience: Census or Sample? The decision about whether to survey all employees or a random sample is an important one. Random sampling can be an effective way of gathering data that is statistically valid for the entire organization but only requires the input of a random sample of employees.

If you need to generate survey reports for multiple departments or other demographic groups within the organization, it may be necessary to survey all employees in order to have enough data to be statistically representative of each demographic group of interest. But if your main interest is in the overall opinions of all employees, then a random sample might be an effective strategy.

Consulting a statistician can be beneficial whether you are conducting a random sample or surveying everyone.

Conducting the Survey: Online Versus Paper? While more and more employees have electronic access, keep in mind that such electronic access is not equally easy for all employees. To avoid respondent bias, it is important to carefully consider the extent to which all employees have equal access to computers to complete an online survey. You might need to allow for a paper survey of employees who don't have electronic access to ensure your data are statistically representative of all employees. One approach to consider is to conduct the survey both online and on paper to give everyone an equal opportunity to participate.

Promoting the Survey. Promote the survey in advance and during the survey administration, and distribute at least one reminder to respondents. This includes communicating with senior management in advance, seeking their support of the survey, and even having senior management promote the survey among their units.

Response Rate. The response rate to a survey is the percentage of the survey audience that completed the survey. For example, if you send the survey to 2,000 people, and 1,000 participate, your response rate is 50 percent. There is no rule that sets a minimum response rate for surveys. If you need to provide reports for small groups of employees (such as department reports), then you likely need a high response rate. If you are primarily concerned with opinions of the overall organization, then your response rate may not need to be high. The response rate is influenced by many factors, and it is only one element in determining the statistical validity of the survey project. Effective response rates for an employee survey can range anywhere from 30 percent to 90 percent.

Response rates are strongly influenced by your methodology for conducting the survey: If you bring people into a room and ask them to complete the survey, you will have a high response rate (80 percent or more). If you send one e-mail invitation to participate in the survey and one reminder e-mail, with little to no promotion otherwise, you will likely have a low response rate (maybe 30 percent).

Qualitative Research

When measuring the effectiveness of internal communications, the most common methodology for qualitative measurement involves focus groups and management interviews. An important decision to make is whether to hire an outside facilitator. There are several benefits to using an outside facilitator:

- Participants are more likely to be candid and open with their comments.
- An outside facilitator will be unbiased and unlikely to get into a back-and-forth discussion with participants about a particular subject.
- The amount of information you can collect through focus groups can be daunting. A trained facilitator can help make sense of this large amount of information.

The main objective of conducting focus groups and interviews is to listen to and learn from participants on a particular topic or issue. You focus the discussion on the things you want to learn about those topics without introducing your own bias or judgment.

The focus group is a controlled discussion, but you have to be careful not to be too controlling. Every group is different in how they provide information, and the moderator has to recognize the participants' priorities and interests in order to draw them out most effectively. The key to success is to listen and ask questions based on what people say, not just based on a prepared script.

Four Types of Focus Groups

1. Problem identification
   - You have limited information about the subject prior to the research.
   - You want to focus on exploration and discovery.
   - This type has the least amount of control in the focus group. It is more of a free-flowing discussion.
2. Planning
   - You have a goal, and now you are working on how to achieve your goal.
   - There is still exploration and discovery in the focus group, but more control around your specific goal.
3. Implementation
   - You have already implemented your plans for accomplishing your goal, and you want to assess them while the project is going on and fine-tune your plans.
   - You want to focus on depth and context of information in the focus group.
   - There is more control in the focus group, asking about specific aspects of your plans and their implementation.
4. Assessment
   - Evaluate what happened in a project and learn lessons for how to do things differently next time.
   - Focus on interpretation of the subject: what worked and what did not work.
   - Generate insights into how and why things occurred.

Participant Criteria and Recruitment Plan. Identify the demographic criteria for participants to best represent your target audience. Do you want opinions from certain job levels, or business units, or work locations? Typically, it is important to hold separate sessions for employees from different job levels, such as nonmanagement, first-level supervisors, and middle managers. Keeping these groups separate enables participants to be as candid as possible. Participants will be unlikely to open up if someone from a higher job level is in the same room.

Focus groups work best with eight to ten participants. In most cases, you should *not* hand-select participants based on anyone's personal preferences. Instead, make the selections by a random process. Do not leave it up to managers to decide whom to send from their departments—they will tend to send you the most positive people they can.

How Many Focus Groups Are Needed? To determine how many you need, start with your target audience: How many different demographic groups exist? If you are interested in differences of opinion according to different demographic groups, then that will determine the number of sessions to conduct. At a minimum, conduct two sessions with each demographic group. If you have multiple business units or major work locations, conduct sessions within each of these groups.

Prepare the Focus Group Script. Identify whether you want a scripted question form or a topic guide.

- *Scripted question form:* Contains exact wording of questions for the moderator to use
- *Topic guide:* Lists subjects or topics, with key words that help prompt the moderator for questions to ask about each topic, most common method for employee focus groups

Advantages of a scripted form include increased confidence because the wording is precise; more efficient analysis; and more consistency when multiple moderators are used.

Disadvantages of a scripted form include that it takes more time to prepare the script and it can be awkward for a moderator if not written in conversational language.

Advantages of a topic guide include that it is faster to prepare a guide; it is more conversational for participants and moderator; and it offers increased flexibility for a moderator to be spontaneous and use questioning skills to maximize understanding of a particular topic.

Disadvantages of a topic guide include increased difficulty in analysis—questions may be asked differently in different groups, making cross-group comparisons difficult at times; and inconsistency between moderators.

Be sure to order your questions in the proper sequence so they flow nicely:

1. Opening or ice breaker questions to set participants at ease.
2. Introductory or big picture questions to encourage participants to start thinking about the subject of the focus group.
3. Transition questions to get to the core material of the focus group.
4. Core subject areas and drill-down questions. Typically, you can expect to be able to cover six to ten core subject areas during a 90-minute focus group

session. Drill-down questions might include, "Can you give me an example?" or "What results when that happens?"

5. Ending questions, such as, "Is there anything you would like to contribute that I did not ask about?"

Conducting the Focus Groups and Interviews. Conducting focus groups and interviews requires a special skill set: you have to be able to remove your own prejudices and opinions and truly listen to the participants. You have to engage them in a meaningful discussion, drill down into more detail at the right moments, and ensure that everyone has an opportunity to provide input. You have to prevent dominant people from controlling the discussion and be able to recognize when the opinions of one person may be influencing the rest of the group.

It is usually not necessary to record employee focus groups. Instead, use a moderator and a second person to serve as a note taker. Recording employee sessions can make participants nervous about being identified, even if it is just an audio recording.

Step 4: Analyze the Data

Making sense of the numbers or qualitative data can be a complex process, one that requires careful attention to detail. Use the analysis to help tell a story about what employees think about communication, and what can be done to improve it. Through your analysis, you want to:

- Seek out the top three to five items that are most important, that have the greatest impact on the organization
- Look for both strengths and areas for improvement
- Look for significant differences among demographic groups

Quantitative Data Analysis

Depending on how many questions you ask and how many demographic groups are listed on the survey, analyzing survey data can be a complex process. It is best to have someone who is good with numbers (preferably with a knowledge of statistics), and to use a software program built for survey data analysis. In general, most survey analysis steps involve:

- *Create charts and/or tables of data* showing responses to each survey question, including responses according to demographic groups.

- Identify a set of criteria for *determining strengths and weaknesses*. For example, you could set a threshold of 65 percent of respondents being favorable to a question to be considered a strength. Or you might use external benchmarking data, and anything above the benchmark is considered a strength.
- Look for *significant differences between demographic groups*. These differences will point out groups of employees who may be doing things very well or those who may need targeted intervention.
- Use *advanced forms of statistical analysis* to help uncover patterns or relationships in the data and to identify the key drivers of effective communication. For example, correlation analysis, multiple regression, and structured equation modeling are forms of statistical analysis that enable you to identify what aspects of communication are your key drivers.

Linking Survey Data to Organizational Performance. With advanced statistical analysis tools, it is possible to draw connections among employee communication and measures of organizational performance, such as employee engagement, productivity, and financial performance. Such techniques require a statistician who can perform complex statistical analysis of your data. The results can provide you with a clear picture of the communication processes that are key drivers in the organization and the role communication plays in the overall effectiveness of the organization.

Qualitative Data Analysis

Analyzing the results of qualitative research is part science and part art. You have to be able to take the stories and descriptions and in-depth discussions that occurred in the focus groups and interviews and interpret that information in a meaningful and accurate manner.

It is helpful during the analysis phase if a systematic process was followed while the focus groups were being conducted. Specifically:

- Ask questions in a logical, sequential format.
- Collect the data in a consistent manner across all focus groups.
- Code the data in a logical format. Look for common themes, ideas, concepts, responses, and code your notes accordingly as these responses occur.
- Verify participants. You can send the session summaries to participants to review and confirm that you accurately captured their input.
- Soon after each focus group (within 24 hours ideally), type your notes for the session, and code the data for key responses or themes.

There can be many pages of detailed notes from focus groups and interviews. To simplify the analysis, follow a procedure for each focus group session and interview:

1. First, *type your notes from each session,* ideally within the first 24 hours after the session.
2. Then, type a *summary of each session.* List the major themes, mood of the group, and overall findings. This can include a summary of key themes for each question or for each major subject area. To the extent possible, include an indication of the strength of agreement among participants on each of your points. For example, "About three-fourths of the group agreed that they do not understand the reasons behind decisions made by their department manager."
3. After all the sessions are completed, prepare a high-level *summary of the entire research,* listing major themes and significant differences from group to group.

Step 5: Report the Results, Take Action, and Commit to Follow-Up Measurement

Communicate the findings and take action. Come to conclusions and make recommendations. Based on your findings, take action to solve the problems—do not let research results sit on a shelf!

Research is a continuing process; it does not end with a one-shot project. Research may generate new questions about things you were not aware of. If research prompts changes in your communications, you will need some evaluation to see the results.

The following steps can help you effectively report the results and develop action plans:

1. *Prepare an executive summary of the results* to be shared with senior management and even employees. Include your recommendations for action and the next steps being pursued.
2. *Report the results to employees in a timely manner.* Do not wait for action plans to be developed. Instead, let people know right away that you completed the research, what key themes emerged, and what will happen next.
3. *Present the results to senior management.* Let them know what the next steps are and how they can be involved to improve the communication climate.

4. *Develop a strategy for taking action* on the research results. Commit to at least three things to do right away. Look for short- and long-term initiatives, and develop strategies for implementing those initiatives.
5. Identify a plan for *follow-up measurement* to monitor your progress and benchmark over time.
6. *Identify people to be in charge* of carrying out the initiatives and tactics in your strategic plan, along with target dates for each task.

Failure to follow these steps will result in a breakdown of trust and engagement in your organization. If employees take the time to provide their input, and the organization fails to acknowledge that input (by reporting results to all employees) and take action on the input, then employees will be reluctant to provide their input in the future, and they will lose trust in management's ability to listen and respond to employees.

Giving feedback to employees about the research findings and taking action on the results can go a long way to building trust, understanding, two-way dialogue, and employee engagement. If employees see that the organization not only listens to their input but responds to it, they will be much more likely to want to participate in the process in the future, and they will feel like they have a say in the organization.

Case in Point: Communications Impact Modeling

Thanks to advances in statistical analysis techniques, communications measurement today can serve two critical functions:

1. *Identify key communication drivers.* Measurement can identify the key communication drivers of business performance and employee engagement.
2. *Predict the impact of communication.* Measurement can serve as a predictive analysis tool by quantifying the impact that communication has on organizational performance and engagement. By doing so, we can predict how performance will improve based on specific improvements to communication.

Using these advanced statistical analysis procedures to measure the impact of communication has generated a similar pattern across organizations: In every case, immediate managers are key drivers of employee engagement and the work environment. Other key drivers we commonly see include senior management, town hall meetings, newsletters, and intranets. Typically, we find that a 10 percent improvement in the key drivers results in a 12 to 17 percent improvement in the work environment and employee engagement. For one client, a 10 percent improvement in the key drivers was predicted to result in a US$15 million increase in revenue.

Companies that have focused their initiatives on improving the key drivers identified by advanced statistical analysis have seen positive results. One regional banking organization focused on three key drivers over a five-year time period: providing more information to employees, helping managers to be better communicators, and involving employees more in the business decisions. Their goal was to improve the internal work environment. Periodic surveys conducted during this time frame showed that the work environment improved by exactly the amount predicted by the communication impact model. What is more, the level of trust among management and employees improved from only 35 percent favorable to 50 percent favorable. There is still room to improve, but things are moving in the right direction as a result of the impact modeling process.

PART FOUR

PUBLIC RELATIONS

CHAPTER TWENTY-TWO

PUBLIC RELATIONS RESEARCH AND PLANNING

Don W. Stacks, Melissa D. Dodd, Rita Linjuan Men

The role of research and planning is essential to any public relations effort. Until recently, this aspect of public relations practice has suffered from what has been described as a lack of measurable outcomes. That is, public relations has been seen as a soft practice (one that focuses primarily on outputs such as news releases) or "publicity," most often an in-house organ or media relations unit that produced press releases and other promotional materials. As such, much of public relations planning was focused on getting a message out to as many constituents as possible, often without much thought to the outcomes that these materials were seeking to influence.

This chapter reviews the research and planning process involved in successful public relations campaigns that cross various corporate communication needs. It examines the research process and focuses on the roles of research in the campaign, such as benchmarking and evaluation of public relations outcomes. The chapter is rounded out by a review of the research methods employed in both gathering data and providing indicators of program success and an overview of the measurement process in terms of return on investment (ROI) and return on expectations (ROE).

Public Relations Research and Planning

Public relations research is no different from any other type of corporate research and should strive to meet several ends. First, it should be driven by the same general organizational research assumptions that drive other organizational areas. Second, public relations research must address achievable and measurable goals. Third, research has specific uses that should match those goals. Fourth, public relations research should be programmatic rather than one-shot case-by-case instance driven. Finally, public relations departments need to have the budget and resources to carry out this research.

Research is the controlled, objective, and systematic gathering of data. It seeks to describe, understand, predict, and control phenomena (Hocking, Stacks, & McDermott, 2002). Basic research begins by describing what the public relations action is and what it seeks to do. Once described, the research can then be used to understand the concern or problem and establish a baseline against which the public relations campaign can be measured and evaluated. Research serves to provide reliable and valid data from which to answer questions of importance to the organization. The keys to how well the questions are answered, however, depend on the research methods employed, the type of data gathered, the reliability and validity of those data, and the systematic collection of the data. This is how social science and business research should be conducted.

There are seven basic uses of public relations research:

1. Public relations research monitors developments and trends as part of the department's environmental scanning function.
2. It examines the current public relations position on an issue or problem.
3. It serves to assess communications activities and functions, such as messaging and corporate credibility, trust, relationships, reputation, and confidence in the organization.
4. It continuously and systematically measures communication effectiveness.
5. It tracks audience perceptions over time.
6. It looks for gaps in the current research that need filling.
7. It evaluates over time the progress made in achieving organizational goals and objectives and offers suggestions for improved decision making.

It should be clear by now that public relations research and planning should be no different from other kinds of organizational research. Research should be planned based on the same decision-making processes found in the organization. It should set measurable objectives that focus on overall business objectives and goals in such a way to correlate with behavior and then determine the strategies to meet them. This process is typically divided into three phases: development, refinement, and evaluation, each having its own objectives in the overall campaign goal.

Best Practices in Public Relations Research and Planning

Best practices of public relations research lie in two broad areas: the use of specific research methods and procedures, and the application of measures that examine both the quality and the substance of public relations activities (Stacks, 2010; Stacks & Michaelson, 2010). To begin with, it is important to set clear and well-defined research objectives so that they can contribute to the measurement and evaluation of the program. This is followed by the application of rigorous research design that meets the highest standards of research methods so that it can provide usable and actionable information. And then, detailed supporting documentation needs to be provided with full transparency of how the research was conducted and what the results yielded.

To assure the quality and substance of research findings so that they contribute to improving the public relations program, a first best practice is to design the research to demonstrate the effectiveness of public relations activities; that is, to show the potential impact of a message or a program and set benchmarks to gauge future performance. Second, it is critical that the research links public relations outputs (for example, newsletters, blogs, media releases) to outtakes (targeted audience and key opinion leader perceptions during the campaign) and outcomes (the impact of outputs on target audience) (Bowen, Rawlins, & Martin, 2010). In addition, research findings should be applied to develop better public relations programs and their impact on business outcomes and organizational effectiveness needs demonstrated. Finally, best practices require that public relations research programs be cost-effective and applicable to a broad range of public relations activities.

Through implementation of best practices, public relations research can provide requisite insights for improved planning and effectiveness of public relations campaigns. From a programmatic perspective, effective public relations planning is accomplished through the following steps:

1. Reviewing secondary research and establishing benchmarks
2. Establishing achievable goals
3. Stating measurable objectives
4. Asking appropriate research questions
5. Employing appropriate research methodologies

6. Conducting programmatic research
7. Having the resources in place and the budget necessary

Reviewing Secondary Research and Establishing Benchmarks

No planning can begin until the problem is understood and the strategic options are known. Planning without first understanding the problem or the internal client cannot be done effectively unless previous research or research carried out by other organizations has been first examined.

Secondary Research. All organizational research must begin with a thorough understanding of what has been done previously. Furthermore, to better understand what has been done and why it was done, secondary research is both necessary and an antecedent to any research planning. Secondary research is research that has already been conducted or data reported. It can take a variety of forms, some public and some proprietary to the organization or to other organizations. Researching public or association databases may be required to understand the problem; academic and public libraries accessible both physically and by Internet provide a rich understanding of the campaign at hand. Bibliographies, case studies, and position papers such as those found at the Institute for Public Relations can be reviewed to provide background. Some secondary research is proprietary to the organization itself and may be found in other departments such as marketing, human resources, or general counsel. A review of secondary and historical material provides a window to both theory and past practices. It also reduces the costs associated with data collection, as it often provides answers to questions without additional and possibly expensive research.

Benchmarking. Secondary research also provides possible benchmarks against which to gauge campaign progress. Without something to gauge against as a baseline, a campaign cannot be evaluated during or afterward with any degree of precision. If secondary data are not available, then data must be gathered prior to kicking off a campaign (baseline) and must be planned for (benchmarks) within the campaign timeline. This is accomplished during the run-up to kickoff, that is, the developmental phase of the campaign. A good public relations department will continually scan the organization for data that can be used to benchmark a public relations problem, thus reducing both research costs and time required to work up to the project.

Establishing Achievable Goals and Stating Measurable Objectives

Before objectives can be stated, goals must be established. A goal is a general outcome expected by the end of a campaign. All public relations goals should reflect the goals of the organization. Thus, a goal statement should have two components: one that clearly indicates the organizational goal and one that includes the public relations goal in meeting the larger organizational goal. Thus, if the organizational goal is to increase productivity, the public relations goal might be stated as: "To help meet organizational goals to increase productivity by establishing effective communications vehicles between management and labor."

Once the public relations goal has been established, the objectives can be stated. It is one thing to say that you want to get something done (a goal); it is much more difficult to state how you will do it (strategy and tactics), with what results (outcomes), and by what date. Thus, an objective is almost always written in the form of cause and effect with outcome. An objective might be "To increase employee contributions to the annual giving campaign from 56 percent to 78 percent through an intranet e-mail push campaign by August 15." The objective clearly states what the problem is (employee contributions to the annual giving campaign), what the current giving and target are, what strategy is being employed (intranet e-mail push), and the date by which the objective is to be reached.

Public relations objectives can be further broken into functional objectives that must be met or evaluated as a campaign progresses. From a logical perspective, the information or messages to be employed in the campaign must first get to the targeted audience and be both understood and accepted. Behavior without a reason is not dependable and is easily countered. Thus, we have an *informational objective* that has to be measured and evaluated. Once the information has been received and understood, one must ask if it motivated the target audience to do what is being requested. Thus, we have a *motivational objective* that has to be measured and evaluated. Third, assuming that the target audience has received, understood, agreed with the message, and been motivated toward our request, we need to find out if the members of the audience are planning on doing what we asked. Thus, we have a *behavioral objective* that has to be measured and evaluated. (See Figure 22.1.)

Figure 22.1 notes there is a loop between the informational and motivational objectives. If the motivational objectives are not being met, an evaluation of the informational objectives must be undertaken to find out why the target audience's attitudes and beliefs have not been changed or reinforced. For each objective there should be one or more research objectives detailing what methodology will be employed, when it should be employed, and what is the expected outcome. For example, a research objective could be "To gather data from employees (target audience) on perceptions of an annual giving campaign (variable of interest or outcome) through an intranet-based web survey (method) between June 1 and 6."

FIGURE 22.1 PUBLIC RELATIONS OBJECTIVES

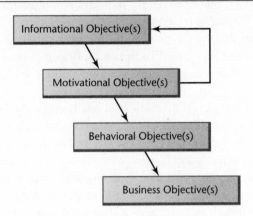

Source: Don. W. Stacks (2010). *Primer of Public Relations Research*, 2nd edition. Used with permission.

Obviously what is being measured during most of the public relations campaign deals with things that cannot be directly observed, with the exception of some informational objectives such as whether the message is actually available to the target public. Thus, measurement, and particularly the measurement of attitudes and beliefs, becomes an integral part of planning a public relations campaign and is covered later in this chapter. Figure 22.1 shows the planning flow for evaluation, from informational to behavioral objectives, and then ends with an evaluation of whether the public relations campaign had an impact on the business or organizational objectives.

Behavioral objectives are particularly important to note here because often public relations evaluations of success in terms of informational and motivational objectives leave organizational leaders unsatisfied. For example, organizational leaders are ultimately not concerned that 80 percent of employees are motivated to increase donations to an annual giving campaign. Rather, they are more concerned with the behavior of increased giving.

Thus, behavioral objectives are detailed in a behavioral model of public relations (Center, Jackson, Smith, & Stansberry, 2008, pp. 13–16). The model describes awareness, latent readiness, and triggering events and their likelihoods of resulting in the desired behavioral outcome. The focus of the model shifts objectives away from awareness as a goal to a behavioral outcome. Additionally, because audiences rarely go directly to the desired behavior based on the message

FIGURE 22.2 PROGRAMMATIC RESEARCH AND
PUBLIC RELATIONS OBJECTIVES

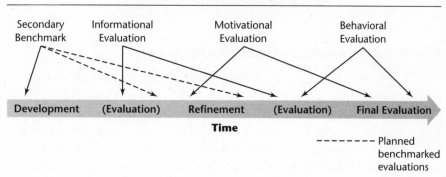

Source: Don W. Stacks (2010). *Primer of Public Relations Research*, 2nd edition. Used with permission.

they receive, the model further explicates intermediate behaviors that may be needed to obtain the desired behavioral outcome.

Figure 22.2 demonstrates how the research should be planned during the campaign. Note that multiple evaluations are conducted that overlap to provide a viable timeline and multiple benchmarks. This allows for strategy or tactic refinement throughout the campaign and provides additional data to compare against business objectives and goals.

Asking Appropriate Research Questions

Research is driven by the kinds of questions asked. In general, there are four basic questions addressed by research: (1) questions of definition (What is it?); (2) questions of fact (Once defined, does it exist and in what quantity?); (3) questions of value (If it exists, how good or bad is it or was it?); and (4) questions of policy (What should be done?) (Hocking et al., 2002; Stacks, 2010). All research must begin with the question of definition. What exactly are we researching? How is it defined or operationalized in both business and public relations objectives? Once we have defined the problem or objective in such a way as to examine it as factual, do we have the quantitative information necessary to establish differences or changes over time—a baseline of sorts through secondary research—or should new research be commissioned? Next, the facts need to be established: How well have we done or, in terms of goodness or badness, what specifically was done well or poorly? Finally, the question comes down to "What should we do?" based on our answers to the first three questions. This is the recommendation that the public relations department takes to the management table for action.

Employing Appropriate Research Methodologies

Choosing an appropriate research methodology depends on the type of questions being asked (Table 22.1). When problem solving or identifying goals and objectives, the questions deal with *definition*. Secondary research is often the best method to employ and may consist of field observation (knowledge gained from communicating with potential audiences or publics or from continuous environmental scanning), previously published research, or case studies. Second, the *facts* must be gathered and benchmarks established against which the results can be evaluated. This requires quantitative methodology to run throughout the campaign: surveys, polls, communications audits, and in the more advanced departments, experiments or simulations that deal with questions of fact. At times it is necessary to conduct qualitative methodology to establish how well the tactics are working by using focus groups, in-depth interviewing, or content analyses that deal with questions of *value*.

In general, we can break the research being conducted into three types. Secondary methods consist of analyses of existing data, most often in the form of published documents. Quantitative methods are scientific, employ large groups of participants or respondents, and with appropriate procedures can be generalized to larger groups through representative sampling. Qualitative methods are concerned with an in-depth knowledge of a few participants or respondents. While quantitative methods seek to establish normative responses

TABLE 22.1 RESEARCH METHODS

Secondary	Qualitative	Quantitative
Case studies	In-depth interviews	Surveys
Industry studies	Focus groups	Polls
Annual reports	Field observation	Delphi studies
Organizational files	Content analysis*	Content analysis*
Informal observation	Experiments or simulations	

*May be either qualitative or quantitative depending on how the content analysis is conducted.

that can be generalized to a larger population, qualitative methods seek to better understand how problems came about or how well tactics were received.

It is necessary to note that well-planned public relations campaigns should employ all three methodologies. This *triangulation* provides the information necessary to drive the "should" (*policy*) question or critically evaluate that question at campaign end.

Qualitative Methods. There are five basic qualitative methodologies found in public relations research. Each provides a wealth of in-depth research but has limited to no generalizability to larger audiences. A way of establishing which method to choose may be a function of the degree of control required in the research. Generally, *observation* is the least controlled and in-depth interviews the most controlled. Observation can be of two types: informal, when no particular notes are taken, and formal, when the observations are noted and analyzed. Environmental scanning in an organization is often undertaken through observation. *Focus group research* asks small groups of volunteers to talk about particular questions through a moderator-controlled discussion that allows participants to tag on to others' statements by employing a schedule of questions and possible follow-up questions. *In-depth interviews* are one-on-one interactions in which the interviewer asks questions of an individual through well-thought-out questions and possible follow-ups. *Content analysis* can have both qualitative and quantitative aspects. From the qualitative, a content analysis takes the messages that have been sent and evaluates them for their impact. That is, a press release may have been sent to the local media and published. A qualitative content analysis would look to see how the press release was positioned and whether it was used as desired.

Quantitative Methods. As a quantitative method, *content analysis* can be used to establish the fact that a message got out. But content analysis can also tell a lot about the message itself: its readability, the number of times a product is mentioned in the media, and other things—for instance, this paragraph consists of 116 words, 50 percent are passive, and it has a readability index of 12.0. (The readability index, calculated as a Flesch-Kincaid Grade Level, indicates that a reader needs at least twelve years of formal schooling to be able to understand the paragraph.) In other words, the content analysis becomes a quantitative method when its use is to establish some form of numeric measure. When we think of quantitative methods in public relations, however, the methods that come immediately to mind are polls and surveys.

A *poll* is a quick, factually based, and often behaviorally focused questionnaire that asks people to react to questions or statements on some metric such as "Yes or No"; "Strongly Agree, Agree, Neither Agree nor Disagree, Disagree, or Strongly Disagree"; or "on a 0 to 10 scale, how do you feel about *X*." The poll provides a way to quickly seek limited information; if representative sampling is used, it may be generalized to a larger audience. A *survey* is much longer and consists of both metric-based questions and open-ended questions that often seek to better understand attitudes. Thus, a question might be phrased in a "Yes-No" format and then followed with a "Why do you say this?" question. Surveys often seek respondent attitudes about the information received, what that information has motivated them to do, and whether they think they will do what has been requested (thus seeking answers to the three basic public relations objectives). Surveys, when conducted with representative sampling, may be generalized to a larger audience. A Delphi study is usually a survey in which the researcher tries to forecast the future based on successive waves of surveys with a panel of experts in a given field as a means of building a consensus of expert opinion and thought relating to particular topics or issues. Delphi studies are not generalizable.

Finally, the *experiment* or *simulation* is a carefully controlled, scientifically oriented methodology that seeks to find answers to basic questions or test hypotheses. Experiments and simulations are few and far between in public relations, partially because of practitioners' lack of training in the social sciences. An experiment or simulation carefully controls the influence of independent variables (things that will cause change in predictable ways) on dependent variables (outcomes of relevance). For instance, the independent variable is the communications channel used (verbal, printed, Internet) to get a message out, and the dependent variables might be the actions taken by the targeted audience or morale indicators.

Quantifying Using Measurement. When planning to conduct public relations research, it is important to think of how that research will be used over the long haul, whether it is for a specific problem or campaign. Hence, the more information that is gathered, the better the prognosis is for success. Part of this will be dependent on the type of data gathered. Public relations research seeks to gather information on what people believe or think—that is, attitudes and beliefs and if they have been created, reinforced, or changed. Attitudes and beliefs are the drivers behind behavior, and public relations has a demonstrated impact on both. The question, however, is how to measure something that by definition cannot be seen. The answer is through carefully created measurement systems.

Measurement systems are designed to create quantitative data that can be used to evaluate how people think. There are four kinds or levels of data:

nominal, ordinal, interval, and ratio. The most basic, *nominal* distinguish between the units being counted, which are often expressed as frequencies, percentages, and proportions. *Ordinal* data not only distinguish but also order the units according to some criteria, such as larger or smaller. Both nominal and ordinal data are categorical data because the quantification places each observation into planned categories.

Interval data are found on a continuum whereby the intervals between data points are assumed to be equal. With interval data, the distance between 1 and 2 is the same as between 2 and 3, which is the same as between 3 and 4, and so on. Interval data are quantified as means or averages, dispersions around the mean or average, and statistically standardized units allowing comparison of seemingly different metric systems. Statistically, interval data are more powerful than either form of categorical data (that is, they explain much more).

A special form of interval data is found when the research is trying to assess attitudes or beliefs. Attitudes and beliefs are generally obtained by asking respondents questions or statements on an "Agree" to "Disagree" continuum. This continuum has a requirement that some form of neutrality be assessed; hence there must be some way for the respondent to say, "I'm not sure." Hence, we find that scalar (attitudinal or belief) data are found on a negative through neutral (arbitrary zero) to positive continuum. Typically, attitudinal and belief measures consist of continua ranging from five to seven equally appearing units. The most often employed attitudinal measure found in public relations research is the Likert-type measure, which asks respondents to respond to two or more statements (see Likert, 1932). A full-scale attitude measure would have several statements assessing each objective (informational, motivational, behavioral).

Finally, *ratio* data not only meet the equal interval criterion but also have an absolute zero point (unlike the arbitrary zero in interval, scalar data). Monetary data are ratio in nature in that they can range from negative through zero to positive amounts, such as found in statements of trade balances or departmental budgets. Ratio data other than monetary or product production figures are not usually found in public relations; instead the focus is on interval or scalar data.

Finally, when conducting research always try to gather data at the most powerful level. You cannot take nominal data and redefine this material as ordinal or interval or ratio. You can, however, take ratio and reduce it to interval, interval to ordinal, and ordinal to nominal. Planning ahead—looking at what data are already available and their types—allows multiple uses of the data, especially when presenting the information to nonresearch or statistical audiences (such as upper management). Always keep in mind to whom you will be reporting as well as from whom you are gathering data.

Conducting Programmatic Research

All research should become programmatic over time. That is, the research a public relations department conducts should be based on previous research and lead to research down the line. Progressive and responsive public relations departments plan their research for the long term. Even during a public relations campaign, planning should be divided into the three stages or phases: development, refinement, and evaluation. At the *development* stage, both the communications and research goals and objectives should be developed. The goals must reflect the overall organization's goals, and the objectives should be actionable and measurable. At this stage a SWOT (strengths, weaknesses, opportunities, and threats) analysis may provide information regarding circumstances, target audiences and their characteristics, and communications strategies and tactics. During the *refinement* stage, research is conducted at planned intervals that validate earlier decisions and provide for corrective action when decisions are found to be off-base through focus group, survey, interview, or observation research. Finally, *evaluation* research determines whether the overall goals of the organization and public relations were met and to what degree. Evaluation research is based largely on performance effectiveness in terms of strategy, outputs from tactics, and behavioral outcomes.

Public Relations Impact on Return on Investment

Any communications manager will inevitably need to account for how the information (data) obtained from research is to be used in making organizational decisions. As previously discussed, much of what public relations researches is labeled "nonfinancial indicators." That is, public relations is often seen as important for establishing expectations from which behaviors will occur.

Contemporary public relations research typically concentrates on five generalized variables: confidence, credibility, relationship, reputation, and trust. Thus, public relations researchers now have the ability to conceptualize relationships to the organization as found in Figure 22.3, and even as a mathematical regression formula: Outcome = $\beta \pm$ [Credibility $\pm$ Relationship $\pm$ Reputation $\pm$ Trust] $\pm$ Confidence + error. Where, β is the starting point (could be benchmark or baseline) and is influenced by the variables credibility, relationship, reputation, and trust; this is modified by target audience confidence within certain amounts of error (Stacks, 2010; Stacks & Michaelson, 2010).

Figure 22.3 provides a simple flow whereby the outcome of interest is influenced by the public relations campaign targeting some or all of these variables.

FIGURE 22.3 PUBLIC RELATIONS IMPACT ON RETURN ON INVESTMENT

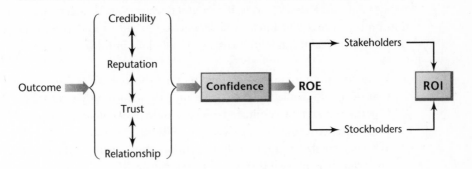

Source: Don. W. Stacks (2010). *Primer of Public Relations Research*, 2nd edition. Used with permission.

For instance, if the outcome is increased trust (for example, increased trust among employees for the organization), then trust is seen as influencing reputation, relationship, and credibility—with confidence an "intervening" variable (one that affects in different ways on the variables being "manipulated" or addressed in the campaign). In turn, these campaign variables establish certain expectations in our targeted audiences, who are defined as stakeholders (for example, employees, customers) and stockholders (people with a financial interest in the company). These expectations are labeled return on expectations, and in turn influence economic decisions (such as increased employee productivity, in a previous example).

It is important for public relations researchers to demonstrate research's impact on both nonfinancial (ROE) and financial (ROI) indicators; this can be incorporated into commonly used management decision-making systems in use today, that is, Six Sigma and balanced scorecard (for more information, see Stacks, 2010). For example, as previously discussed, management is concerned with a cause-effect relationship (outputs → outcomes → outtakes), and public relations research is able to produce this through research and measurement incorporated into currently used management decision-making systems. One method is through incorporating data into a dashboard that provides visual representation of the variables under study. The data are evaluated on a timely basis, can be input into management's system, and helps build credibility with management by demonstrating how public relations is affecting target audiences.

Having Resources in Place and the Budget Necessary

By now it should be clear that planning and research are necessary for effective public relations. Research costs, in terms of resources and budgets, are something that both external and internal customers often fail to understand. Educating the "customer" about research costs generally falls into five areas.

1. What are the circumstances that require the research? Are secondary or historical data available? If so, costs may be significantly reduced.
2. Can the research be conducted with in-house personnel and resources? If this is the case, costs may be significantly reduced.
3. Who is available commercially to conduct the research, what are the costs, and what benefits will they bring to the research?
4. Is the research planned, or is it a budget item?
5. What are the research questions asked?

Conclusion

Effective public relations research and planning require a mindset that focuses on best practiced research as an integral part of departmental budgets and pro-grammatic and continual collection of data. All research planned in public relations should have clearly defined and achievable goals that mirror those of the organization and objectives stated in both actionable and measurable ways. Research should be triangulated and aimed at addressing the research questions appropriate for the problem or opportunity. Finally, effective public relations demonstrates impact on both nonfinancial and financial indicators and must have the necessary resources allocated to research.

References

Bowen, S. A., Rawlins, B. & Martin, T. (2010). *An overview of the public relations function.* New York: Business Expert Press.

Center, A. H., Jackson, P., Smith, S., & Stansberry, F. R. (2008). *Public relations practices: Managerial case studies and problems* (7th ed.). Upper Saddle River, NJ: Pearson Prentice Hall.

Hocking, J. E., Stacks, D. W., & McDermott, S. B. (2002). *Communication research* (3rd ed.). New York: Longman.

Likert, R. (1932). A technique for the measurement of attitudes. *Archives of Psychology, 40,* 1–55.

Stacks, D. W. (2010). *Primer of public relations research* (2nd ed.). New York: Guilford.

Stacks, D. W., & Michaelson, D. M. (2010). *A practitioner's guide to public relations research, measurement, and evaluation.* New York: Business Expert Press.

CHAPTER TWENTY-THREE

MEDIA RELATIONS

Wilma K. Mathews

It has been nearly fifty years since Marshall McLuhan introduced the world to the concept that the medium is the message. He posited that "the 'message' of any medium or technology is the change of scale or pace or pattern that it introduces into human affairs" (1965, p. 8). What McLuhan may not have fully anticipated was the rapidity with which those media would be introduced and the multitudinous ways in which they would be used.

Which leads us to today and the complexities, challenges, and opportunities of media relations as a supportive tool for an organization's overall relationship with the media and other target audiences.

In this chapter, media relations is defined and a number of applications essential to this organizational communication strategy are reviewed.

Defining News

When media were few in both number and delivery systems, news was defined by the editor or producer to meet target audience needs. The audience demographics of a television newscast on a major network directed a news program to focus on government, business, and breaking news such as airplane crashes or natural disasters. That demographic was made up primarily of middle- to upper-class viewers, with middle- to upper-class income and education.

The advent of newer technologies not only ripped those demographics to shreds, it also redefined them, and at the same time created new and additional media to target new demographics.

In short, *news* has come to be defined by the recipient to mean whatever he or she wants it to be.

However large your target audience is, the news value of your information will be decided on a one-by-one basis and will be dependent also on the media through which the target audience member prefers to receive his or her information.

Defining news for your target audience—and, thus, the media—is helped by judging the news value of the information you are sending. Generally speaking, the product, event, issue, personality, or program you are promoting should have one or more of these news values (Missouri Group, 2004):

- *Impact.* How many people are affected by an event or idea? How seriously does it affect them?
- *Novelty.* People or events may be interesting and therefore newsworthy just because they are unusual or bizarre.
- *Prominence.* Names make news. The bigger the name, the bigger the news. Ordinary people have always been intrigued by the doings of the rich and famous.
- *Proximity.* Generally, people are more interested in and concerned about what happens close to home. When they read or listen to national or international news, they often want to know how it relates to their own community.
- *Timeliness.* News is supposed to be new. If news is to be relevant and useful, it must be timely. For example, it is more useful to report on an issue facing the city council before it is decided than afterward. Timely reporting gives people a chance to be participants in public affairs rather than mere spectators.

The explosion of television channels, talk radio, and do-it-yourself online media has altered the definition of *news* into a large group of topics, all guaranteed to attract those greedy for dramatic news:

- *Crisis.* Beyond the usual definitions of natural disasters such as hurricanes and floods, this category now includes oil spills, terrorism, assassinations, and other events not anticipated even three decades ago.
- *Celebrity.* Movie stars, music idols, sports stars, business executives, politicians, royalties—they all are or can become celebrities. Some people are famous for being celebrities and celebrities for being famous.

- *Conflict.* Armed conflicts, such as the Iraq and Afghan wars, remain front page news in many areas. However, people also want to hear stories about the little guy who took on the government (or business, industry, airline, and so on) and won, and they like larger conflicts that often are as much emotional as legal, such as taxes, immigration, or welfare.
- *Controversy.* Squabbles within local government, neighborhood associations, philanthropic organizations—all read and play like soap operas.
- *Crime.* The more unusual the crime or the closer to home, the more appeal it has. The more bizarre the crime or the more unusual the suspect, the more interest it has.
- *Criticism.* The appeal of criticizing a company, educational institution, hospital, or government program comes from a majority of the news audience, as criticism often represents the views of ordinary citizens.
- *Corporate misdeeds.* Whether in good times or bad, investigative reporting about companies' behaviors has large appeal.
- *Crashes.* With video coverage just a cell phone away, a bus, car, plane, or train crash involving your organization is just a few seconds from a post on mainstream media.

Whether you create the news on behalf of your client or organization, or you are responding to developing news, it is essential you understand that your audiences can and will have definitions of news value that may not match yours.

Selecting the Right Media

In many locales, downsized newsrooms have created challenges for business communicators who have relied for years on mainstream media to reach critical audiences. But the advent of social media has brought both opportunities and challenges to counter those shifting dynamics of traditional media and/or to those places that are not yet ready for the full social media onslaught.

For example, respondents ("Global perspectives," 2010, p. 13) to the question "Is social media changing the way communicators in your country relate to the press and the public? If so, how?" said:

> "Even when new media have been absorbed into the communication mix, an integrated approach is far off." Christal P. McIntosh, Bridgetown, Barbados

> "The lack of access is the major factor affecting the use of social media in Liberia." Charles Gaye, Monrovia, Liberia

"Even with a low penetration rate in India of 4.2 percent, compared with television's 50 percent and print's 20 percent, the Internet is proving to be a force multiplier for the latter two. It is not unusual to see communication professionals seed stories via a combined repertoire of social-media-friendly web sites, Facebook, Twitter, YouTube and blogs." Shael Sharma, Mumbai, India

"Traditional forms of media are still the strongest and most popular communication tools." Justyna Piesiewicz, Warsaw, Poland

A 2009 survey of 371 print and Web journalists, conducted by Cision and Don Bates of George Washington University (George Washington University & Cision, 2010), measured the "use of, and attitudes toward, social media for researching and reporting stories" (p. 2). Findings included the following:

- Most journalists—56 percent—said social media was important or somewhat important for reporting and producing the stories they wrote. Journalists who spend most of their time writing for websites (69 percent) reported this the most often, and significantly more so than those at magazines (48 percent).
- Nearly 9 out of 10 journalists reported using blogs for their online research (89 percent). Only corporate websites (96 percent) are used by more journalists when doing online research for a story.
- Approximately two-thirds reported using Social Networking sites and just over half make use of Twitter for online research. Newspaper journalists (72 percent) and those writing for Websites (75 percent) use social networking sites such as LinkedIn and Facebook for online research significantly more often than those at magazines (p. 2).

Do not shift to new media just because it is there. And do not assume that social media is the best and/or preferred method of getting news and information. Make the change because it is the right and best way to reach your target media.

Media Relations Tools

Technology has not just added new media to the mix but has provided ways to help the public relations professional use traditional media relations tools in new ways.

Audio and Video News Releases

Whereas these tools originally were targeted for radio and television newscasts specifically, they now can be posted on company blogs and websites and/or sent to key social media that cover your organization. The releases should adhere to the guidelines as outlined by the traditional and social media you have targeted. In general, the story should be told in 60 seconds either in crisp sound bites (audio news releases [ANR]) and/or terrific visuals (video news releases [VNR]). Always check with the outlet you are targeting to find out what it will or will not accept for use and any length or format it prefers.

Backgrounder and Briefing Information

For many years, you would have to send out an annual backgrounder to your key media. And you would have to prepare and distribute briefing information on a special event, annual meeting, or other key announcement. Now, keep it all on your organization's news media website. The most important element of good backgrounders or briefing packages is the status of the material, that is, Is the material current, up to date, and correct? Do you enter changes in leadership when they happen? What about the statistics on your organization—are they this year's data?

Blogs

Since blogs came into view, they have proved to be an excellent medium for a president or chief executive officer (CEO) to communicate with the media, shareholders, employees, retirees, and other key audiences. You can also create a blog just for the media who follow your organization with the purpose of building or maintaining your relationship with them. If you decide to develop a blog for the media, you must guarantee that you will post often and will respond quickly to any requests that come your way via the blog. Your media blog can contain notices of upcoming events, special holiday or other closures, personnel announcements, and so on.

Editorials, Op-Ed Pieces, Letters to the Editor

The term *op-ed* refers to the page opposite the editorial page and is sometimes called the *opinion page*. Whether the medium is electronic or print, your organization can find places to voice its opinion and/or respond to current events. These 500- to 750-word pieces (always check with the medium to verify the length) usually are ghost-written by the communicator (or speechwriter) in the organization and most often must be developed quickly to take advantage of current interest in the topic. This requires that the communicator must continually scan the media most relevant to the organization and seek out opportunities for an opinion piece.

Editorial Board Visits

Not done as often as in the past, these occasional visits with an editorial board (or its equivalent) not only help the targeted medium's leaders to better understand your organization and its goals, but they also give the communicator a much better appreciation of what challenges the publication or program editors have. These visits also are vital in gaining a medium's support for an upcoming event such as the United Way campaign or a public issue such as a public vote on a bond issue for building new libraries.

Frequently Asked Questions

Frequently asked questions (FAQs) are a must item for the news media site on your organization's website. Journalists always want background and current data on your organization, and this is where they should find it. Keep basic information on hand (officers' names and information; size of organization; customer base; key products and services; locations; history; awards; employment data, and so on). For journalists, there cannot be enough information.

Feature Releases

Not all news and not all coverage are about the hard stuff. Every medium is looking for the softer side of news such as features. You can create both written and video versions of your story and post them on your news media site. What are media looking for? Stories that connect with the general populace, such as profiles of workers who volunteer in the community or workers with unusual hobbies; almost any story about an animal or unusual pet; and oddities such as an unusual collection or an obscure talent.

Interviews

While many interviews take place on the telephone or on Skype, others can take place through Q and A sessions on the main media website, in the CEO's blog, or other preferred medium. Not all interviews have to be in person, but they all should receive thorough preparation. In many cases, specialized training for media interviews may be necessary.

News Conferences

One of the best uses of social media is the news conference or briefing session. For many years, the news conference was an elaborate and expensive event held only to announce really good or really bad news. Now, conferences can be put together and held with minimal time and expenses—to both the organization and the media. What is at issue here, however, is the definition of *news*. Journalists do not like to have their time wasted with invitations to online news conferences that do not have news value. Make sure your information is newsworthy; notify only those journalists and bloggers who have interest in this information; have the right person making the announcement and answering questions; and post the information immediately on your news media site. If key pieces of support material are needed by the journalists, e-mail the material to them before the conference and post it immediately on the website.

News Releases

No media relations tactic has been abused more than the news release. The key is in the *news* half of the equation. Is the information really news? The five *W*'s generally help answer that question: Who is affected by this announcement? What is the problem or solution you are presenting? When will this take place? Where will this be happening? Why are you doing this? Do not forget the *H*: How will this be done? Journalists will ask these questions if you do not address them in the announcement. Pay close attention to guidelines issued by all print and electronic media, and prepare your releases strictly to those guidelines. Perhaps most important: pay attention to the basics—grammar, spelling, and punctuation. A badly written and proofed release is almost guaranteed to be deleted.

Photographs

It seems as though everyone has a still and/or video camera in his or her phone. That does not mean they are all photographers. What works best with the media are those photos that capture what could not have been anticipated, for example, a whale breaching onto a sailboat or a tornado in full form. Also popular are cute or unusual animal photos and stupid human tricks.

Public Service Announcements

While there remain plenty of opportunities to get your nonprofit organization's message played on radio or TV, the onus of the production now resides more with you than with the station. You should provide the material for the public service announcements (PSA), prewritten and timed, keeping in mind that you are writing either for the ear (radio) or the eye (television or website). Ask for examples from the stations you have targeted if you have never created a PSA.

Subject Matter Experts

The plethora of TV and radio talk shows provides a golden opportunity to get your subject matter experts (SMEs) in the public eye. The key is in taking advantage of the day's latest news to seek out the right medium and program for your SME. Whether it is an annual topic (hurricanes) or an explosive new topic (oil spill) or a specialty story in law, medical care, manufacturing, or other area, the gates are open for both new and familiar faces. The key: be the first to feature your SME.

Measuring Your Results

It is not enough just to push your news out the door. As a professional communicator, you will want to measure your results.

Here is the way you do *not* measure your efforts: *impressions*. This measure suggests that if you get a story placed in a newspaper with a controlled and pass-along reading audience of 20,000, then you automatically have 20,000 impressions. You do not. Not everyone will read your story. This measure also is an output-only measure. It does not tell you if people who saw your story will or did act on it. You do not know whether you changed opinions or behaviors. In short, you know virtually nothing about the effect of that story over which you labored so hard.

Try these other measures for overall effectiveness for your client or organization (Howard & Mathews, 2006):

- The relationship you have with reporters, editors, columnists, and freelancers
- The impact your messages have on the publics you wish to reach. (Do your publics react to your messages the way you want them to? Do they understand your messages? Do they buy your product?)
- The number of people you reach via the media

- The way your message is perceived by the public (Do they feel about your organization or product the way you want them to?)
- How many media used your message
- Which media used your message
- An estimated value to the organization of your efforts (Was a boycott avoided? Did you receive favorable editorials? Did the people vote to support your institution?) (p. 194)

Case In Point: More Than Mangos Company Launch

A native of Colombia transplanted to Calgary, Andres Herrera longed for the volume and variety of fresh fruit he enjoyed as a child. After discussing the idea of starting an exotic fruit import business with his wife, Belinda de Wolde, the pair began conducting research, which involved scouring produce markets in Vancouver's Granville Island, Toronto, Montreal, and various ethnic communities, looking for competition and consumer interest. They also met with fruit growers from Colombia, Florida, and the Dominican Republic. Their findings revealed few exotic fruits were entering Canada, although the European markets were importing shiploads of exotic fruit from South America each week. After considering the European market success, conducting an online survey to assess local consumer interest, pitching the idea to family and friends, and consulting with a handful of chefs, in 2007 Belinda and Andres launched their exotic fruit import business: More Than Mangos Inc. (MTM).

Like many small business owners, they had limited funds to start the business. Introducing an unknown entity that required extensive education and promotion, with a limited shelf life and high-end price tag, was a challenge. They also risked attracting controversy from the "100-mile diet" community by flying in products from other continents and competition from large produce wholesalers with solid distribution bases and more buying power.

Belinda and Andres decided to leverage the business through media publicity and use MTM's unique selling points to create a buzz about exotic fruit in a northern climate during the winter months. Starting the business in a community hall in a suburban neighborhood and doing home deliveries in a 1994 Volkswagen cargo van called "Das Mangowagen" helped pique people's interest. It kept costs to a minimum and allowed Belinda and Andres to test the market before expanding into a costly commercial space. They agreed Andres would serve as

---

This case comes courtesy of Gold Quill Award–winner Belinda J. de Wolde, ABC, of Calgary, Canada.

spokesperson; his origins in Colombia embodied the brand and provided an interesting news angle.

MTM's primary audiences were media (city, business, and lifestyle reporters, editors, and columnists); key influencers in the "foodie" community; consumers who appreciate high-end, unique food products; wholesale produce suppliers; executive chefs; produce managers in retail grocery chains; and farmers' market managers and customers. Secondary audiences included ethnic consumers (people who grew up with these fruits) and people who had enjoyed them while traveling.

Andres and Belinda learned from others in the food business that their success depended on volume and appealing to upper-middle-class Canadian consumers interested in unique food products. The restaurant and wholesale produce industries were Andres and Belinda's primary targets, but they needed to establish consumer interest and demand to catch their targets' attention.

As a result, they targeted well-known food editors, columnists, and chefs to endorse their products in special interest publications and used daily news sources to reach consumers interested in exquisite products. By positioning the products as rare, new, exotic, and fresh, they were able to catch the attention of the food community and reporters and editors. Profiling the products through a sustained media campaign heightened consumer awareness and created demand for the fruit among the desired audiences. Word spread quickly, resulting in new business from the restaurant and wholesale communities and increased traffic to their markets.

Introducing new products to consumers requires extensive education and promotion. News coverage, especially broadcast and print, allowed Andres to introduce and explain the fruits' virtues in detail to a vast audience in a short time frame. Features in special interest publications targeted those consumers most likely to purchase exotic fruit. The media relations objectives were

- To develop and maintain a profitable business by introducing exotic fruit to local consumers through mass media and encouraging regular consumption through ongoing awareness and education
- To entice farmers' markets and retail grocery chains to carry exotic fruit through product endorsement by well-known food experts and columnists and increasing consumer demand
- To catch the attention of local chefs through special interest publications and encourage at least ten restaurants and one professional cooking school to order MTM's fruit weekly
- To drive traffic to MTM's markets and increase retail sales by 50 percent in each quarter of 2008 through monthly news coverage and publicity opportunities

- To increase traffic to the MTM website (for online orders, recipes, and product information) by 10 percent per month in 2008 through earned media exposure and the distribution of an online newsletter

The following list summarizes the media relations tactics used to profile and promote MTM during its first year of business. Most pitches to media were done by phone, with Andres highlighting the key messages. He followed up on the phone calls by sending a backgrounder to the writer or reporter and directing him or her to the company website. A formal news release or media advisory was not issued; the MTM owners believed that by positioning the company as a grassroots, entrepreneurial "mom and pop" operation they would have a greater chance of coverage. This approach worked well.

Tactics employed to reach their goals included:

- An initial launch tasting event with media to introduce the fruit to local consumers and promote the weekly fruit market at a community hall
- A sustained media publicity campaign to introduce and profile the product offering to potential consumers: monthly phone pitches to TV breakfast shows, radio talk shows, magazine editors, and city beat reporters for print and broadcast media outlets
- Targeting food writers and columnists for product endorsement
- Pitching to special interest publications that serve the target audiences

Belinda and Andres developed a media event in November 2007 to welcome the first exotic fruits shipment to Calgary and launch the company. Two local television stations arrived at the first fruit sale to film customers sampling the unusual textures and tastes. One of the television stations broadcasted a portion of the six o'clock news live from the sale, which attracted a new herd of shoppers around 7 p.m. They sold all 300 kilograms (more than 660 pounds) of fruit that night.

After the initial launch event, the couple continued to pitch their business to columnists, special interest publications, and broadcast and print news agencies, focusing on the business's unique selling points. Publicity continued throughout the first twelve months of business, at least once a month, resulting in media coverage valued at over CDN$1 million. The coverage included local and regional television and radio features, regional and local newspaper feature articles, and local and regional magazine feature stories.

The news coverage included MTM's key messages:

- MTM is the exclusive Canadian importer of more than fifteen varieties of fresh, natural exotic fruit grown by fair trade farming cooperatives in South and Central America.

- Taste something exotic; exotic fruit is more nutritious than domestic varieties.
- Ripe and ready to eat from South America to Canada in record time—our products are harvested and delivered in three to five days.

With these successes also came some challenges. Competing for space and airtime was tough in the midst of Calgary's economic boom. Positioning the unique news angles and key messages and having Andres make the pitches was critical. Arranging for photo shoots without a permanent storage facility or retail location required last-minute creativity. Belinda and Andres often relied on clients to host media shoots in their facilities until the MTM markets opened. Publicity runs the risks of skewed key messages or controversy and opposition. The fair trade, local farmer angle, and the fact these fruits are not grown in North America, offset the "100-mile diet" debate. Products are perishable and costly; there was an urgent need to attract media attention in a short time frame. Significant money would have been lost if media did not show up. Andres planned to use product reserved for media events as promotional gift baskets for chefs or produce managers if media did not cover the events.

As noted in this chapter, measurement is key to media relations. A combination of formal and informal measurement tools were used to evaluate the impact of media coverage on the business:

- Fruit sales increased steadily from November 2007 to December 2008.
- Andres was invited to join two established farmers' markets in 2008 because of the company's media profile.
- A large produce wholesaler invited Belinda and Andres to a meeting after reading about the business in *City Palate* magazine. This supplier now distributes its fruit to grocery chains in Alberta, Saskatchewan, and Manitoba.
- The Fairmont and Delta Hotel chains, along with eleven other five-star restaurants in Alberta and one professional cooking school, carry MTM products in their restaurants.
- Sales of featured products skyrocketed in 2008.
- Traffic patterns to market locations increased following media mentions.
- MTM consistently experienced a 20 percent increase in visits to their website after each media exposure.
- E-mail inquiries and online orders increased by 50 percent after each media exposure.
- Newsletter subscribers participated in an online survey. Responses indicated most customers have learned about MTM in the media.

References

George Washington University & Cision. (2010). *2009 social media and online usage study.* Available at http://us.cision.com/journalist_survey_2009/GW-Cision_Media_Report.pdf

Global perspectives. (2010). *Communication World, 27*(1), 13.

Howard, C., & Mathews, W. (2006). *On deadline: Managing media relations* (4th ed.). Long Grove, IL: Waveland.

McLuhan, H. M. (1964). *Understanding media: The extensions of man.* New York: McGraw-Hill.

The Missouri Group. (2004). *Telling the story: The convergence of print, broadcast and online media* (2nd ed.). Boston: Bedford/St. Martin.

CHAPTER TWENTY-FOUR

INVESTOR RELATIONS AND FINANCIAL COMMUNICATION

Karen Vahouny

You are evaluating two corporations whose stock is traded on one of the public stock exchanges. They are in the same industry, generate similar revenues, and produce comparable earnings. Yet one company's stock price has been steadily moving up and is viewed as fairly priced, while the other stock trades at erratic prices and is generally regarded as a risky investment. Why?

The answer to this question should be an integral part of an investor relations (IR) program. An investor relations professional blends an understanding of the company operations and financial performance with the ability to communicate effectively with investors. One part of the information mix involves the numbers, which are reflected in the company's financial statements and trends. The other part of the mix is nonfinancial; this also helps influence stock value. The nonfinancial factors include the quality of management, competitive advantages of the products and services, market share, the prospective market growth, and diversification and types of customers, among others. Another facet of an IR officer's role is counseling management on the issues of public disclosure and regulation, providing market intelligence to management and the board of directors, monitoring the valuation of the company and those of its peers, and targeting and cultivating prospective investors. The effectiveness of an IR program is tied to the basic principles of good communication: audience identification and understanding, development of a well-researched plan, the selection and development of appropriate tools and tactics, strong execution, and evaluation and fine-tuning.

Investor relations is "a strategic management responsibility that integrates finance, communication, marketing and securities law compliance to enable the most effective two-way communication between a company and the financial community and other constituencies, which ultimately contributes to a company's securities achieving fair valuation" (National Investor Relations Institute [NIRI], 2004, p. 5). The genesis of investor relations can be traced to 1953, when General Electric's chairman, Ralph Cordiner, began a process to formalize the company's relationship with its shareholders. According to the National Investor Relations Institute (2004), the result of this process was the formation of a new department and the coining of the term *investor relations*.

Why Investor Relations?

Investor relations focuses on helping companies achieve a realistic and fair market value for their stock. A successful investor relations program can help reduce the cost of capital for the company and ensure that shareholder interests are recognized and served.

If a company has 50 million shares outstanding that are trading at $10, the company's market value, or market capitalization, is $500 million. If the share price increases to $12, the company's market value has increased by $100 million to $600 million. The ultimate goal is to increase enterprise value and decrease the cost of capital. Here are two examples illustrating the benefits of a reduced cost of capital:

1. A company wants to use its stock, rather than cash or debt financing, to fund an acquisition.
2. A company wants to raise additional capital through a secondary public offering and use the proceeds for product development and marketing.

The role of investor relations today has changed very little from its original focus in the 1950s, although the tools are more sophisticated.

Shaken Investor Confidence

The collapse among technology stocks following the NASDAQ stock market peak in March 2000 was the first in a number of troubling developments that shattered the confidence of investors. The technology stock implosion stemmed from a buildup of investor expectations that were not backed with financial results. Also uncovered was the unsettling practice of financial analysts who had publicly touted certain stocks but had concerns about those same investments. Adding to investor distrust was the recognition that analyst compensation was tied directly to business generated for their firm's investment bankers.

This represented just the initial wave of investor disappointment. There was more to come. Corporate malfeasance dominated the news as the impact hit individuals and their pocketbooks: Enron, its clouding of financial information, and the downward spiral of its stock; Tyco's senior executives accused of fraud, larceny, and the falsification of business records related to stock sales and bonuses; the list went on to include WorldCom, Global Crossing, and Parmalat, among others, plus some of the investment banks and accounting firms involved in these cases.

These situations touched scores of investors who lost all or much of their wealth and employees whose retirement savings were wiped out. The Sarbanes-Oxley Act passed in 2002 was designed to improve the clarity of financial reporting and strengthen corporate governance, among other purposes.

The Great Recession of 2008–2010 created a new wave of concern about corporate greed, risk taking, and financial oversight that left no country untouched: "Between the fall of 2008 and the winter of 2009, the world's economy and financial markets fell off a cliff. Stock markets in the United States, Asia, Europe and Latin America lost between a third and half of their value; international trade declined by a whopping 12 percent; and the size of the global economy contracted for the first time in decades" (Richardson & Roubini, 2010, B1).

Unfortunately the years to follow did not provide relief for corporate reputations. Stories of excessive executive compensation, particularly in companies that had lost money or performed badly, stirred investor angst and activism. Headlines like "Toyota's shifting stories raise credibility issue" and "Gulf of Mexico: BP loses credibility and trust" continued to erode the public's confidence in business leadership and performance. In coming years, with escalating financial reform and regulation, financial institutions and public company management will increasingly be reviewed and scrutinized, and investor relations will play an important role.

The Numbers

Investors typically use a variety of quantitative tools to determine a valuation, or appropriate market worth, of a company's stock. Investors carefully study a company's fundamentals: the income statement (a summary of revenues, costs, and earnings during a specific time period), the balance sheet (a financial report that shows a company's assets, liabilities, and owners' equity on a given date), and the cash flow statements (reports that analyze changes in the company's cash position). In reviewing these reports, investors make judgments on positive or negative trends that may be emerging. A company's revenues and net income may be growing, for example, but its profit margin (its gross profit divided by sales) may be declining, and investors will question this trend and decide whether the investments being made will generate a higher return in the future.

Ratios, such as price/earnings ratio (P/E, the price of one share of stock divided by its earnings per share) and price/book ratio (the stock price divided by the book value per share, which relates to the value of its assets), are typically used in assessing valuation, but there are a host of other methodologies. In applying these valuation tools, an investor determines whether a company's stock price appears to be fairly valued or whether it is under- or overvalued in relation to its future prospects and to similar companies.

The Story

The quantitative information is an important part of the process of determining whether to invest in a company. But there is another important qualitative factor that goes into the evaluation mix. In investor relations vernacular, this is called the *story*. Investors will make a subjective judgment about a company on the basis of its story.

According to Mavrinac (1997), 35 percent of the investment decision is based on nonfinancial factors. Important performance characteristics include the quality of products and services, strength of the company's market position, the effectiveness of compensation policies, the quality of investor communications, level of customer satisfaction, and strength of corporate culture.

A common theme that spans all the components of a company's story is growth. Whether it is growth of the market, products, or services or the company's position in relation to its competitors, a fundamental question is whether the company has the potential to grow. The premium that an investor places on a company's stock will largely be related to his or her belief in the prospects for growth. Hence, identifying the issues that may have an impact on your company's growth prospects and what interests your target investor should be important drivers of your investor relations program.

Understanding the importance of both quantitative and qualitative aspects of the valuation process is critical to investor relations. If, for example, your company's price/earnings ratio is 10 and all of the firms that would be considered comparable, in terms of industry, product, or service niche, and size, have P/E ratios that are between 20 and 25, you would want to uncover the reasons for your below-average valuation and subsequently develop a strategy to increase your value.

Information Central: The Investor Relations Function and Roles

An investor relations program serves two important constituencies: the investment community and corporate management. The IR professional or staff should function as information central, delivering meaningful information on a regular basis to investors and serving as a clearinghouse for their questions and feedback. The other key role involves providing professional counsel to management on a variety of issues relating to the needs and concerns of the investment community (see Figure 24.1). In fact, an investor relations function maintains a delicate balancing act in supporting the needs and interests of both constituencies. You are employed by and provide counsel and direction to management, while also maintaining relationships with the investment community. There may be times you believe that management's interests may compromise your role of maintaining credibility with the investment community. These are times when investor relations professionals do battle with management, asserting that short-term needs should be put aside in favor of the long-term interests (and institutional memory) of the investment community. For example, management may want to delay revealing an operational problem to its investors or may want to present some information in a much more positive light than the investor

FIGURE 24.1 KEY ACTIVITIES IN INVESTOR RELATIONS

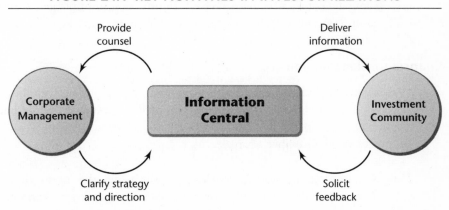

relations person feels comfortable. Although there are times when companies are legally required to disclose certain types of information, there are many situations in the investor relations domain that fall into a gray area, which forces IR professionals to balance their responsibilities to their two constituencies.

Clearinghouse for Investors

Investor relations professionals wear several hats in their dealings with the investment community:

- Providing investors with information about the company. This can range from a brief telephone call, to a multipage document that explains the significance of a recent news item, to a full-day meeting for analysts and portfolio managers at the company's headquarters.
- Identifying and working with reporters in cultivating positive financial coverage and responding to their questions about the company and its performance.
- Identifying institutions and individuals who might be interested in purchasing stock of the company and developing appropriate means to communicate with these investors. Sophisticated screening criteria and online database tools can be used to target new investors based on such criteria as investment style, market capitalization emphasis, geographical region, or industry focus.
- Building positive relationships with current and potential investors. This takes time and effort, but it can pay dividends in the form of increased shareholder support and loyalty.
- Actively soliciting feedback about the company from the investment community. The information from current investors sheds light on how the company's story is being perceived. Information from prospective investors can be extremely useful in strategizing the company's discussion points.

Counsel to Management

In addition to building relationships with and communicating with the financial community, the investor relations professional has another equally important role: as counselor and sounding board to senior management. This valuable activity spans a number of areas:

- Synthesizing investor feedback and prioritizing the issues that require increased management emphasis or clarification in investor communications.

- Compiling data on existing shareholders and their patterns of buying and holding, which can be useful in structuring the ongoing investor communications program.
- Seeking out investor feedback and assimilating their concerns relating to the overall valuation of the company. A strong investor relations practitioner will help management view the company from an objective investor's point of view, which means raising and discussing difficult issues.
- Raising the issues that affect valuation. For example, a company may have a strong reputation and an exciting core business, but one of its divisions is viewed as a negative and nonessential to its strategy, therefore reducing the company's overall valuation. The investor relations professional can reinforce this issue to management; perhaps the answer is the sale of the one division and a renewed emphasis on the core business.
- Assessing the potential impact of an event on the price of the stock and, in the case of negative news, working to minimize the damage through the communications process. If, for example, management learns that its upcoming quarterly financial results will fall below analysts' expectations and it immediately discloses the expected level of shortfall, this could reduce investor concerns and minimize the impact on the stock.
- Providing guidance to senior management—those responsible for speaking with investors—on the public disclosure of information. The Securities Exchange Act of 1934 requires that companies promptly disclose "material" information to the media, that is, events or developments that may affect an investor's decision to buy or sell the stock or may affect the price of the stock. Examples of material information include a change in top management, major borrowings, significant new products, or the closing of a major plant or facility.
- Providing valuable information, based on reviews and analysis of comparable companies, to other corporate departments. IR professionals may learn from investor conferences and conversations with analysts about industry trends or developments in their competitor community—valuable information that can be shared with the strategic planning, marketing, and sales departments.

Figure 24.2 represents the two roles of investor relations: the right portion displays the role as clearinghouse for investors and the left side reinforces the role as counselor to management.

Research and Evaluation

Using information from formal and informal research of investor attitudes and buying and selling data, investor relations should continually make adjustments

FIGURE 24.2 THE TWO ROLES OF INVESTOR RELATIONS

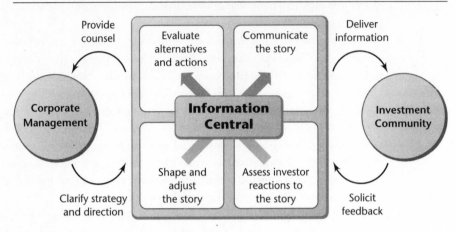

to the IR program. Is the company changing its strategy, resulting in a different type of investor who might be attracted to the new focus? Have the company's acquisitions generated the results that investors anticipated? Do investors understand why the company is using a portion of its profit to invest heavily in sales and marketing? Does the company want to test the water on a new concept or potential product offering with investors to determine how they would react before the step is taken?

These examples illustrate the ongoing nature of investor relations and the need to reevaluate, refocus, and continually communicate with investors about the company's direction. Just as companies are continually making changes to their strategy and operations, the IR program needs to be equally nimble. Figure 24.3 demonstrates the dynamic nature of investor relations and the consideration of such factors as internal and external developments, formal research and evaluation, and investor feedback and expectations.

Credibility

Even if a company has outstanding financial results and a compelling story, there is one thing that can derail even the strongest investor relations program: a lack of credibility. Credibility is king. Investors must believe the company is going to execute the strategy and deliver results in the future. They need accurate information on a regular basis. They use this information to make educated guesses about how the company will perform in the future. Investors who work for financial institutions—for example, analysts who write reports for their firm's

FIGURE 24.3 THE DYNAMICS OF INVESTOR RELATIONS

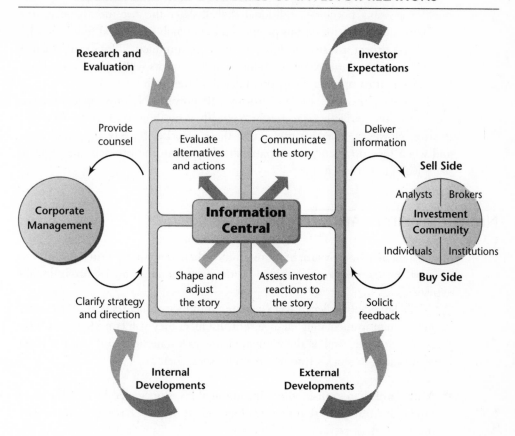

clients, portfolio managers who are managing their client's investments, or fund managers who are selecting stocks for their firm's funds—can be responsible for millions and even billions of dollars, and they rely on complete, candid information from the companies they follow. If they base decisions on incorrect or outdated information, the quality of their investment decisions will be at risk.

Here is an example. A company has been telling its investors for eighteen months that it plans to introduce a new product on March 1. This product has enormous market potential and should generate a strong future revenue and earnings stream for the company. When the company tells investors that it has delayed the product launch by two months, investors immediately want to understand the reasons for the delay. If they are convinced that there are good reasons for the delay and they believe that another competitor will not introduce a similar product during the two-month period, then they are likely to continue to support the company, recommend it to their clients, and continue to hold the stock or possibly purchase additional shares. After the two-month delay, the company announces that it has postponed the launch for several more months. Would you expect investors to have the same commitment? Not likely, because the company has damaged its credibility, and investors will be much less likely to believe that company management is telling the truth.

In investor relations, the no-surprises rule prevails. No one expects companies to execute perfectly or to perform exactly according to expectations every quarter. However, investors prefer that these surprises be kept to a minimum, and when they do occur, a company should explain the problem and what it plans to do to correct it.

Not All Investors Are Created Equal

Understanding the investment community—their investment criteria, communications needs, and so on—should be the cornerstone of an IR professional's activities.

Your financial audience will evaluate a number of factors that an IR practitioner cannot immediately change. For instance, they will consider what business you are in, as well as the company's income statement and balance sheet highlights, and its stock's trading characteristics, such as:

- Number of shares outstanding. Institutional investors generally look for more liquid investments so that their trading activity will not have as much impact on the stock price.
- The float, or number of shares that can be traded by the public (the number of shares outstanding minus the number of shares held by company directors or management). A smaller float means that a company's stock will probably be more volatile, since a large transaction will most likely have an influence on the price of the stock.
- The number of shares held by management (insiders) and the amount of insider buying and selling. A company whose management owns relatively few shares or whose management is regularly selling shares will not be perceived favorably, since this sends a signal that management does not believe that the stock is a good investment.

Many investors focus on companies with certain market capitalizations (or caps). Another important consideration is their investment style. Many investments fall into three main categories: growth, value, or income. Growth investors look for strong projected growth in revenues and earnings. Value investors seek companies that are undervalued in relation to comparable firms. Income investors concentrate on cash flow and dividend payouts.

Investors can be part of the sell side, which means their orientation is to sell the stock to their institutional and individual clients, or the buy side, which includes portfolio and fund managers who buy stock on behalf of their clients or funds.

Analysts and brokers are part of the sell-side audience:

- *Analysts*. Sell-side analysts produce research reports that a number of different investors use. Analysts from larger firms provide research to their firm's retail and institutional sales staffs, who use the reports in their discussions with individuals (in the case of retail sales) and with portfolio and fund managers (institutional sales). A company that works hard to build a strong and open relationship with its analysts will be more likely to have their support during difficult times.
- *Brokers* (registered representatives). Brokerage firms can range from the large national or multinational firms with huge numbers of brokers to regional and small local firms. Brokers use analyst reports and their own data to provide clients with information about companies and whether to buy, hold, or sell the stock.

Investors on the buy side include individuals and institutions:

- *Individuals*. Although some individuals rely on stockbrokers to guide their investments, a growing number have turned to the many online, investor-oriented services available today. These include content providers such as Microsoft and Yahoo!; search engines like Google; news services such as Bloomberg, Reuters, and Dow Jones; the stock exchanges; company financial filings (such as the Securities and Exchange Commission's (SEC) EDGAR, in the United States); individual company websites; and online message boards and chatrooms.
- *Institutions*. Institutional investors, who include portfolio managers and fund managers, rely on information supplied by a range of sources, including analysts and investor relations professionals. Portfolio managers purchase stock for their clients' accounts and oversee their clients' stock portfolios. Fund managers include those who select investments for various funds, including mutual funds and pension funds. Given the potential size of an institutional investor's holdings, this audience can represent an important part of the investor relations program's target audience.

In targeting investors, you want to carefully match investor requirements with the characteristics of your company. If your company is undervalued and has a market capitalization of $500 million (which is considered small), you would not want to target a fund manager who invests only in growth stocks with large market caps. There is a wealth of information, including directories and online services, available to help locate investors who might be interested in your company. In addition, you can collect the names of potential investors through a variety of sources:

- Investors who call your company to request an investor information package or who participate in your quarterly investor conference calls or Webcasts
- Industry conferences or trade shows
- Buy- or sell-side investors who follow similar companies and are quoted in the business or financial media
- Networking at meetings of industry groups or trade associations or at investor meetings or conferences
- The company website, through an investor relations section offering an opportunity for investors to enter their contact information so they can receive company information

Investors are pressed for time, and many companies are competing for their attention. After identifying a list of target investors, you will need to decide how to proceed with introducing them to your company. Some investor relations practitioners add these names to their broadcast e-mail or fax distribution lists. Others may make telephone calls or send short letters of introduction followed by investor information packages that include the company's annual and quarterly reports, a fact sheet or corporate profile, and perhaps trade or business media reprints. These packages should be tailored to the interests of the candidate for investment.

The Importance of Communication

In investor relations, it pays to develop a consistent message and tell it simply, compellingly, and through a variety of channels.

Some companies may view investor relations as an obligation as opposed to an opportunity. The government agency in a given country, such as the Securities and Exchange Commission in the United States, imposes requirements on public companies, and companies must meet those obligations. These include the Form 10-K report (which includes an annual summary of financial results, along with recent historical data), Form 10-Q reports (quarterly financial summaries), Form 8-K reports (which report important events that could have a material impact on value of the stock), annual shareholders' meetings, and news releases that disclose material events or information. Companies that are truly focused on building shareholder value will go far beyond the communication required by law. An active investor communication program can increase shareholder wealth. An *Investor Relations* magazine survey of 1,200 analysts and portfolio managers concluded that companies with the best communication programs recorded above-average shareholder returns.

The Tools of the Trade

There are many communication tools available to reach your investors. Creativity in your communications materials and effective targeting of potential investors are critical, since you are trying to cut through the clutter and catch an investor's attention. You do not need to use all of these tools (with the exception of those required by law); this list is a starting point in developing a plan. In addition to considering your audience's preferences, you will want to factor in management goals, the priorities of your investor relations program, your staff talents and resources.

Annual Reports

Many companies view annual reports as an opportunity to go beyond the information mandated in the Form 10-K, the legally required annual report for public companies filing with the SEC. Their goal is to create a report that integrates the corporate themes and strategy, highlights for the year and plans for the future, along with the business and financial information that summarizes the annual results and gives investors a clear picture of the organization's health. Many companies believe that the annual report is the single most important vehicle for communicating the company's vision, strategy, progress, and future plans, and significant time and resources are dedicated to producing a report that reflects this belief.

Some experts (Morgan, 2008), however, argue that annual reports have become less important in the communications arsenal, particularly with the speed and popularity of electronic channels. Investors also have criticized the time and cost involved with producing elaborate annual reports. Against this background, many companies have opted for the use of the 10-K wrap, which combines a chairman's letter, perhaps some highlights, charts or graphs, and the 10-K report under one cover.

The Form 10-K has been evolving as well, most notably with the importance of the section known as the MD&A (Management's Discussion and Analysis of Financial Condition and Results of Operations). This has become a more prominent and expansive section of the Form 10-K following the problems that led to the adoption of Sarbanes-Oxley regulation, with investors and regulators demanding more clarity and straightforward language to better communicate the issues that have affected the company's financial results.

Regardless of the format, the report should focus on current and prospective investors. Some companies also consider the needs of other constituencies, such as employees and customers, as they develop the approach and content for their annual reports.

Quarterly Reports

Although Form 10-Q reports are required by the SEC, some companies create more expansive quarterly reports that are designed to complement their annual reports. These may include a brief letter to shareholders, operating highlights from the quarter, financial statements, news, and photography. Many companies have decided to eliminate comprehensive quarterly reports in favor of using a combination of 10-Q reports and quarterly financial news releases.

Annual Meeting

The purpose of the annual shareholders' meeting is to conduct necessary business matters such as voting on bylaws changes, the board of directors, the issuance of new stock, and other matters. Prior to the meeting, shareholders are sent a copy of the proxy statement, and many choose to vote by proxy rather than in person. Companies also can use the annual meeting to project a core theme or message about the company, review accomplishments for the year, showcase products or services, and encourage shareholder questions about the company.

Internet

There is a growing trend for investors to rely on company web pages as a starting point for their investment decisions. Many companies include investor relations sections on their websites that include downloadable Forms 10-K and 10-Q and other filings, as well as information on company management, financial and other news releases, historical financial results, stock charts, and a host of other data. Many websites offer investors the ability to ask questions electronically; to request information that could be e-mailed, faxed, or mailed; and to enter their contact information in order to receive regular company updates.

Investor Presentations

Many companies develop their presentations in PowerPoint format, with executives combining prepared comments with the computer-based presentations to deliver their message in a small group, larger conference, or Webcast format. The investor presentation has become a critical way for companies to communicate their corporate story to the investment community. The presentation should address the questions, "What's exciting about this company and its future, and why should I want to invest?"

One-on-One and Group Meetings

One-on-one and small group meetings are an essential part of the outreach effort, both to maintain regular, personal communication with major shareholders and introduce the company management to prospective investors. Although financial data are important, many institutional investors, such as analysts, fund managers, and portfolio managers, look for personal interaction with the chief executive officer and chief financial officer. They rely on these opportunities to get a clearer picture of the company, its persona, the executives' commitment to growth and shareholder value, and their excitement and enthusiasm about the company's prospects. Investors also use these events to probe deeply into what is driving the financial results and assess management's command of their operations and their position in the industry. These meetings can range from one-on-one, informal discussions in an investor's office to breakfast, lunch, or dinner presentations for larger audiences at broker forums.

Investor Conferences, Road Shows, and Analyst Tours

Companies often present at conferences sponsored by brokerage firms, particularly if the analyst from that firm has included the company or plans to include it in written coverage. These conferences can include the firm's institutional clients, their own brokers, and high-net worth individuals. In addition, there are independent conferences that showcase firms in a given industry group or market capitalization range.

Investor road shows allow members of senior management to travel to targeted locations to meet and update groups of current and prospective investors. Analyst tours and analyst days are often used by larger companies to host a large number of analysts and institutional owners. It may be more cost- and time-efficient to host a group of analysts rather than traveling to meet individually with each one, particularly if a company wants to communicate something immediately and consistently.

With the passage of Regulation FD (Fair Disclosure) and the requirement to avoid selective disclosure (giving information to one set of investors and not others), many companies broadcast their investor meetings and analyst days live on the Web.

Investor Kits

These kits are used to introduce prospective investors to the company. Investor kits could include one or more of the following: a short introductory letter, annual and quarterly reports (and/or Forms 10-K and 10-Q), proxy statement, advertising reprints or trade or business article reprints, and a fact sheet that includes a compilation of the major financial data, stock characteristics, and corporate strategy information.

Fact Books

These are used to present the same type of information as a fact sheet but in much more detail. Fact books are used to give analysts and institutional investors expanded company information in summary form. Given the growth in the use of computer-generated presentations, some companies have replaced the fact book with a hard-copy booklet of their investor presentation.

News Releases

A company's news releases that summarize the quarterly financial results are an essential ingredient of the investor communication program. These releases are issued prior to or at the same time as the quarterly filings and are used as a basis for the discussion in investor conference calls. Generally, financial news releases include a summary of financial highlights as well as charts that compare the current period's income statement, balance sheet, and cash flow data with comparable prior periods. Some companies use the financial news releases as an opportunity to include a summary of the business, quotations from the chairman or chief executive officer, and a discussion of trends demonstrated by the financial results. The investor relations or media spokesperson must be prepared to explain financial details and provide background to financial reporters immediately after dissemination of the release. Being able to respond to the reporter's deadline is essential. News releases are a low-cost vehicle to give investors regular updates about the company.

Conference Calls

The majority of public companies host conference calls with their investors immediately after the quarterly financial results are announced. Telephone conferences also can be held after major news events, such as an acquisition or divestiture, a major stock restructuring, or a product launch. These conference calls allow management the opportunity to summarize the events and financial summary and allow investors to ask questions. In addition to providing a telephone dial-in number, many companies broadcast their quarterly calls through live Webcasts. Regular telephone and e-mail contact with current or prospective investors is an essential part of the investor relations program.

Advertising

Advertising is another communications opportunity, ranging from corporate image advertisements in national or business media to more targeted, investor-oriented advertisements or advertorials. Some companies use reprints of advertisements in mailings to investors, at investor presentations, or at annual shareholders' meetings.

Media Relations

A strong media relations program supports the investor relations effort. You want to build relationships with appropriate reporters and editors who cover your industry or geographical area. You will want to initiate coverage through a telephone call or media pitch letter that meets the reporter's interests. A strong trade press article often can attract visibility with a more targeted core audience for your industry. Sending a copy of a positive reprint, by mail or e-mail, to investors and including media articles in your investor kits is often used to supplement the investor relations efforts.

Social Media

Social media channels have become another source through which investors can find information about companies they are evaluating. These channels may be more informal than the others, but they are no less important from the standpoint of corporate disclosure.

One example validating the impact of social media and its relevance for investor relations came from Dell. "The company inadvertently posted its YouTube interview with CFO Brian Gladden discussing Q2 results before issuing the press release to the wire services. The video got noticed and the news spread on trading blogs and tweets, which were picked up by Bloomberg news. The stock shot up 6 percent on 23 mn shares in a 21-minute rollercoaster ride before the company was able to rush out its release" (Allen, 2009, para. 10).

The investment community is using YouTube, Facebook, Twitter, and blogs. For example, bloggers, journalists, investors, and investor relations officers with Twitter accounts are sending earnings call announcements, live commentary during earnings calls, and links to a variety of sources (Metzker, 2010).

Factoring social media into your investor relations planning is essential. Consider how other IR officers from comparable companies are using social media to share information, encourage dialogue, or reinforce messages. You also can review Seeking Alpha and StockTwits.com to get a sense of the investor-oriented social media environment.

Best Practice Investor Relations Function

Award-winning IR professional Jeff Mobley is senior vice president of investor relations and research for Chesapeake Energy Corporation, one of the largest producers of natural gas in the United States. Mobley held an unusual position of covering Chesapeake as an investment analyst before joining the company as its chief IR officer. His transition was a success: in 2010, Chesapeake was recognized for Best Investor Relations in the Energy Sector and Best Investor Relations Website in *IR* magazine's annual awards program. Mobley also won awards from *IR Global Rankings* the same year: Best IR Program in North America and Best IR Officer in North America. What made these two awards even more prestigious was that they were considered "Investors' Choice" awards, meaning they were voted on by investors, analysts, and capital market professionals.

Having worked on the investment side and now on the corporate side, Mobley offers a balanced perspective on best practices:

- *Transparency in financial guidance.* "Our quarterly news release that outlines financial results and our investor presentation provide extremely detailed guidance and great depth into our operating and financial performance."
- *Comprehensive content.* "This centers around providing in-depth information about our company and about the entire energy sector. Our goal is to make

the information easy to access and easy to understand," he adds. This includes a major emphasis on the website, and Mobley personally has led its redesign efforts.

*   *Responsiveness.* "It is important to be as prompt as possible in responding to investor questions," says Mobley. "I answer my own phone and return calls as quickly as possible, whether I'm in office or traveling." Mobley uses e-mail, phone, and BlackBerry to stay connected.

One of the analysts who covers Chesapeake agreed with IR Global Rankings' assessment of Mobley as a top IR officer. Jeff Robertson of Barclays Capital cited Mobley's commitment to being transparent, accessible, and knowledgeable. Robertson explained that Chesapeake provides a lot of information and that the information is easy to use. "Jeff Mobley is extremely responsive; he gets back to you quickly and if he doesn't have an immediate answer he'll find it and call you back."

Mobley noted, "I try to approach my communication with investors from the standpoint of walking in their shoes—that is to consider what I would most want to know about Chesapeake from an investor's perspective."

Integrating Investor Relations and Corporate Communications

Integrated communication has been a major professional development priority in recent years. It is clearly in the corporation's best interest for both IR and corporate communications professionals, regardless of organizational structure, to be as knowledgeable and as versatile as possible. Many companies have integrated investor relations and corporate communications into one central department to ensure that the corporate brand is leveraged among all constituents and to maximize the skills and resources of all staff involved in these functions.

Some organizations believe that a centralized communications department that integrates both investor and public relations staff enables the company to communicate with all audiences more effectively. Although investors represent one stakeholder group with certain specific information needs, a company can develop and use the same underlying messages, customizing and personalizing them to meet specific audience needs. Integrated messaging (the use of consistent messages across various constituents) can reinforce and help ensure that they are heard and understood. One way to accomplish this is by having the key communications and IR people work together to develop and update the key corporate messages.

Linking the investor relations and communication activities can result in:

- Developing and communicating consistent overall themes and messages
- Reaching investors through events and activities typically falling in the marketing communications domain such as trade shows
- Enhancing communications with employees, who may own company stock through stock purchase or retirement savings programs
- Developing products for one audience that could be used effectively with investors
- Sharing information to enhance each function; data that IR gathers on competitors shared with the in-house sales and marketing organization, and customer reactions to a new product relayed to investors
- Ensuring that there is a formal, well-defined process for the dissemination of material information news and an established crisis team to manage negative news and its potential impact on the value of the stock

Global Trends

The 2008 and 2009 global market downturn has affected the activities of investor relations professionals throughout the world. Bank of New York Mellon (2009) in its survey analysis of IR practices worldwide reported that 90 percent of all respondents increased or maintained the same level of communications with analysts and investors due to financial market volatility. Some of the other trends that were reported included:

- The most frequent shift of IR messaging related to credit concerns.
- North America was the region with the highest tendency to have shifted its IR messaging on credit concerns, followed by Western Europe. Asia Pacific was the least likely to have shifted messaging on this topic.
- The United States remains the most frequently visited roadshow destination.

The survey also reported:

- The top three IR goals for 2008/2009 were (1) ensure exercising effective disclosure, (2) being a part of strategic decision making, (3) diversification of the shareholder base.

- The top three measures for IR department effectiveness were (1) informal feedback from the investment community, (2) effective use of senior management's time, (3) number of one-on-one meetings with the investment community.

   Investor relations practices outside the United States vary significantly. Stock listing requirements, disclosure policies, targeting and communicating with investors, regulatory oversight, and reporting frequency and format are among the various aspects of investor relations that can be affected by the legal, regulatory, and cultural practices of a given country.

   Neil Stewart, editor-at-large for *IR* magazine, notes that the 2008–2009 financial crisis spurred an intensified shareholder interest—transcending geographic borders—in the quality of the balance sheet and cash flow statements.

- The United Kingdom has been leading the way in shareholder engagement; that is, boards of directors taking a much more active role in investor relations. The UK has developed a stewardship code (outlining responsibilities for institutional investors) and a corporate governance code (including the position of an independent chairperson or outside director on the board and the need for increased scrutiny of executive compensation). The European Union has developed a position paper on governance, which includes risk management, disclosure, institutional investor engagement, board voting disclosure, and shareholder transparency and identification. This is a likely precursor for a new code that would guide European investor relations activities.
- South Africa has been extremely proactive in its review of corporate governance and the development of a new governance code, a model for the work in Europe. In addition, all public companies that are listed on the South African stock exchange are now required to issue a corporate social responsibility (CSR) report in combination with their financial reporting.
- Canada has been a leader in CSR reporting, particularly in the environmental area. The country also has been a "hotbed" for expanding use of social media in investor relations.
- Brazil has made great strides in corporate governance, with its companies producing some of the best CSR reports in the world.
- The Asia-Pacific region, due to the strength of its economy, is developing its own model for investor relations. New, successful IR societies have emerged in Malaysia and Thailand, for example, and Singapore is seen as an incubator for strong corporate governance standards.

The End Result of a Strong Investor Relations Program

A successful IR program can be characterized by less volatility in the price of the stock, a value that increases with performance, the respect of the investment community, and the ability of the company to return to the market for additional capital. Some of the desired results, which can be used for benchmarking and evaluation purposes, include:

- A changing shareholder base: getting the investors you want
- Analytical coverage by analysts who have intimate knowledge of the company and actively support the stock
- Lower volatility, with the stock price moving up steadily with minimum fluctuation
- Positive coverage in the media that is read or seen by investors
- A fair valuation of the stock
- Ultimately, a lower cost of capital

References

Allen, B. (2009, October 8). IR in the age of social media. IR Magazine. Retrieved August 18, 2010, from www.thecrossbordergroup.com/pages/1913/Breaking+news. stm?article_id=13661

Bank of New York Mellon. (2009, January). *Global trends in investor relations*. New York: Bank of New York Mellon.

Mavrinac, S. C. (1997). Estimating the value of IR: What's it really worth? *Investor Relations Quarterly, 1*(1), 24–39.

Metzker, C. (2010, March). *Investor relations update*. Vienna, VA: National Investor Relations Institute.

Morgan, J. D. (2008, October 28). 2008 annual report survey. *NIRI's executive alert*. Vienna, VA: National Investor Relations Institute.

National Investor Relations Institute. (2004). *Standards of practice for investor relations*. Vienna, VA: National Investor Relations Institute.

Richardson, M., & Roubini, N. (2010, April 11). Starving the beasts of Wall Street. *The Washington Post*, B1, 3.

CHAPTER TWENTY-FIVE

GOVERNMENT RELATIONS

Connecting Communication to the Public Policy Process

John Larsen, Anna Marie Willey

Government relations is a critical component of a healthy democratic process. It is part of the pluralistic nature of our society that expects—and even demands—various levels of participation in the public policy process. Conducted ethically, underscored by credible background research, and triangulating among corporate objectives, government intentions, and the public interests, government relations is a fundamental pillar of good governance for an organization that needs to understand and navigate the complex legislative and public policy process. At root, the practice of government relations is predicated on surrounding oneself with the best possible and current information on a relevant

The authors gratefully appreciate chapter input and perspective from these individuals: Silvia Cambie, Director, Chanda Communications, London, United Kingdom; Mary Lynn Carver, ABC, Senior Vice President, Communications and Public Affairs, University of Maryland, Medical Center/Medical System-Baltimore, Maryland, United States; Russell Grossman, Director of Communications, Department for Business, Innovation and Skills, Government, United Kingdom; Alan Lane, VASGAMA, International Communications Counsel, United Kingdom; James D. Lynch, ABC, Vice President of Communications, American Express Company, New York, USA; Michael Nord, Commercial Attaché, Danish Trade Council, Amsterdam; Matti Ojanen, healthcare and government affairs consultant, London, United Kingdom; Randy Pettipas, President and CEO, Global Public Affairs, Calgary, Alberta, Canada; Sam Rowe, Cutsforth Consulting Services, Brussels, Belgium; Roy Suter, Head, International Government and Industry Affairs, Zurich Insurance Company, Zurich, Switzerland; Marvin A. Tort, Project Director, Think Tank Inc., Philippines; and Ling Wang, Public Affairs Director, Abbott China.

issue and then using that knowledge to shape the types of policy alternatives that support business objectives. It allows governments to make the best possible decisions and to tap into sources of information that may not otherwise be available to them. Government relations practitioners need to understand the intricacies of the public policy process, the political pressures involved, the values embedded in public sentiment, and the perception triggers exploited by traditional or social media.

In communications, the word *dialogue* is often misappropriated and is instead represented by a process that is essentially monologue. Accordingly, one of the key tenets of good government relations is that every effort is made to create meaningful two-way communications, or dialogue, between government and your organization. That two-way street strives to develop policies that are both fair and effective while allowing for necessary consultation with affected stakeholders. To underscore transparency, government relations officials should be registered as required by a jurisdiction. And, an effective lobbying effort should rest on the credibility of the information provided. Although relationships between organizations and government may open doors, the decisions made should be based on the legitimacy and veracity of the information brought into the policy domain.

This chapter provides an overview of the process of government relations and considers its practices across a number of cultures.

Defining Government Relations

Government relations is a term that is often misunderstood, occasionally shrouded in a sense of mystery, and sometimes regarded with uncertainty. But, at its core, government relations is a relatively straightforward activity that revolves around an organization's intent to understand a government's position on an issue while also advancing the organization's position relative to that issue. Government relations has sometimes been given uncomplimentary, and unfair, treatment in public opinion circles. Very often the term *lobbyist* is used pejoratively, without recognizing that government relations practitioners are entrusted with sharing the types of information, experience, and ideas that lead to the development of better public policy. In exactly the same way that any number of citizen or issue advocacy groups influence government officials, public relations professionals work to bring important and broader context to the policy decision makers.

Inherent in all government relations activity is the expectation that it will be conducted openly, with transparency, and in accordance with a professional code of ethics. Whether it is being conducted by in-house corporate representatives or external consultants, the government relations practitioner must continually triangulate between their organization's strategic goals, a government's priorities, and the legitimate public interest. As such, the IABC (International Association of Business Communicators) *Code of Ethics* (2005) applies to any government relations activity, and most often any government relations activity is further governed by various lobbying acts. Implicit is the assumption that all communications will be honest and truthful, but there is also the expectation that government relations will be fulsome in their information, thereby avoiding any charges of selective disclosure and misrepresentation.

Government policy has a significant impact on the way organizations conduct business. With growing regulatory controls, it is increasingly important that business has a direct channel of input and insight into the people who can affect operations, customers, and whose decisions affect an organization's bottom line. All communications and interactions with government of any level needs to be managed with the greatest trust and integrity, ensuring that there is no conflict of interest and most important that there is compliance within all codes of ethical standards.

Government relations often allows the interests of various groups, which may otherwise be too fragmented to be properly heard and integrated into the public policy context, to represent their views through a professional coalition. Whether conducting lobbying activity as a single organization or collectively, the key steps for success include:

- Knowing the issues
- Knowing who the key stakeholders are within government
- Understanding the public policy debate and the government's position
- Ensuring the allocation of appropriate resources to follow up
- Knowing which timing is most effective to maximize the strategic effort
- Predetermining measurements and evaluation of your work

Models of Government Relations

Navigating the needs of municipal, provincial, and federal governments can be complex, and there are numerous structures to meet the challenges. The most effective type of government relations occurs when a proactive approach is taken.

If government relations is not conducted proactively, organizations may be forced into an adversarial position with government wherein they may consider various pressure tactics to get their points across. Any of these tactics, including presenting positions to opposition parties, assessing internal political debate, or monitoring the media to measure government reaction, are often less effective techniques in the long run.

Government relations can not be seen as an occasional activity, predicated solely on addressing individual issues as they arise. It needs to be built on a respect for the importance of developing lasting and honest relationships among an organization and various levels of government. The process allows organizations to monitor and evaluate the trends and issues that will ultimately affect the bottom line. Proactive advocacy of your organization's position toward government should be professional and focused on key facts to help shape decisions and recognizing that—although there may be much your organization wants to say—there is far less time for politicians and government officials to review the full scope of information. Bottom line: keep your information relevant, honest, short, and convincing.

In-House Function

The government relations function can be housed within a communications branch, report directly to a chief executive officer, or managed in another way. Regardless of structure, staff must be seen as senior level and strategically focused. Typically, responsibilities include:

- Establishing liaisons with key government officials—an ongoing relationship-building activity
- Monitoring issues within an organization by developing a proactive issue identification, prioritization, and decision-making framework
- Assisting with correspondence development—helping to shape the types of strategic messages that inform decision makers and drive public policy
- Setting up meetings with key partners in government
- Participating in events that provide further insight into government priorities and potential policy
- Reviewing contracts to ensure regulatory and/or policy compliance
- Hosting visiting dignitaries—government officials who seek to better understand your organization and your contribution to public policy creation
- Providing regular reporting for members of your organization's executive team and governing bodies
- Completing any legislatively required reports to demonstrate understanding of, and accountability relative to, government expectations

An essential element for any government relations structure is that the insight of the government relations personnel is proactive and welcomed as a contributing member of a senior management team.

Contracted Function

If an organization chooses to enlist the services of a consulting firm or lobbying group, the services may be somewhat more focused. Lobbyists are engaged to help position the organization's strengths and provide better context should an issue be emerging. Whether the outreach is conducted by a representative from your organization or by an external consultant, it is equally important that the government relations representative put as much energy into understanding the official position of government as it is for that person to represent the organization's perspective. When key stakeholders are more conversant about an issue, they are able to communicate better within a crisis situation both internally and externally. Caught uninformed about an issue facing an organization, key stakeholders can easily go on the defensive, and the situation can escalate.

Government As Key Stakeholder

As these comments demonstrate, regardless of the model chosen, communicators from around the globe uphold that governments need to be considered as key stakeholders:

"It is key to anticipate the future and shape the existing regulatory framework by an ongoing constructive dialogue with government stakeholders who essentially determine the rules of engagement for corporations," said Roy Suter, Head, International Government and Industry Affairs, Zurich Insurance Company, Zurich, Switzerland.

"In more ways than one, most if not all organizations fall under some form of government control, regulation, supervision, management, oversight, or cooperation, to the extent that even the smallest of organizations require some form of national or local licensing and/or permission to exist if not operate and to transact with the public," said Marvin A. Tort, Project Director, Think Tank Inc., Makati, Philippines.

"Governments are also an important link to getting new public policies approved and thereby paving the way for new private initiatives. The last 20 years of outsourcing government responsibilities also make government important stakeholders for business," said Michael Nord, Commercial Attaché, Danish Trade Council, Amsterdam.

"There is virtually no business not affected by Government policy. Your judgment has to be on the resource you put in locally versus trade associations or employer bodies, with whom Government spends a lot of its time and resource," said Russell Grossman, Director of Communications, Department for Business, Innovation and Skills, UK Government.

"These days, corporations are expected to take position on global issues and to work together with government and other organisations to find sustainable solutions," said Silvia Cambie, Director, Chanda Communications, London, United Kingdom.

"Business needs a clear regulatory framework in which to operate, and if it wants to plan long-term it needs to know what is on the horizon and what initiatives governments are planning," said Sam Rowe, Cutsforth Consulting Services, Brussels, Belgium.

"Depending on business/organization type, governments potentially have a huge influence on their license to operate, as well as an impact on regulatory and legislative frameworks which affect businesses," said Matti Ojanen, health care and government affairs consultant, United Kingdom.

"The regulatory environment absolutely affects a company's ability to serve its customers, manage its employees and drive revenues and profits for its shareholders. If regulators and government officials are not in your primary or secondary audience analysis, then it is very important to go back and include them. It's a must for success today—and tomorrow," said James D. Lynch, ABC, Vice President of Communications, American Express Company, New York City, United States.

Importance of Research and Evaluation

Communicators around the globe note the importance of basing their government relations programs on solid research. Research underpins the importance of knowledge for all stakeholders: understanding of a government's agenda, being cognizant of the stakeholders' positioning within mandate, its progress on commitments, the issues capturing the attention of the day, preferences of decision makers, action drivers, and pace. Governments engage in various types of communications research, including public opinion surveys and focus groups on numerous initiatives prior to launch or during rollouts.

Organizations should position themselves to understand how their actions can affect government's social or economic agenda, or even both. They should also be sensitive about how an organization's issue can be perceived by government decision makers.

Organizations can undertake research to answer some of these key questions to help inform government decision makers. For example:

- Will the decision of our organization affect any of government's priorities?
- Will there be any impact on specific audiences?
- Will there be budget implications for government?
- How will the organization's decision affect the environment or any social or health agendas?
- How will the organization's decision affect the economy?
- Is there a need for broader base consultation?
- Is there any minority interest affected by the decision?
- Is there a potential for any demonstration as a result of the organization's actions?
- Is there a comprehensive communications strategy developed with government related to the issue or rollout?

As part of a government relations program, practical monitoring could include:

- Monitoring progress on issues regularly to ensure your organization receives crucial feedback as to areas which may require more attention or resources
- Monitoring sufficient research on issues to prepare for all potential outcomes, thus mitigating any potential risks
- Monitoring needs of a local society—form alliances—and engage in two-way symmetrical communication with target audiences.
- Monitor efficiency of budget spending on the program's outcomes

The cornerstone to any successful communications effort is evaluation. First, how did the government relations effort affect legislation? Was new policy introduced, old policy amended, or a process for review implemented? Second, what were the financial implications? What was the return on investment for the overall government relations taken? Third, what was the reputational component of the lobbying effort? Do key audiences better understand the issues, your organization's position, and the various points of public interest?

Important Processes for Government Relations Activities

Government relations activities typically fall into two categories: communicating with government decision makers and protocol.

Communicating with Government Decision Makers

It is important to know how government coordinates its decision-making process and manages formats for such decisions. For example, if a government cabinet is needed to make a final decision, is there a format they follow for such a decision, and if so, has your organization provided detail in the cabinet's preferred manner of receipt? Have all the questions within the template for decision making been addressed?

There are elected and nonelected decision makers, all of whom can affect organizations and communications activity. It is important to develop working relationships and build these relationships on honesty and trust. For example:

- Briefing key officials to help with ensuring that the background of an issue is well known by decision makers
- Ensuring your organization has developed succinct, relevant, and timely information for government officials.
- Communicating without overly technical information or industry jargon
- Ensuring there is a common communication protocol for crisis communications
- Maintaining contact lists
- Striving for a win-win situation and working to bring a solution to the table that recognizes the government position

Protocol

If an organization has an opportunity to work with government, it should be aware of the protocol of the government and the advance timing required. Particular attention should be paid to:

- *Scheduling of events.* Many key officials have agendas blocked for months, and advance planning is paramount.

- *Formal agenda development.* Consult carefully with government officials on expectations of meetings or events. Know early what is expected in terms of dignitary speaking roles.
- *Logistics.* Ensure that dignitaries' needs are managed as a priority and with precision, from parking arrangements, name tags, meeting of guests at entrance, accommodating dietary requirements, addressing onsite concerns.
- *Support material.* Ensure that there are adequate briefing materials available in advance of any discussions.
- *Media relations.* Ensure that there is a coordinated media relations approach and coordinated effort for postdiscussion or event interviews.
- *Evaluation.* Set up an opportunity to debrief about activities and do appropriate correspondence or follow-up.

Government Relations Structures

Government relations programs are structured in many different ways. Here are some examples:

- Head of government relations department reports directly to the chief executive officer (CEO). There is direct access to the government relations public policy expertise; guidance and networks allow the CEO to promptly and effectively discharge such duties.
- Regional heads of the government affairs department have close reporting lines to the various regional (business) executives of the organization.
- Government relations personnel are placed in regions based on the nature of the business.
- Government relations staff within a country reports directly to general manager with dotted line to government relations function in the region or headquarters.
- Policy officials have some defined role in engaging in stakeholder relations.
- Senior managers have target companies assigned to connect with.
- Stakeholder team has assignments for overall strategy, coordination, and channels.
- Lead line management tasked with the connecting with appropriate sectors of government.

Whatever process is chosen, pre-location training and familiarization with a culture is important for government relations practitioners, especially before arrival at the site. Government relations are based on deep levels of trust and the practitioners' understanding of the culture. Roles and responsibilities must be clearly defined. This will ensure there is consistency and coordination of approach to move the business objective forward.

Important Considerations

These ten elements comprise turning points in government relations programs witnessed by communications professionals from around the world as:

1. Ensuring open and transparent communication: listen carefully; address concerns quickly
2. Using all communication channels in the preferred manner of receipt for audiences
3. Networking and establishing credibility with key officials, assisting in identifying solutions
4. Establishing internal buy-in and appropriate internal resources
5. Building strong research capacity for mandate, policy, operational environment, issues, advocacies, and impact on stakeholders
6. Displaying strong leadership
7. Establishing measurable objectives aligned to audience needs; ensuring evaluation; clarifying what you are attempting to do—that is, impact on legislation, regulatory environment, policy, public opinion; allowing sufficient time to achieve results
8. Respecting language, cultural, religious, and philosophical protocol and differences
9. Ensuring an integrated approach that goes beyond issue management to include corporate social responsibility and reputation management
10. Bringing awareness of global issues and the role played by the respective government in addressing them

These ten factors limit the success of government relations programs:

1. Lack of network with external stakeholders and poor targeting of objectives
2. Lack of knowledge or organizational credibility—leaders not trained to communicate
3. Lack of internal executive buy-in for programs and initiatives to improve communication and relations with the government
4. Inability to understand the priorities or mandate of the public institution. Lack of research and understanding of government operation, experience,

analytical methodology and program management capacity, and unwillingness to compromise on advocacies and issues

5. Failure to quickly and extensively identify potential points of conflict and agreement, and potential leverage for and against the organization
6. Failure to measure outcomes
7. Gaps in internal process alignment; setting unrealistic expectations
8. Delays or limited capacity to engage in proactive work
9. Lack of experience or expertise when dealing with governments in foreign countries
10. Lack of coordination between government relations and reputation management

The following two case studies provide evidence of government relations communications.

Case in Point: Canada: Client "Green"

Whereas in the United States there are many billions of dollars available through private foundations, in Canada this is not the case: there are a limited number of smaller foundations that provide support for a multiplicity of initiatives and interests.

Client "Green" is a small Canadian foundation that worked with larger U.S. foundations. Both were interested in protecting a unique area of land that was host to rare species of flora and fauna. Interested in pursuing a new model of working with the government, the small Canadian foundation proposed an innovative Private-Public Partnership (P3) model to leverage funding from governments through the commitment of U.S. foundation funding supplemented by smaller-scale Canadian philanthropic funding.

Client "Green" had worked for many months with the federal and provincial governments to sell the idea and attract federal and provincial funding. There were general interest and general commitments, but no money was secured. After many months of work, there was also a change in government, from a government seen as more pro-environment to one seen as less interested or open to supporting environmental initiatives.

This case is used with permission from Randy Pettipas, President and Chief Executive Officer, Global Public Affairs, Calgary, Alberta, Canada.

With the change in government, Client "Green" retained the services of a government relations firm that specialized in environmental matters. The lead consultant had an environmental policy background, a strong sense of the people, specific language and ideas of the government party, and several years of understanding government's decision-making process.

A presentation package and briefing notes were developed that considered the language of the governing party and connected with themes and issues of interest. A broad contact plan was initiated, focusing on key players in various departments. Very senior volunteers from the business and government communities in both the United States and Canada were identified to help answer questions of key government contacts. A desire to fund the project began appearing, but one question that emerged that was difficult to manage: the amount of money desired from the federal government (in the tens of millions of dollars) would likely come from multiple sources, so a single departmental "champion" would need to be identified.

After several months of contact and building interest in the idea, principally on the part of the client but complemented by lobbying, the only ministerial champion to emerge was willing to contribute a much lower sum of money than desired, leaving the foundation funders struggling and ready to walk away from a deal. However, just as negotiations progressed, the minister-champion was moved to a new post. A new minister was announced.

The new minister-champion identified the project as a key initiative, based on public policy fit, and then supported the original amount requested. This was matched by both the provincial and private foundation funding.

The outcome was based on much hard work and was built on several strategic requirements:

1. Alignment of a project with the political and policy interests of the government
2. Alignment of groups and key decision makers applying the necessary pressure to make a convincing case about the importance of the project
3. Naming an able, trustworthy, and high-profile spokesman to make the case
4. Identification of an able champion in the cabinet or at the senior bureaucratic level who could bring together others to support the initiative
5. Importance of building the groundwork with reliable information that reflects scientific research and public opinion polling support regarding the project
6. Patience and consistent work to keep the issue alive despite personnel changes within the system
7. Timing and being present with an answer when governments are faced with a way to align actions with a commitment

Case in Point: United Kingdom: Government Relations within Communications

This case study describes how an international brand saved its market share and reputation through a systematic approach to relations with the national government.

South America is a fascinating and exotic place. It is made up of many different cultures, all of which have their own ways of running their countries. Doing business there can be both rewarding and at the same time provide a cautionary tale.

Such was the case with a global energy company that had operated successfully in a South American country for many decades. Government relations were long established, and the company took great care in its relations with key people at the center of power. Yet, as this case study shows, nothing can be taken for granted.

There was a sudden change of government. This led to power moving from a side of the Congress in tune with international business to politicians who favored more control over foreign multinationals in the country.

The company operated a chain of gasoline service stations across the country. It enjoyed a healthy market share. The new government was planning to nationalize part of the market held by multinationals, allowing it more control over its economy. The company viewed this as a threat to parts of its business, to its revenues and its future in the country.

Senior management, led by the CEO, went on the offensive. The company's network of government contacts was seen as the route to informing the proposed government policy.

The company developed the background for briefing key decision makers on why the company thought the legislation would damage the company and its role in the country. Central messages to be communicated were

- Competition in the gasoline retail market allowed a level of service and product quality to international standards.
- Global companies brought best practice, high levels of health, safety, and environmental care along with revenues that provided government with a strong tax base and financial support for communities.

This case is used with permission from Alan Lane of VASGAMA, International Communications Counsel, United Kingdom.

Key decision makers were contacted at all levels known to the company to tell its story. The CEO took a leadership role and ran a high-profile campaign. The company placed advertisements in the national media outlining the importance of this decision. Support was sought from other multinationals facing the same issue. A concerted approach to influencing government legislation was seen as more effective.

Underlying the corporate campaign was a simple message: Multinationals had for decades been a positive force for the country. The new legislation now posed a threat to this legacy.

The issue went to the top of the government's agenda. There was much internal debate. After months of contemplation, the government revised its legislation to address the issues raised.

The results were a proposed government role in the retail market, scaled down but allowing a national influence to be secured. Meanwhile, the global companies retained what they saw as an adjusted but workable market share.

Conclusion

Effective government relations is a fine synthesis of art and science—balancing public perception and policy reality. Key to success of government relations operations is an understanding of the complex public policy environment in which your organization operates. Every organization is affected by decisions of government, whether they are realized or not. For government relations efforts to be truly effective, they need to be part of an ongoing and proactive issue research and outreach program. Such a program needs support from the executive table and must be understood and respected by those within government decision-making circles. The successful government relations practitioner today is the one who can triangulate among corporate aims, government responsibilities, and the broader public interest. Once initiated, all government relations activity needs to be carefully monitored, evaluated, and refined to meet the expectations of an ever-changing public and political environment.

Reference

International Association of Business Communicators. (2005). *IABC code of ethics for professional communicators.* Available at www.iabc.com/about/code.htm

CHAPTER TWENTY-SIX

REPUTATION MANAGEMENT

Building, Enhancing, and Protecting Organizational Reputation in the Information Age

Alistair J. Nicholas

Sadly, the first decade of the twenty-first century is likely to be remembered for the number of corporate scandals and not the technological advances and better living that open markets have enabled. There have been enough instances of individuals and organizations failing to do the right thing, leaving one to question whether the current generation of business and political leaders is morally bereft. Certainly too many of today's politicians and captains of industry have crossed ethical boundaries in pursuit of power or profits. But what is striking is how easy it is to uncover and expose wrongful behavior. Thanks primarily to modern communications technology, and in particular the pervasiveness of social media, individuals and organizations now find themselves under a microscope that forces them to behave with greater sincerity, openness, and transparency.

Arguably a paradigm shift has occurred. Today a culture that demands organizational (and individual) transparency permeates society. We expect truth, openness, and nothing short of total integrity of political leaders, captains of industry, and the organizations they lead. At a minimum, we require them to live up to our standards; and, when their espoused principles and values exceed the minimum, to match them as well. The technology of modern communications and globalization, the 24/7 news cycle, and social media have empowered the public to demand a better deal.

Organizations must ensure they live up to their principles or risk their reputations. And reputation is everything. Shakespeare put it best: "Who steals my purse steals trash … ; /But he that filches from me my good name/ … makes me poor indeed." This chapter explores the concept of reputation, how it is built, enhanced, and protected by communicators.

Building Reputation: Integrity is Everything

Before discussing how to build a reputation, it is useful to determine what reputation is. From the perspective of organizational communications: "Reputation means how positively, or negatively, a company or similar institution is perceived by its key stakeholders—the people or entities that the company or institution relies on for its success. For many for-profit companies, typical stakeholders might include customers, employees, suppliers, or financial analysts. For government or political entities … stakeholders are, above all, the electorate" (Gaines-Ross, 2008, p. 6).

Given that an organization has a number of stakeholders, it is likely that its reputation means different things to each. Indeed, it is conceivable that what makes a good reputation for one stakeholder might diverge entirely from what makes a good reputation for another stakeholder. Consider, for example, that investors are concerned primarily with the financial reputation of a company, while customers are more concerned with its reputation for producing high-quality, safe products, while the wider public is concerned with ethical behavior.

An organization must be able to balance its reputational repertoire. Financial performance must be measured against its treatment of its employees, the safety and quality of its products, governance matters, and, increasingly, how the organization behaves as a member of civil society.

This yields a simple definition of *reputation* as the sum of what an individual or organization is. Reputation management, then, is the totality of all the positive things done by an organization to enhance its various, and sometimes competing, stakeholders' objectives. A good reputation for a company means strong financial performance based on continuously and consistently delivering to the market quality products and/or services while acting in accordance with accepted social norms and standards of ethics and delivering on its own promises to its customers and the wider society.

Reputation is ultimately about the integrity of an organization. Clearly an organization's reputation is based on two factors: acting in a way that is consistent with its stated values, and acting in accordance with the standards of the societies in which it operates.

Reputation Monitoring

One definition of *reputation* often given is that it is what is said about you *after* you have left the room. Therefore, a valuable communications officer knows what is being said about the organization by its various stakeholders. Insights into what is being said about an organization can be garnered in several ways, under the umbrella of reputation monitoring.

Because public relations (PR) is about two-way communications, the PR department should have an ear to the ground and know what key stakeholders may be thinking or saying about the organization. Several means of reputation monitoring are available to today's communicator. Media monitoring is probably the first and oldest means available. A good communications department will have extensive media-monitoring capabilities. These are often outsourced to media-monitoring companies that cover traditional print and broadcast media as well as new media.

If your media monitoring is collecting a lot of positive stories about your organization, the organization's reputation is most probably in good standing. But in truth there should be a balance of stories garnered, including some that may be less than flattering. These should not be dismissed or ignored. Rather, a good corporate communications officer will ensure that the negative stories are communicated to senior management, so that the organization can see what is being said about it and investigate any shortcomings that might exist between the image it wants to have and the perception key stakeholders are forming about it.

If negative issues are already being talked about openly in the published media, it may be too late to protect the organization's reputation. This makes it important for the communications officer to be able to pick up on the chatter of journalists before chatter becomes a newsworthy story. A good communications officer should also be an intelligence gatherer for his or her organization. This means having strong relationships with key journalists covering the organization's industry to pick up important information about perceptions of the organization before the media start publishing negative stories.

A more formal way to obtain information from journalists is to conduct a *media audit* for an organization. This is usually done by constructing a blind survey and asking key journalists covering the respective industry to complete it. It is better if such blind surveys are conducted by public relations firms or independent consultants in order to maintain confidentiality; this is likely to yield more objective responses from journalists involved. Such surveys ask journalists to rank companies in the industry against certain criteria, or they include open-ended and qualitative items such as "Name the company with the best/worst reputation. Why?"

Communications officers can go further with such formal surveys and conduct audits of other stakeholder groups. For example, it is common to survey government officials, political staffers, investors, and customers. Market research companies can be engaged to assist with larger-scale surveys. Modern communications technology and social media can also be utilized.

A *reputation perception audit* is critical to identifying the gap between an organization's reputation and where the organization would like its reputation to be. Once the gap is identified, the organization can put in place appropriate strategies to close the perception gap. After all, an organization wants to be perceived by its stakeholders the same way its leadership envisions it to be. The goal is to achieve integrity of purpose and perception.

Enhancing Reputation

Assuming an organization has achieved reputation success, that it has built a solid reputation, the next task is to enhance that reputation. The best way to do this is through a strategic corporate social responsibility (CSR) program. *Strategic* implies a well-designed program that is more than philanthropic activities. Giving money away is not the same thing as engaging with key stakeholders on socially important matters. Similarly, cause-related marketing is not the same thing as corporate social responsibility. *Cause-related marketing* refers to businesses partnering with nonprofit organizations or charities to raise awareness of issues and assist their causes by associating products with those specific causes. Both philanthropic activities and cause-related marketing can help enhance a company's reputation, but they are not as effective or credible from a reputation management perspective as corporate social responsibility.

CSR by comparison can go to the very heart of organizational reputation. It is about acting in accordance with the law. It is about ethical behavior. And it is about building sustainable businesses and supporting sustainable business practices. This applies especially to organizations that act in socially responsible ways when the legal standards of a country or the norms of society do not demand it. For many, CSR is about acting responsibly with respect to the environment. CSR is considered a triple bottom line: people, planet, and profit.

Companies that use strategic CSR programs to enhance their reputations often go beyond the minimum expected of them. Such companies initiate projects that extend their commitment beyond the purview of their own operations and immediate business impact to have an impact on the wider societies in which they operate. For example, many multinational corporations operating in developing nations have been instrumental in establishing schools to raise literacy rates or vocational learning centers to enable adults to acquire skills that are needed in a fast-changing world.

Strong CSR programs are increasingly seen as ways to attract and retain good staff in both advanced and developing economies. This is of significance as global talent pools shrink and the competition for high-performing employees intensifies. "Clearly, a more strategic approach to CSR warrants greater ownership of the initiatives by employees. They yearn to play greater roles—in effect, to become co-creators of CSR value" (Bhattacharya, Sen, & Korschun, 2008, p. 41).

In the future, CSR will have a more prominent place in the corporate communications tool kit than it enjoys even today. More than anything else, it is CSR that will enhance the reputation of an organization.

Protecting Reputation

When Tony Hayward took over as CEO at BP in 2007, he promised he would improve the company's safety record following a 2005 accident at the company's Texas City refinery that had killed fifteen workers and injured 180 others. But the Deepwater Horizon accident that killed eleven oil rig workers and caused the massive oil spill in the Gulf of Mexico in 2010 has put pain to that claim, particularly as it appears that BP was cutting corners on safety to achieve profitability faster. For example, documents were produced by the U.S. Congress House Energy and Commerce Committee showing that only six centralizers were used on the rig, despite a recommendation by Halliburton that the company should use twenty-one centralizers (King & Gold, 2010).

It would appear that BP was waiting for a major accident to happen. The disaster and the reputational crisis in which BP is embroiled were avoidable. If people had taken note of the signs, the accident and spill could have been avoided. All that was needed was a simple mechanism to identify and deal with problems before they erupted into full-blown crises. The failure of BP to put in place adequate safety measures on the Deepwater Horizon and the subsequent poor handling of the crisis will make this incident the textbook case study of how not to handle a crisis for many years to come. Could BP have taken any steps to better protect its reputation?

Build a Good Radar System

Take, for example, a client who suffered many reputational crises that always seemed to take it by surprise. The communications department of the company had no idea of the risks it faced and could only react as crises *went hot* in the media. As it transpired, the internal management of the organization operated with a silo mentality and was very dysfunctional. Various departments did not communicate with each other, and the communications department was consequently in the dark about the organization's risk exposure. The communications team would only become aware of financial problems or court cases when it read about them in its daily media clips. This meant the communications department could only react to the crises. But every issue that it faced in the media was already known to others in the organization long before the media reported the stories.

To amend this, I counseled the organization's communications department to put in place some mechanisms to determine potential risks and create early warning systems. As a first step, all department managers were surveyed to determine the potential risks, the worst-case scenarios. From the results, a risk matrix was constructed that plotted the risks according to the likelihood of occurrence in correlation to the potential impact on the organization's reputation if the risk materialized.

Next, a crisis management committee was convened to monitor and reassess the organization's risk exposure on a biweekly basis. The committee included the head of corporate communications, chief financial officer, chief operating officer, head of marketing, head of corporate affairs, and head of legal affairs; these managers' areas were the most likely to know about potential risks.

These first two steps enabled us to get ahead of the curve and prepare for potential crises well before they were reported in the media and intervene and correct organizational behavior that was raising our risk profile and threatening organizational reputation; at worst, we were able to prepare crisis scenarios and related boilerplate statements in case the stories broke before we could intervene. Either way, we were not going to be caught off-guard again.

A third step was to establish a mechanism so that frontline employees felt comfortable about reporting problems to the organization. To help overcome this fear of reporting problems, we established an e-mail address and an old-fashioned letter box in each office to which staff could send their concerns anonymously. These frontline workers often knew about problems from their customer networks long before senior management was aware of the problems; we had to create a culture of concern about the organization's reputation and encourage frontline workers to report issues before they became full-blown crises for the organization.

As a final step to protecting the organization's reputation, regular crisis management training sessions and drills were implemented, particularly for those executives who might be required to act as spokespersons for the organization during a crisis. The purpose of this activity was to test and improve the organization's crisis management systems and processes so that if the company was caught in a crisis situation, its crisis management team would be able to respond appropriately.

Today social media and the tools to monitor social media are a great addition to the communicator's tool kit as early warning systems for identification of potential crises. Some years ago my firm was brought in to conduct a media interview skills-training program for a client. In the course of researching the client on the Internet, we stumbled across a blog by one of its employees in which the employee was discussing an issue of sexual harassment in her office that involved one of the company's managers in China. Senior management at the client company was unaware of the situation, as it was not reported due to fear of reprisal. The employee had only mentioned it to a friend in the office who had chosen to vent about her friend's dilemma on her personal blog. Had the issue gotten worse or been uncovered by the media, it could have proven very damaging to the reputation of the company. Fortunately, we were able to raise the issue to senior management, and they intervened and addressed it before it reached reputation-damaging proportions.

The tools exist for monitoring reputation-threatening risks. Communicators need to use them and take responsibility for ensuring that companies are aware of the issues before they develop into full-blown crises. Communicators need to keep an eye on the radar screens of their companies.

Reputation Repair

The truth is, most companies come back from crises and manage to rebuild their reputations—even the worst of crises. Consider now textbook examples like Johnson & Johnson's handling of the Tylenol contamination case in 1982 and the *Exxon Valdez* oil spill in Alaska in 1989. How fast and how well a company reacts to a crisis will determine the degree of the impact on its overall reputation and how long it will last. The future of BP following the Deepwater Horizon accident and oil spill in the Gulf of Mexico remains uncertain.

But the cases of Arthur Andersen and Enron, companies that vanished following their crises, seem to be more the exceptions that prove the rule that companies can return from the brink:

Most large companies that lose reputation have the opportunity, resources, and residual goodwill to recast their companies with new CEOs, new boards, new partners, and new visions, as did Tyco, WorldCom, CA, AIG, Royal Ahold, Parmalat, Skandia, and Vivendi, to name just a few. For big players such as these, the issue is usually not so much a question of whether recovery will happen but how soon recovery will take place and whether recovery will return the company to its former glory (Gaines-Ross, 2008, p. 27).

Gaines-Ross goes on to say, "Decades need not pass before lost reputations are restored. Business decision makers estimate that, when recovery is properly managed, approximately three and a half years are required for a company to rebuild its damaged reputation" (p. 27).

Apart from the speed of the response to a crisis, critical factors that are likely to play into the rebuilding of a reputation are sincerity of the organization's response during the crisis and whether it showed empathy or understanding for the plight of those affected or concerned about the crisis. To rebuild its reputation after a crisis, a company needs to show true remorse for the crisis and demonstrate real action taken to ensure that the crisis will not occur again—or at least that the chances will be greatly reduced.

Case in Point: Good Health Pharmaceuticals

Good Health Pharmaceuticals Corporation (GHP) [this is a fictitious case to illustrate reputation management concerns] is a leading pharmaceutical corporation, one involved in developing new drugs as well as manufacturing of a range of medicines for life-threatening conditions.

Although the company has been investing in and operating in China for close to twenty years, it has not been able to differentiate itself from other foreign pharmaceutical companies in the market. Despite millions of dollars of investments and several manufacturing plants across the nation, it is largely seen as just another foreign drug manufacturer making and selling product in China and taking profits out of the country. Indeed, the company has on occasion been hit by media crises, either in relation to product quality issues or in relation to ethical issues around some activities of its sales and distribution network partners (none of whom are direct employees of GHP). In these instances the media has portrayed the company as a foreign investor that has double standards in the China market: it does not act as responsibly as it does in European and North American markets.

To counter this perception, the company has put in place several cause-related marketing programs. For example, as the company is involved in trialing new HIV/AIDS drugs in the south and west of China, it has initiated, in partnership with some nongovernmental organizations, education programs on HIV prevention in those regions. But such efforts are not resonating well with the media and other key stakeholders, who see the programs as linked too directly to the company's own products.

While GHP knew that the market's perception of it was poor, it had not conducted any research to determine how specific stakeholders perceived it or to determine which stakeholders could be relied upon to support it, particularly in a crisis situation. Therefore one of the first steps toward building its reputation in the market was to have a market research firm conduct audits of its various stakeholders to see how they perceived the company and what was expected from the company as a corporate citizen of China.

The survey provided statistical evidence of the gap between how the company was perceived by various stakeholders and how the company wanted to be perceived. One interesting finding was that the company's employees in the market perceived it very differently than the way management thought it was perceived.

The survey provided hard data on the perception gap that previously was known only anecdotally by senior management. These data were critical to moving senior management to focus on the issue and commit to solving what was ultimately a reputation problem.

Reputation strategy and messaging workshops were conducted nationwide, with managers across various divisions and business units brought in to determine a corporate position. While managers of various units were focused more on their businesses, it was necessary to achieve buy-in across all units for a corporate reputation communications strategy that would include a social responsibility program for China.

Eventually it was decided that the company needed to establish its credentials as fully committed to the market by engaging in activities important to the market. The company additionally decided that it needed to involve its own staff in some of those activities so that they could have firsthand experience with the company's commitment to the market and ownership for the company's CSR programs.

One of the first steps for the company was to establish a *strategic cause-related marketing campaign* that extended the company's reach to a broader audience than the existing cause-marketing programs of the company, which were largely focused on specific regions or particular diseases. The company's market research had shown the emergence of a specific demographic in China that was coming under considerable quality-of-life pressure related to health: women ages 35–55. These women were termed *sandwich-class women* because they were caught in the middle of many health issues—their children's, husbands', parents', and their own. That research indicated that these women felt no one was looking after their interests and that they often could not find basic information to help deal with the health issues faced by their families.

The company decided to make these women a focus by putting in place mechanisms to communicate directly with this group: a column with a leading national newspaper and a regular segment on a national TV talk show targeting this group of women were negotiated to deliver important health and well-being information to them. Later, as social media took off in China, blogs and micro-blogs were used to reach this key stakeholder group. The result of the program was that this key group started to feel a connection with the company—a connection that would ultimately influence their buying decisions.

The company recognized that this was only a cause-related marketing program and that by itself it would not be sufficient to turn around overall perception of the company. It was decided also to establish a *community outreach program* to directly involve employees of GHP. A mechanism was established for staff to suggest projects the company could assist with in their local neighborhoods. Preference would be given to projects that the staff would become directly involved in and that would go beyond mere corporate philanthropy. In other words, it was decided to avoid situations of just giving money to causes, no matter how good those causes were. Projects that won company support included programs to place exercise equipment in small neighborhood parks and schools; staff gave their time to run classes or seminars on the benefits of healthier living through regular exercise or were involved in establishing community sports teams or running sports workshops. This program was very successful because it involved employees directly and enabled them to see that their company was committed to the communities in which it was involved.

The third element of the strategy was to put in place a more *extensive corporate social responsibility program* that would demonstrate the company's commitment to China at a national level. A serious problem facing China is keeping children, particularly girls, in rural areas in school beyond the sixth grade. Many children drop out to help supplement their parents' incomes and usually end up working in low-paid, unskilled jobs. At the same time China has a shortage of qualified nurses. GHP therefore partnered with a well-known nursing college by providing scholarships to needy students from rural areas and by providing input into the curriculum from the perspective of a pharmaceutical company—something directly related to their value proposition. Additionally, the company provided scholarships at the middle and high school levels to children in rural areas who demonstrated an interest in nursing careers. While it was accepted that not all children receiving scholarships would enter nursing, it was seen as an important initiative to keep children in school longer. To ensure key stakeholders were aware of the program, local government officials and media were invited to scholarship award ceremonies at which a local manager of GHP awarded the scholarships to the successful students.

While it took several years to achieve, the company's approach successfully changed the perception many of its stakeholders had held. The company stopped being seen as just another foreign company trying to make money in China and started to be perceived as a company with local interests at heart. Even the local media changed its view of the company and, when crises arose from time to time, the nature of the reporting shifted from accusing GHP of double standards in the market to focusing more on the specifics of the issues of the time.

A more strategic approach to reputation management by GHP clearly changed the company's fortune in China.

Conclusion: The Secret of Reputational Success Is Sincerity

The public is looking for integrity from its leaders, political institutions, businesses, and other organizations. The public has, through technology and increased interaction with each other—thanks to social media—the tools to hold individuals and organizations to account.

Acting unethically, failing to live up to espoused values, or failing to meet the expectations of society will prove damaging to the reputation of an organization. Reputation management therefore is about ensuring that organizations act with full integrity. Today's sophisticated and socially aware consumers will accept nothing less.

Simply put, a reputation is built by doing what you say you are going to do—by integrity. It is enhanced by going the extra distance and helping to build a civil society—even globally—according to the values of the organization and in keeping with the social standards of the organization's key markets. And, after being established, a reputation must be vigilantly protected; once broken, it is not easily rebuilt.

Reputation management matters, pure and simple. Communications officers need to put in place the strategies to enhance reputation and the systems and procedures to protect it.

References

Bhattacharya, C. B., Sen, S., & Korschun, D. (2008). Using corporate social responsibility to win the war for talent. *MIT Sloan Management Review, 49*(2), 37–44.

Gaines-Ross, L. (2008). *Corporate reputation: 12 steps to safeguarding and recovering reputation.* San Francisco: Wiley.

King, N. Jr., & Gold, R. (2010, June 15). BP crew focused on costs: Congress. *Wall Street Journal* (Eastern ed.), p. A1.

CHAPTER TWENTY-SEVEN

MEASURING PUBLIC RELATIONS PROGRAMS

Mark Weiner

Every day, the imperatives of business affect public relations (PR) investment decisions, as bottom-line thinking is the current reality. While some organizations and public relations executives thrive in this new environment of accountability, the absence of profession-wide standards, the vagaries of where to begin, and the dearth of guidance from internal and external clients leads to a shared state of anxiety and uncertainty: senior management does not know enough about PR to provide direction, and PR executives do not know enough about measuring the value of PR or its return on investment to take the initiative. The result is stasis: timid, conventional approaches yield predictable, unspectacular results.

The inevitable outcome of being in such an indeterminate state is that while you are there, the world accelerates without you. Just as pain is your body's way of signaling itself to do everything possible to help make you well again, the same holds true for business. It is better to feel *the pain* at the onset (and for only a short time) so that the process for improvement can begin. Unfortunately, most PR professionals seek to mute their symptoms or, worse, ignore them.

Much can be gained when the rigor of science is married to the art of public relations: meaningful and positive business outcomes, market supremacy, and professional advancement. Companies that dominate do so because they understand and master their environments. The world's most admired companies did not earn their reputations without carefully studying themselves in the mirror and then acting on what they saw—the ugly as well as the beautiful. The only passage out of uncertainty is a direct one.

Companies and public relations professionals who enjoy the benefits of PR research and evaluation begin by embracing the process fully: they relish their victories because their wins are validated and can be merchandised more credibly. They also understand that uncovering shortfalls is a natural result of the process and allows course correction. As a result, they lead with confidence and certainty. That is the substance of this chapter.

The Science of Public Relations

Traditionally, public relations is rooted in the social sciences. Edward Bernays, often cited as the father of public relations, pioneered PR's use of psychology and other social sciences to design campaigns of public persuasion. He called this scientific technique of opinion molding the "engineering of consent" and described the PR counselor as a practicing social scientist. To assist clients, PR counselors would use research and evaluation as a primary facet of PR.

Professional PR associations emphasize research and measurement in their credos and mission statements. The International Association of Business Communicators (IABC), for example, defines itself as an organization whose mission is to help members to "make business sense of communication. Think strategically about communication. Measure and clarify the value of communication. Build better relationships with stakeholders" (2005, para. 2).

As part of its definition of public relations, the Public Relations Society of America (PRSA) identifies PR as follows:

As a management function, public relations encompasses the following:

- Anticipating, analyzing and interpreting public opinion, attitudes, and issues that might impact, for good or ill, the operations and plans of the organization.
- Counseling management at all levels in the organization with regard to policy decisions, courses of action, and communications, taking into account their and the organization's social or citizenship responsibilities.
- Researching, conducting, and evaluating, on a continuing basis, programs of action and communication to achieve the informed public understanding necessary to success of an organization's aims. These may include marketing, financial, fund raising, employee, community or government relations, and other programs.

- Planning and implementing the organization's efforts to influence or change public policy. Setting objectives, planning, budgeting, recruiting and training staff, developing facilities—in short, managing the resources needed to perform all of the above. (2005, para. 4)

The examples of Bernays, IABC, and PRSA suggest that scientific measurement is a critical component of public relations. Unfortunately, PR as it is routinely practiced regards formal research and measurement as afterthoughts. According to the sixth Communication and Public Relations Generally Accepted Practices (GAP) Study, conducted in the third and fourth quarters of 2009 by the Strategic Communication and Public Relations Center at the University of Southern California Annenberg School for Communication, roughly 4 percent of total PR spending is invested in research and evaluation.

Fortunately, given the magnitude of the opportunities and the enormity of the challenge facing business today, there is a better way, well within the reach of nearly every PR person.

What You Need to Know about Public Relations Research

There are three forms of research in public relations: primary research, which centers on conducting original research; secondary research, which is based on the mining of preexisting data and information; and statistical modeling, which seeks to create some greater learning through the unified statistical analysis of disparate sources of data, both primary and secondary.

Primary research usually involves a process of questioning respondents for the benefit of their observations and opinions to help the researching organization achieve greater insight. The type of primary research that yields objective, statistically reliable results is known as *quantitative research*. When quantitative research is done properly, the findings can be projected to a larger population. Quantitative research gathers data in a variety of ways, but the most common methods are surveys.

The other form of primary research is known as *qualitative research*, which is most commonly conducted in the form of focus groups. Focus groups are collections of a dozen people or so who are encouraged, under the direction of a facilitator, to share their opinions, frustrations, likes, and dislikes of the subject under discussion. Focus groups are useful for ideation, but their results cannot be projected to a larger population. When properly used, qualitative research is staged as a precursor to quantitative research to improve its relevancy and efficacy.

Secondary research usually involves the analysis of data previously collected and archived within the organization or another repository. It may also include reviewing the findings of previously conducted research to develop an understanding of existing practices or trends in an industry.

Statistical modeling is a process used in marketing and PR analytics to mathematically explain historical results and predict future outcomes. These analytics focus on probabilities and trends based on a number of variables that are likely to influence future behavior. In marketing, for example, a customer's gender, age, and purchase history might predict the likelihood of a future sale. To create a predictive model, data are collected for the relevant predictors, a statistical model is formulated, predictions are made, and the model is validated (or revised) as additional data become available. In PR, statistical models are most often used to uncover the effect of PR and its interaction with other marketing and communication agents, as well as such external factors as the weather and population, on sales or some other behavioral outcome. Models of this type, known as *marketing mix models*, seek to provide insight into what drives purchasing behavior.

Research Tools for Effective Public Relations Measurement

While there is an array of research applications for public relations, we focus on three fundamental tools for scientific measurement and evaluation of public relations: news content analysis, survey research, and statistical modeling. While public relations is more than media relations, and the motivation for PR research is more than proving value and improving performance, the three areas explored here represent the most common forms of PR research and evaluation and reflect the most common motives.

Content Analysis

One popular application of secondary research is news content analysis, a method for tracking the activities or outputs of a PR program. Outputs might include news conferences, special events, news releases, and speeches. "News content analyses are a research technique of studying media in order to systematically and objectively identify the characteristics of the messages" (Weiner, 1990, p. 110).

Content analysis begins with gathering print, broadcast, and Internet content through the use of a traditional or online media-monitoring service or by simply combing the Web or hard copy media yourself. The content usually contains a variety of themes and messages, which are coded for references of interest to a particular organization. Once coded, the resulting data are analyzed to determine trends and opinions. For example, in the case of a new car introduction, PR researchers scan consumer and trade press clippings, broadcast transcripts, and online car buff blogs for references to a campaign in which the new model is promoted as being safe, luxurious, and fun to drive. They catalogue and analyze the intended references along with any unintended or negative references to determine trends and perceptions relevant to that model car, its brand, and its manufacturer.

In practical terms and in its most common form, content analysis is used as a means to report on the volume and quality of news coverage during a specified period of time. The resulting data are presented at consistent intervals. Typically these reports include information such as the name of the content source, the date the story ran, the circulation or audience, a register of the messages contained, and its overall tone. The content analysis is used to prove and improve the return on investment in PR.

Media Tabulations. As shown in Figure 27.1, even simple forms of news content analysis can be used to provide insight. In this example, which shows frequency and reach from one quarter to another, we can glean some indication of the direction of the PR program.

FIGURE 27.1 QUARTERLY NEWS CONTENT ANALYSIS PROVIDING COMPARISONS OF FREQUENCY AND REACH

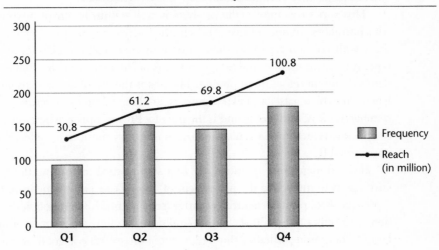

FIGURE 27.2 MEDIA TRACKING PROVIDING COMPARISON DATA OF MEDIA COVERAGE

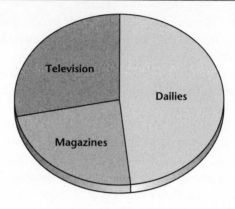

As simple as these data are, we can see at a glance whether the program is trending up or down, and we might also be able to attach the timing of certain outputs to the corresponding results. The second quarter saw an increase of almost 100 percent over the prior quarter. Was there a publicity campaign or a special event underway during that period of time? Another simple measure is tracking by media type. In Figure 27.2, the pie chart indicates that nearly 50 percent of the news generated on this subject came from daily newspapers. If newspapers were the focus of this campaign, that might reaffirm the plan. However, if most of the campaign's resources were directed toward magazines, you might need to review and adjust.

This sort of simple media analysis is well within reach of anyone in PR who has access to spreadsheet and charting software. Simply create a spreadsheet with column headings such as date of coverage, circulation, and media type. It is worth mentioning here two forms of PR measurement that are highly debated and therefore questionable. The first is the use of an advertising equivalency, in which case a dollar figure is applied to news coverage on an if-purchased basis, and the second is the use of a PR multiplier, wherein circulation or ad value is factored or multiplied by an arbitrary number to reflect the added impact of PR.

Beyond measuring quantity, the first step toward measuring the quality of coverage is to introduce the assessment of tone. Tone can be measured using a 3-point scale of positive-neutral-negative (see Figure 27.3). Although the illustration exemplifies a 3-point scale, the 7-point scale offers a higher level of granularity to determine whether the high volume of coverage is good or bad.

FIGURE 27.3 IMPACT MEASURED ON A THREE-POINT SCALE

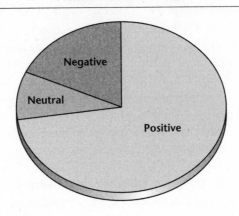

FIGURE 27.4 TRACKING THE TONE OF MESSAGES

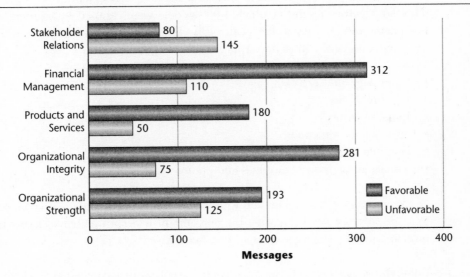

Message Tracking. A still more advanced level of analysis tracks the presence and the tone of individual messages contained within a news item. Figure 27.4 shows five messages that might be used to describe any organization. At PRIME Research, we call these messages *core messages*.

Of the five messages shown in Figure 27.4, a mix of messages appears to be working according to plan, and some messages warrant improvement: Quality products and services is being delivered in the highest proportion of positive-to-negative (about 3 to 1), but the volume of coverage ranks only 4 out of 5. If messages about the quality of products and services are important, these results suggest that the PR team reinforce these good results to generate even higher volumes of positive coverage. Conversely, stakeholder relations needs help, as negative coverage outpaces positive at a rate of almost 2 to 1. On the positive side, organizational integrity is a solid performer, as is financial management. The theme of organizational strength can be improved.

While this level of message analysis can be done in house, it requires a degree of involvement and objectivity that most organizations find difficult to undertake.

Linking Media Coverage to Recall and Awareness. Most PR people and the executives to whom they report would agree that media coverage is but a means to an end. The following elements have been determined to affect recall and awareness in a number of studies, the original of which was undertaken by the research team at AT&T under the leadership of Bruce Jeffries-Fox (n.d.). Through rigorous testing in which 1,000 people were exposed to a variety of news items and later tested for recall and awareness, the following factors were determined to be the most powerful:

- Front page/cover/splash page
- Headline/lead
- Initial mention
- Size/length of mention
- Dominance over competing companies and brands
- Visuals in the form of graphics and photos

When worked in combination with the simpler measures listed—frequency, tone, presence of key messages—the outcome provides a number of levers to push and pull to achieve greater success (see Table 27.1).

Competitive Tracking. To take the content analysis to a contextual level, add competitors to the mix. This is a point at which complexity and cost may become considerations, so we recommend two ways to reduce the volume of clips and the time required to analyze them. First, identify the media that matter. Rather than tracking every publication and TV show, select only those that are known to be the most important among the target audience. Second, identify just those competitors worth tracking; that usually reduces the list to two or three: your company, the market share leader (if it is not you), and the market innovator,

TABLE 27.1 ANALYSIS OF IMPACT SCORE FACTORS TO DRIVE BUSINESS OUTCOMES

Impact Score Factors	Frequency	Percentage (%) of Total Clips
Front page	10	11
Headline	21	21
Exclusive mention	5	8
Significant mention	6	8
Lead mention	5	8
Visual/graphic	2	5
Percentage positive or neutral tone	120	95

or the company that may be responsible for changing the landscape of your category. An example in the automobile area might be Buick, Toyota, and Scion, respectively.

As the complexity increases, so does the capacity of the analysis to drive learning and insight. At this point, a process known as *message engineering* becomes possible. The theory is that if a message is important, frequently seen, and positive, then simply reinforce the effort. If a message is important, frequently seen, and generating negative tone, then fix the situation.

Survey Research

Surveys are a quantified assessment of a person or a group toward a subject, developed as a result of previous influences. Most survey research involves questioning and probing among a representative sample of individuals. Carefully designed questionnaires are usually administered in a structured manner to uncover attitudes, needs, or preferences.

While there are many types of surveys, here are three that you can begin using today: the executive audit, the media demographic audit, and the journalist audit.

The Executive Audit. The first requirement for determining value in terms of generating a return on expectation is met through the application of an executive audit of the senior executives who underwrite public relations programs. The audit is a clean-slate approach to uncover what PR underwriters seek from public relations—delivering key messages to target media, increased awareness, or even increased sales—matched with the executives' assessment of current PR performance. Delahaye conducts thousands of executive interviews each year, and the results indicate that PR investors have a good understanding of what measures are reasonable, meaningful, and measurable. Interestingly, executive assessments of current PR practices indicate that public relations departments tend to overdeliver on what PR underwriters value least (media clippings) while underdelivering on what they value most (raising awareness and delivering key messages to target media). Once these preferences and assessments are discussed and understood, more formal standards may be established against which value can be clearly demonstrated.

The executive audit, a form of qualitative research, is a brief telephone survey of internal public relations clients who have a primary impact on PR strategy, goal setting, and evaluation. The purpose of the survey is to provide the feedback needed by PR professionals to continually improve departmental and personal performance in meeting the needs of key executives. Reports are used to open up and formalize dialogue between PR professionals and their internal clients.

The executive audit measures the attitudes, preferences, needs, and expectations of top management when working with their PR departments. The survey concentrates on such issues as how internal clients feel about the role of public relations in achieving their objectives, what they feel are the most and least important PR activities, tactics, outcomes, and measures. Another battery of questions addresses the current performance of the PR department on each element, how PR success is best evaluated, and how executives rate your efforts against what they know of competitors.

The executive audit results are used to accurately assess client attitudes, preferences, needs, and expectations for public relations effort in terms of:

- Professional attributes such as good writing and media skills
- Activities and tactics such as media relations and strategic PR guidance
- Achievement of client and companywide objectives
- Media considered most credible or most important
- Messages considered most credible or most compelling
- Helping to define the standards by which public relations effectiveness is measured (and what drives success in the opinion of this key audience)
- Determining the extent to which public relations now satisfies these preferences, needs, and expectations

- Setting the stage for ongoing dialogue in terms that are meaningful, educational, and consensus building

Media Audit. One of the most critical steps in any communication endeavor is that of targeting: the process of identifying and reaching the audience that is considered the optimal subject of your effort. Targeting should be considered in terms of the audience primarily and the media secondarily. Most PR targeting falls under the categories of either Rolodex targeting, which is calling the journalists who are in your Rolodex, or coffee table targeting, a purely intuitive process based on what the publicist determines must be on the coffee table of the target.

The media audit is a form of secondary research that provides detailed analysis of national and local print and broadcast media viewership, listenership, and readership. Rather than simple circulation, the audit provides detailed information regarding targeted audience reach:

- Demographics, geographics, and psychographics
- Products and services owned and planning to purchase (including brand names)
- Leisure activities
- Media involvement

The media audit is used by PR professionals to manage their media relations plan more strategically in targeting, positioning, and return on investment. Since the media audit has detailed information about your target audience, you can make the most of limited PR resources by targeting only the most productive print and broadcast media.

The value of public relations is also more meaningfully and easily communicated within the marketing mix because the audit goes beyond conventional PR wisdom to provide customer-driven planning and evaluation. For example, a luxury car manufacturer may use the audit to target luxury car owners, but only those expressing intent to purchase a new luxury car within the next twelve months. The car manufacturer can target by a number of criteria: brand, price range, domestic or import, and intent to purchase within the next twelve months. Further refinement comes by indexing versus age, income, and other variables.

Journalist Audit. The journalist audit, a form of qualitative research, is a brief telephone survey of journalists at your *media that matter* who have a primary impact on the success of your PR programs. The purpose of the survey is to provide the feedback that PR professionals need to continually improve the quality and quantity of media coverage by meeting the needs of key journalists.

The journalist audit measures the attitudes, preferences, needs, and expectations key journalists have when working with PR departments. The survey concentrates on such issues as what PR activities and attributes are important to journalists and how you are doing in light of what journalists say is important and in comparison to competitors and peers. Another battery of questions addresses journalist preferences for notification, communications, news conferences, and special events.

The journalist audit results are used to accurately assess journalists' attitudes, preferences, needs, and expectations for your public relations effort in terms of:

- Professional attributes (for example, responsive, accessible)
- Activities and tactics (pitch calls, releases, events)
- Which of your competitive set is best, what they do that makes them best, and how you compare to the best on a variety of attributes
- Helping to define the standards by which public relations effectiveness is measured (and what drives success in the opinion of this key audience)
- Determining the extent to which your public relations efforts now satisfy these preferences, needs, and expectations versus competitors
- Setting the stage for continual improvement as evidenced in how the journalists treat your organization editorially and how your organization performs in the next annual journalist audit

Statistical Modeling

Marketing mix modeling, an example of statistical modeling, is an analysis that draws data from disparate sources and then integrates them to provide insight into the ongoing process of marketing. Using traditional databases like sales, advertising GRPs (gross rating points), or content analysis, researchers merge these data to create more complete views of the marketplace and estimate the impact of advertising, PR, pricing, merchandising, competitive activity, seasonality, and other factors on sales. Given an understanding of what drives sales, we can explain past results and influence future sales.

As new approaches and more powerful technologies become available, our ability to properly assess and accurately forecast marketing performance has never been greater. It is in this new environment that the line is being drawn through management's use of two words—*Prove it*—and soon you may have no other choice but to do so.

The need for and the increased access to marketing intelligence has not led to a sea change for marketers yet. Television advertising, promotions, and direct marketing continue to command significant spending, and their need to demonstrate and generate a positive return on investment (ROI) is scaled to the level of investment. As such, the day is coming when each of these marketing functions will be judged on its ability to deliver value. Those consuming the greatest resources will feel the most pressure first.

On the basis of relative spending, public relations may seem like a lower priority. But in terms of ROI, PR may be the most critical: marketing mix modeling analyses have repeatedly demonstrated that PR delivers a superior ROI, and an investment in PR often delivers a lift to other forms of marketing.

PR has the most to gain in this new environment. But in order to achieve some higher level of primacy, PR departments have to change the way they work. Success will be contingent on PR's willingness to work in a more integrated fashion with other marketing agents and use proven research techniques to demonstrate clearly a positive and meaningful ROI. In this setting, marketing decisions will be based on what drives results.

Companies whose names you would recognize in categories as diverse as retail, automotive, telecom, consumer packaged goods, financial services, and motion pictures are feeding advanced news content analysis into sophisticated marketing mix models to make the PR-to-sales connection. In its own right, the content analysis gives PR people the feedback they need to do a better job in delivering a high quantity of quality media coverage. But when content analysis results are fed into a statistical model along with other marketing data, in order to tweak out the relative power of advertising, direct marketing, telemarketing, and trade marketing, the result is an ROI road map based on a common lexicon. Data points are the common thread interwoven throughout the marketing fabric. These savvy companies apply what they learn by shifting their emphasis within the marketing mix to drive the optimal combination of marketing-for-sales. It will not be long before PR is planned on the basis of what drives sales rather than what drives buzz.

Conclusion

Clearly understanding the value and ROI of public relations holds huge promise for marketers in general and public relations professionals in particular. While the result of this type of measurement often brings increased budgets and staffing, it also provides companies with opportunities to focus precious resources on those programs that deliver. The savings derived from cutting nonperforming programs means that human and financial resources can be reallocated in ways that help PR departments reduce budgets while generating even better results.

References

International Association of Business Communicators. (2005). *Information: Vision, mission and structure: How IABC can help you.* Retrieved July 6, 2005, from www.iabc.com/info/about/vision_mission_structure.htm

Jeffries-Fox, B. (n.d.). Toward an understanding of how news coverage and advertising impact consumer perceptions, attitudes and behavior. Available at www.instituteforpr.org/files/uploads/News_Ad_Impact.pdf

Public Relations Society of America. (2005). *About public relations: Official PRSA definition: What it does.* Retrieved July 6, 2005, from www.prsa.org/_Resources/Profession/index.asp?ident=prof1

Weiner, R. (1990). *Webster's new world dictionary of media and communications.* Upper Saddle River, NJ: Prentice Hall.

PART FIVE

MARKETING
COMMUNICATION

CHAPTER TWENTY-EIGHT

MARKETING COMMUNICATION

Lorenzo Sierra

Growing up in Tucson, Arizona, in the 1970s and 1980s, I was a member of Tucson's burgeoning Latino American community. Like most other consumers of that era, I marveled as more and more product choices became available to me.

Although there were more choices, marketing approaches remained as they had in the 1950s. Marketers continued to deliver their messages using the same tactics that made America's post–World War II economy the strongest on the planet. The faces and messages were largely Anglo. In essence, marketers of that day did not see me as special.

In the early 1990s, marketing messages were beginning to feature faces and places that looked like mine, using the language (Spanglish, a colloquial version of English and Spanish) my friends and I were speaking.

In my youthful naiveté, I figured marketers were specifically addressing American Latinos out of the goodness of their hearts. Little did I know that it was not compassion or enlightenment that led to culturally relevant messages; it was survival.

In this chapter, we discuss marketing communication, target marketing, and other disciplines applied to marketing communication.

Ask and You Shall Receive . . . Several Answers

What is marketing communication? The definition of marketing communication often depends on whom you are talking to.

Let us define *marketing communication* here as all communications activities an organization undertakes to promote its agenda to its audiences. From a deliverable standpoint, it might be advertising, public relations, or a coordinated face-to-face campaign. The medium is irrelevant. The point is that your organization has something to say or sell to a well-defined audience, and you want the audience to take some sort of action.

Marketing communication is many things to many people. It is sometimes difficult to say what it is not. One need only review the International Association of Business Communicators (IABC) *Code of Ethics* (2005) to determine what marketing communication is not. For example, marketing communication is not:

- *Spin.* Communications professionals engaged in marketing communication have truth as the foundation for all communication. Using falsehoods or half-truths in order to spin an event goes against everything professional marketing communicators stand for.
- *Illegal.* Marketing communications professionals will not use their messages to advance illegal activities.
- *Unethical.* Marketing communications professionals must adhere to the highest ethical standards. We are the voices of our organizations and must be sensitive to cultural values and beliefs.

There are many activities and media that fall under the marketing communications umbrella, each with advantages and disadvantages. The choice is yours on when and how to use each medium. The best foundation for all media is your creativity and your honesty.

Contextual Target Marketing

My philosophy regarding marketing communications has evolved. Since 2005, an increasing number of U.S. companies have instituted a "Hispanic" marketing campaign.

More often than not, companies' initial communication with me is as a Spanish speaker. Unfortunately, my Spanish is not so polished.

Even though companies were marketing to me primarily as a Latino American, my cultural/ethnic heritage was not the reason I had interest in their products or services. That is when I realized that all marketing communications interactions are done within a given context. That I am a Latino American may be the primary reason I buy a certain brand of tortillas. Being a generation Xer may be the primary reason I watch a particular television program.

We have so many demographic traits that define us as individuals. For example, in 2010, marketers can appeal to me as a gen Xer, Latino American, college graduate, sports fan, environmentalist, political liberal, apartment renter, car enthusiast, golfer, wine drinker, and on and on. As marketing communications professionals, it is our job to understand the demographic traits that make up our audiences and appeal to those traits that best allow us to achieve a meaningful connection.

For maximum loyalty and engagement, however, you must appeal to your audience's core intrinsic values. Intrinsic values are not outward traits like demographics. These are the beliefs that define the audience. For example, in America it is not uncommon to see a home services company (plumber, carpenter, and so on) identify itself as a Christian company. They do not hide their theological dispositions. Although being Christian is a demographic trait, *faith* is an intrinsic value—and for many, it is their most pertinent value.

In this example, being a Christian does not necessarily mean you have faith. But if faith is part of a person's core beliefs and he or she believes a particular plumber shares those beliefs, all things being equal (price, quality, dependability, and so on), shared beliefs will make for a loyal customer.

For a real-world example, consider Jeremy Schacter, the owner of 76 Mortgage, a mortgage brokerage in Phoenix, Arizona. Schacter has been in business since 2005. "A loan is a loan," Schacter says. "If someone needs a loan, I provide that service."

However, as a politically liberal person, Schacter has chosen to advertise and align himself with a fledgling liberal-leaning radio station. "I am in line with what they talk about," Schacter said. "I relate to it." As a result, Schacter says, he has attracted clients who share his values and beliefs.

Within the context of his relationship with his customers, Schacter attracts people based on demographic traits such as Democrat, gay, higher income. But because he is also connecting with some customers on one of their highest intrinsic values—liberalism—he is able to grow his business with people who are aligned with him on a core intrinsic belief.

To that end I created the contextual target marketing (CTM) approach (see Figure 28.1). Contextual target marketing is an approach wherein organizations promote brand loyalty by marketing to participants' self-identified demographic traits within the context of the customer relationship.

FIGURE 28.1 CONTEXTUAL TARGET MARKETING

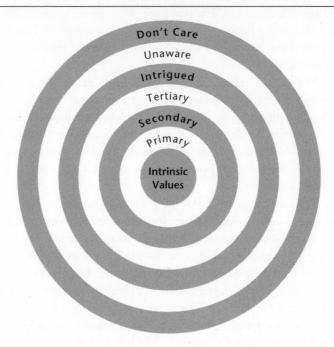

In this model, the closer you get to the target, the more bonded you are to your constituents. The outermost section represents the vast majority of the general populace. They simply do not care if you exist. Do not take this to mean that they dislike your product or service. They may be loyal to another product. They may not need your product or service. Most likely, you will never win over these people. Marketing to them is a waste of time, money, and effort.

In the next level, these potential consumers are unaware of who you are or what you do. They are inside of the "don't care" ring because they are potential constituents for any given product or service. Here, you can undergo great efforts to reach those who have never heard from you. Here, your efforts will yield miniscule results.

While working for a Fortune 100 health insurance firm from 2006 to 2010, part of my role as a marketing communications professional was to disburse my location's share of charitable dollars. I often received calls from people seeking sponsorships for their charitable events. They often said, "This is a good way to get your name out there."

Had they done their research they would have known that the number of people who could actually sign off on a group health insurance policy is very small. Getting my company's name "out there" was never a high priority for me. To me, it was fine if my company had low brand recognition among the general populace. My task was to increase brand recognition and familiarity among those directly tied to the health insurance purchase.

However, if instead, I worked for a soft drink company, I would very much like to have my name "out there," reaching those who are unaware of my soft drink company's existence.

The "intrigued" level is where marketing efforts start to show potential results. Here, potential constituents have a limited awareness of your product or service. When discussing this target area, I refer to a personal experience with a Hawaiian restaurant in my neighborhood.

I am certain that in your personal lives you have driven past a business many times and thought about finding out more. Such was the case with this Hawaiian restaurant. I always promised myself I would check out the restaurant online or stop by and review the menu. With the demands of work and home, I never got around to it. Yet, I was intrigued.

One day, I got home and the restaurant had taped a flyer to my door. Reading through it, I found that the restaurant connected with me on a key self-identified demographic trait: frugality. On the flyer the restaurant included a "Buy one, get one free" coupon for an entrée. That was enough to get me in the doors.

Once there, I was impressed with the food, the atmosphere, and the service. The restaurant was locally owned by people from my neighborhood. There is where my tightest bond was made. One of my intrinsic values is supporting locally owned small businesses. Because I bonded on several areas of the target area, I have since become a loyal customer.

Marketing communications professionals must understand the traits of the people who are intrigued with their product or service. If you believe you can communicate to them in a meaningful manner, you must make every effort to do so.

The next three target areas on the chart represent the self-identified demographic traits that bond constituents to your product or service. Your job is to determine the traits that, within the context of the business relationship, make for more dedicated constituents.

When explaining these three target areas, I often use the example of the last time I bought a car. When I was in the market for a car, my primary demographic trait was that of "father." I wanted a car that was safe and had enough room to haul a tuba. Please note that within the target bands can be more than one demographic trait, but you should keep your primary at one trait unless the two traits complement each other.

Although "business leader" was almost a primary demographic trait for me, I decided to make this secondary. As a professional who often transports customers or potential customers, I needed a car that had at least a bit of elegance. Of course, this demographic trait was at complete odds with another of my secondary traits: frugality. My tertiary demographic traits included:

- *Environmentalist.* I wanted something with good fuel economy.
- *Local business supporter.* I wanted to buy from a locally owned dealer.
- *Gen Xer.* I wanted an age-appropriate car. I did not want an "old man" car, nor did I want one of those boxy things millennials drive.
- *Latino American.* I wanted to support a business that was affiliated with my local Latino chamber of commerce.

I bought a Chevrolet Impala. With quality safety features and lots of room for my son's tuba, it met my "father" demographic trait. With upgraded features and a modern design, it met my "business leader" demographic. As a domestic auto, it was less expensive than some foreign competitors, which addressed my "frugality."

On the tertiary traits, the car has a FlexFuel feature that allows me to use alternative fuels. I bought it from a locally owned lot. The salesman was a member of the Latino chamber of commerce. On the age issue, my high school–aged boy claims that it is, in fact an "old man" car, but then again, *everything* I own is an "old man" item in his eyes. Regardless, I believe my car is age appropriate.

By now, you have noticed that I did not address my "bull's eye" or my intrinsic values target. Because I rarely buy a car, I did not need to be reached at that level to become my car lot's customer.

Now here is the secret about reaching your constituents' intrinsic values: you cannot *market* your way to that level. Reaching a constituent's intrinsic values is all about the way you conduct your business—it is who you *are*.

Communications guru Thomas J. Lee, a leader in communications leadership, advocates for three things that give organizations an opportunity to reach the highest levels of engagement:

1. *Words.* This is the outward communication an organization creates to define itself. It may be its website, its advertising, its marketing brochures, its signage, or anything that identifies the organization to it constituents.
2. *Deeds.* This is the behavior of the organization. It is how the organization interacts with its constituents.

3. *Raison d'être*. This French term, which means "reason for being," is arguably the most important of the three. It is the reason you are in business. It should be your organization's driving force.

In many ways it is the deeds and raison d'être that allow you to reach your constituents' intrinsic values.

My favorite example of a business I am completely loyal to because it reaches me at my intrinsic values is the Fair Trade Café in Phoenix, Arizona. Fair Trade is a locally owned coffee shop located in the downtown area. Here are the bonds that have tied my loyalty:

- *Tertiary*. Ethnic minority: Fair Trade is a registered minority- and woman-owned business. Frugal: Fair Trade offers a "Buy ten, get the eleventh free" card. Because I often host meetings of up to four people, I reach ten very quickly. Commuter: It is located off a train stop.
- *Secondary*. Business leader: Fair Trade is a member of an organization on whose board I sit. Bohemian spirited: Even though I am a little older and a lot less cool than the young adults and students who frequent Fair Trade, the artsy vibe and sense of community appeals strongly to my inner artist.
- *Intrinsic value*. Fair Trade, like me, is very socially conscious. They buy beans only from certified fair trade suppliers. Their coffee comes from organic plantations. They pay and treat their employees fairly.

Because of all these things, I am a very loyal customer. I go out of my way to go there. I promote it on consumer websites about restaurants. I frequently take guests there. They in turn have their meetings there.

Having reviewed contextual target marketing, you may find that you and your organization already operate in this manner. If you, as a marketing communications professional, feel like you are already operating in this manner, I encourage you to use this model to explain to upper management why you do the things you do.

Shall We Do the Fandango?

Today, marketing communications professionals have more ways to get their messages to their audiences than ever before: from cell phones, iPads, e-mail, wireless broadband, personal computers to all the other devices that have promised to make us more efficient. Marketing communications professionals still make good use of traditional tools like print, audio, and video—although with all the current Internet options like YouTube, Skype, and iTunes these media have an almost unlimited number of places to live.

Some of the greatest advances for marketing communications professionals have been in the field of technology. Rarely does a fiscal quarter go by without the introduction of new or upgraded technology that allows people to communicate more effectively with one another. But technologies are not communication.

In 1965 H. Marshall McLuhan coined the phrase, "The medium is the message." As Web-based technologies began to emerge, many of my peers used this phrase to justify the need for their respective organizations to jump on the website bandwagon. Never mind that they really had nothing to say.

I will concede that audiences can arrive at certain impressions based on the context in which they receive a message. For example, in an era when government spending is perceived to be out of control, it would be foolish for a governmental agency to distribute a communiqué via first-class mail and printed on high-quality paper with many original photographs. Instead of absorbing and contemplating a message, the audience—in this case taxpayers—will only focus on how much it cost to produce the piece rather than on the message.

To illustrate my point about media, I often refer to my love of classic rock music. As a big fan of the British rock band Queen, I've listened to "Bohemian Rhapsody" on a vinyl album, on an eight-track tape, on a cassette, on a CD and, most recently, on my iPod Touch. Sound quality and convenience may have improved over time, but regardless of *how* I heard it, the plain fact remains: it has been and always will be a great rock song. If you can focus on making great *songs*, your messages will lead your audiences to action.

Keep in mind that technology is just a way to get a message to your audience. Without a credible message that contains information valuable to the receiver, it does not matter what method of delivery you use. Once the novelty of a technology has worn off, all you have is your messages.

Many of the technologies that marketing communications professionals use today are mainly one-way deliveries of messages. In order to become the best possible marketing communications professional, you must develop your most valuable tool: the ear.

Speak the Word

In an increasingly competitive global marketplace, an organization's ability to listen is often the determining factor between success and oblivion. Marketing communications professionals must take the time to truly listen to the wants and needs of their organizations' audiences.

Bolívar José Bueno is a marketing communications prodigy who coined the term *cult branding* (Bueno & Ragas, 2002). In our technology-driven era, Bueno knows exactly where marketing communications power lies: with the customer. "The customer is totally in control," he says. "Marketers need to realize that customers are the brand" (personal communication, May 2005).

Customers in this sense are not only consumers but internal organizational stakeholders. Each customer has his or her perception of an organization. Each experience that person has with the organization has an impact on his or her perception of the brand.

The marketing communications professional's task is to understand the elements of a positive brand experience for all customers. Once you understand the audience's expectations, you must develop messages that will resonate with each customer segment.

"The process now is to allow the customer to coauthor [your branding] with you," Bueno said. "Companies that listen to the customer—with a creative experience that is driven by the customer—end up creating very powerful brands."

Bueno and Ragas (2002) cited nine brands that have transcended traditional brand loyalty to develop a cultlike following among customers and employees. These organizations, through their brands, make extraordinary efforts to listen to the customer.

"This presents a problem for lazy companies, to be honest with you," Bueno said. "Listening is an active process. We're [marketing communications professionals] going to have to develop better ways of listening to our customers" (personal communication, May 2005).

To increase the desirability of their brands, marketing communications professionals must develop ways of engaging internal and external customers in the messaging process. "The modern marketer has to bring the customer into the boardroom," Bueno said. "They have to bring an advocate of the consumer inside" (personal communication, May 2005).

One of the cult brands featured in Bueno's book is Apple. Bueno cites the maker of Macintosh computers, the iPhone, and the iPod as one of the first to bring consumers into the brand-building process.

I mentioned internal and external customers in the preceding paragraphs. It is vital that marketing communications professionals not only have a firm grasp on the pulse of the consumer but also have a firm grasp on the pulse of the internal constituent.

"To me, selling in is more important than selling out," Bueno said. "You can read a hundred business books on what makes a company successful and no one has ever listed managing people as one of the factors that makes a company successful. Guess why? No one likes to be managed. No one wakes up and says 'I can't wait to get to work to be manipulated by my boss'" (personal communication, May 2005).

Bueno goes on to say that employees will give maximum effort when they feel as though they are part of something bigger than themselves. This is especially true if the employee can see how his or her contribution fits into the bigger picture.

"When your employees buy in, your customers buy in too," Bueno said. "You can have the greatest marketing program. You can have the best product. You can have the best displays and everything else. It comes down to the person who is in direct contact with the customer. If they do not treat the customer the way the customer wants to be treated based on your industry, you have blown the whole program" (personal communication, May 2005).

But how do you develop messages that result in desired action? Most marketing communications professionals enter the profession through the creative end of the skill spectrum. That is, at their core, many marketing communications professionals are writers. Good writing is the foundational skill that all marketing communications professionals must possess. But it is growing increasingly difficult to get and keep the attention of the countless audiences. To develop effective messages, marketing communications professionals must look outside the profession for assistance.

The Science of Persuasion

Like any other good marketing communications professional, Bueno takes his professional development seriously. As a busy professional, he makes time to continually learn. But you will not find Bueno at marketing communications seminars or conferences. "I spend my time going to conferences on quantum mechanics and physics and psychology," he said.

Nevertheless, you do not have to sign up for the closest seminar on Newtonian dynamics. But it is definitely worth your time to study disciplines outside traditional marketing communications. Marketing communications professionals who glean useful information from sociology, psychology, anthropology, and other disciplines will be able to differentiate themselves from other professionals.

Marketing communications professionals are familiar with the basic communications model: Sender-Message-Receiver-Feedback. Another model that should be in every professional's toolbox is Maslow's (1954) hierarchy of human needs, a pyramid of motivational elements that lead a person to self-fulfillment.

The base block of the pyramid is physiological needs. These are the biological needs of eating, sleeping, and drinking that keep us alive. Once physiological needs are met, the person seeks to achieve safety needs. Humans crave security. Next are love and belonging, followed by esteem needs. The peak of the pyramid is self-actualization, which happens when a person attains a level where he or she seeks to become self-fulfilled. In other words, he or she has a purpose for being.

For marketing communications professionals, this model presents the ideal methodology for developing messages. You can develop truth-based messages that describe the essence of your organization based on levels of the pyramid.

For example, an employee's safety needs can be communicated by showing how the organization takes great strides to ensure safety. This is done by communicating policies that show that the company will not tolerate any form of abusive behavior. Of course, the organization must adhere to those policies to establish and maintain credibility.

According to Bueno and Ragas (2002), the foundation of the power of cult branding is derived from Maslow's hierarchy of needs. From it, Bueno and Ragas developed the "Seven Golden Rules of Cult Branding." Based in extensive research, the seven rules lay the groundwork for any organization to develop a cult brand:

1. Consumers want to be part of a group that is different.
2. Cult brand inventors show daring and determination.
3. Cult brands sell lifestyles.
4. Listen to the choir and create cult brand evangelists.
5. Cult brands always create customer communities.
6. Cult brands are inclusive.
7. Cult brands promote personal freedom and draw power from their enemies (Bueno & Ragas, 2002, p. 17).

Despite the simplicity of the seven rules, most companies are unable to implement the rules in a manner that would take their brand to cult status.

As we embrace more scientific ways of developing messages, there are long-standing hurdles to overcome. Marketing communication professionals are often seen as the "newsletter editors" or "PR people." We use our art to craft messages that persuade our audiences to action. But over the years, researchers have proven that persuasion is not just the tool of the charismatic or charming. There is science behind persuasion.

Persuasion can be empirically described by six principles developed by Arizona State University psychology professor Robert B. Cialdini (2001). Cialdini says that one does not need to be born with a world of charisma to be a persuasive person. All you have to do is understand and practice his six principles:

1. *Liking.* Do you have the type of disposition that makes people naturally like you?
2. *Reciprocity.* Do you give the way you would like to receive?
3. *Social proof.* Can you rally people (preferably influencers) to your cause?
4. *Consistency.* Do you ask others to be accountable for their commitments?
5. *Authority.* Do you have the expertise to be credible?
6. *Scarcity.* Can you make people feel as though they are "in the know"?

As with all other communication, the persuasive tactics should be used with the highest ethical standards. Far too often, especially in political campaigns, professionals use persuasive tactics to mislead or misinform.

No Day but Today

At one time marketing and marketing communications practices may have been seen as fads or buzzwords. They are now well-defined specialties within the organizational communications field.

To be most effective, all elements of marketing communication must work in synchronization. Gone are the days when the advertising, public relations, internal communications, and marketing departments operated independently. Customers today have neither the time nor the patience to figure out what an organization is and stands for.

Marketing communications professionals have the opportunity to become increasingly valuable to their organizations. The first step is to understand that the creative disciplines cannot thrive in a vacuum. They cannot meaningfully exist if they are not perfectly aligned with the organization's raison d'être.

As marketing communication evolves, no matter how advanced our delivery systems are or how much audience research we do, no one will listen if we have nothing to say, regardless of how loud we say it.

References

Bueno, B. J., & Ragas, M. W. (2002). *The power of cult branding: How nine magnetic brands turned customers into loyal followers (and yours can, too).* Roseville, CA: Prima.

Cialdini, R. B. (2001, October). Harnessing the science of persuasion. *Harvard Business Review, 79*(9), 72–79.

International Association of Business Communicators. (2005). *IABC Code of Ethics for Professional Communicators*. Available at www.iabc.com/members/joining/code.htm

Maslow, A. H. (1954). *Motivation and personality*. New York: Harper.

McLuhan, H. M. (1965). *Understanding media: The extensions of man*. New York: McGraw-Hill.

CHAPTER TWENTY-NINE

THE ENGAGEMENT OF BRANDS

D. Mark Schumann

He walks through the store with purpose, knowing he has little time; he knows precisely what he wants. His purchasing plan begins with his loyalty to a brand, familiarity with a product, comfort with its reliability and endurance, satisfaction with how it makes him feel. Completing this purchase creates satisfaction, as he remains confident that he will experience what he expects. Disappointment is not a part of the brand proposition for which he enthusiastically and financially commits to support.

Brands are amazing things. They drive how we choose, what we purchase, why we react, what we remember, and when we share. We begin our days enjoying our favorite brands of coffee, absorbing news from our favorite sites, bloggers, or broadcasts, eating specific brands of yogurt or cereal, driving in the cars we identify with to places of work we support. Nothing separates us from our brands. We love them. We are them.

We experience, as consumers of brands, just what brands can do. Every visit to a store is a living laboratory in how people react to brands. Every interaction with a brand offers lessons in how brands connect emotionally with consumers. Every conversation with a salesperson teaches us how brands simplify explanations of value or promises of experience. And every encounter with a sponsoring organization helps us learn the ultimate power of brands to articulate big ideas upon which reputations are built as places to buy, places to work, places to connect. And, as communicators, we learn the power of brand as shorthand for what a company wants to say—a simple, compelling way to explain why an organization must exist, why a product or service must be purchased, and why a positive memory must be captured and shared. We are taught, every day, how brands engage.

This chapter addresses how the elusive, mysterious nature of a brand can create a sense of emotional identity and connection that reaches beyond logical explanation. We review five key steps to brands that engage and discuss a few pivotal brands as well as fundamental exercises in branding.

A Memorable Brand: Southwest Airlines. So much has been written over the years about Southwest Airlines and the *freedom* its approach to business creates. And, as a partner to Southwest for some twenty years, I've had the chance to experience the authenticity of their relationships. What makes Southwest work, then and now, is their willingness to look at themselves in the mirror, see who they are, live who they are, and not try to be anything else. They live by the "What you see is what you get" rule. And, as customers, we love the ride.

Consider How Brands Work

Brands are more than tag lines, more than logos, more than creative illustrations. They capture the essence of the relationships between organizations and stakeholders—customers, investors, employees, communities—as they articulate the fundamental value that relationships deliver.

So, for a brand to work, it must successfully journey through five stages of experience. First, the brand must be *seen* and be *heard.* Before a brand can be remembered, which is essential, it must be noticed. And this reaches beyond simply being recognized on its own—as, perhaps, a clever collection of words or images—to instantly creating a connection between a message and a value articulated. A brand must be seen or heard in the context of how its message should be *received.* So, for example, when an organization as brand savvy as Disney uses its brand as part of a message to its stakeholders, it carefully considers how the brand can advance the connection, not simply publicize the transaction.

Second, the brand must *inspire* or *motivate* a stakeholder to try something; perhaps a customer to make a purchase, an investor to consider a stock, a potential employee to consider an opportunity. That inspiration or motivation directly results from the value the brand conveys as articulated in the value proposition that it communicates. The brand must convey a call to action to the recipient to take the steps to try the brand, to find out, firsthand, what the experience can mean.

Third, the brand must be *experienced*. A strong brand is not simply a collection of attributes; it transports a user to a place, whether labeled a magic kingdom or the friendly skies, a distant yet accessible destination where the brand dominates. Such an experience can be an organization's best defense against criticism; when I sit in a car I love, for example, the experience helps me avoid hearing how the company may be criticized for what it does or how it works.

Fourth, the brand must be *shared* and will be shared between consumers, as reports of experiences quickly travel from person to person. We want brands to be shared, in fact, as we look for word of mouth to advance a brand's persona and reputation. That means, as we create a brand, we must look for opportunities, for experiences that consumers will want to share and, when they share, for them to pass on what we want them to say about the brand.

Fifth, we want consumers to *advocate* for our brands so that, if times get tough, or competition heats up, our customers stand by what we deliver, how we work, and why we exist. This relationship between a brand and consumers is fundamental to our work; if a brand is not reaching to create advocates, then it is simply not doing its job, and it might as well simply label a product or service rather than be a crystal-clear articulation of an organization's value.

To journey through these five stages, a brand must define and establish the value provided through the customer experience, with *systems* and infrastructure in place to support and reinforce this value proposition, and the *marketing* implemented to articulate and publicize the value proposition and invite customers to participate. Otherwise, a brand may simply be an empty collection of words and visuals that may sound and look good but say and mean very little.

A Brand Exercise. To focus on the brand you want to develop, take a moment to consider your favorite brands. What experiences do they promise customers? What *big ideas* do they represent? How do they simplify the value, opportunity, and results you expect? And how do they influence you at every touch point? Then, with these thoughts in mind, take a look at your organization's brand. What do you promise to customers? How do, in turn, your customers view your reliability and authenticity? How does your brand emotionally engage your customers? And what relationship does it help you develop and nurture with your customers?

Focus on Brand Fundamentals

To journey through the five stages just described, a brand and its sponsoring organization must do many things right, exceed expectations in several ways, and surprise and delight consumers. But before a brand can please, it must work. Before a brand can engage, it must embrace the fundamentals to achieve in order to have any chance to inspire.

The Brand Must Work

Reliability of brand is fundamental. It does not matter how compelling or catchy the brand phrasing may be if the product or service does not match what is described. Southwest Airlines, for example, creates its own permission to have fun in the skies because it delivers reliable value in the skies, as expressed in a brand message for the company in the 1990s: "We are serious about having fun."

The Brand Must Be Unique

No brand will successfully travel through the five stages if it is continually confused with others in the same space. Just consider the challenges in the fast food industry, for example, where so many offer what may be seen as so much the same thing. And look at the consistent success of McDonald's, the marketing genius, at always finding a compelling way to separate itself from the pack while remaining true to itself.

A Reliable Brand: FedEx. Ultimately, FedEx does not sell transportation, or delivery, or convenience. It sells peace of mind. And when you drop off a package to be delivered, you pay for the sense of relief that comes from knowing it will get there and, if a problem occurs, that FedEx will do everything it can to make it right. As FedEx has expanded the scope of its brand, it may have found it challenging to transfer that brand equity to other offerings, but ultimately the core of its value proposition is sound. It sells and it delivers a sigh of relief.

The Brand Must Be Real

One reason a Southwest or a McDonald's creates strong relationships with consumers and inspires enduring loyalty is who these companies are; they rarely try to be anything else. When we dine at McDonald's we know what we are getting, our expectations are managed, our experience is proven. When we fly Southwest, we behave in a manner the brand trains us to do, which is precisely how the brand and the relationship with consumers are designed.

The Brand Must Be Replicable

If brand integrity is fundamental to Southwest and McDonald's, how the brand can leverage and reach a mass audience is key to financial success. Southwest, perhaps more than any company in recent years, successfully clones its brand in state after state many miles from its Texas heritage. And, as McDonald's reaches across the world and expands its daily menu, it never veers too far from what got it there in the first place. These companies know who they are and how to repeat the magic.

The Brand Must Be Personal

Relationships are, at their core, personal expressions of commitment, and any brand relationship between a consumer and a company is ultimately personal. I drive my Jeep because I believe Jeep cares about how it designs its products, how it serves its customers, how it responds to what I need. It is a personal relationship that effective advertising and experience reinforce. But at its heart, my brand loyalty is all about me, and the brand that reaches that part of me will be rewarded with my commercial loyalty.

An Evolving Brand: Hewlett-Packard. It feels like a new company. Its products feel current, timely, perhaps cool. And while it may be the granddaddy of the Silicon Valley, something about Hewlett-Packard (HP) feels very today. It is not just how it markets itself, which is excellent, or the product mix it offers, which is wide and ever growing. Somehow, HP convinces us as customers that the possibilities are endless because the products are so good. Its reliability is at the core of its effectiveness and at the foundation for its dreams.

Reach For the Big Ideas

For a brand to journey successfully through the five stages, it must do more than simply communicate the attributes of a product or service. Any brand wants to be remembered positively and wants to affect sales successfully. There is less chance of that happening, frankly, if the brand promise is all about the product or service. Such a focus can limit the impact of the brand to the specific transaction of the moment, with little opportunity to build relationships. And, to create advocates for a brand, relationships are key.

That is where the big idea comes in: to encourage, through positive brand experience, consumers to commit to the sponsoring organization's larger agenda.

For example, when Nike uses a phrase, "Just Do It," the impact reaches beyond the attributes of a specific product. When Sony expresses, "Make. Believe," the inspiration to connect involves more than today's purchase. It is a way to embrace a larger mission for which the company is destined.

The importance of the big idea, in fact, puts pressure on organizations to be about more than simply what they sell, and that frequently reaches into a sense of corporate social responsibility. To create real brand advocates, the scope of interest must reach beyond the product to the relationship, to engage the consumer in the cause for which the organization is committed. So it is no surprise today, as consumers are more aware of responsibility to a broader world, that organizations seeking their support travel the same direction.

A Brand Exercise. To get started in the right place on your brand work, take a moment to assess what work you have done or your organization has recently done. When is the last time you looked at the effectiveness of your brand? What resulted from this study? How do your intentional efforts to advance your brand compare to what unintentionally happens to your brand (such as through customer experience, hits on your reputation or bad publicity)? How satisfied are you with how your customers perceive your brand? How effectively does it drive sales? And how reliable is your employee engagement in delivering the brand experience your customers expect? How you answer these questions can help you determine where, among the ideas in this chapter, you should begin to focus.

For a big idea to sustain, however, it must be rooted in one or more of three brand fundamentals. First, the brand must be grounded in *operational soundness* to ensure that it delivers what it promises. No big idea can sustain if the day-to-day deliveries are inefficient or ineffective. Second, the brand must articulate the value of *excellent products and services* that bring the brand promise to life. No big idea will sustain if the products are not very good or the services are not very memorable. People will see through that in a flash. And, third, the brand experience must create *intimacy with customers* that forges a lasting relationship between the customer and the organization. That means, to sustain a big idea, an organization must be seen as being open to customer feedback, responsive to customer concerns, and willing to engage customers in its mission.

Years ago, I was leading a brand focus group at a hospital. Like many organizations in the health care arena, this institution was suffering from a market identity crisis. How, simply, could it compete in a crowded space where everyone promised everything? So the institution decided to rebrand itself and, rather than focus on what it is or what it does, it focused on what it could mean, which can be a very smart strategy. But it neglected to preserve its roots, and when the new brand was launched, employees felt lost, as if suddenly they were working for a hospitality resort instead of a hospital. And, as one worker expressed, "We make sick people well, what's wrong with that?"

And, guess what? The hospital tossed out the fancy brand work and simply expressed their purpose: "We make sick people well." Some ideas are naturally big.

A Comfortable Brand: Kimberly-Clark. It may not be the most glamorous of companies despite the designer touches on its paper products. And it may not be the first mentioned when it comes to dramatic new ideas that change the world. But when it comes to brands that you would simply like to take home with you, what better place for a consumer products company to land? KC thrives because KC simply does what it does so well, innovating enough to keep current, as it reliably and efficiently produces all that we have come to count on.

Follow All the Steps

It is too easy, when working in brand, to want to get right to the development of the tagline, the few words that will create fame and fortune. Such words work only if they are the product of diligent thinking, listening, and imaging. And the process works only if you follow all the steps of the process. Here is an overview.

Do Your Homework

When you first gather as a team, or work as an individual, to develop or rehabilitate a brand, start with the basics. First, immerse yourself in your organization's promises to customers and how, up to now, you express that promise. Go through every possible piece of background information on the brand development process followed in the past, as well as any available customer research, to fully understand the thinking, purpose, and promise behind the brand and what it should mean to customers. Study, as well, your current value proposition—how it was developed, what it articulates, how it differentiates—to fully embrace the brand challenge ahead.

Scope the Expectations

In the brand world it can often be tempting to try to cover too much ground and accomplish too many things. To follow all the steps means, as well, to limit the number of steps. So, based on the homework you complete, determine what is reasonable for you to accomplish within the constraints of time and resources. Set those expectations. If a full redo of the brand is needed, scope that out; but if the challenge is simply the application of a current brand, or the rehabilitation or retrofit of a brand, focus in those directions.

Clarify the Value Proposition

No matter the scope of the brand exercise, it must begin with a thoughtful and realistic assessment of the value proposition for authenticity, clarity, and relevance. It is very easy, in the brand world, for a value proposition, over time, to promise everything except everlasting life. Take the time to ensure the proposition is simple, real, and reachable, and adjust as needed. The test for a solid value proposition is simple: Does it make you want to stop everything and buy it now? If not, keep working.

Simplify the Tagline

Next, after reviewing and revising the value proposition, take a close look at existing taglines for how current, clear, and compelling they may be. It is very easy for taglines to become dated, especially those that strive for cuteness about clarity. Lasting taglines endure because they simplify. They are elegant in how few words they use, and how few meanings those words try to convey. Only when a creator tries to do too much with too few words can a tagline get too busy.

Build the Brand Architecture

With a renewed value proposition and tagline in place, it can be too easy to jump right to the tactical and start slapping the new brand on everything that moves. Stop. Before you paste that puppy anywhere, take the time to develop an overall architecture for how you are going to use the brand. This is fundamental blocking and tackling, as tactical as today's weather report, as essential as a balanced checkbook. Such a brand architecture should include specific means and channels to ensure the ongoing consistency of how the brand is marketed, how to use the brand as the framework for all messaging, how to *bring the brand inside* to be relevant to employees, how to embed the brand in the fabric of the organization, and how to nurture the brand as the company continues to mature.

A Brand Exercise. To focus your creative efforts, follow these simple ideas to get started developing a brand tagline. First, before you begin to connect any words, simply list the key words that describe what your brand promise should mean to your customers. Next, add to this list simple phrases that describe how your customers should feel after they experience your product or service. And then list the key commitments your brand should, and one hopes does, make to your customers. From this collection of words, articulate a potentially lengthy brand promise from which, as you then focus on the words, you shorten into a compelling tagline. To help you get started, simply complete this sentence:

> At [insert name], we promise to deliver [insert experience and result] to our customers so, in turn, they tell their friends [what you want your customers to remember and share about the brand experience] and believe [what you want them to believe about the big idea] about our organization overall.

Follow a Launch Strategy

Central to the effectiveness of the brand architecture is the impact of the brand launch (or, as appropriate, relaunch). This is not as simple as putting up visuals and applying a new logo in every possible place. First, a meaningful strategy must engage leadership in their roles in promoting the brand. Senior leaders are, no surprise, poster children for what a brand embraces, and their messages and behavior will be viewed through the brand lens. Second, an effective launch will begin to embed the key messages of the brand *before* it is visually introduced. And, third, the launch should maximize the impact by focusing on the stakeholder experience, not simply announcing or presenting the new visual identity.

Create Brand Guidelines

A brand will last only if its use is carefully monitored. And so, for any brand, the do's and don'ts must be clearly established and documented to ensure the consistent use and application of the brand for multiple communication and media approaches. This includes brand application guidelines to ensure the consistency of what people see and hear in the employer brand: attributes, tone and feel; brand message guidelines to support all messaging to potential and current stakeholders; brand connection guidelines on how to bring the brand to life through various programs; and brand development guidelines to follow when developing new sub-brand messages that must support the overall brand.

A Thrilling Brand: Apple. Its accomplishments are so widely known and recognized that to repeat them seems redundant. But perhaps no company consistently demonstrates as much brand self-awareness as Apple, a company once left for dead, marginalized into the sidelines, only to reemerge as the brand and marketing powerhouse in its industry. Apple does not simply sell, it defines, and it creates new demand for whatever it invents and sets reasoned expectations for whatever it delivers. By engaging its customers in its journey, it creates a level of brand goodwill others envy as its loyal customers willingly endure the growing pains simply to be a part of the experience.

Find the Words Before Creating the Visual

It is also easy, when working in brand, to put the cart before the horse, or to focus on the visual identity before thinking through the words. The danger in rushing through the words is that the visual representation will only be as effective as the reinforcement it provides. While a powerful visual can articulate an organization's identity and purpose, it must connect to something larger in people to motivate customers to buy. And that comes through the meaning of the words, not simply the flash of the visual. So, before painting the pictures, make sure the words express some fundamental things that the visuals can illustrate.

Why the Company Exists

Take a look at any successful brand, and the question, Why do we exist?, never enters the conversation. We know why Disney is here, McDonald's, and Southwest. But we may wonder how other brands last if they violate our trust, or fail to meet our expectations, or simply no longer matter. The brand must capture why this organization is necessary, why it matters, what it provides that customers would sorely miss. To last, a brand must find a lasting place in a customer's imagination, and that brand must reinforce its hold on that place with every expectation.

What We Stand For

Beyond why the organization exists, the brand must express what the company will fight for, be unwilling to compromise about, be trusted to consistently provide. Of course, when making such statements, the organization must have the processes and people in place to deliver, because the consumer is easily disappointed, and nothing disappoints faster than companies that fail to deliver on what they say they stand for, whether that be reliability, safety, or environmental respect. A brand is only as strong as the commitment of the organization that stands behind it.

An Embracing Brand: International Association of Business Communicators. A few years ago, when the International Association of Business Communicators (IABC) embarked on its own rebranding effort, the association followed the fundamentals outlined in this chapter as it strove to articulate a relevant value proposition, express a big idea, focus on the fundamentals, and follow all the steps. Plus it reached beyond describing who it is today to articulate a vision for what the association and the communications profession can mean for many years. As a result, it not only created a memorable brand, an embracing brand, it also reinforced the fundamental lessons of an effective brand development and launch.

What We Promise Customers

At every interaction with a brand, customers will ask, "What's in it for me?" and "What have you done for me lately?" And the answers to those questions reach beyond a description of the transaction—what a specific purchase will generate for the customer—to describe how the relationship between the consumer and the organization will strengthen as a result of the commercial exchange. Consider the promise as an invitation to the consumer to participate in a long-term relationship with the organization. With every purchase, the family ties simply strengthen.

How Employees and Customers Connect

The stronger the relationship between organization and customers, the more at home customers may be with how the organization manages its business. And that can directly reach to customers observing and assessing the relationship between the employees and the organization. As customers become advocates for the brand, many customers, as the relationship progresses, see themselves as advocates for the employees, too, especially those who embody what customers believe the brand is all about. As this occurs, you may see more personal commentary in customer feedback tools as customers let you know when they think you should be treating your employees differently.

Conclusion

As communicators, we search for ways to contribute, for issues that inspire us, for content that stimulates our curiosity. There are, in business, few opportunities as rich and essential as how organizations brand. This is a fundamental area that needs the best people in our community to contribute their best thinking. The ideas in this chapter are just the beginning. Enjoy the journey, the challenges, the opportunities. There is nothing like a well-built brand.

CHAPTER THIRTY

CUSTOMER RELATIONS

Smart Organizations Think Like Their Customers

Morgan Leu Parkhurst

Smart organizations in the twenty-first century are not satisfied with having customers who are, well, satisfied. These organizations want relationships based on mutual loyalty and a common understanding—traits that go beyond mere satisfaction. Such organizations do not work hard for the sake of working hard. They work smart for the sake of the consumers they represent. These same organizations recognize that satisfied customers in today's market are consumers who do not see the difference between similar products and services of competing organizations. If given a choice between Company A and Company B, they do not have a preference because they are satisfied either way. This scenario rightfully scares smart organizations that want customers to remain loyal in spite of competitive offers.

Smart organizations achieve this by doing something most companies fail to do well. They think *like* their customers, not *for* them. They strive to understand their customers as well as they know themselves. These organizations build a singular connection with consumers that competitors cannot match. The relationship is not susceptible to like-marketing and advertising from competitors because of its uniqueness. Smart organizations also recognize that customers do not simply buy products and services but also ideas and messages. Therefore, they keep an open mind about what it means to think like a customer.

This chapter explains how the smart organization utilizes the skill of professional communicators to develop methods for getting to know customers better and to meeting their needs. Without professional communicators, this competitive approach is difficult, if not impossible, to implement.

Remember to Forget the Golden Rule

Before delving into customer mindsets, their unique behaviors, and what is needed to better understand them, clear your mind of an age-old, counterproductive habit: treating others the way we would want to be treated. It is time to forget the Golden Rule. Why? Because thinking like a customer means treating customers the way they want to be treated, and not the way we *think* they want to be treated. Relating to the needs of the customer is paramount, even if the needs are different than what the organization expects. The Golden Rule is ineffective in business communications because it:

- *Assumes the customer is like the organization.* This dangerous thinking allows companies to impose their own biases without being held accountable for what the public really thinks. For example, during memory care training, health care professionals were asked what they believed the greatest fear was for someone just diagnosed with dementia. Everyone collectively agreed it was the loss of memory. Research suggested otherwise; it was the fear of losing control over one's life. Had professional health care communicators focused their marketing on preserving one's memory rather than on being able to control one's own care, they would have failed to connect with their audience.
- *Presumes the customer has the same information the organization does.* This is a critical issue. Communicators have the benefit of knowing the intent of the message being created. Customers do not have access to the same behind-the-scenes data. This can make customers feel disadvantaged. As a result, they bring very different thought processes into the mix. Although a message is well intended, accurate, and important, it can be misunderstood once it is disseminated to the public.
- *Creates stagnation.* Often in company meetings someone will recognize there is insufficient information about the customer. Heads will be scratched, moments of panic will ensue, and finally someone will say, "Let's go with this. It's what I would want if I were them." Communicators who follow this approach miss a critical opportunity to deepen the customer relationship.

The communicator who goes beyond the Golden Rule to understand the consumer's mindset will catapult ahead of the competition, pleasing customers who are not accustomed to being thought of on their own terms. Letting go of the Golden Rule is daunting for organizations that have come to rely on it as a business model. It is challenging for communicators who must now rethink existing strategies. But as consumers take control of their destinies in the marketplace, companies need to acclimate to this change.

Segmentation Is the Key to Thinking Like a Customer

Looking at the world through the eyes of the customer is not easy. Segmenting audiences into primary, secondary, and tertiary categories helps professional communicators stay organized. How clusters are organized and labeled will vary by organization. Some organizations cluster their audiences by demographics, psychographics, purchase price, revenue generated, or some other identifier that is important to the company. If an organization already has customer groups identified, then the following information can be used as an auditing tool. If an organization has never gathered customer information, then start with demographics of the people the organization wants to reach. Determine the ages, income and education levels, zip codes, ethnicities, and religions as well as any other important characteristics. Look for commonalities and contrasts of the people in these groups. Typically, there will be clusters of people in the data who share similarities. Each cluster will likely illustrate a possible market segment.

In addition to charting demographics, it is important to study the customer's psychographics—his or her behaviors and motivations to make purchases. While demographics provide a shell for understanding consumers, psychographics provide the bulk of what is needed to better understand their mindset. Psychographics get to the heart of what the customer wants from the selling organization. For example, when a consumer buys a car, he is buying more than just transportation. He could be buying any number of things, such as comfort, convenience, an image, or peace of mind. When dealerships sell cars, they need to communicate about more than transportation. The salespeople need to relate to the underlying reasons people purchase cars. It is that thought process that underscores the value of psychographics.

If information is missing, consider setting up a questionnaire, survey, focus group, one-on-one interview, or informal observations to gather what is needed. If possible, avoid relying solely on data that are based on national or international averages unless the organization reaches that far. Often this broader research is too general or skewed for one region. For example, the midwestern region of the United States typically has lower cost of living, salary, and unemployment rates than do the eastern and western coasts. Therefore companies in this region have to be careful in assuming that national research accurately reflects what is happening locally.

Once psychographics and demographics are gathered and customer groups are at least loosely identified, write down the information. Leave nothing out. Include the good, the bad, and the very, very ugly. Note any remaining missing information. The example following demonstrates what a car dealership might write for a customer cluster:

- *Primary Audience 1 Cluster:* Men and women, ages 30–43, married with 2–3 children under age 16, household income of $100,000, 55555/55545/55535 zip codes, 2–4 years higher education, race and religion vary.
- *What Is Known About This Group?* Finance more than 50% of total cost of vehicle, purchase mini vans, need space and desire comfort. Vehicle is extension of family image but purchaser is price sensitive. Researches vehicle options before visiting lot. Makes multiple visits before purchasing. Visits more than one dealership, considers more than one make and model. Does not want to be taken advantage of or given a hard sell.
- *What Needs to Be Learned?* What causes them to visit more than one dealership before making a purchase? What do they dread most about purchasing a vehicle?

This is repeated for Primary Audience 2 (if there is one) all the way through tertiary audiences. It is important to remember that this information represents only parts of whole data. Some groups may not be large enough to merit marketing. Others may represent outliers, typically small clusters of people who are on opposite ends of the spectrum. Going through the process of thinking like a customer allows an organization to identify the audiences it wishes to retain and those it wishes to terminate. The process also identifies weak spots that need to be strengthened. An organization should retain customers when there is a mutually beneficial relationship. Once that relationship has been established, it is time to go full force in making it even stronger.

Analyze Profitability to Improve Focus

While analyzing customer clusters, pay attention to how profitable these groups are. Markets evolve and so do customers. It is not uncommon for once-profitable groups to start lagging and new customers to take hold. Some organizations choose to cluster according to purchase price or revenue generated, followed by demographics and psychographics. The previous exercise is still applicable; however, the dealership's cluster would look something like this example:

- *Primary Audience 1 Cluster:* Purchasers of mini-vans $25,000–$40,000
- *What Is Known About This Group?* Men and women, ages 30–43, married with 2–3 children under age 16, household income of $100,000, 55555/55545/55535 zip codes, 2–4 years higher education, race and religion vary. Finance more than 50% of total cost of vehicle, purchase mini-vans, need space and desire comfort. Vehicle is extension of family image but purchaser is price sensitive. Researches vehicle options before visiting lot. Makes multiple visits before purchasing. Visits more than one dealership, considers more than one make and model. Does not want to be taken advantage of or given a hard sell.
- *What Needs to be Learned?* What causes them to visit more than one dealership before making a purchase? What do they dread the most about purchasing a vehicle?

If profitability is an issue with certain clusters, there are options. The organization can redirect marketing efforts to the profitable group in an effort to garner more business and focus less or not at all on the unprofitable groups. The organization recognizes it has been targeting the wrong groups and needs to focus on more appropriate markets. Redirecting budget, time, and other resources to the profitable groups allows the organization to think more like them and develop methods for increasing profit. Another option is to market to the less profitable clusters. Remember, less-than-profitable groups should not be immediately discarded. Often there is a profit opportunity. Thinking like these customers is necessary to understand what is currently missing in the relationship that prevents profitability. It is crucial to remember that an organization can tweak its expectations to meet consumer needs, or it can terminate the relationship if continuing would be a detriment to either the organization or the customer.

Profitability is a vital component for an organization to be successful, but looking merely at numbers for numbers' sake oversimplifies what is complex in the customer relationship. Studying demographics and psychographics in conjunction with profitability provides a cross-referencing tool. Profitability can be matched with certain target groups and behaviors. This process identifies whether the right types of audiences are being reached or unnecessarily overlooked.

Although it is acceptable to cluster according to purchase price, purchase frequency, or overall revenue generated, it is important to take into consideration the cost to acquire and retain the customer. Assessing profitability keeps the organization from working for free. It is important that when thinking like a customer, the organization is able to remain solvent. In the previous cluster example, the dealership needs to assess the costs associated with selling to this audience group in relation to what the dealer spends per purchase.

Tie Messages to Consumer Values

Studying demographics, psychographics, and profitability is logical when thinking like a customer; however, this research is not the endpoint. More detail and insight are needed to create a complete picture. Professional communicators need to connect this data with the attributes, consequences, and values associated with the company's products and services. Without this connection, communications fail to resonate with consumers.

Means–end chaining, developed by Thomas J. Reynolds and Jonathan Gutman in 1979, is a process by which attributes of products and services are linked to consequences and then tied to consumer values (Shimp, 2007). This concept provides the connection professional communicators need. Means–end chaining illustrates that for each set of attributes are resulting consequences. It is possible that each attribute might create more than one consequence. For example, a compact car might offer excellent fuel economy and low insurance rates. One attribute (the compact size) provides more than one consequence (fuel economy and low insurance rates). Furthermore, each consequence might be the result of more than one attribute. Fuel economy might be the result of the car's compact size; however it could also be the result of the car's hybrid design. One consequence (fuel economy) has more than one attribute (compact size and hybrid design). For professional communicators to successfully weave their way through this web, they need to know their audiences well.

These attributes and consequences are then linked to values. If consumers value saving money, leading with a car's attributes (compact, hybrid design) and their consequences (fuel economy and low insurance rates) is effective. It is not uncommon for consumers to be unaware of what they value most; therefore professional communicators need thorough research to make accurate decisions. Table 30.1 illustrates this means–end chain.

The means–end chain in Table 30.1 illustrates what would be done for products. To understand how this works for services, look at the process of buying a car. The consumer stress surrounding car purchases becomes a classic opportunity for the dealership to think like the customer and grow the business as a result. Leaders find out what makes the process stressful. They refer back to their customer cluster. They want to know what causes prospective buyers to

TABLE 30.1 EXAMPLE OF THE MEANS–END CHAIN FOR PRODUCT MARKETING

Attributes of Car	Consequences to Consumer	Consumer Values Tapped by the Attributes and Consequences
Compact size	Fuel economy Low insurance rates	Saving money
Exterior color	Low insurance rates	Saving money
Hybrid design	Fuel economy	Saving money

TABLE 30.2 EXAMPLE OF THE MEANS–END CHAIN FOR PROCESS OR SERVICE MARKETING

Attributes of the New Car Dealership Pricing System	Consequences to Consumer	Consumer Values Tapped by the Attributes and Consequences
What-you-see-is-what-you-pay pricing	Up-front pricing No haggling Time saved	Honesty Being treated fairly
No-commission sales team	No haggling No pressure to buy unaffordable vehicle	Being treated fairly

shop around and what bothers them most about the shopping experience. They learn that consumers lack trust in the dealership because the salespeople are rewarded based on sales and commissions, attributes of the car-buying process.

The dealership encounters negative attributes that need to be eliminated. Thinking like a customer now, it cuts out commission-based pay for sales employees. In place of commissions, the dealership now offers what-you-see-is-what-you-pay sticker pricing (attribute). There is no more haggling over prices (consequence) and time is saved now that the sales staff does not have to get approval for negotiations (consequence). The sales team earns income based on the number of cars sold but not on the price point per sale (attribute). Therefore, the salesperson does not haggle (consequence) and has no financial incentive to incite the consumer to buy what he or she cannot afford (consequence). Ultimately, this model taps consumers who value fair treatment and honesty. Table 30.2 illustrates how a means–end chain works for the new pricing system.

Will some of the sales team quit, desiring commission-based pay because they thrive in that system? Absolutely. The dealership expects this and accepts it as a positive outcome. The dealership continues to think like its customers by only hiring people who are willing to work under the new system. This change creates a culture in which consumers and employees can rely. Although not everyone will be won over (including consumers who enjoy haggling), the customers who like the system will remain loyal to it. The organization does not worry about customers who dislike the new system, much like they do not lose sleep over employees who leave. They focus on customers who appreciate the new system, will refer others as a result, and increase overall profit.

Critics of the idea might suggest that a model like this will not sustain itself. However, dealerships like this are successfully being developed throughout the United States. Professional communicators are then called in to help redesign messages communicated to the public. It is not easy to convince purchase-wary individuals that the company has changed. However, the professional communicator is the key to ensuring customers understand the change and how it benefits them.

If it is unclear whether changes are being effectively communicated, simply ask the audiences. If answers are not readily coming, ask again. Consider asking in a different way. If surveys do not produce the response rates needed, put together a focus group. Do whatever it takes to get the information. Without it, informed decisions are nearly impossible. Efforts become nothing more than elaborate guessing games.

Tailor How Messages Are Communicated to Audiences

As professional communicators go through the means–end chain, they must review *how* they are relating to audiences. Are the media used, the words selected, and the images captured complementary to consumer values? Or does the communication piece focus entirely on attributes and corporate boilerplate? Most companies fail to effectively think like their customers because they design programs around what they want to share rather than what customers want to hear. The smart organization will tailor communications and the method for transmission to what customers want. They adopt new mentalities, acquiring the kind of customer loyalty and profitability their competitors can only dream of.

A U.S.-based computer technology consulting company found that small, no-cost changes could make a significant difference in engaging audiences more effectively. For this company, the primary audience was its employees. These employees worked in the field at client sites, often visiting headquarters only a few times per year. As a result, keeping them engaged in the company was critical and difficult to do. Many employees felt more connected to their client sites than they did company headquarters. The human resources department decided to hold an annual employee meeting in addition to other events so that field consultants could connect with one another, learn more about the company, and stay abreast of their benefits packages. Because everyone worked remotely in a variety of locations, communicating about the event was a challenge.

Initially, communications were sent to home addresses. Response rates were low in spite of initial interest in the concept. As the RSVP deadline neared, the human resources department convened to discuss the next step. They agreed to convert the print communications to digital form and e-mailed them to the consultants at their client sites. Fearing backlash from the consultants about communications overload, the human resources team was surprised to have a response rate of almost 100 percent in 24 hours.

While this may appear to be an oversimplified example, it illustrates how uncomplicated tailoring communications can be. Aside from time to convert the communications to digital form, there was no additional cost. From that point on, communications were managed electronically, saving the organization time and money.

When organizations have multiple audiences, budget constraints may make it unrealistic to plan separate communications for each group. This is especially true when the overall message, such as a new product offering or change in service, is the same. Communicators can combine various means–end chains into one message as long as it remains organized and easy to follow. For example, the car dealership might have point-of-sale booklets for each vehicle model sold on the lot. If consumers value to varying degrees safety, self-image, and product quality, one booklet will address the attributes and consequences that connect to those values. The salesperson goes through the guide with prospective buyers, highlighting parts of the booklet that seem most relevant to the buyers. If there are conflicting or completely different needs between customer groups, then separate communications may be necessary. For example, colleges frequently have separate communications for high school graduates and for their parents.

Tailoring messages makes business communications more effective and credible. Professional communicators feel more confident they are on the correct track. They can use this process as a litmus test for how well they are reaching audiences. Customers can build trust with the organization as it strives to meet their needs.

Determine Which Relationships Should Last Forever

Throughout the process of thinking more like a customer, communicators often come across audience groups who do not fit with the company's culture. In spite of the company's attempts to think like these customers, the organization finds that continuing the relationships would be detrimental to either itself or the customers. For example, an independent communications consultant might need to fire a client who does not pay for services. She might also have to reassign a client who requests services she does not provide. In the first scenario, it is detrimental to the consultant to work for free. In the second scenario, it is necessary for the customer to find a different consultant. If professional communicators are faced with this unpleasant reality, they need to ask themselves the following questions before taking any permanent action:

- *Can the company find a reasonable method for connecting with these audiences to maintain the relationship?* It is possible the audience is desirable but there is a barrier between the audience and the organization. This audience believes in the company's message but does not feel extremely satisfied. It is possible that consumer values are not being properly tapped or the tools for communicating with the audience are not fitting. Simply changing how this group is reached (moving from direct mail to electronic mail) could remove the barrier. Discussing other attributes, consequences, and values as well as expanding company offerings could enhance communications with this group.
- *Is there a benefit to keeping this audience that has not already been identified?* It is easy to develop tunnel vision, assuming audiences need to fit into predetermined guidelines set by the company. The problem with this thinking is it prevents the company from seeking new opportunities. Audiences who do not seem to fit the norm often provide other benefits. Sometimes they represent a new market. Other times, they have more indirect benefits. For example, they might not buy from the organization but they refer people who do. Getting to know these audiences better is beneficial for the organization, in spite of the extra effort it requires.
- *Can the organization identify trends within the undesirable groups to avoid marketing to them and others like them in the future?* If after going through the first two steps there are still undesirable audiences, professional communicators must take the time to identify what is ill fitting with the groups. Reviewing clusters can help communicators detect trends as well as warning signs that signal a poor fit. This is necessary so that future communications are tailored to desirable groups only.

Frightening as it is to part ways with customers, the idea behind thinking like a customer is to identify those who will love the company back and participate in a mutually beneficial relationship. Consumers are willing to love organizations in return, and those who do are the audiences to maintain. They are the most profitable and likely to sing the organization's praises to the community, offsetting lost revenue from groups no longer targeted. Truly successful companies know customer relationships are about quality instead of quantity.

They also know that the practice of quality customer relations does not mean giving in to every whim a consumer might have. Like any healthy relationship, there are appropriate, clearly established boundaries that both parties respect. It becomes a culture, exactly like the car dealership that revamped its sales process to meet consumer needs. The dealership does not give products away for free, although consumers might like that. But the dealership can modify operations to enhance the customer experience. Developing a mutual relationship based on fairness takes time, but it is worth the effort. Smart organizations know this and strive to build these opportunities every day.

Success for the Twenty-First-Century Communicator

Changes in corporate thinking become a valuable opportunity for the twenty-first-century smart communicator. This type of communicator helps build an equally smart organization that thinks like and communicates effectively with its customers. Being able to stay the course is a significant part of achieving this. All too often, good intentions end up unfulfilled as the realities of day-to-day obligations overtake efforts to lead competitors and connect more deeply with customers. To improve the odds, it is important for the smart communicator to:

- *Create a communications plan.* Thinking like a customer does not happen overnight, nor is it without challenges. Delineating a course based on a realistic timeline for seeing results helps connect initiatives with organizational goals. Regardless of an organization's size, a written plan is needed to keep efforts organized. Communicators also need to refer back to the plan throughout the process and establish times for progress reporting.
- *Identify possible setbacks.* Budget limits, time constraints, and lack of support or understanding from management can slow the process of thinking like customers. There will be setbacks no matter how well planned the initiative. Being honest within the team about what could go wrong encourages proactive behaviors that prevent as many problems as possible.
- *Decide what the response will be for each setback identified.* There will likely be different responses for each derailment. Acknowledging what the first step would be in each scenario helps keep the overall effort moving forward in the event hypothetical setbacks become reality. Some setbacks are more

detrimental to the effort than others, but it is important to chart courses of response for each instance.

- *Name the persons or teams who are responsible for leading communications efforts.* Clearly stating at the outset who will be responsible for each effort encourages open dialogue about what is expected. This also provides an opportunity for people to share concerns they have as well as ideas that have not been included in the overall plan.

Although the communicator can develop a plan, identify setbacks, establish new courses of action, and ensure initiatives are completed, there is another component to successfully competing in the twenty-first century. The communicator, as well as the organization, must *want* to think like the customers who are being represented. Without the organization's and the communicator's desire to know these groups more intimately, the relationships cannot grow well. It is the smart communicator who facilitates this growth internally and externally, bringing people together to create mutually cherished relationships.

Reference

Shimp, T. A. (2007). *Advertising, promotion, and other aspects of integrated marketing communications.* Mason, OH: Thomson-Western.

CHAPTER THIRTY-ONE

MEASURING MARKETING COMMUNICATION

Lin Grensing-Pophal

For too long, marketing communicators have convinced themselves—and sometimes their superiors—that it is too difficult, if not impossible, to measure the results of their communications activities. Nothing could be further from the truth. Even in strong economic times, companies are concerned about controlling costs and increasing revenues. Effective marketing communications can achieve both of these goals.

Businesspeople know that *you cannot manage what you cannot measure*. Evaluation is an important part of any communications initiatives, and its initiation needs to occur during the planning phase. Evaluation should be built into any communications plan from the outset.

In 2009, the Lenskold Group conducted a study that indicated that chief executive officers (CEOs) and chief financial officers (CFOs) are making even greater demands than ever before for marketers to show a potential return on investment (ROI). That should come as no surprise. After all, companies would be foolish *not* to want to achieve measurable results from their marketing efforts. Still, according to this study, only about 24 percent of the respondents indicated that they calculate marketing profitability, ROI, or similar financial measures to assess marketing effectiveness—and that number remained steady from the previous year.

For marketing communications professionals hoping to make their mark in an increasingly competitive business environment, the ability to demonstrate measurable results from their work can help them both personally and professionally. Unlike their colleagues in sales, for instance, they are often challenged to point to tangible evidence of the value of their work.

This chapter describes processes for measuring the results of marketing communications and evidence of the value they provide.

What to Measure

The first important question is *what* to measure. There is a lot out there, and marketers need to be wise in the decisions they make because not everything needs to be measured. In fact, Albert Einstein has been noted as saying that not everything that counts can be counted and not everything that can be counted, counts.

Marketers will want to measure both high-level activities that give a sense of the effectiveness of the marketing efforts as a whole and activities related to individual communication initiatives. Developing a marketing plan and updating it regularly, generally on an annual basis, can provide a good frame of reference for overall marketing effectiveness.

On an individual project basis, the first clue about what to measure can be found when you begin planning your marketing efforts. What is your goal? Why are you communicating? If the goal is to increase awareness, then you will want to measure awareness. If the goal is to increase understanding, you will want to measure understanding. If the goal is to generate inquiries, you will want to measure the number of inquiries you receive. Sometimes your goal may be multifaceted. You may want to generate awareness, understand preferences, *and* generate inquiries. In any event, the first step in measuring marketing communication is your communications goal.

Progressively Better Results

Diffusion theory (Rogers, 1962) is a model that examines how people process and accept information and can be a good tool to use when considering how to measure the effectiveness of marketing communication activities. There are five steps or stages in the diffusion model:

1. *Awareness:* The point at which consumers become familiar with a product or service.
2. *Interest:* The point at which consumers become interested in the product or service.

3. *Evaluation:* The process a consumer goes through that involves considering the product or service as something he or she might wish to buy.
4. *Trial:* The point at which the consumer actually tries the product or service.
5. *Adoption:* The consumer is pleased with the product or service and considers himself or herself to be a customer. At this point the consumer is also likely to engage in positive word of mouth for the product or service, recommending it to others.

Media is used differently in each of these stages as the marketing communicator attempts to first generate awareness and interest and then encourage evaluation and trial. During the awareness and interest stages, mass media is very important. It is a communication vehicle that allows messages to be conveyed to very large groups of people, but because of the brevity of these types of messages it is designed more to attract attention (for example, generate awareness) and pique interest. The next two stages—evaluation and trial—require more information. At this point personal contacts become important. Media relations is also often used at this stage in the consumer-buying process.

Marketers are generally concerned with whether a message was received, whether opinions or preferences were changed, and whether behavior was changed—for example, a purchase decision was made.

Marketers typically measure awareness and interest through consumer surveys, which give an indication not only of the awareness and interest in a company's products or services but comparative information about competitive products as well. As media activities are implemented, research can be used to indicate whether awareness and interest are increasing and at what levels compared to interest in competitive products.

Trial and adoption can be measured through consumer behavior. Have they responded to a free trial offer for a product? Have they made a purchase? Have they made a second purchase? How often do they make purchases? What was the date of their last purchase?

Checkpoints for Measuring Marketing Communication

Research is used as an important input at several points in the marketing process. Based on research, marketers may recommend changes to program strategies and/or tactics, targeted audiences, media and messages, and or the organization's products, services, policies, or procedures.

In marketing messages, evaluation may be focused on both implementation and outcomes. Evaluation of implementation will focus on such things as whether the target audience is being reached as planned. Marketers generally evaluate such things as the number of messages sent, the number of messages appearing, the number of people who received the messages, and the number of people that paid attention to the messages.

During a campaign, progress will be monitored and adjustments made as necessary to ensure that the targeted audience is reached. This process is *formative evaluation*. Ultimately, though, marketing communicators will be interested in outcomes: Did the communication achieve results? Outcome evaluation is *summative evaluation*. Objectives and results are compared to evaluate the success of the communication effort.

Four broad categories of marketing communication measurement revolve around:

1. *Audience coverage:* Whether the intended audience was exposed to the communication
2. *Audience response:* How the audience responds to the message (often evaluated through pretesting)
3. *Campaign impact:* Overall impact of all of the communication efforts involved in a marketing campaign
4. *Environmental impacts:* Communication does not occur in a vacuum, so marketers are also interested in environmental factors that may have affected results; for instance, the sales of umbrellas positively affected by weeks of rain

Pretesting of communication efforts is often used to make adjustments prior to the implementation of a campaign. This is especially true when significant investments will be made in the campaign. Pretesting may use readability testing methods to determine whether the messages are readily understood by target audiences. Focus groups are also frequently used to get a more subjective indication of how target audiences may react to a campaign. A health care organization pretesting a new campaign that involved a series of television commercials decided to pull the commercials when it was found that focus group participants were offended by messages that seemed to imply that people from the Midwest were overweight and lived on diets of beer and bratwurst. Since focus groups are qualitative, quantitative surveys may also be used to pretest communications to get a more statistically significant indication of response.

Post-testing also generally uses quantitative surveys to measure changes in awareness and attitudes after consumers have been exposed to marketing messages.

SMART Goals

Of course, it is impossible to successfully measure the effectiveness of marketing communication efforts without a good understanding of what the marketing communication goals were in the first place. Surprisingly, it is not uncommon for marketing communicators to embark on a communications effort with only a general idea of what they hope to achieve; the goals, they feel, are implied. While this may be true to a certain degree, the more specifically marketers can identify their goals during the planning process, the better they will be able to evaluate effectiveness of both implementation and outcomes.

The acronym SMART provides a helpful frame of reference for considering the establishment of goals. While there are often variations in the definitions for this acronym, generally goals should be

S   Specific
M   Measurable
A   Agreed upon
R   Realistic
T   Time-framed

At the end of a marketing communications effort, the marketing communicator and the client each should be able to independently say whether or not the goal was met. Without agreement up-front based on specific desired outcomes and a time frame for these outcomes, the likelihood of one or both of these parties being disappointed is high. Here is a quick example to illustrate:

The marketing communications coordinator for a dental office was asked to develop a marketing campaign to increase the number of new patients. She worked with the clinic administrator and one of the dentists on the project, which involved the use of radio and direct mail to raise awareness of and encourage consumers to sign up for appointments. After three months, the clinic administrator reviewed patient records and determined that twenty-five new patients had been seen. The marketing communications coordinator was happy with the results; the clinic administrator and the dentists were not. The problem? They had not discussed and agreed upon measures of success at the outset of the project. In addition to helping to manage expectations, establishing clear and specific goals at the beginning of a marketing communication project can also help the marketing communicator determine just how much and what type of communications to use. A goal of gaining twenty-five new patients would require a different level and mix of communications than a goal of gaining two hundred new patients, for instance.

Whether embarking on a major multimedia marketing campaign, or simply sending out an e-mail offer to a list of existing customers, establishing a specific, agreed-upon goal during the planning process is critical.

Clarifying Your Communications Goals

The time to establish communication goals is during the communication-planning process. At the outset, the communicator should have some idea of the results desired from the communication effort. Based on those results, then, the next step is to determine how the communicator will measure whether the results have been achieved. It does not have to be a complex process—it just needs to be measurable. In addition, the goals do not need to be significantly lofty. For example, you want to become involved with social media. You decide to set up a Facebook fan page, and your goal is to generate five hundred fans in a six-month time frame. Your boss suggests that this does not seem to be a very meaningful goal—why is the number of fans important? Well, you say, being visible on Facebook and generating fans can help boost your company's image as technologically savvy and could attract a younger customer demographic. Assuming these two goals are important to the company, and were agreed upon as appropriate measurements of success, how would you measure whether you had successfully achieved them?

- To determine whether the company's target audiences' impression of it as being technologically savvy increased due to participation on Facebook, the company might establish a baseline measure through a survey of its customers, implement the Facebook fan page, reach a point of five hundred participants, and then conduct another survey.
- To determine whether it had attracted a younger customer demographic (and assuming it collected this type of information), the company would first have to define *younger* based on some age range, then measure the number of customers in that age range before and after the Facebook campaign.

Comparing results following a communications activity to historical results can be a good way to evaluate the impact that a communications effort has. A sports medicine clinic, for instance, had traditionally used local newspaper advertising to generate appointments for the spring clinics, but the marketing communications coordinator felt the same, if not better results, could be achieved by communicating directly with patients from the health care system. Instead of newspaper ads, direct mail and e-mail were used to communicate about the appointments. Visits increased over the prior year, and there were no immediately identifiable environmental circumstances that might have contributed to the change.

Measuring the effectiveness of marketing communication activities does not have to be extremely complicated, take a lot of time, or involve high-level statistical analysis skills. It is critical, however, that some effort at specifying communication goals and taking steps to measure whether or not those goals were achieved is important for marketing communicators to be able to establish the value of their efforts.

Shel Horowitz, author and marketer, says:

> I use very easy, low-tech measuring tools. When a client books some work, I ask, "How did you hear about me?" When I'm running a live event, I ask for a show of hands of who heard about the event from various methods. In this way, I'm able to capture 80 or 90 percent of the data with no work and no money spent. Sometimes they may not remember the original source, but I'll learn they've been on my newsletter for a year or two. Even these very simple things have helped me a great deal. For instance, back when my business was primarily local, I went into three different phone books just outside my core geographic area. One paid off; the other two were a complete waste of money. But by knowing they weren't pulling (and knowing that the copy had proven well closer to home), I didn't keep spending hundreds of unnecessary dollars every year. (2010, personal communication)

It truly can be that simple. The important thing for any marketer is, again, to know the goal from the outset and to include evaluation in the overall communication plan.

Challenges of Marketing Communications Measurement

Your individual communication efforts do not exist within a vacuum. Sometimes there is a direct correlation between your communication efforts and identified results; sometimes there is not. For example, sales growth may seem like a good indicator of whether marketing communication has been effective. But, keep in mind that there are several external factors that can affect sales growth that should also be considered. For instance:

- *The activities of your competitors.* If competitors are running specials during the same time period that your ads are running, their efforts could cause your results to be lower than they might have been otherwise.

- *Economic climate.* For instance, a plant closing that affects a large number of people in your sales community can negatively affect sales.
- *The product/service experience.* Your communication efforts may generate interest, but if the product experience does not meet consumer expectations, sales will be negatively affected.
- *The efforts of your sales force, retail staff, and other employees.* The enthusiasm and morale of your employees reflected in their efforts to meet or exceed sales goals will affect growth.

Despite the complexity of measurement, however, it should *always* be part of any communication effort. Recognizing the limitations of measurement, it is still appropriate to identify—at the outset—what results are expected and how you will identify, to the best of your ability, whether your communication efforts contributed to the achievement of those results. Some examples:

- Track sales levels against communications efforts to determine whether there are any bumps in sales volume that correspond to specific tactics.
- Identify sales levels before the introduction of a campaign and determine whether those levels improved following the campaign.
- Develop communications messages designed to overcome a misconception among consumers about your product. Measure perceptions before and after the implementation of your communications.

Most marketing communications efforts take advantage of the power of integrated marketing communications, using several different communication tactics to achieve results. Obviously, trying to identify which of these individual tactics accounted for which specific results can be extremely challenging, if not impossible.

Measurement by Media

A wide range of media options is available to marketing communicators, and that range of options is growing significantly all of the time—particularly with the advent of the Internet and online marketing. In the old days marketers had limited choices in television networks, local newspapers per market, and radio stations. Those days are gone. Disaggregation of the media market offers benefits in terms of more choices and more opportunities to target very specific market segments; it also represents challenges for marketers in terms of keeping up with all of the available choices and making good decisions about which media mix to use.

The best way to measure the effectiveness of any marketing communication effort would be to remove all intervening variables that could impact results and focus only on a single communication and its impact. That is not likely to happen in the real world. Instead, marketers do the best they can to measure the effectiveness of their use of media by initially selecting media that best covers their target audience, by establishing a goal or outcome that they will track, and then by comparing results before and after the communication. There are some ways that marketing communicators can attempt to measure individual media efforts, however. For example:

- Using coupons in print advertising.
- Creating a special offer made only through one type of media—radio, for instance.
- Using different media in different market areas with the same offer and comparing results in each area.
- Using different phone numbers or different e-mail response addresses for different ads in various media—or different offers.

In short, there are a variety of relatively simple and creative things that marketing communicators can do to attain some level of the measurement of effectiveness of various types of media efforts. Measuring individual media efforts can be challenging, though, and will always have some degree of uncertainty.

One type of marketing communication tool, though, can provide a higher level of specificity in terms of how well it performs: direct marketing. Direct marketing, whether conducted through the traditional postal route or online, allows marketers to specifically measure response and also provides the opportunity to test various types of offers and messages to see which worked best. Direct marketing offers both the ability to specifically target and effectively measure the response of consumers to directed marketing efforts.

Internet marketing has become a major focus on many companies' marketing communication activities, offering even more opportunity for measurability than direct marketing. In its infancy, Internet marketing generally involved counting clicks, just as many social media marketing activities are currently focused on generating followers or friends. Of course, counting clicks is a fairly ineffective means of determining marketing communication effectiveness. Like direct marketing, Internet marketing offers marketers the opportunity to measurably track results. Free tools like Google Analytics allow marketers to evaluate a wide range of metrics that can show exactly how consumers traveled through the awareness, interest, trial, and purchase process—and where they may have been lost along the way.

Campaign Measurement

While measuring individual communication efforts is important, and measurement should be built into any communication activity, it is also important to measure overall campaign effectiveness. It can be very difficult if not impossible to parse out the individual impacts of media used in a multimedia campaign. Instead, marketers will use a combination of media intended to achieve desired objectives and then measure the overall impact of the activities at the end of the campaign.

However, one important way that marketing communicators can build in an element of measurement to a multimedia effort is to be very specific in identifying a target market and selecting media based on its ability to specifically reach the intended market segments. This would be part of the formative evaluation process.

An annual marketing planning process can be used to measure campaign effectiveness and, when combined with consumer research, can combine benchmarks against which to measure and monitor success on an ongoing basis. The steps involved would include:

1. Identify specific marketing communication goals—e.g., "We wish to be viewed as the highest quality restaurant in our market area," or "We wish to have the highest level of awareness among our competitors in our market area." There may be multiple communication goals.
2. Establish a benchmark. Conducting a quantitative survey among a representative sample of the target audience can provide a benchmark of levels of awareness, preference and perception across a variety of measures.
3. Target areas for focus. Based on the results of the survey, identify those areas where you would like to see improvement.
4. Develop a marketing communication plan designed to use a variety of media to communicate specific messages geared toward affecting the measures you have selected.
5. Implement the tactics.
6. Remeasure results.

While this is certainly an overly simplified description of the process, it does outline the general steps that would be involved in evaluating marketing communication efforts across a broad range of communication tactics. In short, the whole is greater than the sum of its parts.

Emerging Issues in Marketing Measurement

Social marketing tools like Facebook, Twitter, and LinkedIn have become extremely popular in the early twenty-first century, and many marketing communicators are eager to explore the benefits these tools can provide. But, just as with using any other type of marketing communications tool, it is important to measure effectiveness.

Measuring the ROI of social media is a hot topic among communicators in the twenty-first century. While most feel compelled to be involved in social media to some degree, many are challenged with the need to somehow demonstrate the effectiveness of social media activities. There are limited, if any, out-of-pocket costs associated with these activities, but time of course is money. Company leaders are often skeptical of the value that social media may provide, so having methods in place to track effectiveness is very important.

An important point to be made here is that using social media is really no different from any other communications activity in terms of how effective measurement should work. At the outset, communicators need to identify their goals, track costs, and then measure results to see whether the goal has been achieved.

Some goals are better than others, but the process of engaging in social media may be more evolutionary than revolutionary. Initially, a goal might be to generate a certain number of followers. There is nothing wrong with that goal. It is a starting point and certainly measurable. But, ultimately, there needs to be some business purpose around generating those followers.

Amanda Chaborek is director of communications and community relations at Cleary University and was formerly in a similar position at Detroit Country Day School. In both positions, she took specific steps to measure, monitor, and report on the effectiveness of marketing communication activities, including social media efforts on both Facebook and Twitter. A Facebook fan page was created in September 2008 and a Twitter account established in February 2009. By tracking both the number and demographics of Facebook fans, Chaborek can tell which represent her target market and can take steps to engage—and measure engagement with—these followers (see Figure 31.1).

Chaborek also tracks post quality, which is a measure of the percentage of fans that engage when content is posted to the Cleary page calculated on a rolling seven-day basis. The number of stars assigned (5.5 as of June 9, 2010) is an indication of post quality compared to similar pages (for example, pages with a similar number of fans).

In addition to measuring the effectiveness of social media activities, Chaborek also measures media relations and public relations efforts. Monitoring these activities and reporting them to administration is a good way to provide tangible evidence of the value of her communications efforts.

FIGURE 31.1 MEASURING FACEBOOK ACTIVITY

305 Total Fans on June 07   ⬆ **2** Since June 06

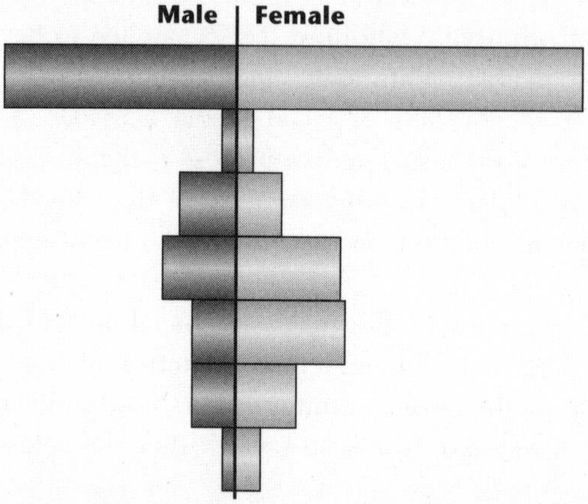

	Male	Female	
	39%	**58%**	
13–17	2%	2%	4%
18–24	9%	7%	16%
25–34	12%	17%	29%
35–44	7%	18%	25%
45–54	7%	10%	17%
55+	2%	4%	6%

Top Countries		Top Cities		Top Languages	
United States	293	Southfield	47	English (US)	294
Canada	4	Detroit	30	English (UK)	4
United Kingdom	2	Brighton	21	English (Pirate)	3
Australia	1	Flint	11	German	1
Spain	1	Troy	11	French (France)	1
France	1				
Philippines	1				

Case In Point: American Greetings

American Greetings Corporation is a leading manufacturer of social expression products. It generates annual revenue of approximately $1.7 billion, and its products can be found in retail outlets domestically and worldwide. American Greetings has the largest collection of electronic greetings on the Web, including cards available at www.AmericanGreetings.com through AG Interactive, Inc., the company's online division.

AG Interactive drives millions of unique visitors from paid search and other online media sources. Their goal is to convert this traffic using online registration for a free trial subscription (which later converts to a paid subscription to AmericanGreetings.com).

In the past, this online traffic funneled into the www.AmericanGreetings.com home page, or a single, MVT (multivariate testing)–optimized landing page. The marketing team knew they needed to launch aggressive landing page testing in order to lift conversion rates, but they faced some executional roadblocks. Implementing testing on the one landing page was slow and arduous, with a multi-month feedback loop to the marketing team. Experimentation with alternative design and content was slower still. When learning was extracted from this process, it was months behind and often gave little reliable cause and effect determination.

In order to lift online conversions and reduce cost per acquisition, American Greetings needed to develop context-specific landing pages, experiment more broadly with content and layout, and view test results and analyses in real time. They decided to use a product called LiveBall, a cloud-based landing page software platform available through Ion Interactive to measure results. Within the first three months of testing, American Greetings moved from a single, optimized landing page to more than forty unique landing pages, each context specific to its source of traffic. Three entirely different design formats were tested with twelve different price points across more than two hundred different audience segments. American Greetings found that it was able to increase conversations by speaking specifically to each segment.

Each unique landing page format was quickly customized and messaged to match closely with the pay-per-click ads that were sending traffic. The testing resulted in an almost immediate 30 percent increase in conversion and a subsequent 20 percent decrease in cost per acquisition. New tests are always in the works at American Greetings. The conversion goal for 2010 was more than 40 percent higher than 2009 and 2011 is targeting another 33 percent lift over 2010. American Greetings' experience clearly demonstrates the many measurement opportunities that marketers are afforded through the use of online marketing techniques.

References

Lenskold Group. (2010). *2010 B2B lead generation marketing ROI study*. Available at www.lenskold.com/content/LeadGenROI_2010.html

Rogers, E. M. (1962). *Diffusion of innovations*. Glencoe, IL: Free Press.

INDEX

About the International Association of Business Communicators

The International Association of Business Communicators (IABC) is a global network of over fifteen thousand communication professionals in ninety countries, one hundred chapters, and ten thousand organizations. Established in 1970, IABC ensures that its members have the skills and resources to progress in their careers, develop and share best practices, set standards of excellence, build credibility and respect for the profession, and unite as a community. IABC members practice the disciplines of corporate communication, public relations, employee communication, marketing communication, media relations, community relations, public affairs, investor relations, and government relations.

Programs

IABC sponsors several conferences through the year in addition to its annual world conference. To further the education of communication professionals, IABC offers monthly teleseminars and Web seminars. IABC honors the best in the profession with the Gold Quill Awards program and the accreditation program. IABC also maintains an online job board.

Publications

The publishing division of IABC offers a range of resources—both in print and online—on a wide variety of organizational communication topics. IABC also publishes the award-winning bimonthly magazine *Communication World* and a monthly online newsletter, *CW Bulletin*. IABC's content resources are easily accessible via its innovative and powerful online library, Discovery. www.discovery.iabc.com <http://www.discovery.iabc.com>

Research

The IABC Research Foundation is a nonprofit corporation dedicated to the support and advancement of organizational communication by delivering research findings vital to the profession. The Foundation translates leading-edge communication theory into real-world practice, helping communicators be effective and visionary in their work. Established in 1982, the Foundation is building a research portfolio aligned with a new research agenda. The Foundation offers grants for communication research in support of this agenda. Learn about the International Association of Business Communicators at www.iabc.com.